About the Author

Michael Griffis is an author, trader, speaker, and business owner. His MBA from Crummer Graduate School of Business at Rollins College was the first step down his multi-faceted career path.

The MBA program emphasized economics, forecasting, and marketing. Its case-study style forced him to write more in a single semester than he had written in his entire Computer Sciences undergraduate program at the University of Florida. (As you may know, coders aren't normally noted for their English composition skills.) Mike's experience in the MBA program was his first hint that he enjoyed writing and was at least competent if not inspired.

Mike first became an active trader — for his own account — in the mid-1980s. He later became a stock broker who helped businesses and individuals manage employee and personal investments. Today he is again trading for his own account.

Mike has business interests in two marketing agencies that help clients address traditional and Internet marketing challenges. Through these agencies, he's able to incorporate his economic knowledge and skills with economic indicators to help clients fine-tune their marketing forecasts. He first began writing about stocks online when the Internet was new and shiny. You can now find him at `www.mikegriffis.com`.

by Michael Griffis, MBA
Coauthor of *Trading For Dummies*

John Wiley & Sons, Inc.

Economic Indicators For Dummies®

Published by
John Wiley & Sons, Inc.
111 River St.
Hoboken, NJ 07030-5774
www.wiley.com

Published by John Wiley & Sons, Inc., Hoboken, New Jersey

Published simultaneously in Canada

For general information on our other products and services, please contact our Customer Care Department within the U.S. at 877-762-2974, outside the U.S. at 317-572-3993, or fax 317-572-4002.

For technical support, please visit www.wiley.com/techsupport.

Wiley also publishes its books in a variety of electronic formats and by print-on-demand. Some content that appears in standard print versions of this book may not be available in other formats. For more information about Wiley products, visit us at www.wiley.com.

Library of Congress Control Number: 2011936924

ISBN 978-1-118-03762-1 (pbk); ISBN 978-1-118-16387-0 (ebk); ISBN 978-1-118-16388-7 (ebk); ISBN 978-1-118-16389-4 (ebk)

Manufactured in the United States of America

10 9 8 7 6 5 4 3 2 1

Dedication

This book would never have been without the love, support, and assistance of my wife Susan. I'm also deeply indebted to Zeki and Harley, the feline duo whose endless fascination with all things laptop led to endless comic relief.

Author's Acknowledgments

I would like to express my gratitude to my editors at John Wiley & Sons, Inc., including acquisitions editor Michael Lewis, project editor Chad Sievers, copy editor Amanda Langferman, and technical editor Steve Russell, who made this book possible and made me sound like a better writer than I really am. Although I couldn't have done it without their help and oversight, any errors or oversights are my responsibility alone.

Publisher's Acknowledgments

We're proud of this book; please send us your comments at http://dummies.custhelp.com. For other comments, please contact our Customer Care Department within the U.S. at 877-762-2974, outside the U.S. at 317-572-3993, or fax 317-572-4002.

Some of the people who helped bring this book to market include the following:

Acquisitions, Editorial, and Vertical Websites

Senior Project Editor: Chad R. Sievers

Acquisitions Editor: Michael Lewis

Copy Editor: Amanda M. Langferman

Assistant Editor: David Lutton

Editorial Program Coordinator: Joe Niesen

Technical Editor: Steven Russell, PhD

Editorial Manager: Michelle Hacker

Editorial Assistant: Rachelle Amick

Art Coordinator: Alicia B. South

Cover Photos: © iStockphoto.com / Lebazele

Cartoons: Rich Tennant (www.the5thwave.com)

Composition Services

Senior Project Coordinator: Kristie Rees

Layout and Graphics: Claudia Bell, Samantha Cherolis

Proofreaders: John Greenough, Jessica Kramer,Bonnie Mikkelson

Indexer: Valerie Haynes Perry

Special Help: Heike Baird, Christine Pingleton, Jessica Smith

---

Publishing and Editorial for Consumer Dummies

Kathleen Nebenhaus, Vice President and Executive Publisher

Kristin Ferguson-Wagstaffe, Product Development Director

Ensley Eikenburg, Associate Publisher, Travel

Kelly Regan, Editorial Director, Travel

Publishing for Technology Dummies

Andy Cummings, Vice President and Publisher

Composition Services

Debbie Stailey, Director of Composition Services

Contents at a Glance

Table of Contents

Part II: Making Money, Spending Money: Employment and Consumer Indicators 65

Introduction

Economics is one of those subjects that students either get instantly or seem to struggle with forever. Fortunately, the subject of economic indicators doesn't share this stigma.

This book is written for people who have no intention of becoming economics experts. Rather, it's for investors, business leaders, business managers, business leader wannabes, and the rest of you who are looking to improve your business plans and investment strategies with the help of the economic indicators you see and read about on a regular basis in the news. This book provides everything you need to know to determine the current economic situation and maybe even forecast the economic future.

Many people have misconceptions about economic indicators. *Economic Indicators For Dummies* is here to dispel those misconceptions and make your analysis easier. In doing so, this book uses plain terms and avoids economic jargon whenever possible. It covers all the background knowledge you need to know and shows you how to put economic indicators to use right away for your investment and business planning.

About This Book

This book presents economic indicators in a logical order, progressing from general, high-impact indicators to more specialized economic tools. The discussion for each indicator tells you what it is, what it means, and how you can use the information it provides. But before diving into specific indicators, this book starts with a brief introduction of the specialized terminology you need to know and a review of the basic analytic concepts used to create economic indicators.

You don't have to read this book from cover to cover. Each chapter is intended to stand on its own. Feel free to jump to the sections that interest you most. Plan to use this book as a reference as you begin to use economic indicators in your business and investment plans.

Conventions Used in This Book

I've used some standard conventions throughout this book to help you understand concepts a bit better. Here's what you need to know:

- I use *italic* to highlight key terms and to add emphasis to certain words or points. (Don't panic! I provide definitions for all key terms right after I first use them.)
- I use **boldface** to point out keywords in bulleted lists and the action part of numbered lists.
- I use `monofont` to make web addresses stand out. If you see an address that has broken across two lines, just type in what you see. I haven't added any hyphens or other punctuation.

  Sometimes, when the web address is unusually long, I use a special shortened address from bit.ly in place of the official address. The bit.ly address still takes you where you want to go; it's just easier to type in.

Furthermore, the Internet is the easiest way to stay up-to-date with most of the indicators discussed in this book. So I provide a reference table, like the one shown in Table 1-1, for each indicator and an explanation to follow. That way, you know how to stay up-to-date with every indicator I discuss in this book.

Table 1-1 Name of the Economic Indicator

Release Schedule	*Agency*	*Web Address*	*Sensitivity*
Release frequency and specific dates and times, if applicable	Source	`www.web-address.com`	Market impact

- **Release schedule:** The frequency of the indicator's publication — weekly, monthly, or quarterly. If the release happens on the same day of the month, I list it here. For those indicators that are released on an inconsistent schedule, I describe the release schedule in the text.
- **Agency:** The organization responsible for the indicator. If the source is an agency within a department of the U.S. Government, I list both the agency and the department. If the source is a private organization, I list just the organization's name.

- **Web address:** The URL of the economic indicator. The address you see in this column is either the full address or the shortened bit.ly address.
- **Sensitivity:** A ranking that attempts to anticipate how investment markets generally react to the indicator's release. Please be aware that investment market reactions depend on many circumstances. When an indicator reports a surprising result far outside of its expected range, investment markets are likely to react regardless of that indicator's general sensitivity ranking. The three rankings I use in this book are
    - **High:** Investors and traders pay close attention to highly sensitive indicators. Unexpected results almost always result in strong market reactions.
    - **Moderate:** Investors and traders pay attention to moderate indicators. Unexpected results occasionally result in strong market reactions.
    - **Low:** Few investors or traders pay close attention to low-ranked indicators. Although unexpected or surprising results rarely occur, when they do, market reaction may be strong. In this book, I include only those low-sensitivity indicators that provide information that you can't find elsewhere.

  Note that I don't include a Sensitivity column in the data tables for international indicators (see Chapters 17 and 18). These indicators have little impact on markets outside the country.

Foolish Assumptions

As I wrote this book, I made a number of assumptions about your basic knowledge of general business concepts and investment markets. Most employees, employers, business leaders, and even business students have the basic background necessary to understand the business concepts I discuss in this book. Although I assume that you're familiar with the business world, including how products are bought and sold, I don't assume that you have any specific business or economics expertise.

I also assume that you have a basic understanding of investing, including stock and bond investments or mutual fund investing. If you're familiar with your company's 401(k) retirement plan, you should have enough background knowledge to dig into this book.

Finally, I assume that you know how to operate a computer and use the Internet. Most of the resources discussed in this book are available online, so you need access to the Internet to take advantage of the information you find in this book.

What Not to Read

Digging into the world of economic indicators leads to lots of information that's surprising, unusual, or just plain odd. Few of these extraneous tidbits are crucial to your understanding of economic indicators, but I include some of them anyway because they're fun. Feel free to use them to liven up your next dinner party. You can find this fascinating but ultimately superfluous information in sidebars, which you can identify by its black border and light-gray background. Also, I've flagged some highly technical information with a Technical Stuff icon. Generally, this level of detail is useful but not crucial for your understanding or for using the indicator.

How the Book Is Organized

To make this book as user friendly as possible, I break it down into six logical parts. The six parts are as follows:

Part I: Figuring Out the Economy

Although you don't need a background in economics to use this book, you may want to review the basic concepts, like economic recession and growth, before you jump into the discussion on indicators. This part offers a refresher on the terminology you encounter in this book and defines some of the most common economic jargon in noneconomic terms. (You can also refer to the glossary at the end of this book for a refresher on economic terms.) In addition, it provides an overview of the analytic concepts and math you need to understand to get the most out of the economic indicators you follow. Don't worry; this isn't high-level math. If you can use a calculator or a spreadsheet, you'll be fine. Lastly, this part includes a quick review of stocks, bonds and other investment markets.

Part II: Making Money, Spending Money: Employment and Consumer Indicators

Consumer spending is the driving force behind the U.S. economy. Knowing how much money consumers have to spend, seeing where that money comes from, and discovering how much consumers are actually spending provide the basis for understanding how the economy works. You also need to know how many people are working and how many are looking for jobs. After all, people who don't have jobs likely don't have money to spend, and a lack of spending definitely impacts the economy. You also need to know what people are buying because some purchases are more sensitive to the economy than others. In addition, you may want to know how consumers are feeling about their financials because customers buy more when they're feeling optimistic.

Part III: The Essence of Business: Product and Service Indicators

Not too long ago, the U.S. economy was based on its manufacturing strength. Although the economy still has a large and robust manufacturing sector, the service sector has grown much larger. Identifying the kinds of products and services being produced in the United States provides another way to look at the economy. Tracking the largest economic sectors — including healthcare, automobile manufacturing, and housing — is an excellent way to determine the economy's current health.

Part IV: Inflation, Productivity, Interest Rates, and Commodities: Oh My!

Many things can send the economy off its growth track. Inflation, rising employee compensation costs, and falling productivity can all hamper economic growth. Of these, inflation is usually the most worrisome. It affects the price of everything, including food and energy costs, wages, and the cost of borrowing money. Monitoring the economy for signs of growing inflation or falling productivity can help you prepare should either ever occur.

Part V: International Intrigue: Indicators beyond the United States

The U.S. economy is the largest economy in the world, at least for now. However, it isn't the only economy. Many foreign countries provide excellent economic indicators, and some even publish them in English. This part provides a brief overview of some worldwide economic indicators that you may want to watch.

Part VI: The Part of Tens

The final part of the book is a hallmark for the *For Dummies* series — the Part of Tens. In it, you find advice that helps you create your own personalized ten-step checklist for monitoring the U.S. economy to help you improve your business plans or your investment returns. You also find ten techniques for making your knowledge of economic indicators pay. At the end of the book, you find a glossary that defines some common economic terms.

Icons Used in This Book

For Dummies books use little pictures, called *icons,* to flag certain chunks of text. Here's what these icons mean:

Watch for these little bull's-eyes to get ideas for using your newfound knowledge of economic indicators to improve your business or investment planning.

If you see this icon, you know whatever text appears next to it is particularly important for you to remember. Don't skip it!

This icon highlights information that delves deeper into a particular topic. You may find the technical stuff to be interesting, but it isn't crucial to your understanding of the concept being discussed.

Although the world of economic indicators isn't fraught with danger, sometimes a misinterpretation can lead to a costly mistake. You don't find many warnings in this book, but when you see one, look out!

Where to Go from Here

You're ready to enter the exciting world of economic indicators. You can start anywhere in this book because each chapter is self-contained. But if you're totally new to economics and economic indicators, starting with Chapter 1 is the best way for you to understand the basics. If you already know the basics, have a good understanding of math, and have a firm grounding in analytical concepts, then jump right in to Parts II through VI. Have fun and enjoy your trip into the fascinating world of economic indicators.

Part I
Figuring Out the Economy

"Well, after establishing a new baseline index, the economy's looking up."

In this part . . .

If you're looking for a quick refresher on economics and wondering why you should want to follow economic indicators, you've come to the right place. Here you can explore concepts like economic growth and recession, the business cycle, and the relationship between investment markets and the economy. You also find explanations for the analytic concepts you need to know and definitions for some of the jargon used in economic indicators. In addition, this part introduces you to several different kinds of indicators and explains how they're used.

Chapter 1

Introducing Economic Indicators

In This Chapter

- Defining economic indicators
- Looking at what the indicators tell you about the economy
- Figuring out how to track and use indicators to meet your needs

Everyone has a financial interest in the economy. Although you may not think about it every day, your country's economic system has a direct impact on your financial well-being. After all, the economy is made up of you, me, and all the people who buy products and services; the companies that create those products and services and deliver them to their consumers; the factories and equipment used to make the products; the facilities needed to offer the services; and of course, the government.

So you see, everyone has an economic role to play. Whether you're a business leader, an employee, an investor, or a consumer, your actions affect the economy and the economy affects you and your finances.

If you're thinking, "Wow, I should really start paying attention to the economy," you've come to the right place! Economic indicators can help you measure the performance and health of the economy and forecast its future. As a bonus, economic indicators can even help you improve your investment returns, your business plans, and your financial health. This chapter serves as a jumping board into the pool of economic indicators. Here I give you a basic overview of the topic so you can navigate your way through the rest of this book.

Understanding What Economic Indicators Are

Can you picture NASA's Mission Control Center? Today it's all flat-panel displays and subdued lighting, but it used to be a system of big industrial panels with blinking lights, gauges, levers, dials, push buttons, and at least one bright-red phone. Each one of those lights and gauges displayed some tiny piece of information that was crucial to whatever mission NASA was working on at the time.

The economy is a bit like NASA's Mission Control Center. Each economic indicator is a metaphorical dial, light, or gauge that provides information about some part of the economy. One dial shows how many people are working, and another shows how many are unemployed. One gauge shows how many cars were manufactured last month, and another tells how high interest rates have grown. These metaphorical dials and gauges show you what's happening in the economy right now.

Although no single Mission Control Center exists for the economy, you can use a collection of economic indicators to see what's happening economically. And although you can't push a button and make the economy change course (at least not by yourself), you and your fellow citizens do have some say about the economy through the purchasing, employment, and other business decisions you make on a daily basis.

When you decide to buy a car or not buy a car, start a business, hire new workers, or even take a new job, you have an effect on the economy. When a lot of people make the same decision and push the same economic buttons, noticeable changes happen in the economy.

Economic indicators show you what's happening in the economy. Most indicators examine and report only a tiny slice of the economy, but several of them provide information about the whole economy in one report. By using a combination of both types of indicators, you can tell where the economy has been and where it's headed.

The following sections provide a bit more insight into how to read economic indicators and what they can tell you about the economy.

Reading the economy through economic indicators

The economy isn't complicated, but the experts who spend their days studying it have devised their own private jargon to describe it. Unfortunately, their terminology often obscures the economy's simplicity. But the economy doesn't have to be confusing. You can use economic indicators to help you read what's happening in the economy.

Several types of economic indicators exist. Some record one kind of data, like the number of people filing for unemployment insurance, and then tabulate and publish the results. Others survey consumers to see how they're feeling about their financial health. Still others massage the data they collect, using complex mathematical formulas, to try and create easy-to-interpret numerical indexes that represent (or *indicate*) the level of things like inflation and consumer confidence.

These different indicators are often categorized by their ability to forecast. *Leading indicators* turn up or down before the economy, so they're generally considered to be good forecasting tools. *Coincident indicators* are useful for identifying the economy's current health, and *lagging indicators* tell where the economy has been.

Find out more about economic jargon as it relates to indicators in Chapter 2. There you also find a brief refresher on the math you need to understand to correctly interpret some economic indicators. It's not high-level math, so don't worry if math isn't your strongest subject.

Cycling through economic ups and downs

You can use economic indicators to give you a clear picture of what direction the economy has gone and where it's going. Economic indicators demonstrate when the economy expands, like during economic growth, and when it falls, like in a recession.

Economic indicators help identify the following pattern of economic expansion and contraction as it happens over and over again:

- At the beginning of an economic recovery, you see an abundance of underutilized production equipment and even some factories that have been idle. A lot of people are looking for work, interest rates are generally low, and the supply of raw materials needed to make new products is high.
- As the economy expands, most people who want a job can find one, factory equipment is put to good use, and idled factories are restarted.
- At some point during the expansion, some raw materials become hard to find. For example, say the lumber used for new-home construction becomes scarce. The price of the lumber goes up as a result, and so do the prices for new homes. As the expansion matures, companies may have a hard time finding the skilled workers they need to continue growing the business. Raw material and labor scarcity leads to rising commodity prices and higher wages.

- Economic growth slows down. The Federal Reserve observes the rising prices and the potential for inflation. It responds by raising interest rates. As a result, credit gets more expensive, and some people have a harder time qualifying for new mortgages or new car loans. Sales of big-ticket items and new-home construction slow down.
- The economy is still growing but perhaps a little more slowly than before. Employers become cautious. If sales slow, employers slow production. Layoffs may not be imminent, but if sales remain soft, job losses are all but inevitable.
- The contraction begins. When the nightly news starts featuring stories about rising prices and higher interest rates, people start to worry. Worried consumers hold off on bigger purchases. Instead of flying to an expensive resort, some vacationers take local vacations. Some consumers delay new car purchases as long as their old ones are running fine.
- The pace of growth may slow so much that the economy actually shrinks. When that happens, businesses are forced to lay off production staff, which causes workers to have less money to spend. Even consumers who are still employed start saving rather than spending.
- As the economy slows, interest rates fall. Prices for things like houses and raw materials also fall. During a recession, the economy takes at least a few months, and sometimes much longer, to find its footing again. But the good thing is it will do so eventually.

Chapter 3 shows the interaction between the stock market, the economic cycle, and the business climate. It also shows the types of indicators that can help investors and business managers plan for the economic future.

Identifying What Indicators Indicate

Though some economic indicators try to report on the big economic picture, most look at only a tiny vignette. For example, one indicator looks at the kind of products people are buying. Another shows if workers are able to find jobs easily. Still others report on current interest rates, the rate of inflation, and the availability of credit for businesses and consumers. This section looks at the specific types of economic conditions that economic indicators measure and report.

Tracking consumer spending

One area economic indicators measure is how much money consumers spend. Consumer purchases drive most of the economy. In fact, if you include the amount the U.S. Government spends on behalf of individuals for healthcare, about 70 percent of all spending is for consumer purchases.

Several types of economic indicators focus on consumer spending. Here's what they measure:

- **How much consumers earn:** Before consumers can spend anything, they have to earn money. Thus, the strength of the job market is a very good indication of the strength of the economy as a whole. As long as the market for jobs is robust, the economy is generally growing. A faltering job market is one of the best signs that an economic peak is near. I discuss which indicators track employment conditions in Chapter 4.
- **How confident consumers feel:** People spend money when they're feeling confident about the future; they hold onto their money when they're concerned about their job or financial situation. The best way to find out how consumers feel about their finances, their jobs, and the economy is to ask them, which is exactly what consumer surveys do. Consumer sentiment is a very good indicator of people's future spending patterns. Turn to Chapter 5 to get the lowdown on consumer economic surveys.
- **How consumers spend their money:** Another way to keep up with the economy is to watch consumers' income and spending patterns. Personal income indicators show you how much money people bring home each month. However, the amount of money consumers have to spend isn't a good determinant of how much they will spend. Sometimes consumers spend more than they make. Other times they choose to spend less than they earn.

Watching how much consumers actually spend and what they're buying can give you a better overall picture of the economy. For example, if people are feeling uncomfortable about their jobs or if they're worried about the economy, they're probably not going to empty their wallets at the shopping mall. And they're certainly not going to remodel the kitchen or take on a new car loan. Retail sales statistics show you what consumers are actually buying each month and how much they're buying. Turn to Chapter 6 to find out how to keep track of both consumer income and spending.

Looking at the big picture

The most direct way to evaluate the economy's health is to look at the whole thing and then compare its current condition to the last quarter or the last year. That's exactly what the Gross Domestic Product (GDP) report does. It reports the total value of everything businesses produce and the earnings of both businesses and consumers.

The GDP report distills economic data from a wide variety of sources, including other economic indicators, into a single report. In fact, it tries to distill the entirety of the economy into a single number. Then it shows the underlying economic details in extensive data tables to explain how the GDP was determined. Unfortunately, this important report is only available quarterly.

But when it does come out, it's an excellent indicator for showing the economy's current health. You find everything you need to interpret and use the GDP report in Chapter 7.

For another big-picture look at the U.S. economy, follow the actions and pronouncements from the U.S. Federal Reserve. The Fed (that's what those in the know call it) manages the money supply for the United States. Part of its responsibility is to keep inflation from getting out of control. The Fed's reports and actions are very good indications of the economy's current and future condition. Chapter 8 shows you how to keep a close eye on the Fed.

Eyeing manufacturing

Consumer products fall into two broad categories: the things people use or consume every day and the things that are supposed to last for a number of years. In economic jargon, these categories are called *consumer staples* and *consumer durables,* respectively, and you can use economic indicators to keep tabs on both of them.

- **Consumer staples:** Also called *nondurable goods,* they include things like food, beverages, toothpaste, medicine, bath soap, paper towels, and cosmetics. Although these purchases make up the largest percentage of consumer product spending, they don't tell you much about the economy.
- **Consumer durable goods:** These products include kitchen appliances, laptop computers, home entertainment systems, and even automobiles. These products are rarely urgent purchases. People don't really need a new refrigerator as long as the old one is still working, which is why durable goods purchases are considered discretionary. Durable goods purchases show how freely consumers are making discretionary purchases.

When you look at the economy from the point of view of the durable-goods manufacturers, you get an entirely different perspective than from the consumer's perspective. Are orders for cars and refrigerators going up, or are inventories growing? Are the factories having problems getting enough raw materials to keep the factories busy, or is the supply chain meeting requirements?

You can watch toothpaste inventories all you want, but the real action is in durable goods. Chapter 9 shows you how to track current sales orders, inventories, and the raw material supply chain for durable goods manufacturing.

Another way to stay up on manufacturing is to ask manufacturers. Business people love to talk about business, which is why business surveys are so compelling. They give you an insiders' view of the business world. Surveys of manufacturing industries are the most economically sensitive, although you can also find surveys for service industries. If you want to know what's really happening in the world of business, go to Chapter 10, where you find out how to find and interpret the premiere business survey results.

Counting up the number of bought, sold, and newly built homes

You find another excellent indicator of the economy's health right in your own neighborhood. Have you tried to sell your house lately? Did you have to chase away the buyers, or did your home sit on the market for months or longer?

Even if you're not personally in the market to buy or sell a home, housing indicators tell a great deal about the economy's health. Are new homes being built? If so, how many? Are houses selling quickly, or do buyers have the upper hand?

Housing indicators are very sensitive to the economy's health. If the economy is doing really well, the housing market is often strong, too. In a healthy home-building market, home builders can keep a large team of skilled tradesmen and laborers employed and the factories of home-building suppliers busy. More to the point, a healthy market for new homes means that consumers are willing to make very large, long-term financial commitments. You can build on your knowledge of the local and national housing markets and stay up-to-date with housing indicators in Chapter 11.

Monitoring inflation

Some indicators also track inflation. The economy almost always has a little inflation, which is a good thing. A little inflation is like an economic fertilizer that keeps the economy growing. However, in this case, the economy is like a houseplant. Too much fertilizer is unhealthy for houseplants, and too much inflation is unhealthy for the economy.

Inflation makes the money you earn worth less and the prices you pay go up for no good reason. In other words, you see price increases that aren't caused by changes in consumer purchasing habits or the availability of products. High inflation is the number-one concern of bond investors because it erodes the value of a bond's interest payments. As inflation creeps higher, the bond's value falls. Chapter 12 covers the most useful inflation indicators.

Measuring productivity

Businesses can improve profitability in a couple of ways. They can cut material costs, or they can improve productivity. Cutting costs works but only up to a point. If the manufacturer cuts costs so deeply that doing so harms the product's quality, then the increased profitability will be very short-lived.

The better long-term approach is to improve productivity. If businesses can get more production and more product from the same number of employees, they're basically tapping into free money. They get more product to sell, and the per-product costs fall.

As long as the machinery or employee training needed for productivity improvements costs less than the value of the productivity gains, it's an easy investment for any business to make. As long as businesses give their employees the tools to produce more and then fairly compensate them for the productivity improvements, everyone is happy.

Productivity improvements are as important to the economy as they are to the individual business that's making them. Growing productivity means that the economy can generate more product and profit from the same number of employees. Productivity improvements generally raise the standard of living for everyone and are a good indication of a healthy, growing economy. Chapter 13 explains how different indicators measure productivity and how you can use them.

Looking at loans and commodity purchases

Almost everyone borrows money. Consumers use personal credit to purchase goods and services and longer-term credit to buy durable goods. Of course, most homeowners also borrow money to buy their homes.

Businesses borrow money, too. They use short-term loans to finance things like inventories and accounts receivables, and they use longer-term loans to buy production machinery and finance construction or purchases of factories and office facilities.

The interest rates that consumers and businesses pay for short-term loans rise and fall with the economy. Rates generally rise during economic expansion and fall during a recession.

One important indicator of the economy's health measures the difference between short-term and long-term interest rates. Short-term rates are normally lower than long-term rates, but when short-term rates get close to long-term rates, you can usually assume the economy is in poor health. Sometimes short-term rates actually rise above long-term rates, and when that happens, you'll usually see a recession in the near future. To find out more about business finances and interest rates, see Chapter 14.

Sometimes businesses use credit to buy raw materials, like oil, corn, wheat, lumber, and even silver and gold, that they need to produce consumer and business products. The markets call these types of raw materials *commodities.* You can tell a lot about the economy by watching commodity prices; see Chapter 15 for details.

Following worldwide economies

The United States is one of the world's largest exporters, but it imports a lot more products from overseas than it exports, which is why the United States has a trade deficit. While exports are a clear boost to the U.S. economy, imports aren't. Check out Chapter 16 to find out how to track foreign trade and trade deficits.

Though the United States may be the largest economy in the world (at least for the moment), many other countries have large and important economies, too. Not all these countries use the same accepted methodologies for reporting and data gathering as the United States, but you can find enough similarities between them and the U.S. methods that you can use the tools identified in this book to evaluate the economic indicators from other countries. Plus, many of these countries publish their reports in English. Travel on over to Chapter 17 to see several examples of first-class economic indicators from foreign lands.

Some countries are still trying to establish their economic reputations. These economies are growing rapidly, but they don't always provide the same level of economic information that you find in the United States. Countries like China, India, and Brazil have very large, growing economies, but some of their economic reports are hard to interpret. The good news is that their economic reports are improving, and some are even published in English. For the intrepid traveler, these emerging economies offer plenty of investment opportunities, so get your travel documents in order and head to Chapter 18, where you find a map for keeping up with these emerging markets.

Knowing How to Start Following Economic Indicators

As an investor, I use economic indicators to develop my strategic investment plan. They help me evaluate the risk level in the economy and identify where opportunities may exist. (As a stock trader, I use a few additional tools to make specific buy-and-sell decisions. They're not a secret. See the latest edition of *Trading For Dummies*, the book I coauthored with Lita Epstein, for an in-depth review of my buy-and-sell methodology; it's published by John Wiley & Sons, Inc.)

The type of investing I do requires that I check my investments frequently. In fact, I check my investments every day, sometimes a little more frequently, and I evaluate my strategy every week. My weekly checklist looks like this:

- **Evaluate the current economic situation.** Have there been any major changes in the economic situation? Which economic reports have surprised investors? Do I need to adjust my strategy or risk outlook?
- **Evaluate the current condition of the stock market.** I analyze stock sectors and the technical condition of the market.
- **Evaluate my current investment positions.** Have the fundamentals of any of my companies changed? Are any of my existing positions likely to change their technical condition during the next week?
- **Evaluate alternative investment candidates.** See whether I'd like to own any stocks other than the ones currently in my portfolio.
- **Decide how and when to implement any portfolio changes.** Make my plans for how and when to buy or sell.

If any of this is Greek to you, you really need to read *Trading For Dummies*. If it sounds like I'm promoting my other book a bit too much, I'm only doing so to help you understand how I use economic indicators. From my perspective, economic indicators are risk-analysis tools. I use them to identify the current state of the market and to predict whether that condition is likely to change. After all, if the current condition is likely to change, I need to change my investment positions.

The following sections help you get started with using economic indicators to meet your investment and business planning needs. They explain how to analyze the economic indicators you choose to follow and how to stay up-to-date with them so you don't miss anything important.

Analyzing the data

Keeping track of different economic indicators doesn't mean you have to quit your full-time job. You just need to know how to analyze and decipher the data and then put what you learn to use. Becoming an economic analyst takes a little practice, but you don't have to spend every minute of every day looking at economic reports to understand what's happening in the economy. I certainly don't.

I spend between 30 and 60 minutes each week on this part of my investment plan. You may need a little more time, but you may also be able to get by with less, at least after you get a feel for the analysis process.

At the beginning, following all the economic indicators that you think are important to your business or investment strategy may seem overwhelming, so start small. Select ten indicators to follow. If ten prove to be unworkable, start with two or three. Pick the two or three indicators that you think will be most beneficial to your business or to your investing portfolio (see Chapter 19 for details). Then add to your list as you become comfortable with the reports and what they're telling you.

I recommend that you keep records of the indicators you choose and your thoughts as you read them. Track your analysis over time. Record which indicator caused you to make a specific decision. Identify which predictions and decisions you get right and which ones you get wrong. In either case, try to figure out why you were right or wrong and write it down.

After you've tracked your analysis for a little while, you'll really get the hang of it. You'll find that your analysis is at least as good as the talking heads on TV. And because you've selected specific indicators to suit your business or investment, your analysis will likely be even better than theirs!

Soon you'll find that the news reports simply provide too little information to be useful for your analysis efforts. Then you'll be well on your way to making your own reliable economic forecasts.

Tracking economic indicator release dates

Keeping up with economic indicators is fairly easy. Several prominent websites post release dates for the economic reports coming out during the current week (these dates are collectively called the *economic calendar*), and some of them even include summaries of the indicators after their release. Check out these sites for details:

- **Bloomberg:** www.bloomberg.com/markets/economic-calendar/
- **MarketWatch:** www.marketwatch.com/economy-politics/calendars/economic
- **Briefing.com:** www.briefing.com/Investor/Public/Calendars/EconomicCalendar.htm

When you're first starting out, you may want to rely on one or two of these calendars to keep track of the indicators you've chosen to follow. However, I've been doing this long enough that I really don't have to use these calendar tools that often. The release dates for the main indicators I follow have become second nature to me. Besides, you can request to have most indicators sent to you by e-mail.

Keeping track of the economic indicators published by the U.S. Government is especially simple. Here are the two primary sources for government indicators:

- **Economics and Statistics Administration:** You can sign up to receive e-mail reports from the Census Bureau and the Bureau of Economic Analysis (BEA), including the GDP report, the New Residential Construction report, the Personal Income and Outlays report, and others. Just go to www.economicindicators.gov.
- **Bureau of Labor Statistics News Service**: You can sign up for e-mail alerts regarding indicators like the CPI, PPI, Employment Situation report, and more. Just go to www.bls.gov/bls/list.htm.

Additional sources for e-mail reports are available. Most of the publicly available reports allow you to sign up for automatic e-mails whenever the report is released.

Chapter 2

Explaining Economic Jargon

In This Chapter

- Looking at the main types of economic indicators
- Analyzing the data and making adjustments
- Identifying the timeliness of different indicators
- Considering consensus forecasts and revision reports
- Figuring out how money and interest rates affect the economy

Economists may seem like strange visitors from another planet. After all, they use terms and techniques that are more or less foreign to the rest of us, and they have a seemingly unnatural knack for making accurate forecasts and analyses. But although economists speak in a language all their own, with a little effort, you can figure out what they're talking about. After all, if you're going to use economic indicators to improve your investment or business decisions, you need to understand what some basic economic terms — like indexes and moving averages — mean.

This chapter introduces you to the economist's lingo. It walks you through the nitty-gritty of economic indicators and shows you how to use the work of economists to compare the past to the present and maybe even catch a glimpse of the future.

Identifying Types of Economic Indicators

As you start your investigations into *economic indicators* (statistics or reports that describe something about the economy that's generally useful for economic forecasting or analyzing economic performance), you'll find that they come in a remarkable variety. The most common types are tables, surveys, and indexes, all laden with data.

This section provides an overview of the major types of economic reports or indicators. It looks at their strengths and weaknesses, as well as their value to investors and business leaders.

Summarizing economic results

A lot of economic reports simply report the data in *summary tables*. These reports tally and categorize the results from the previous week, month, or quarter. Examples of this type of report include the following:

- **Gross Domestic Product (GDP) report:** The quarterly GDP report describes the value of all products and services produced in the United States. (I discuss GDP in Chapter 7.)
- **Unemployment Insurance Weekly Claims Report:** The U.S. Department of Labor collects unemployment data from every unemployment agency in every state and presents it in this report the following week. (I cover unemployment in Chapter 4.)

In some cases, just collecting the data can be a gargantuan task. For example, the GDP report collects data from dozens of sources and distills it into a single large report. That all this information is even close to correct is astonishing.

The results you find in reports like the GDP report are sometimes adjusted for seasonality or indexed for inflation. Other times the results are annualized to make comparing them with other reports easier. I explain these data adjustments later in this chapter.

Surveying for information

You're probably familiar with the concept of a survey even if you've never participated in one. A typical *survey* asks a certain number of people what they think about a particular topic. You see surveys used for product-preference tests, consumer-satisfaction reports, and political forecasts. Economic surveys ask questions that help you gauge attitudes on economic topics like consumer confidence and the U.S. manufacturing business.

Economic surveys are remarkably *prescient*, meaning that they often provide a very good forecast of things to come. For example, when you ask consumers about their finances, you get a sense of their hopes and fears. If people are afraid for their economic futures, they're unlikely to make significant financial commitments, and the economy will suffer as a result.

Likewise, when you ask business owners or purchasing managers about their businesses, you get a good feel for how their businesses are doing now. If you ask enough business people, you can gain tremendous insight into the economy's future.

Examples of economic surveys include the following:

- **Surveys of Consumers report:** Several surveys of U.S. consumers, like the University of Michigan's Surveys of Consumers report, ask consumers how they're feeling about their economic future. This turns out to be a very good way to predict the future of the whole economy. (See Chapter 5 for more on this and other consumer surveys.)
- **Manufacturing ISM Report On Business®:** Purchasing managers know a great deal about the purchasing habits of their companies and about the sales pipeline. Monthly surveys, like the Manufacturing Institute for Supply Management (ISM) Report On Business®, help investors keep abreast of this important economic sector. They also provide an excellent predictor of the future economy. (Chapter 10 covers the Report On Business®.)
- **Tankan survey:** Surveys aren't limited to U.S. consumers and businesses. The Tankan is a wide-ranging survey of Japanese businesses that asks about their sales channels, inventory, exports, and lending rates. Like the domestic surveys, the Tankan survey is an excellent forecasting tool for the Japanese economy. (See Chapter 17 for details on the Tankan and other worldwide economic indicators.)

Surveys have to be carefully constructed or else their results can be misleading. The following sections highlight some issues surveyors must consider.

Surveying samples

For a survey to offer perfect results, it would have to survey the entire population, or at least a very large part of it. Conducting a survey that big is not only difficult but also very expensive. To make things more manageable and affordable, surveyors select a small sample of the population to stand in for the whole population.

Surveyors can conduct surveys over the phone, on the Internet, by mail, or face to face. As long as the survey's designers get the sample right, the survey can be a good indicator of the future (see the next section for details on getting the sample right).

To make surveys as useful as possible, statisticians have developed tools to help estimate how many people need to be surveyed for you to have some degree of confidence that the survey results are accurate. Generally, the larger the sample, the more confidence you can have in its results.

Constructing a valid survey

For the survey results to be meaningful, the survey sample must be made up of people with characteristics that proportionately match the population as a whole. For example, if you're trying to figure out who's going to win a national presidential election and you survey only democrats (or only republicans), your survey won't produce useful results. You need to survey the right proportion of republicans, democrats, and independents, and you need to exclude people who aren't likely to vote.

Statisticians use the following concepts to design surveys and to describe the usefulness of their results:

- **Random sample:** Although surveyors must design their sample so that its makeup is proportionate to that of the whole population, they must also select their participants randomly. If surveyors hand-select participants, the value of the survey results decreases dramatically.
- **Confidence interval:** The *confidence interval* is a numerical measure used to construct a survey. It describes the likelihood that the actual survey results will be representative of the true survey results you'd get if you were to survey the whole population. The survey developer uses the confidence interval to determine the number of participants required for the results to be statistically valid. Typical confidence intervals are 90 percent, 95 percent, and 99 percent. A larger confidence interval (99 percent compared to 90 percent) usually requires a larger sample size.
- **Margin of error:** The *margin of error* is generally half the width of the confidence interval (although this is an oversimplification, it's all you need to know for the purposes of this book). For example, if you construct a survey with a 95 percent confidence interval, the margin of error is 2.5 percent. If a survey asks people to choose a preference between one product or one candidate and another and the answers differ by only one percentage point, then the result is not statistically significant because it falls within the margin of error. In other words, you can't make a valid conclusion based on this survey result. A larger sample size produces a smaller margin of error.

For more info on any of these concepts, get a copy of *Statistics For Dummies* by Deborah Rumsey (John Wiley & Sons, Inc.).

Indexing the economy

Indexes are helpful for measuring economic conditions because they allow you to use a single economic statistic to evaluate a large quantity of data.

You're probably familiar with the concept of an index because indexes are used so often to describe the performance of the stock market. The Dow Jones Industrial Average Index, the Standard & Poor's (S&P) 500 Index, and the Nasdaq Composite Index are famous indexes that track the stock market throughout the trading day.

Few people understand exactly what the S&P 500 Index is or how it's calculated, but most people know the market is doing well when the S&P 500 Index is up and doing badly when it's down. However, just because the S&P 500 Index is up doesn't mean that every stock is higher for the day or even that every stock in the S&P 500 is up for the day. The S&P 500 Index is simply an average that reports the aggregate performance of a basket of stocks.

Although few people treat stock market indexes like traditional economic indicators, they're calculated just like any other index. To create an index, analysts take a large quantity of data and use a formula to turn that data into a single aggregate value that represents all the data.

Examples of economic indexes include the following:

- **Consumer Price Index (CPI):** This baseline index measures price inflation. Check out Chapter 12 for the skinny on CPI.
- **PMI (formerly known as the Purchasing Managers Index):** This diffusion index measures the strength of U.S. manufacturers. It's created by using the data from the Manufacturing ISM Report On Business® survey. I cover PMI in Chapter 10.
- **Consumer Confidence Index:** This baseline index is based on the data gathered in the Conference Board's Consumer Confidence Survey. See Chapter 5 for more on this index.

What's the difference between baseline and diffusion indexes? Read on to find out.

Finding the baseline

A *baseline* is a reference value. In a *baseline index,* the baseline is a known measure that you can use to compare future (or previous) index values.

The index creators define the period, usually a single year, used as the baseline. It's somewhat arbitrary, but for most economic indicators, the baseline period is usually within five years or so of the current period. A baseline value is then constructed by collecting data from the baseline period and converting that data into an index value.

Baseline indexes allow you to compare large amounts of complex information across long spans of time. You can easily measure the economic results from future years against the baseline year. Specifically, you can use baseline indexes to measure inflation, consumer confidence, and the economy as a whole. Baseline indexes allow you to easily see how fast the measured value is growing.

The baseline value, at least for economic indicators, is usually 100. If the baseline index moves from 100 to 110, you know that the index has grown by 10 percent. If the index reaches 200, the index has doubled, or grown by 100 percent.

For the CPI, the baseline value is 100, but instead of representing a single year, the CPI's baseline period spans from 1982 to 1984. In March 2011, the reported CPI value was 223, meaning that the price level had more than doubled since the baseline was established. (See Chapter 12 for more on CPI.)

Although most economic indexes set the baseline value at 100, any value can be used. For example, in disciplines other than economics, zero may be used for the baseline. In any case, results above the baseline tell you that the measured value is larger or better than it was in the baseline year. Results below the baseline tell you that it's smaller or worse.

Diffusing information indexes

A *diffusion* shows how much something has spread away from the center. For example, one survey may ask whether sales orders have increased, decreased, or remain unchanged. The *diffusion index* shows how far and in which direction the answers differ from the unchanged response.

You see diffusion indexes most often in conjunction with survey data, but you encounter them in other types of indicators as well. The PMI is an example of a survey-related diffusion index.

To see how to calculate a diffusion index, consider the hypothetical survey question of whether sales orders increased, decreased, or remained unchanged. Assume that 100 people were surveyed and 40 said sales increased, 40 said sales didn't change, and 20 said sales decreased. Then follow these steps:

1. **Assign a value of +1 to each of the responses that said sales increased, a value of zero to each of the unchanged responses, and a value of –1 to each of the decreased responses.**
2. **Add the survey results together to create the diffusion index.**

In this example, the index equals 20:

Diffusion index = (+1)(40) + (0)(40) + (–1)(20)

Diffusion index = 20

The diffusion index value is positive, or above zero, so you know that sales increases were greater than sales decreases. You don't know the magnitude of the increased sales, but you do know that they increased.

In the sales order example, zero is the midpoint for the diffusion index, but it doesn't always have to be. For instance, some diffusion indexes use 50 as the midpoint. In cases where 50 is the midpoint, the scale is usually 1 to 100, with 50 representing 50 percent. As long as you understand what the midpoint stands for, its value is immaterial.

You can use other methods to calculate a diffusion index, but the basic concept is always the same: The value of the index diffuses away from the center value as more responses favor one answer over the other.

Understanding How Economists Analyze the Data

Economic analysts rely on a number of tools to make economic indicators more useful. Having a basic grasp of these tools can help you better understand what the indicators mean and how analysts come up with the data. This section reviews the most common of these analytic tools.

Measuring growth

One of the first things any analyst wants to know is how fast the economy, or any economic measure, is growing. The most common way to look at growth is to use the *growth rate,* or the percentage growth from one period to the next.

Growth rate is a simple tool, and it's as easy to calculate as any percentage calculation. Take a look at the economic results in Table 2-1 for the fictional Republic of Freedonia.

Table 2-1 Freedonia Economy, 2005–2010

Year	*Economy (In Thousands)*	*Growth (In Thousands)*	*Growth Rate*
2005	$10,124		
2006	$10,315	$191	1.89%
2007	$10,021	–$295	–2.86%
2008	$10,168	$148	1.47%
2009	$10,475	$306	3.01%
2010	$11,009	$534	5.10%

From Table 2-1, you can see that the Freedonia economy grew in four out of the five years. However, the economy was smaller in 2007 than it was in 2006, which means that the economy declined for that year.

The third column, labeled Growth, shows the actual amount of growth or decline. In 2010, actual growth was $534,000. The economy grew to $11 million from $10.475 million in the previous year.

In this example, the 2010 total shown in Table 2-1 is $11,009. But the results in the table for the Economy and Growth columns are reported in thousands of dollars (the column headings tell you this). So you have to multiply $11,009, the 2010 result, by 1,000, to get the actual result of $11.009 million. This reporting technique is very common in economic reports.

For each economic report you review, make sure you know what the numbers in the report represent. If the report says the results are in thousands, multiply each number by 1,000. If the results are in millions, multiply by 1 million.

To compare Freedonia's economic performance in 2010 with its performance in previous years, you may look at the actual growth values; however, using the growth rate is more common.

Here's how to calculate the growth rate:

$$\left[\left[\frac{X_1}{X_2}\right]-1\right]*100 = \textit{growth rate}$$

In this equation, x_1 represents the data for one period (one year, in this example) and x_2 represents the data for the previous period (the previous year).

To calculate the 2010 growth rate from Table 2-1, use the 2010 data for x_1 and the 2009 data for x_2, like so:

$$\left[\left[\frac{11{,}009}{10{,}475}\right]-1\right]*100=5.10\%$$

You can perform this calculation for the remaining years in Table 2-1. Your results should match the percentages you see in the Growth Rate column. Then you can compare Freedonia's economic growth in 2010 to the growth rates from the previous years in Table 2-1. Calculating growth rates is particularly useful when you're comparing results from recent years with those from long ago or when you're trying to compare one country's economic growth with that of another country.

Using the growth rate puts everything on a common percentage scale. Imagine if you were to compare Freedonia's economic growth with that of the United States. Because the U.S. economy is measured in trillions of dollars rather than millions like Freedonia's, the U.S. numbers would completely overwhelm Freedonia's. Comparing the two economies by using the growth rate makes these comparisons more useful.

Annualizing reported data

Some economic reports provide economic data every week, some every month, and some every quarter. As a result, you often need to compare data from economic reports that are published at different frequencies.

Comparing monthly or quarterly data to annual data requires that you convert one set of data to approximate the frequency of the other. The most common way to do so is to adjust all the data so that they approximate the annual results; this technique is called *annualizing* the data. In other words, you convert the monthly or quarterly data to their approximate annual equivalents. To see what I mean, look at the quarterly report of Freedonia's economy in Table 2-2.

Table 2-2 Freedonia Economy, Quarterly Results

Year	*Economy (In Thousands)*	*Growth (In Thousands)*	*Growth Rate*	*Annualized Growth Rate*
2008 Q4	$10,168			
2009 Q1	$10,186	$18	0.17%	0.69%
2009 Q2	$10,293	$107	1.05%	4.27%
2009 Q3	$10,461	$168	1.63%	6.70%
2009 Q4	$10,475	$13	0.13%	0.51%
2010 Q1	$10,575	$100	0.96%	3.88%
2010 Q2	$10,700	$125	1.18%	4.81%
2010 Q3	$10,853	$153	1.43%	5.86%
2010 Q4	$11,009	$156	1.43%	5.86%

Table 2-2 shows the condition of Freedonia's economy at the end of each quarter, along with its quarterly growth rate. If you want to compare the quarterly results with Freedonia's annual results, you need to convert the results to make them comparable. The idea is a little like finding a common denominator when you're dealing with fractions. In this case, you have to convert the quarterly data to its approximate annual equivalent.

Fortunately, many economic reports annualize the data for you. For those that don't, the calculation process is fairly simple. You just have to take the results from a monthly (or quarterly) report and recast them as though they occurred over the span of a year.

To annualize any data set, you need three pieces of information:

- **x_1:** The result for the most recent period (or the ending result for the period you're annualizing).
- **x_2:** The result for the preceding period (or the beginning result for the period you're annualizing).
- **n:** The number of periods per year. For example, if you're looking at quarterly data, the number of periods per year is 4. For monthly data, it's 12, and for weekly data, it's 52.

The equation for annualizing data looks similar to the equation for calculating growth rate. The only difference is that you have to raise the fraction by the exponent or power *n,* as shown here:

$$\left[\left[\frac{X_1}{X_2}\right]^n - 1\right] * 100 = \textit{annualized growth rate}$$

The math for annualizing data isn't terribly difficult, but having a calculator or spreadsheet handy can help you keep everything straight and can make the process go faster.

If you want to use Excel to calculate annualized results, use Excel's POWER formula. To use year-to-date results, you need to adjust the exponent in the preceding equation. If the year-to-date results are based on monthly data, change the exponent so that $n = 12/m$, where m is the current month (1 for January, 2 for February, and so on). For quarterly year-to-date data, the exponent $n = 4/q$, where q is the current quarter (1 for the first quarter, 2 for the second, and so on).

Distinguishing between percent, percentage points, and basis points

For those of you with a strong math background, the distinction between percentage change and percentage points is old hat. For everyone else, it can be a source of confusion, so here's a quick refresher:

- **Percent**: Sometimes called *percentage, percentage change,* or *percentage difference, percent* expresses a number as a fraction of 100. For example, 55 percent (or 55%) is equivalent to 55/100 (55 divided by 100), which is also equivalent to 0.55.

  Using percent is a simple way to describe the relationship of one number to another. In the Freedonia example in Table 2-1, Freedonia grew from $10,475,000 in 2009 to $11,009,000 in 2010. In percentage terms, Freedonia grew 5.10 percent.

- **Percentage points**: While *percentage* describes the relationship of one number to another, *percentage points* describe the relationship of one percentage to another. The difference between 4.10 percent and 5.10 percent is one *percentage point* (5.10 – 4.10 = 1.0).

  The distinction is important. After all, the *percentage difference* between 4.10 percent and 5.10 percent is 24.39 percent. The percentage difference calculation is the same as the growth rate calculation. In this case, it's ((4.10 ÷ 5.10) –1) × 100 = 24.39.

- **Basis points**: 100 basis points equal one percentage point. Basis points are commonly used in discussions about bond interest rates and stock indexes. The difference between 4.10 percent and 5.10 percent is 100 basis points.

Smoothing data with moving averages

Sometimes economic data are very volatile. Looking at the data and determining an underlying trend isn't easy. Even if you plot the data on a graph, you may see lots of dots on the chart and no obvious pattern. In fact, the data may appear to be completely random. In such cases, determining what the data are saying is quite difficult.

Figure 2-1 shows an example of a volatile data set. It shows a plot of the Unemployment Insurance Weekly Claims Report data (I discuss this indicator in Chapter 4). The week-to-week changes in this data series may not show an obvious trend.

As you can see from the graph in Figure 2-1, the weekly unemployment data are extremely volatile. Even when the data are declining, as they are here, it's hard to tell by looking at the graph. Not surprisingly, it's just as hard to tell by looking at the raw data.

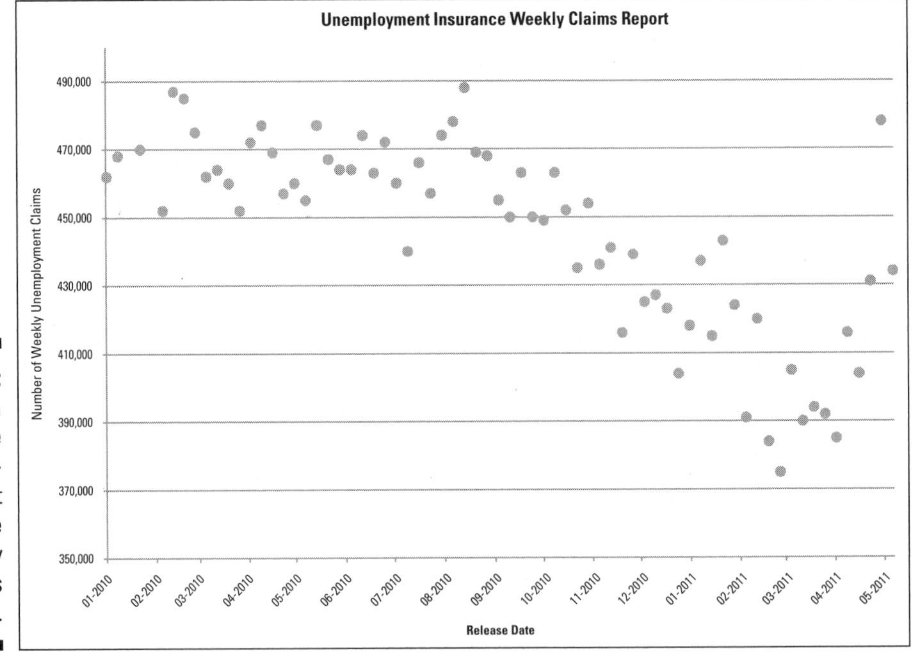

Figure 2-1: Data from the Unemployment Insurance Weekly Claims Report.

The most common tool analysts use to deal with the volatility issue is called a *moving average.* A moving average can help you visualize trends in the data that may not be obvious otherwise. Several types of moving averages exist; I describe two common ones in this section.

Note: Many other techniques for weighting a moving average exist, though economists rarely use them in their analyses. If you'd like to know more about exponential moving averages, check out *Trading For Dummies* (John Wiley & Sons, Inc.), the book I coauthored with Lita Epstein.

Simple moving averages

The *simple moving average* (SMA) is the most common moving average used for economic data. You also see it used in other applications like stock chart analysis. An SMA has the advantage of being both simple to calculate and easy to understand. It's a good choice when you need to smooth volatile data. For example, this technique is so common that some economic indicators, like the Unemployment Insurance Weekly Claims Report, provide the moving average for you. For others, you have to calculate it yourself.

If you were to apply a simple four-week moving average to the Unemployment Insurance Weekly Claims data shown in Figure 2-1, the result would look like Figure 2-2.

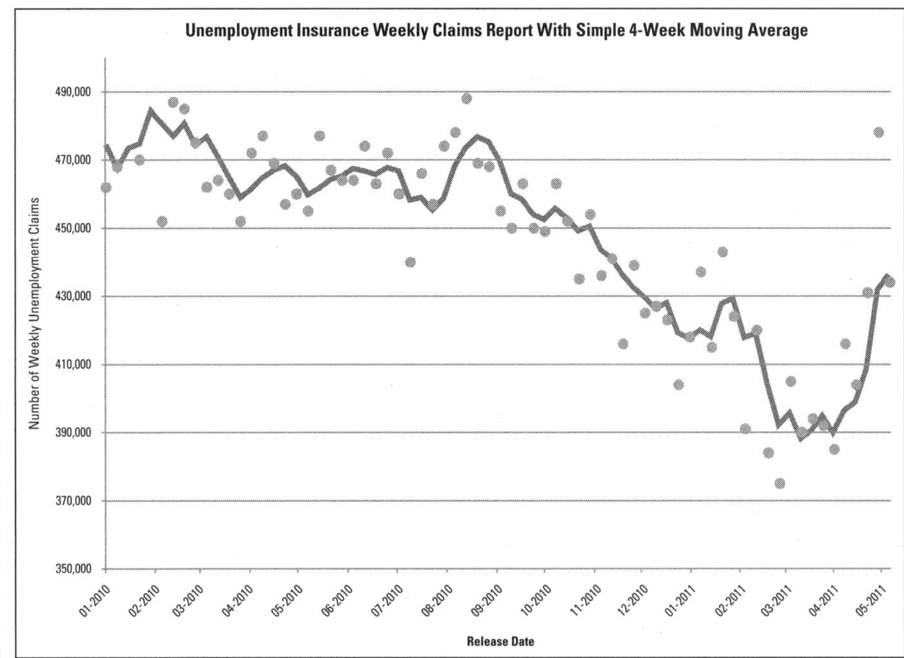

Figure 2-2: Applying a simple four-week moving average to a set of data.

As you can see, the trend in Figure 2-2 is much clearer than the one in Figure 2-1. Until April 2011, the number of people filing claims had been declining steadily. That decline is good news for the unemployed people. However, the jump in April and May is more than a bit worrisome for the economy.

Calculating a moving average is simple. To find a four-week moving average, start with the first four weeks of data, add them together, and then divide the sum by four. The result is the first point on your moving average. Then you move one week ahead and do the same calculations. For every week of new data that you add to the average, you drop one off the oldest week of data.

Although doing all the moving average calculations by hand is a bit tiresome, it's really easy in a spreadsheet program like Excel. Use the AutoSum function for the first four weeks, divide the result by four, and then copy the equation for each subsequent week.

Exponential moving averages

Another moving average that some analysts find helpful is called the *exponential moving average* (EMA). An EMA is a type of *weighted* moving average. It uses the x-value to serve as the weighting factor. Weighting a moving average means that the most recent data receive more importance than the older data. Each new data point is added based on the weighting factor. The importance of each data point is greatest when it's first added; its importance diminishes over time.

To find an EMA, you start the series with a *seed value.* The seed value can be the first data point in the series, or it can be an average of the first few data points. Then you apply the smoothing factor to the seed and add each subsequent data point to the series. The equation looks like this:

$$EMA_{today} = EMA_{yesterday} + x * \left(Value_{today} - EMA_{yesterday}\right)$$

$$Where: \qquad x = \frac{2}{period + 1}$$

Yesterday and today can stand in for any time period. For example, if the data is weekly, interpret *today* to mean this week and *yesterday* to mean last week.

The *period* used to calculate the value x is the moving average period. For example, if you were to use the same four-week moving average period as you use in the SMA example, the *period* would be 4 and the value for x would be 2/(4+1) (or 2 divided by 5), which equals 0.40.

Choosing the best moving average to use for your data

Distinctions between an SMA and an EMA are clear, so if you're trying to decide which one to use, consider the following points:

- The SMA is a true average for the selected time period. For most economic applications, a simple moving average is the more common choice. Just be sure to select the period of the moving average based on your analytic purpose. If you're trying to identify long-running trends, choose a longer period for the moving average. If you're trying to identify turning points in the data, choose a shorter period.
- A weighted moving average like the EMA tends to react more quickly to recent data changes, but it also has a memory. The EMA doesn't drop any data points; it only diminishes their importance. Analysts often consider the EMA's memory a benefit. However, the EMA's memory also means that the starting seed value always has some impact on the EMA value, even if the seed's impact diminishes over time. If you change the value of the seed, you change the value of the EMA. If the underlying data change because of seasonal or inflation adjustments, the EMA seed will likely change, too. When using an EMA, be sure to keep a long-running record of the data and the seed value.

Massaging Economic Data to Make the Results More Useful

Many economic indicators adjust the data before publication. The goal is to make comparisons between current and previous periods more useful. Indexing for inflation and adjusting for seasonality are two of the most common adjustments made. I discuss both in this section.

Adjusting for inflation

Economists (and most everyone else, for that matter) expect product prices to rise or fall based on the availability of the product. The more product that's available, the lower the cost, at least theoretically. Likewise, when products become scarce, prices tend to rise. However, when product prices rise because of monetary issues — too many dollars — the rise in price is called *price inflation*. Inflation causes problems for consumers, investors, and businesses. It also makes economic analysis more difficult.

Most economic analyses use dollar values rather than physical quantities as the basis for economic comparisons. If inflation devalues the dollar, those analyses become less useful, which is why so many economic reports are adjusted for inflation.

Analysts can use several different techniques to remove inflation's impact from economic data. This section looks at the two most popular ones.

Indexing for consumer prices

You're probably familiar with cost-of-living adjustments. They're common in government programs like Social Security and Medicare, but you also see them in collective bargaining agreements and some private contracts.

Cost-of-living adjustments help make sure Social Security and other government program benefits keep pace with rising prices. Where do these adjustments come from? The most commonly used indicator for cost-of-living adjustments is the Consumer Price Index (CPI).

The value of the CPI is based on the price of a standardized basket of consumer products. In the case of Social Security, the value of the payment owed to beneficiaries is adjusted by the amount that the CPI rises each year. The adjustments are calculated based on the value of the CPI at the end of the third quarter each year. This type of adjustment is formally called a *price escalator.* In lay terms, it's called *indexing for inflation.* (I discuss the CPI and inflation in detail in Chapter 12.)

The math for calculating the inflation adjustment is usually straightforward. Just multiply the value to be adjusted by the CPI's growth rate. The result is the adjustment value. Whether you add or subtract the adjustment value depends on the application. For example, if you're adjusting Social Security benefits, you add the adjustment to the benefit.

Chaining dollars

For economic analysis, some adjustment techniques are generally better than others at indicating inflation's true economic impact. The most prominently used inflation adjustment for U.S. economic indicators is called dollar chaining.

For *dollar chaining,* analysts first collect economic data, using current prices (the current market values) for products and services. Then they separate the economic data into two components: price and quantity. Their goal is to segregate the price components, leaving only a standard value for the quantity of goods and services. Finally, they express this standard quantity value as an index number, based on a reference year that's equal to 100.

This approach allows analysts to estimate the quantity changes of goods and services separately from annual changes in price. In addition, economists believe this method eliminates the influence of relative price changes (the price of one product relative to the price of another) from the base year calculation. The math is complex, but the end result is a good measure of inflation's current economic impact.

The U.S. Bureau of Economic Analysis (BEA) first adopted the dollar-chaining technique in 1996 and has been using it ever since. If you want to find out more about the math used in this technique, check out this link on the BEA website: `www.bea.gov/scb/pdf/2003/11November/1103%20Chain-dollar.pdf`.

Adjusting for seasonal fluctuations

Some parts of the economy rise and fall with the seasons. For example, retail sales and retail employment are strongest just before the Christmas holiday. Housing construction ramps up in the spring and tapers off during the fall. Fresh fruits and vegetables are most expensive during the winter when fresh produce is scarce.

Many economic reports are adjusted to account for these seasonal fluctuations, which are often lumped together and called *seasonality.* The goal of seasonal adjustments is to reveal the true strength or weakness of the underlying economic data, without having the seasonal fluctuations obscure the underlying trend. When you remove seasonality, monthly or quarterly results become a whole lot easier to compare.

Most reports, such as the Employment Situation report, provide both the actual data and the data with seasonal adjustments. That way, you get to choose which data series you use for your analysis.

Considering the Timeliness of Economic Indicators

Some economic indicators are pretty good fortunetellers; they anticipate what's going to happen in the economy and provide advanced warning of coming changes. Others describe the state of the economy as it exists today, and still others tell you where the economy has been. This section looks at these three types of indicators.

Leading indicators make forecasts

A *leading indicator* signals changes before the economy even knows things are changing. Some leading indicators are very good at identifying upcoming recessions. Others are very good at showing when a recession is likely to end. Unfortunately, few do both well.

Leading indicators aren't perfect oracles. Sometimes they're right, but other times they're wrong. So don't think of them as infallible predictions. Instead, think of them as signs of things that *may* happen, and then do more research to see if you can find other signs that say the same thing.

Examples of leading indicators include

- **Housing indicators:** Home building often precedes economic recovery and decline. The housing market offered one of the early warnings that the economy was in trouble in 2007 and 2008. However, it didn't recover as the economy regained its footing in 2009 and 2010. I discuss housing indicators in Chapter 11.
- **Consumer and business confidence surveys:** Surveys are often good economic forecasters. I discuss consumer surveys in Chapter 5 and business surveys in Chapter 10.
- **Employment indicators:** Declines in employment (or increases in unemployment) often precede the onset of an economic recession. However, as the economy begins to recover from a recession, employment often lags behind. I go over employment indicators in Chapter 4.

Note: Although the stock market isn't considered an economic indicator, it does have some predictive power. Stock market indexes like the S&P 500 and the Nasdaq Composite have a history of declining before an economic recession and trending higher before an economic recovery. Of course, no indicator is perfect. The stock market forecasts many more recessions than actually occur.

Coincident indicators are no coincidence

Economic indicators that mirror the performance of the economy are called *coincident indicators.* Although they aren't good for forecasting the economic future, they offer plenty of information about the current economic condition.

Examples of coincident indicators include

- **Gross domestic product (GDP):** The quarterly GDP report is almost the definition of a coincident indicator. Its purpose is to show how big the current economy is and how fast it's growing. It reports the total value of everything made or sold in the United States. I go over this extensive report in Chapter 7.
- **Personal income:** Personal income is a part of the Personal Income and Outlays report and is one of the monthly inputs used to calculate GDP. Although consumer spending tends to lead the economy, personal income grows and falls along with the economy. I discuss personal income in detail in Chapter 6.

Lagging indicators can't foretell the future

You may be wondering what the point of having a lagging indicator is. After all, a *lagging indicator* only tells where you've been. Well, that's the point; lagging indicators are useful to analysts because they confirm that the economy has turned a corner and started to expand or decline.

Employment may be the most obvious example of a lagging indicator, at least part of the time. Though it's very good at identifying when the economy is likely to enter a recession, it's very slow to recover after the economy has started to expand. So employment is both a leading indicator and a lagging indicator.

Looking into the Future with Consensus Forecasts

Forecasting is hard, especially when you're forecasting the future. Whether it's the weather, the stock market, or the economy, telling the future with any degree of accuracy is difficult.

That said, people still try. Turn on the business news. Analysts tell you what their favorite stock is going to do tomorrow. Fund managers describe how the market's going to react to the most recently released economic indicator. And economists are always forecasting the economy's growth rate for the coming year.

The track record for these folks is rather unremarkable. Studies done by the U.S. Federal Reserve show that no forecasters are consistently right. You may as well listen to the weatherman.

However, if you take the results from a lot of forecasters and average them together, you may do better than following any single one of them. That's the idea behind *consensus forecasts* (sometimes called *consensus opinions* or *consensus estimates*); they average many individual forecasts to create one consensus value.

If you want a closer look at consensus forecasting, specifically where some of the more reliable sources are and how to check the accuracy of them, the following sections can help.

Finding consensus forecasts

One of the games investors play is trying to guess the value of upcoming economic reports. Several firms provide private consensus forecasts for a fee. If you're not looking to spend any money, you can find some free consensus forecasts at the following websites:

- **Bloomberg:** Go to `www.bloomberg.com/markets/economic-calendar` and click on the individual economic reports to find the consensus estimates.
- **MarketWatch:** Go to `www.marketwatch.com/economy-politics/calendars/economic` and look in the Forecast column to find MarketWatch's consensus estimates.
- **Briefing.com:** Go to `www.breifing.com/investor/calendars/economic/` for a list of consensus estimates for reports issued during the coming week.

Analyzing the accuracy of the consensus

Consensus forecasts are at least somewhat more accurate than most individual forecasts. Although consensus forecasts aren't perfect by any means, they generally outperform any individual's forecasts over time.

The caveat is that you still have to give consensus forecasts a lot of leeway. But as long as you understand that the actual result may differ from the consensus estimate by many basis points (and sometimes by whole percentage points), the consensus forecast is often your best choice. (See the sidebar

"Distinguishing between percent, percentage points, and basis points" if you're not sure of the difference between basis and percentage points.)

If your business plans or investment strategies require precise forecasts of the economy, you're playing a dangerous game. Even if you correctly forecast the upcoming GDP or inflation report, that indicator isn't necessarily a perfect measure of the current economy or a good forecast of the economic future. Play it safe; use these economic forecasts as a guide to adjust your planning, not as the be-all-end-all of your investments.

Amending and Modifying Data with Revision Reports

Economic data are rarely set in stone. Often, early economic reports are based on incomplete facts. So as new information is collected, the data in previous reports are revised. This type of revision is very common.

Another type of revision — called a benchmark revision — has a more significant impact. I go over both types of revisions in this section.

Revising previous reports

The first release of an economic report is commonly identified as *preliminary*. When new or missing data are gathered, the preliminary report is revised. Revising is a common occurrence, so you can expect that most economic reports will be revised periodically.

Some reports have only minimal revisions based on new data, while other adjustments to preliminary reports can be extensive. In fact, some reports see changes that are significant enough to affect many months or even years of the indicator's previously reported data.

Investors and business leaders (as well as economists and policy analysts) regularly make decisions and plans in the face of incomplete information. That's why they want to see the data reports as early as possible, even if those reports will be revised later. After all, something is better than nothing. You can wait for the revised data if you prefer, but most investors and business leaders make portfolio and businesses decisions based on the early reports. They may have to revise their plans when the data are amended, but that's a decision for a later date.

Changing benchmarks

People change. Buying and spending habits change. Old products become obsolete as new products make their way into the marketplace. Periodically, the agencies responsible for publishing an economic report must reexamine the assumptions they made when they created the report, adjust the methods used to collect the data, or decide to change the report's layout. Adjustments made to take into account these changes in the marketplace are called *benchmark revisions.* Although all reports may be subject to benchmark revisions, those that are adjusted for seasonality and especially those that are adjusted for inflation are more frequently revised.

How benchmark revisions work

Benchmark revisions are different from simple data revisions. A benchmark change can modify the structure of the report, reclassify data definitions, or provide new data presentations. For instance, the tables in a report may be updated for newly developed products. Benchmark updates may even require revisions to data from previous reports, sometimes causing those reports to undergo significant changes dating back many years.

Benchmark adjustments are made periodically to most economic indicators. The frequency of benchmark changes differs by the report. The indicators most affected are surveys based on sampled populations. Surveyors need to frequently realign their sampled populations with the underlying population to make sure the survey techniques capture statistically valid results. This type of benchmark revision often occurs annually. For example, the Employment Situation report, which I discuss in Chapter 4, undergoes an annual benchmark revision. The CPI benchmark for seasonal adjustments is also updated every year (see Chapter 12). Other reports schedule benchmark reviews every five or ten years.

For analysts, benchmark changes represent both a blessing and a curse. After a benchmark change, some or all historical data must be adjusted to conform to the new benchmark. At best, this adjustment process can be confusing. But it can also help clarify in some situations. For example, in 2009, a benchmark revision for GDP made the 2001 recession look less severe than originally thought. This same revision showed that the 2007–2008 recession was more severe than original estimates.

Some benchmark changes can be radical. For example, during the 1997 benchmark exercise, the U.S. Bureau of Economic Analysis (BEA) converted all of its record keeping from the Standard Industry Classification (SIC) to the North American Industry Classification System.

Introducing a new benchmark on the block

The GDP report used to undergo extensive benchmark revisions every five years or so. A recent change to the GDP revision process (made in 2010) means that the GDP report's benchmarks will be revised much more frequently. The BEA calls this approach *flexible benchmarking*. The new flexible benchmark revisions are intended to accompany the traditional annual revisions but also to more quickly improve the GDP report to more accurately reflect the U.S. economy.

These new changes to GDP may include changes to data definitions and presentations, as well as the introduction of new methods for estimating data. You can reasonably expect the BEA to roll out this type of flexible benchmark to other indicators during the coming years.

Cha-Ching: Money, Interest Rates, and the Economy

The concept of money shows up throughout this book, so I want to clearly define the concept here. Most people look at the currency in their wallet and consider that to be money. Well, it is, but currency is only one form of money in the U.S. economy.

Economists define *money* as currency plus some of the deposits at banks and credit unions. In other words, there's a whole lot more *money* than *currency* circulating through the economic and banking system. I delve deeper into the money discussion in this section (see Chapter 8 for even more info).

Understanding the Fed's monetary measures

Economists use the term *demand deposits* to describe bank deposits that can be withdrawn without notice to the bank. In the United States, a checking account is an example of a demand deposit. But demand deposits make up only one part of the money supply. Other types of deposits considered in the money supply include money in savings accounts, some money market deposits, travelers' checks, certificates of deposit, and bank deposits with the U.S. Federal Reserve. (Note that IRA and other retirement accounts aren't included in the money supply.)

You need to understand the types and values of money to follow some economic indicators, including the FOMC statement, and some of the Federal Reserve's actions (which I discuss in Chapter 8). The Federal Reserve tracks and reports money supply values, using a language all its own. The following two categories of money are the most important in terms of economic indicators:

- **M1:** M1 consists of currency held by the public, travelers' checks, and demand deposits at commercial banks, credit unions, and thrift institutions.
- **M2:** M2 consists of M1, plus savings accounts, money market accounts, some certificates of deposit, and money market mutual funds; it excludes IRA and other retirement account assets.

Setting short- and long-term interest rates

Interest rates have a direct impact on the economy's ability to grow. Low rates generally facilitate economic growth, while high rates generally impede growth.

In general, the marketplace sets interest rates. When businesses and consumers need to borrow money, the interest rate is directly dependent on how much money is currently available to lend and on expectations about future inflation. The longer the term of the loan, the more inflation will affect the interest rate. Consumers with high credit scores and businesses that have a long history of stable cash flows or that can offer significant collateral qualify for the best interest rates on their loans. Those that present a greater default risk are charged higher rates.

The U.S. Federal Reserve has some influence over all rates. After all, it controls the value of one very short-term interest rate, the federal funds rate, and it controls how much base money banks must keep in reserve. These controls affect the base rate for all loans. (I discuss the federal funds rate in depth in Chapter 8.)

Chapter 3

Understanding the Big Picture: The Economy and Its Footprints

In This Chapter

- Cycling through the economic landscape from periods of growth to recessions
- Surveying the four main financial markets
- Identifying the ins and outs of economic reports
- Determining an indicator's market impact, timeliness, and relevance

Before digging into individual economic indicators, you may want to take a step back and view the big picture. What exactly is the economy, anyway? Put simply, it's you and me and all the other people who go to work, buy things, make things, and sell things. It includes businesses, banks, shoppers, contractors, and employees. In short, the *economy* is the accumulation of all business transactions throughout a particular country (or the world, if you're talking about the global economy). You can make this definition a whole lot more complicated if you want to, but why do that when the simple definition is at least as good and offers the benefit of clarity?

Of course, no matter which definition you use, the economy also includes the government. After all, most bureaucrats long for a starring role in the economy. In fact, they generally want their fair share of every business transaction in order to keep the government's coffers full.

Although the economy's natural tendency is to grow, it never grows straight ahead, so you need to pay careful attention to where it's been and where it's heading as you make your investment decisions. This chapter looks at the regularly recurring economic patterns of growth and recession. It also shows you how economic indicators report on the condition of the economy, how some indicators fall in and out of fashion with the times, and how you can use economic indicators to improve your investing and business strategies.

Taking a Closer Look at the Business Cycle

History may not actually repeat itself, but it sure comes close. The history of economies is littered with manias and depressions. In fact, economies go through *business cycles* and travel the road from boom to bust so frequently that you'd think they'd occasionally try a different route, but they never do.

One boom differs from the next, but you can count on people to eventually buy too much, overextend themselves (and their pocketbooks), and have to pull back. One boom gains momentum from excitement over the new fangled Internet, which makes shopping a cinch. All you have to do is start a new Internet company and you're sure to get rich — right? Escalating housing prices drives the next boom. And the one after that? Who knows?

The economy's booms may not end in exactly the same way, but every expansion so far has ended in recession. After all, the economy has to slow down to recover from all the spending that occurred during the boom.

The following sections explain in greater depth what business cycles are and how the economy moves up and down.

Identifying the phases of the cycle

Some economic experts quibble about the definition of an economic cycle. In fact, some even claim that the economy isn't cyclical at all and is instead a system of economy-wide fluctuations.

Call it what you will, the *economic* or *business cycle* is a useful way to describe the not-quite-cyclical phenomenon of expansion and contraction — boom and bust — that occurs over and over again in the economy. As you can see from the graphic depiction of a business cycle in Figure 3-1, cycles of boom and bust are easy to identify, at least in hindsight.

Each phase of the business cycle has recurring characteristics:

- **Peak:** At the business cycle's peak, most businesses are thriving and prices increase along with personal income. Unfortunately, all is not well. Interest rates climb as investors and the Federal Reserve worry about the risk of rising inflation. New-home construction slows a bit as higher prices and higher interest rates make homes less affordable.

Unemployment starts to creep up as the construction industries and related businesses slow.

- **Recession/contraction:** After a peak, the economy slows down. Sales of consumer goods, especially durable goods like cars and kitchen appliances, begin to slow. Businesses respond by slowing production and possibly laying off workers. Personal incomes fall as unemployment rises. Interest rates fall.

The popular definition of *recession* is an economic decline that falls short of a depression. This isn't very useful, given the imprecise definition of depression, so some economists clarify by saying that a recession must be two or more consecutive quarters of economic decline.

- **Trough:** The economy eventually slows its decline as it tries to find its footing. Lower interest rates eventually stimulate consumers to start shopping. One of the first signs of an economic trough is often bargain hunting for houses. Housing doesn't always lead the economy out of a recession, but it does often enough that the housing market is well worth your attention.
- **Recovery/expansion:** As the recovery blooms, industrial output picks up, as does demand for durable consumer products. Employers are reluctant to hire at the beginning of a recovery; instead, they ask their existing workforce to work overtime. Eventually, jobs become more plentiful as businesses become confident that the economic expansion is going to last.

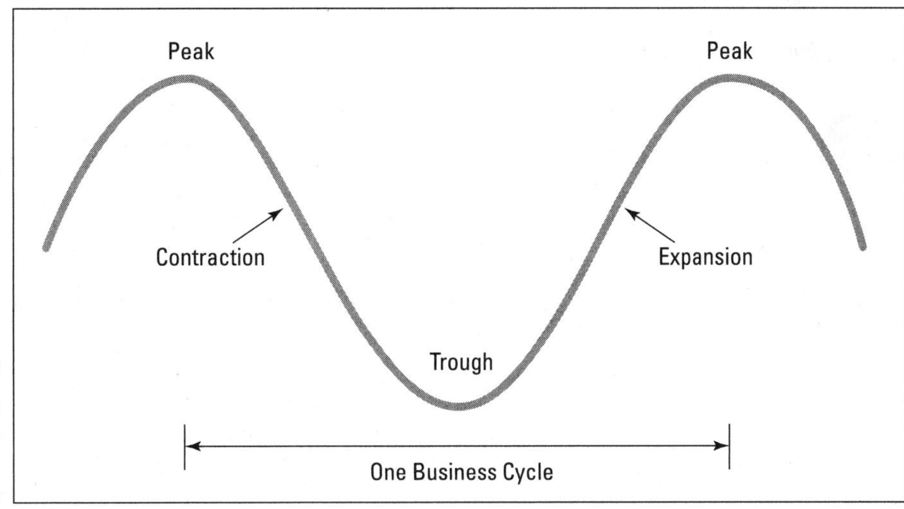

Figure 3-1: The business cycle.

Better late than never: Identifying recessions and recoveries

Before the 1930s and the Great Depression, any economic downturn was called a *depression.* Today most of these downturns would be considered *recessions* instead. Neither term really has a formal definition. Some economists consider any severe, sustained economic downturn to be a depression. Others claim that the downturn must last three years or more or account for at least a 10 percent decline in economic activity before it can be considered a depression. Regardless, the United States hasn't seen anything like the Great Depression (the period from 1929 through 1933 when the economy was cut roughly in half) or its aftershock in 1937 and 1938 when the economy declined by more than 18 percent.

The National Bureau of Economic Research (NBER) is the final authority on the matter. The NBER's Business Cycle Dating Committee (BCDC) identifies economic peaks and troughs in the United States. The BCDC looks at the economy's entire output of goods and services, employment, personal income, and industrial production to determine when a recession begins and ends. The NBER doesn't provide a formal definition for *recession,* but researchers know it when they see it (although they use the term *contraction* rather than *recession* and *expansion* rather than *recovery*). The BCDC believes its research approach provides a better indicator of when the economy is in expansion or contraction than using only one or two economic indicators (see the rest of this book for details on individual indicators).

Unfortunately, the BCDC isn't quick about making its announcements. Case in point: By the time the NBER declared the start of the 2007–2009 recession, it had been underway for 12 months. Likewise, in September 2010, the NBER announced that the recession had ended in June 2009, 14 months after the fact. Plus, when the NBER makes a declaration, it's not the final word. The bureau's pronouncements are always subject to revision, though they rarely occur.

You can keep up with the NBER's economic announcements on the NBER website at `www.nber.org/cycles/main.html`, and you can find a record of the economic cycles going back to 1857 at `www.nber.org/cycles/cyclesmain.html`. This particular site shows economic peaks and troughs by listing the number of intervening months from one peak to the following trough.

Although the NBER definitively identifies a recession's beginning and end, it delivers its reports so late that they're of little use to investors or business leaders (which is why savvy investors track the economy and economic indicators on their own).

By staying abreast of and anticipating these economic trends, you can identify when the economy has become overheated and improve your performance as an investor or business manager. You probably can't duplicate the thoroughness of the National Bureau of Economic Research's (NBER) economic analysis, but you can arrive at a conclusion that's remarkably similar.

As an added benefit, you can act on your personal assessment long before NBER publishes its report. (See the nearby sidebar for more on the NBER.)

Growing into expansion

For the economy to grow, people have to buy things. The more people buy, the faster the economy grows. After all, consumer spending attributes to a very large portion of economic growth. From toothpaste to automobiles, consumer purchases drive domestic production along with demand for foreign product imports. Service industries like healthcare and restaurants also depend on consumer spending to grow and prosper. Consumer spending causes companies to make more products, hire more workers, expand production facilities, and provide more and better services. (See Chapter 6 for details on consumer spending and Part III for the lowdown on business products and services.)

To spend, consumers need money. More jobs and better-paying jobs provide consumers with the money they need to spend. Of course, consumers can also borrow money to continue their spending habits. As long as personal incomes are increasing, lenders are usually willing to lend money to consumers for housing, automobiles, travel, or anything else they want to buy. From the economy's point of view, where the money comes from doesn't matter; what matters is that it comes. (Just remember that when consumers borrow to fuel their spending, that spending — and the subsequent economic growth — can't last forever.)

Slowing into recession

As the economy grows, investors and the Federal Reserve start to worry about inflation. The Federal Reserve's primary defense against growing inflation is to raise interest rates. Higher interest rates make borrowing money more expensive for consumers and businesses. (See Chapter 12 for more on inflation and Chapter 8 for more on the Federal Reserve.)

As the monthly payments for purchases rise, people start to pull back on spending. Big purchases, like houses, cars, appliances, and furniture, are the first to go. As interest rates rise, people can't qualify for the loans they need to buy these items.

As consumer spending slows, the economy heads for its peak and, ultimately, for a recession. Then the cycle starts over again.

Stimulating with government spending

The government has a few levers it can pull to influence the economy. The main one is setting interest rates at the Federal Reserve, but many economists argue that government spending can also stimulate economic demand.

Unfortunately, the effectiveness of government spending for stimulating economic growth is still up for debate. One camp points to the recent trillion-dollar stimulus packages and says that the 2007–2009 recession would've been much worse without the stimulus. The other camp argues that the trillion-dollar borrowing caused the recovery to remain sluggish, hampered private investment, and kept unemployment high.

There's little doubt that, in certain cases, government spending can be good for the economy. But the argument for increased government spending might be more persuasive if the government hadn't had to borrow the stimulus money. Besides driving the deficit higher, the stimulus borrowing may have crowded out private investments. After all, the economy has only so much money to slosh around. If it all goes toward government spending, the private sector will get squeezed.

Although increased government spending can create government jobs, little evidence suggests that government stimulus spending leads directly to increasing private sector employment. Thus, in most situations, government spending is a poor substitute for private investment.

Reviewing the Key Financial Markets

Today most people are at least familiar with the major investment markets. Although investments in stocks, bonds, and commodities used to be the province of the very rich, growing numbers of Americans now have at least some assets invested in 401(k) and other retirement programs.

The investment markets are very sensitive to the state of the economy and the business cycle. Hence, economic indicators are very useful tools for investors because they can help you see where the economy is now and where it's heading. Armed with this information, you can improve your investment results.

This section looks briefly at the impact the economy and the business cycle have on the major investment markets.

Investing in stocks

When most people think of investing, they think of stocks. When you own *stock* in a company, you own a small portion of that company. Hence, stocks are also called *equity investments* because stockholders own an equity position in the company.

Many investors today hold mutual funds and exchange-traded funds (ETFs) instead of holding stocks directly. Although these approaches are significantly different from directly owning stocks, the general concepts are the same. Funds that invest in stocks rise in value as prices for the funds' underlying stock positions appreciate.

Like the business cycle, the stock market has repeating tendencies, and different stock sectors perform well during different phases of the business cycle. You can use the Sector Rotation Model, which was first published by Sam Stovall, the chief investment strategist for Standard & Poor's, to help identify the stages of the stock market and the current stage of the business cycle. Figure 3-2 illustrates the Sector Rotation Model.

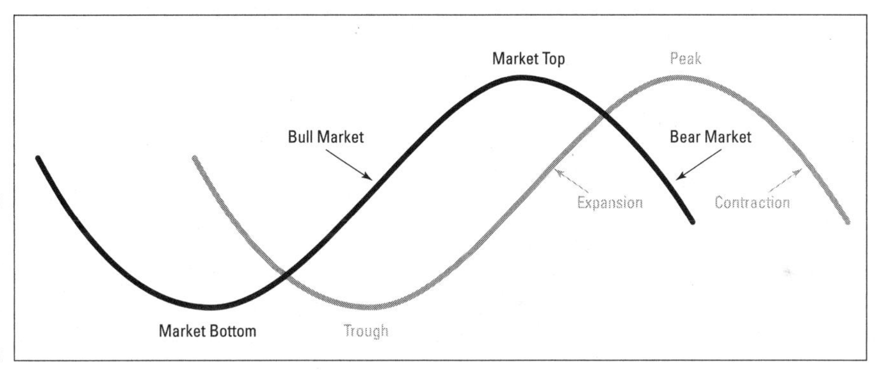

Figure 3-2: The Sector Rotation Model.

You can't set your watch by this model, but you can get some general clues about the state of the stock market and the overall economy by tracking different stock sectors.

The Sector Rotation Model divides the stock market into the following four broad stages:

- **Market bottom:** The values for broad stock market indexes like the Dow Jones Industrial Average and the S&P 500 are at their lowest. The market bottom coincides with the lowest prices for many stocks.
- **Bull market:** Prices for most stocks and broad stock market indexes are rising.
- **Market top:** The values for the broad market indexes and for many stocks are at their highest.
- **Bear market:** Prices for most stocks and broad market indexes are falling.

During these four stages, you often see recurring patterns in which certain sectors of the market perform better than others. These patterns intersect with the economy and business cycle. Here's an example of how the stock market and business cycle generally correlate:

- **Early bull market:** The stock market tends to lead the economy. During an early bull phase of the market, stock prices for many stocks begin to rise. However, the economy is still in recession. The business cycle is still declining and heading for a trough. The stock market generally anticipates the coming improvement in the business environment.

  So-called cyclical stocks and technology stocks are often the leaders in an early bull market. *Cyclical stocks* are those that perform well when the economy is doing well. Investors try to get in on the early action, causing the prices of these stocks to rise. Cyclical stocks include steel manufacturers, construction companies, auto manufacturers, and consumer durable goods companies. Technology industries include software companies, network and communication equipment suppliers, computer companies, and semiconductor manufacturers.

- **Middle bull market:** As stock prices continue to climb, the economy reaches its trough as it gets ready to come out of recession and begin its recovery. Industrial stocks often do well in this environment. These stocks include aerospace companies, farm and construction equipment manufacturers, industrial equipment suppliers, and machine tool manufacturers.
- **Late bull market:** The economy begins its recovery while stock prices continue to rise. Basic material stocks start to perform well. These stocks include industries such as agricultural and specialty chemicals, aluminum and other industrial metals, as well as oil and gas producers, refineries, and other energy producers.
- **Market top:** The economy is doing really well, but stock investors are beginning to get nervous. Experience tells them that the expansion won't last. But at the same time, stocks of energy companies and precious metal companies begin to do well. The stocks of energy companies are doing well because the demand for energy is growing, which pushes energy prices and energy stock prices higher. Prices for precious metals are rising because investors are getting nervous about the possibility of inflation, and precious metals (and, to a lesser extent, the stocks of precious metals companies) can be a hedge against that risk. (Be aware that the stock market doesn't always get the timing right for this phase of the business cycle. Investors are a skittish bunch and have been known to cause more than a few sell-offs before the economy actually heads into recession.)
- **Early bear market:** The economy hasn't peaked yet, but experienced stock investors are heading for the exits. Instead of cashing out completely, they often put their money in relatively lower-risk or less-volatile stocks, like those of companies that produce things that people use every day (basic consumer staples, in other words). Food and beverage companies, pharmaceutical manufacturers, cosmetics companies, and

manufacturers of household products like soap, shampoo, dishwashing detergent, and toothpaste are all examples of basic consumer staples. The share prices of many stocks are falling, though stocks of consumer staples companies tend to hold value and sometimes rise in price during this period.

- **Middle bear market:** The economy has peaked and is now heading for a recession (or contraction). Stock prices continue to fall. However, stocks of service providers, like healthcare companies, auto parts retailers, drugstores, and food wholesalers, tend to hold their value in this environment.
- **Late bear market:** The recession is in full swing. Investors are looking for a place to park their assets. Stocks of financial companies, including banks and insurance companies, often do well in this environment, as do stocks of dividend-paying utilities, such as electric companies, gas companies, and water service companies.
- **Market bottom:** The business cycle is still in recession. Investors are looking for the next big thing. In anticipation of a new bull market, transportation stocks and cyclical stocks begin to perform well again.

Although the Sector Rotation Model's main purpose is to help investors identify the current state of the market, it's also useful in helping economic forecasters gauge the state of the economy. It's by no means a perfect tool, but it does offer insight into the current state of the economic cycle.

Holding bonds

A *bond* is basically just a loan. Borrowers issue bonds, and the investors who buy the bonds lend money to the bond issuers. The borrower gets the money upfront. In exchange, the lender — the bond buyer — receives interest payments until the bond matures (zero-coupon bonds are one exception to this rule; I discuss them later in this section). At the bond's maturity, the lender receives the final interest payment, along with the repayment of the original principal amount of the loan.

For a variety of reasons, risk-averse investors favor these fixed-income investments over equity investments. That's not to say that bonds are without risk. Even the highest-rated bonds are subject to price fluctuations as interest rates rise and fall. But bond investors are generally more concerned with the continued stream of interest payments rather than the current price of the bond because many bond investors hold their investments until maturity.

The biggest worry bond investors have is inflation. Bonds and bond prices are extremely sensitive to inflation because the value of the interest payment declines whenever inflation is high. In a low-inflation environment, interest rates tend to stay low and bond prices stay high. As inflation concerns rise, so do interest rates. This direct relationship with inflation makes bonds very sensitive to the business cycle and the economy. (See Chapter 6 for details on inflation and Chapter 14 for details on interest rates.)

Here's a very brief survey of the types of bonds that are available, listed in order of their risk profile:

- **U.S. Treasury securities:** The United States borrows a lot of money. Even so, U.S. securities are considered to be among the lowest-risk loans in the world; so low, in fact, that the risk of default is almost nonexistent. The U.S. Treasury handles all these loans. Short-term and long-term loans go by different names:
  - **Treasury bills:** These very short-term loans have maturities of one year or less. Treasury bills don't pay interest. Instead, the Treasury sells them at a discount to face (par) value. At maturity, the investor receives their face value.
  - **Treasury notes:** These loans have maturities of one to ten years. Treasury notes are interest-bearing securities.
  - **Treasury bonds:** Probably the best known of the Treasury securities, these loans have maturities that range up to 30 years.
  - **Treasury Inflation-Protected Securities (TIPS):** These bonds are for inflation-wary investors because they're indexed for inflation. If inflation goes up, so does the biannual interest payment. If deflation rears its ugly head, the bond's interest payment falls. At maturity, the bondholder receives either the face value or the inflation-adjusted principal, whichever is higher.
- **Municipal bonds:** The federal government isn't the only government borrower. States, counties, cities, school boards, and various government agencies, like airports and water utilities, all use debt to finance various projects. When these state and local government entities borrow, their bonds are called *municipal bonds,* or *munis.* Interest on munis is sometimes tax-free. The federal government doesn't levy income taxes on munis, and state governments rarely tax in-state munis, although states may tax out-of-state munis. The two types of munis are
  - **General obligation bonds:** The full faith and taxing authority of the government municipality that's borrowing the money backs these bonds. They're often the lowest-risk munis and, therefore, offer the lowest interest rates.
  - **Revenue bonds:** Instead of backing the bond with the full faith and credit of the borrower, the government backs some bonds with the revenue stream from a specific government asset. Examples include civic arenas, airports, and water utilities. These asset-backed munis may be riskier and, therefore, pay a higher interest rate than traditional general obligation munis.

- **Corporate bonds:** Corporate borrowers also use the bond market to raise capital. Corporate bonds range from very low risk to relatively high risk:
    - **Investment-grade bonds:** Some institutional investors, such as insurance companies and pension plans, may invest only in bonds with a relatively low risk of default. That's why bond issuers hire bond-rating agencies to evaluate the risk of each bond and bond issuer and to assign the bond a rating based on their evaluation.
    - **Noninvestment-grade bonds:** Also called *junk bonds,* noninvestment-grade bonds have a higher risk of default. They pay higher interest rates to compensate for the higher risk to the lender.

Most bonds in the United States are issued for a fixed interest rate and a fixed term to maturity. In addition to these traditional bonds, some borrowers offer the following variations on the bond theme:

- **Callable bonds:** These bonds give the issuer the right to repay the bond before maturity. Both munis and corporate bonds are sometimes issued with the call option.
- **Convertible bonds:** The convertible feature of some corporate bonds allows the bondholder to exchange the bond for a fixed number of shares of the company's stock.
- **Floating rate notes:** These bonds have a variable coupon rate, which means that the interest payment is adjusted based on a reference rate like the London Interbank Offered Rate (LIBOR) or the federal funds rate.
- **Zero-coupon bonds:** These bonds don't pay interest. Instead, they're sold at a discount to their face value. The investor receives the face value when the bond matures. Treasury bills are an example of zero-coupon bonds.
- **Inflation-adjusted bonds:** These bonds are linked to an inflation-rate measure, such as CPI. Usually, the principal value is adjusted based on the CPI; the interest payment is then calculated from the inflation-adjusted principal amount. Although not common, corporate and muni inflation-adjusted bonds are sometimes issued. TIPS bonds are an example of inflation-adjusted bonds.

Trading commodities

The commodities markets span a wide range of products. Commodity products are either purchased directly from the producers or sold through a standardized exchange. Though transactions can occur in several different ways, the most economically sensitive markets include the following:

- **Cash markets:** Commodity producers and purchasers sometimes buy and sell commodities by using *cash market* (also called *spot market*) transactions. The buyer pays the current market price, sometimes called the *spot price,* and the seller expects payment upon delivery. There are a few centralized cash market exchanges for trading high-volume commodities like gasoline and natural gas. However, most transactions are handled directly by the buyer and seller, through local cooperatives, or through a specialized commodities broker. More commodities trade in cash markets than in futures markets.
- **Futures markets:** A *futures contract* is a standardized form of forward contract that's bought and sold on a futures exchange. *Forward contracts* specify the commodity, the quantity, and the delivery terms. *Futures exchanges* (such as the CMEGroup, formerly the Chicago Mercantile Exchange) provide physical and electronic trading facilities, much like stock exchanges. Each futures exchange sets its own contract standards; however, in the case where multiple exchanges trade the same commodity, contracts are generally similar.

  Examples of commodities traded on futures exchanges include

  - **Agriculture:** Soybeans, wheat, corn, cotton, orange juice, coffee, sugar, meat, and livestock
  - **Industrial metals:** Copper, aluminum, and steel
  - **Precious metals:** Gold, silver, platinum, and palladium
  - **Energy:** Crude oil, gasoline, and natural gas

Commodity producers and users often use commodities markets for *hedging* (a technique used to offset or minimize the risk of adverse price movements). Prices of these agricultural and industrial commodity products are generally very sensitive to both inflationary pressures and the economic cycle. (See Chapter 15 for more on commodities and the markets in which they're traded.)

Tracking currencies

The value of a currency, like the Japanese yen or the U.S. dollar, is directly tied to the strength of the local economy. In the case of the U.S. dollar, its value is high when the U.S. economy is strong and growing. It's low when the U.S. economy is in decline. Inflation also has a significant effect on the U.S. dollar. When the United States experiences inflation, the value of the U.S. dollar declines. These relationships between the local currency and the local economy hold true for all currencies.

Cashing coupons

The interest payment on a bond is sometimes called the *coupon* or *coupon payment*. The term *coupon* is a holdover from the days when bond certificates were issued with coupons attached. The bondholder would clip the coupon and cash it at the bank.

Bonds with coupons attached were generally known as *bearer bonds*. Unlike most bonds today, bearer bonds are unregistered. In other words, nobody tracks the ownership of the bond. The bearer bond's interest coupon is payable to the holder of the bond. Due to changes in the U.S. tax code, newly issued bearer bonds are generally not available in the United States.

If you've ever traveled overseas, you intuitively understand the nature of currency trading. When you go to the bank to exchange dollars for an upcoming trip, sometimes your dollars buy more of the foreign currency and other times they buy less. For example, assume that you're a U.S. resident. If you book your trip when the dollar is strong but it falls by the time you take the trip, your trip becomes more expensive even if overseas prices remain constant.

The idea of investing in currencies is similar to exchanging dollars for a trip, but it generally takes place on a much larger scale. Large currency investors, such as banks, exporters, and importers, primarily use the highly leveraged foreign exchange markets to hedge against currency exchange risk.

For example, the United States imports a great deal of product from overseas producers. U.S. importers pay for imports with dollars. If the value of the dollar falls, relative to the local currency, the overseas producers can lose money on the transaction because of the change in the exchange rate. The exporter can protect against that loss by selling dollars in the foreign exchange market.

Speculators and central banks also have a role to play in currency trading. Speculators that trade currencies hope to profit from changes in exchange rates. Central banks use the foreign exchange markets to manage the money supply (see Chapter 8 for details). Individual investors may also invest in currencies by using mutual funds and exchange-traded funds.

Figuring Out What's What in Economic Reports

Each month, dozens of economic reports are released from a variety of sources, both public and private. The U.S. Government is the largest publisher of economic data about the U.S. economy. Fortunately for you and me, it makes its research reports and most of its data freely available on the Internet. Privately generated reports are often available by paid subscription, but some publishers provide excerpts to the public at no charge.

In the following sections, I explain what information is essential in the reports and how they're assembled so you can focus on just what you need.

Finding what's important in each report

Some economic reports are quite simple in terms of what information they present, but many of them are chock-full of data tables, charts, graphs, and analyses. You quickly realize that there are too many reports and too much data for one person to fully grasp. Fortunately, you don't need to follow every report, and you don't need all the information that appears in each report. Many economy reports provide a quick summary that highlights the most important changes. Some, however, require you to dig into the data tables to find the crucial bits. As I describe each indicator throughout this book, I show you where to find the most useful information.

To help you determine what's important for your needs, I offer suggestions for reports that are useful for different types of investors and business managers later in this chapter. This book also provides tips for creating and using your own set of economic reports in Chapters 19 and 20.

You can try to read all the reports, but you risk becoming paralyzed by the data. Avoid analysis paralysis and don't try to track every indicator when you start out. Pick the indicator that's most pertinent to your task, find out how it works, and start following it. Then pick another one. Most people can get what they need by following ten or so indicators. You may need more than that, or you may need fewer. Either way, I recommend that you add one indicator to your quiver each week or month until you're confident in your analytic skills. If you're not sure where to start, keep reading. This book helps you prioritize which reports are right for you and your needs.

Unfortunately, economic reports aren't perfect. Sometimes they contradict each other, and they rarely paint a perfectly clear picture of the current economic situation or provide a perfectly reliable forecast of the future. I recommend that you first evaluate the potential impact of any contradictory or incomplete information. If the potential impact is high (in other words, if you or your business stands to lose a lot of money if the information is correct), then do what you must to reduce the risk. Otherwise, wait for additional information before making any big decisions.

Seeing how reports are assembled

Most U.S. economic reports tackle only a small part of the U.S. economy, such as employment, personal income and spending, or inflation. But reporting for even these small slices of the economy takes a remarkable amount of research and data.

To get a better idea of how economic reports are assembled, consider the Employment Situation report from the U.S. Bureau of Labor Statistics (BLS). The BLS bases this report on the following two very large surveys:

- **Household Survey:** This monthly survey covers about 60,000 households throughout the United States. Researchers ask about the employment status for each person living in the household.
- **Establishment Survey:** This monthly survey collects employment data from about 140,000 businesses, nonprofit organizations, and government employers.

The BLS collates and disseminates the results from these two surveys about a week after the surveys are complete. Although the BLS may revise the reported data in a subsequent release, many investors and business leaders pay close attention to the first release of this report.

Measuring the entirety of the U.S. economy is a gargantuan undertaking. To create the Big Kahuna of economic reports — the Gross Domestic Product (GDP) report — the U.S. Bureau of Economic Analysis (BEA) assembles and distills numerous economic measures, including consumer purchases, personal income, industrial production, business inventories, and current interest rates.

Showing Economic Fashions without the Runway

Just as fashions change with the seasons, economic indicators fall in and out of favor with changes in the economic climate. Investors and business leaders are likely to care about different economic reports based on the current economic cycle and the particular markets they're involved in. For example, as an economic expansion matures, investors are keenly aware of the housing and employment reports because a decline in either may indicate the first cracks in the expansion.

During an economic decline, on the other hand, investors aren't likely to care much about employment statistics because employment is usually the last indicator to recover after the economy begins its expansion.

Several factors determine when investors and business leaders are most interested in a specific indicator. Of course, the indicator's predictive ability in a specific part of the economic cycle is one of the main considerations. Another is how quickly the indicator is made available and how frequently its reports are revised. The following sections discuss these factors and show how different types of investors react to different types of indicators.

Understanding market sensitivity

Indicators move in and out of fashion. The state of the economy affects how investors and the market react to economic indicators. For example, as long as inflation reports show low inflation, those reports generate very little reaction or interest in the investment markets. But when conditions for inflationary pressures rise, inflation indicators rise to the top of the watch list, and investors, particularly bond investors, start digging into consumer and business price data from many sources to ferret out any hint that inflation is becoming a problem.

Investors are a skittish bunch when things are going well. When the economy is growing, the job market is strong, and stock prices are rising, investors and traders start watching for unwelcome surprises. You can gauge how sensitive an economic report is and how it impacts the investment markets with a sensitivity rating. I use the following ratings in this book when discussing economic reports:

- **Low:** Rarely impacts the investment markets
- **Moderate:** Occasionally impacts the investment markets
- **High:** Regularly impacts the investment markets

Sometimes an economic indicator is so important to the market that investors collectively hold their breath while waiting for the data's release. Other times, investors meet the same indicator with a collective shrug. How the market reacts to the indicator really depends on the current economic cycle. For example:

- **During a recession, investors look for indications that things are getting better.** They focus on the stock market indexes and the Sector Rotation Model, housing reports, and reports of durable goods like automobiles and kitchen appliances.
- **As an economic expansion matures, investors watch for signs that the economy is becoming overheated.** They look for rising interest rates, rising inflation, signs of increasing unemployment, and constraints at manufacturing production facilities.

Bad news rarely comes as a complete surprise. When everything in the economy looks great, the first hints that something is amiss usually come from predictable places. For example, when interest rates get too high, folks have a harder time qualifying for mortgages and the number of housing starts usually drops as a result. Or after employment and the economy have been growing for some time, an employment report that shows no job growth may be the first sign that an expansion is coming to an end.

Determining an indicator's accuracy and timeliness

If you want to follow economic indicators, you need to know when they're released and how accurate they are. Most indicators are released once a month, but some are released once a week, others are released once a quarter, and a few are released only once a year.

But knowing the publication schedule is only part of the equation. Don't forget about accuracy and timeliness. Some economic indicators are rushed out the door before all the data are fully collected. But even with the uncertainty that accompanies these reports, investors and business leaders are eager to know the preliminary results. Updated reports are usually released a month or two later. Other reports aren't released until months after the data are collected. The information in these reports is usually more accurate but not nearly as timely.

Economic reports rarely have the capability of being both accurate and timely. Given the choice, most investors and business leaders would choose timely preliminary results over accurate but delayed results. Even if a report will be revised later, investors want to know what data have been collected so far. I identify those timely indicators that are subject to significant revisions throughout this book.

Seeing who's interested in what

Some investors and business leaders are interested in one kind of economic data, while others follow completely different indicators. Although generalizing these preferences perfectly is impossible, you can easily match the type of investor with their economic interests. The following sections tell you which investors are interested in which indicators.

Stock investors

Stock prices are a reflection of corporate profitability and profit growth, which are directly related to consumer spending. So, of course, stock investors focus on economic indicators that may signal changes in consumer spending patterns. The indicators of most interest to stock investors, in order of their market sensitivity, timeliness, and importance to the stock markets, include

- **Employment reports:** Employment is a key indicator for tracking consumer spending patterns. If employment levels fall, consumer spending won't be far behind. Employment reports include the Employment Situation report, the Unemployment Insurance Weekly Claims Report, and the ADP National Employment Report®. (See Chapter 4 for details on employment indicators.)
- **Consumer confidence:** Consumer confidence is another good indicator for anticipating future consumer spending. Reports include the University of Michigan's Consumer Sentiment Index, the Conference Board's Consumer Confidence Index, and Bloomberg's Consumer Comfort Index. (I discuss consumer confidence surveys in Chapter 5.)
- **Income and spending:** The Personal Income and Outlays report and the Retail Trade report provide information about the current spending habits of consumers. (See Chapter 6 for details.)
- **Inflation:** Consumer and producer price indexes provide insight into inflation's effect on the economy. Rising inflation means that consumer prices are trending higher, which generally means that consumers may have to scale back purchases of products and services. (See Chapter 12 for the lowdown on these indexes.)
- **Manufacturing:** The Manufacturing ISM Report On Business® provides detailed insight into the condition of manufacturing industries throughout the United States. This report is highly correlated with the economy (see Chapter 10 for details). The Industrial Production and Capacity Utilization report is also a key manufacturing indicator that stock investors keep track of (see Chapter 8 for details).
- **The economy as a whole:** The GDP report is the quarterly summary of all goods and services produced in the United States. It includes consumer spending for domestically produced products as well as imported products. Although it's issued quarterly, it provides important insight into the economy and consumer spending. (See Chapter 7 for everything you need to know about the GDP report.)

Bond investors

Inflation and interest rates are the primary concerns of bond investors. As interest rates rise, the value of bond holdings falls, and inflation is one of the key drivers leading to higher interest rates. During periods when interest rates are high, bond investors look for the economy's turning point so they can lock in the high interest rates and profit as bond prices rise while interest rates fall. Although stock and bond investors may look to some of the same reports for information, their reactions couldn't be more different. The indicators that bond investors find most interesting, in order of their market sensitivity, timeliness, and importance to the bond market, include

- **Interest rates:** The Federal Reserve is responsible for setting interest rate targets in the United States, so bond investors are very interested in their deliberations. To stay up-to-date with the Federal Reserve and interest rates, bond investors follow the Federal Open Market Committee (FOMC) report, which I discuss in Chapter 8, and the yield curve, which I discuss in Chapter 14.
- **Inflation:** Consumer and producer price indexes provide insight into inflation's effect on the economy. Rising inflation is a red flag for bond investors. (See Chapter 12 for details.)
- **Employment reports:** Strong employment isn't a good sign for bond investors. They much prefer falling employment levels. Like stock investors, bond investors follow the Employment Situation report, the Unemployment Insurance Weekly Claims Report, and the ADP National Employment Report®, but they're hoping for results that are quite different from those that stock investors want to see. (See Chapter 4 for information on employment reports.)
- **Housing:** A strong housing market is a sign of a strong economy. So, naturally, bond investors perform best when housing is weak. Housing indicators that bond investors keep track of include the New Residential Construction report, the New Residential Sales report, and the Weekly Applications Survey. (See Chapter 11 for details.)
- **Income and spending:** Bond prices tend to rise as income and consumer spending fall, so bond investors keep close tabs on the Personal Income and Outlays report. (See Chapter 6 for details.)
- **The economy as a whole:** Bond investors are interested in the GDP report for its take on the economy and also for a specialized inflation gauge called the personal consumption expenditures (PCE) deflator. (See Chapter 7 for details.)

Currency traders

Those brave souls in the highly leveraged and volatile foreign exchange (currency) markets look for information that can cause the value of the U.S. dollar to trend higher or lower. In general, the dollar rises in value during periods of strong economic growth and falls during economic recessions.

Investors with an interest in the U.S. dollar are likely to follow the same indicators that stock investors follow. Foreign investors in the U.S. dollar prefer higher interest rates, but they don't like high inflation because it harms the value of the dollar.

The report that currency traders find most pertinent is the U.S. International Trade in Goods and Services report, which reports the number of U.S. imports and exports and the current account balance, commonly known as the trade deficit. Exports are especially important because they have a direct bearing on the value of the U.S. dollar: As exports rise, the demand for dollars rises. (See Chapter 16 for details on this report.)

Commodities traders

The interests of commodities traders lie mainly in the prices for agricultural and industrial commodities. As inflation heats up, prices for these commodities also rise. Industrial commodities like metals, lumber, and energy are more sensitive to the economic cycle than their agricultural counterparts. As the economy grows, so do industrial commodity prices. On the other hand, pricing for most agricultural products is more sensitive to weather patterns than to the general economy.

Expect commodities traders to follow the same indicators that stock investors follow. In addition, commodities traders stay abreast of the production and demand reports for individual commodity products, such as the U.S. Geological Society's Gold Report, the Department of Energy's This Week in Petroleum, and the U.S. Department of Agriculture's outlook reports for individual agricultural products (see Chapter 15 for details on these reports). Of course, commodity prices are an exceptionally good indicator of the supply and demand for any individual commodity. Rising prices indicate high demand, limited supply, or a combination of the two. Falling prices show falling demand, an abundant supply, or both.

Part II

Making Money, Spending Money: Employment and Consumer Indicators

"Hubris appears to be in decline while sarcasm remains strong in active trading..."

In this part . . .

In this part, you find the most basic, high-impact information you need to analyze the economy. At the heart of it all is consumer spending, which forms the basis for the whole U.S. economy. Without consumers, businesses and the economy have little reason to exist.

To help you understand the importance of consumer spending, Part II looks at the employment picture in terms of where consumers get their money, how much money they have to spend, and what they spend it on. It also shows you how economic indicators measure consumer feelings. After all, happy consumers spend more money than worried consumers.

Chapter 4

Counting Jobs and Unemployment

In This Chapter

- Getting acquainted with the Employment Situation report
- Noticing weekly claims for unemployment insurance
- Understanding the ADP National Employment Report®
- Looking at the Conference Board Help Wanted Online index
- Monitoring massive layoffs with the MLS report
- Following the Monster Employment Indexes

A robust, growing economy causes employment to rise. More employees bringing home larger paychecks mean more spending on consumer goods and services. High unemployment, on the other hand, is the result of an economic downturn. Fewer workers mean less spending and a slowing economy.

As an economy grows, any drop in employment is an avalanche warning. This drop doesn't signal that the economy will immediately slide off a cliff, but one false step can bury the economic expansion and cascade the economy into recession.

When employment levels start to change, investment markets, business leaders, and Federal Reserve policymakers take notice and turn to economic indicators related to employment. As the business cycle matures (see Chapter 3 for details), pay close attention to the employment statistics in this chapter. Each statistic provides insight into the job market and offers useful information about the changing economy. Use the insight to adjust your portfolio or business strategy in a way that minimizes the damage when a growing economy inevitably cools.

In this chapter, I discuss three big-picture reports and also point out some additional sources you may want to review. I list these indicators in order of impact to investment markets and the general business climate. Each succeeding indicator can help fine-tune your understanding of the job market and its impact on the economy.

Tracking the BLS Employment Situation Report

If you're looking for that single economic report that makes traders jump and that turns placid markets tumultuous, look no further. The Bureau of Labor Statistics (BLS) *Employment Situation report* is the single most important indicator for investors and traders. Informally known as the *jobs report,* it provides timely insights and surprises about the job market, unemployment, and employee compensation.

Changes in the total number of people employed provide one of the earliest indicators that the economy is changing. Traditionally, economists categorized employment as a lagging indicator. But today's savvy investors and business leaders look to the Employment Situation report for early hints about the economic future.

This monthly report is especially timely because it's released only one week after it has been tabulated. Investors try to anticipate this report's results, but they're hard to predict. Although the report is subject to revision, investors and business leaders carefully watch for its initial release.

Table 4-1 tells you what you need to know to follow this report.

Table 4-1 Employment Situation Report

Release Schedule	*Agency*	*Web Address*	*Sensitivity*
Monthly: First Friday of each month, 8:30 a.m. ET	U.S. Bureau of Labor Statistics (BLS), Department of Labor	`www.bls.gov/news.release/empsit.toc.htm`	Very high

In the following sections, I walk you through the Employment Situation report and highlight the most important details beyond the headline numbers, including where you can find useful surprises. I also discuss the way investment markets typically respond to this report.

Counting workers and the unemployed

If you want to know how many people have jobs, how many are working full or part time, how many are looking for work, and how many have given up ever finding a job, take a look at the Employment Situation report.

In this report, you can find the following information for the prior month (along with any revisions to the two previous reports):

- Average hourly compensation
- Average hours worked
- Number of new jobs created
- Total employment
- Unemployment rate

The BLS uses two distinct surveys to accumulate this employment data: the Household Survey and the Establishment Survey. Both try to gather the same information, but they use different approaches. One survey asks people whether they have jobs. The other asks employers how many people they employ. I explain both surveys and tell you how the BLS adjusts the data for certain factors in the following sections.

Surveying households: The Household Survey

The unemployment rate that the Employment Situation report lists every month is part of the BLS Household Survey. The U.S. Government asks approximately 60,000 households about their employment status. Each person 16 years or older is categorized as being employed, unemployed, or not in the labor force.

For purposes of the Employment Situation report, the BLS counts only the civilian population and excludes the military. The *total labor pool,* which is formally known as the *civilian workforce,* is the sum of all employed and unemployed persons:

Total labor pool = Employed + Unemployed

Everyone else is considered to be outside the workforce.

The BLS calculates the unemployment rate by dividing the number of unemployed people by the total labor pool:

Unemployment rate = Unemployed ÷ Total labor pool

The BLS then reports the employment and unemployment information by age, race, ethnicity, sex, marital status, and education.

Employed or unemployed?

Classifying people as employed or unemployed seems straightforward, but it's not as simple as you may think. Here's the gist of the classifications:

- **Employed:** The BLS classifies people as *employed* if they're at least 16 years old and have performed any paid work during the survey period. This classification includes people working in their own business, in their own profession, or on their own farm. It also includes people who worked without pay for at least 15 hours in a family business or farm.
- **Unemployed:** The BLS classifies people as *unemployed* if they had no full-time or part-time employment during the survey period, they were available for work, and they looked for work during the previous four weeks. Note that the BLS doesn't consider a person's eligibility for unemployment benefits when classifying a person as unemployed.

If a person isn't working but didn't look for work during the previous four weeks, the BLS doesn't count that person as unemployed. Instead, it classifies her as a *discouraged worker.* Discouraged workers are tabulated and reported in the Household Survey of the Employment Situation report under the category *Persons not in the labor force.*

Surveying businesses: The Establishment Survey

The Establishment Survey, sometimes called the *Payroll Survey,* takes a different approach from the Household Survey when gathering employment information. For this survey, the BLS interviews about 140,000 businesses, not-for-profit organizations, and all levels of government, asking about their payroll. Excluded are members of the military, self-employed people, and domestic workers. (*Domestic workers* are those employed in a home to care for a child, serve as a companion to a sick or elderly person, perform housekeeping, or carry out other domestic chores.)

When surveying businesses, the BLS asks about

- The number of jobs created
- The number of hours worked
- Hourly compensation

The BLS tabulates the Establishment Survey data, adjusts the numbers for seasonality, and reports both the raw and seasonally adjusted data. (Check out the later section "Adjusting data for seasonality" to find out how seasons affect the job market.) The BLS also breaks down the employment data by industry and geographic region.

Seeing the differences between the Household and Establishment Surveys

As you may expect, the Household and Establishment Surveys produce similar, but not identical, results. Table 4-2 shows the significant differences in the ways the data are collected.

Table 4-2 Differences in the Household and Establishment Surveys

Household Survey	*Establishment Survey*
Includes agricultural (farm) workers, domestic workers, and self-employed individuals	Doesn't include agricultural (farm) workers, domestic workers, or self-employed individuals
Distinguishes between full- and part-time employment	Doesn't distinguish between full- and part-time employment
Counts people on unpaid leave as being employed	Doesn't count people on unpaid leave as being employed
Limited to workers 16 years old and older	Not limited by age
Includes only U.S. residents	Includes residents of Mexico and Canada who are working in the U.S.
Counts a person as employed only once even if that person holds more than one job	May double- or triple-count a single person if that person holds two or more jobs

The two surveys rarely provide dramatically clashing conclusions. When the conclusions occasionally contradict, you may have to dig deep into the data to unearth the discrepancy's source. Taken together, the two approaches used to collect the Employment Situation data provide an excellent look into the health of the U.S. job market.

Adjusting data for seasonality

Seasonal changes in the labor pool occur regularly and can be very large. For example, when students take summer jobs, they can swell reported employment levels. In the same manner, the ranks of temporary retail workers usually swell during the holiday season. These changes can have a large, but temporary, impact on the reported employment numbers.

Seasonal changes in employment happen with enough reliability that the BLS can easily anticipate the change and correct for these seasonal differences. The BLS adjusts most of the data reported in the Employment Situation report for seasonality; the few unadjusted items are noted in the report.

Exploring the reliability of the Employment Situation report

Instead of talking to every U.S. household or business, the BLS samples a small portion of the population and extrapolates the survey results onto the population as a whole. This sampling technique usually gives a good estimate, but it's not perfect.

The sampled population offers what statisticians call a *90 percent level of confidence.* You don't need to hide from this horrible flashback to your college statistics class. All this phrase means is that you have to think about a range of values rather than the single reported value.

For example, a good rule of thumb is to estimate that the number of jobs reported in the Establishment Survey is accurate to plus or minus 100,000 jobs. If total employment reportedly grew by 50,000 jobs, you should interpret that to mean that the economy either lost up to 50,000 jobs or it grew by up to 150,000 jobs. The implication is that when job growth is reported to be less than 100,000 jobs, you can't say with complete confidence that more jobs are available that month. If the number is exactly 100,000, for example, all you can say is that a 90 percent chance exists that the number of jobs has either shrunk by up to 50,000 or grown by up to 150,000.

Revising the data and the benchmarks

When the BLS first reports survey data, consider those numbers to be preliminary. The BLS will likely revise the data in the next two reporting periods as new and updated survey results are tabulated. The BLS tends to revise the Establishment Survey more than the Household Survey, often because small businesses respond late to the survey.

The BLS reworks its benchmark data regularly. (*Benchmark revisions* can modify the methods used to collect the data, update the reports' layout, or change the underlying assumptions made when creating the report; see Chapter 2 for more details.) The Establishment Survey benchmark is recalculated every year to better represent the types of jobs currently seen in the marketplace. The Household Survey benchmark is generally updated on a ten-year cycle to adjust for the population changes reported in the decennial U.S. Census.

Tallying the unemployed outside the United States

If you'd like to compare U.S. employment rates with those of other countries, the BLS International Labor Comparison (ILC) program can help. The ILC program adjusts employment data from foreign countries to make direct comparisons more practical. For more information, go to `www.bls.gov/fls`. Also, check out Chapter 17 for details on unemployment outside the United States.

Highlighting key parts of the jobs report

The Employment Situation report starts with an excellent executive summary called the *News Release.* This summary highlights the most recent jobs data translated from Statistician into plain English. In addition, the BLS issues the *Commissioner's Statement on the Employment Situation* to the Joint Economic Committee of the U.S. Congress. The Commissioner's Statement discusses the strengths and weaknesses in the U.S. job market. It's even briefer than the executive summary. (After all, it's for Congress.) You can find the most recent Commissioner's Statement at `www.bls.gov/news.release/jec.htm`.

Although these two summaries provide an excellent overview of the U.S. job market, I recommend that you look beyond the summaries and really dig into the Employment Situation report. In addition to the aggregate survey data and summary tables, you find a discussion about the sampling techniques, details about the differences between the Household and Establishment Surveys, and a discussion about seasonal adjustments.

You also find answers to frequently asked questions and detailed explanations about the report, as well as in-depth information taken from the Household and Establishment Surveys, including

- Average weekly hours and overtime hours by industry
- Employees by industry sector
- Employment status of the Hispanic or Latino population
- Employment status of the population by race, sex, and age
- Employment status of the population that's 25 years and older by educational attainment

A real-world example illustrates why digging deep into the Employment Survey can pay off. Late in 2010, the total nonfarm payroll fell by 95,000 jobs. During that reporting period, the U.S. Government laid off more than 500,000 census workers, and state and local governments dropped another 100,000 jobs. However, private-sector employers reported job growth. If you looked only at the top-line nonfarm payroll number, you would have missed the good news that was obscured by the huge drop in government employment.

The following two sections make reading the Employment Situation report easier by explaining the two summary tables it contains.

Reviewing Summary Table A

The Employment Situation Summary Table A (see an example of this table in Figure 4-1) provides a detailed overview of the Household Survey results. (Refer to the earlier section "Surveying households: The Household Survey" for more on these results.) Summary Table A includes the following information:

- Duration of unemployment
- Employment status for the civilian noninstitutional population
- Number of people not in the labor force
- Number of people working part time
- Reasons for unemployment
- Unemployment rates categorized by age, race, and sex

HOUSEHOLD DATA
Summary table A. Household data, seasonally adjusted
[Numbers in thousands]

Category	Nov. 2009	Sept. 2010	Oct. 2010	Nov. 2010	Change from: Oct. 2010-Nov. 2010
Employment status					
Civilian noninstitutional population	236,743	238,322	238,530	238,715	185
Civilian labor force	153,720	154,158	153,904	154,007	103
Participation rate	64.9	64.7	64.5	64.5	0.0
Employed	138,381	139,391	139,061	138,888	-173
Employment-population ratio	58.5	58.5	58.3	58.2	-0.1
Unemployed	15,340	14,767	14,843	15,119	276
Unemployment rate	10.0	9.6	9.6	9.8	0.2
Not in labor force	83,022	84,164	84,626	84,708	82
Unemployment rates					
Total, 16 years and over	10.0	9.6	9.6	9.8	0.2
Adult men (20 years and over)	10.4	9.8	9.7	10.0	0.3
Adult women (20 years and over)	8.0	8.0	8.1	8.4	0.3
Teenagers (16 to 19 years)	26.8	26.0	27.1	24.6	-2.5
White	9.3	8.7	8.8	8.9	0.1
Black or African American	15.6	16.1	15.7	16.0	0.3
Asian (not seasonally adjusted)	7.3	6.4	7.1	7.6	-
Hispanic or Latino ethnicity	12.7	12.4	12.6	13.2	0.6
Total, 25 years and over	8.5	8.3	8.2	8.4	0.2
Less than a high school diploma	15.0	15.4	15.3	15.7	0.4
High school graduates, no college	10.4	10.0	10.1	10.0	-0.1
Some college or associate degree	9.0	9.1	8.5	8.7	0.2
Bachelor's degree and higher	4.9	4.4	4.7	5.1	0.4
Reason for unemployment					
Job losers and persons who completed temporary jobs	9,965	9,401	9,108	9,498	390
Job leavers	929	807	854	862	8
Reentrants	3,221	3,436	3,512	3,451	-61
New entrants	1,270	1,187	1,273	1,238	-35
Duration of unemployment					
Less than 5 weeks	2,774	2,891	2,657	2,828	171
5 to 14 weeks	3,517	3,350	3,458	3,359	-99
15 to 26 weeks	3,075	2,336	2,519	2,576	57
27 weeks and over	5,901	6,123	6,206	6,313	107
Employed persons at work part time					
Part time for economic reasons	9,225	9,472	9,154	8,972	-182
Slack work or business conditions	6,684	6,733	6,232	6,038	-194
Could only find part-time work	2,238	2,456	2,572	2,569	-3
Part time for noneconomic reasons	18,354	18,234	18,211	18,365	154
Persons not in the labor force (not seasonally adjusted)					
Marginally attached to the labor force	2,323	2,548	2,602	2,531	-
Discouraged workers	861	1,209	1,219	1,282	-

- Over-the-month changes are not displayed for not seasonally adjusted data.

Figure 4-1: Employment Situation Summary Table A.

Dealing with the annual influx of millions of new workers

Every year in the United States, millions of students graduate from high school. Almost 3 million matriculated in 2009 alone. Some of these students enter the workforce immediately, some go to college full time, and some work part time during their college years. Regardless of the exact timing, most students enter the labor force not too long after their graduation date.

The number of new graduates generally overwhelms the number of new retirees each year. So the job market needs to grow at a rate sufficient to absorb several million new workers every year. You can estimate that the job market needs about 200,000 new jobs every month just to absorb these new graduates. Any number less than that means the unemployment pool will grow.

Retiring baby boomers may eventually change this dynamic. Boomers were born after World War II, from 1946 through the early 1960s. The oldest boomers reached retirement age in 2011. Some economists predict a shortage of workers to fill positions vacated by retiring boomers perhaps as early as 2015 to 2020. Factor in the healthcare needs of the aging U.S. population, and you can see why the job market may be robust for future graduates.

Studying Summary Table B

Summary Table B summarizes the Establishment Survey results. (Refer to the earlier section "Surveying businesses: The Establishment Survey" for more on this specific survey.) Figure 4-2 shows an example of this table, which includes the following information:

- Average hourly earnings
- Average weekly hours worked
- Employment by selected industry
- Number of new jobs added since last month

Deciphering employment numbers

Savvy investors and business leaders find useful nuggets regarding employment numbers in the Employment Situation report. Although economists usually consider employment a lagging indicator, modern businesses would disagree. They're sensitive to changes in purchasing patterns. Employees are the largest expense for most businesses, so the first sign of trouble often causes managers to quickly lay off workers to cut costs. These layoffs usually start to happen well in advance of a recession's start. So how can you figure out what these numbers mean and how they can potentially impact your investments? The following sections explain.

ESTABLISHMENT DATA
Summary table B. Establishment data, seasonally adjusted

Category	Nov. 2009	Sept. 2010	Oct. 2010[P]	Nov. 2010[P]
EMPLOYMENT BY SELECTED INDUSTRY (Over-the-month change, in thousands)				
Total nonfarm	64	-24	172	39
Total private	75	112	160	50
Goods-producing	-33	-10	3	-15
Mining and logging	7	7	11	3
Construction	-15	-11	3	-5
Manufacturing	-25	-6	-11	-13
Durable goods[1]	-23	5	-4	-5
Motor vehicles and parts	-4.6	-0.9	1.2	-1.5
Nondurable goods	-2	-11	-7	-8
Private service-providing[1]	108	122	157	65
Wholesale trade	-6.2	4.5	10.0	4.7
Retail trade	8.8	-3.9	13.0	-28.1
Transportation and warehousing	7.2	16.5	0.7	11.6
Information	-12	-7	-1	1
Financial activities	2	4	0	-9
Professional and business services[1]	106	28	50	53
Temporary help services	94.7	27.3	34.7	39.5
Education and health services[1]	31	26	64	30
Health care and social assistance	26.1	34.2	39.9	23.1
Leisure and hospitality	-21	38	-10	11
Other services	-6	17	30	-8
Government	-11	-136	12	-11
WOMEN AND PRODUCTION AND NONSUPERVISORY EMPLOYEES AS A PERCENT OF ALL EMPLOYEES[2]				
Total nonfarm women employees	49.9	49.6	49.6	49.6
Total private women employees	48.4	48.1	48.1	48.1
Total private production and nonsupervisory employees	82.4	82.4	82.4	82.4
HOURS AND EARNINGS ALL EMPLOYEES				
Total private				
Average weekly hours	33.9	34.2	34.3	34.3
Average hourly earnings	$ 22.39	$ 22.68	$ 22.74	$ 22.75
Average weekly earnings	$759.02	$ 775.66	$779.98	$780.33
Index of aggregate weekly hours (2007=100)[3]	91.1	92.6	93.0	93.1
Over-the-month percent change	0.7	-0.2	0.4	0.1
Index of aggregate weekly payrolls (2007=100)[4]	97.2	100.2	100.9	101.0
Over-the-month percent change	0.8	0.0	0.7	0.1
HOURS AND EARNINGS PRODUCTION AND NONSUPERVISORY EMPLOYEES				
Total private				
Average weekly hours	33.2	33.5	33.6	33.5
Average hourly earnings	$ 18.80	$ 19.11	$ 19.19	$ 19.19
Average weekly earnings	$624.16	$ 640.19	$644.78	$642.87
Index of aggregate weekly hours (2002=100)[3]	97.9	99.7	100.1	99.9
Over-the-month percent change	0.7	0.1	0.4	-0.2
Index of aggregate weekly payrolls (2002=100)[4]	123.0	127.3	128.4	128.1
Over-the-month percent change	0.8	0.2	0.9	-0.2
DIFFUSION INDEX (Over 1-month span)[5]				
Total private	46.8	54.5	58.0	52.0
Manufacturing	45.7	52.4	43.9	43.3

Figure 4-2: Employment Situation Summary Table B.

Interpreting payroll changes

Month-to-month changes in nonfarm payroll, as shown in Summary Table B (refer to Figure 4-2), make the biggest ripple in the job market. Consumer spending drives the U.S. economy, so more workers mean more people with more money to spend. Fewer workers mean less spending. The correlation is clear, so carefully watch for changes in nonfarm payroll.

Anticipating big changes from the jobs report

Average weekly hours is one statistic in the Establishment Survey that those in the know follow. The Establishment Survey size is so large that small changes in the reported number foreshadow big changes coming in the economy. This statistic can be volatile, so many investors use a three-month moving average to smooth out the average weekly hours statistic. (See Chapter 2 for how to use moving averages.) Three months may not make a trend, but many investors and traders watch for changes in these three-month moving averages to anticipate future economic activity.

Although the actual value of average weekly hours isn't as important as the month-to-month changes, you can use certain guideposts. When the average weekly hours statistic is less than 41 hours, many interpret the drop to be a sign of economic weakness. A number less than 40 hours signals the potential for a recession. A number greater than 41.5 hours usually indicates economic growth, and 42 hours or more is economic rocket fuel.

For those of you keeping score at home, you may have noticed that the average weekly hours in Figure 4-2 is 34.3. The number is less than 40, but it's up from a year earlier and up from September. It doesn't take an advanced statistics degree to realize that November 2010 was a terrible time for job seekers.

Relaying employers' intentions

The Diffusion Index shown at the bottom of Summary Table B (refer to Figure 4-2) is a source of valuable job market insight. (See Chapter 2 for details about diffusion indexes.) The numbers in this index indicate whether employers are planning to hire workers in the near future. A reading of 50 shows that half of employers plan to add workers and half of them plan to reduce staff. A number greater than 50 indicates that more employers plan to add workers; a number less than 50 shows that more employers plan to reduce employment.

Predicting market reactions due to employment changes

Investors carefully watch the Employment Situation report for unexpected changes. You see the most dramatic market reactions when an unexpected drop in jobs occurs after the economy has experienced growth for an extended period. After all, unexpected employment weakness is often the first sign of an economic downturn. On the other hand, I can't recall employment strength ever leading an economic recovery. Why? The economy can improve on the strength of productivity gains long before businesses start hiring or recalling workers.

The following sections discuss how you can expect bond, stock, and commodities markets to react to the Employment Situation report.

Gauging the reaction in the bond market

The bond market has what often seems like a perverse reaction to employment news. What's good news for workers and the economy is bad news for bonds. For instance, when the number of jobs available takes an unexpected jump, you can expect the bond market to sell off in anticipation of rising interest rates. Investors anticipate that the Federal Reserve will raise short-term interest rates to keep the economy and inflation from overheating. (See Chapter 8 for details about the Federal Reserve and its role in the economy.) When unemployment rises, you can expect bond prices to rise, too, which coincides with falling interest rates.

When employment surprises occur, it's a good time for bond investors to reevaluate their portfolio positions, because a drop in jobs is usually profitable for bondholders. If the job market is really shedding jobs, it's a good time to look at longer-maturity bonds. You may also consider repositioning some equity (stock) assets into the bond market because long-term bond prices are more sensitive to interest-rate changes. As long as interest rates are falling, holding long-term bonds can be very profitable. In fact, in this environment, long-term bonds can even outperform an equity portfolio.

Pegging the reaction in the stock market

Stocks and bonds generally move in opposite directions in reaction to the Employment Situation report. Stock market investors love growing employment numbers and even love when employees work more hours and get paid more. The reverse is true as well, however. Falling employment is bad news for the stock market.

At the beginning of a new bull market (when stock prices begin to rise), the jobs report doesn't show much improvement in employment. Eventually, though, rising jobs can serve as a delayed but confirming indicator that the economic cycle is moving toward growth. Stock investors need to pay close attention to the jobs report after a period of economic growth. An increase in employers who unexpectedly lay off workers is often an early indicator that the economy is cooling. Stock investors should begin making plans to allocate some assets away from stocks and into bonds when this cooling occurs.

Noting the reaction in the commodity markets

Commodity prices are rarely affected by employment reports. However, one circumstance may cause prices of a few commodities to react. When employment growth stokes fears of an overheating economy, the threat of inflation can drive some precious metal prices higher. Of course, all commodities are subject to inflationary pressures, but other commodity markets rarely react directly to the jobs report. Check out Chapter 15 for more information on commodities.

Looking at Unemployment Insurance Claims

Investors and business leaders carefully watch the *Unemployment Insurance Weekly Claims Report* for early clues about the job market and employment trends. (Note that the Conference Board Index of the Leading Economic Indicators also uses the data in this report; see Chapter 10 for details.)

The Unemployment Insurance Weekly Claims Report is often the first indication that something is amiss in the job market. It can be a timely warning to alert business leaders and investors about changing job market conditions. For example, investors can watch this report to catch the signs that an economic recession is beginning. Here's the life cycle of a recession: A large number of people lose their jobs, and those unemployed people have less money to spend. Others become fearful of losing their jobs, and fearful consumers spend less and save more. Retailers notice the spending drop and reduce their inventories. Manufacturers make fewer products when retailers buy fewer goods, and they may even lay off additional workers.

Table 4-3 provides what you need to know about the Unemployment Insurance Weekly Claims Report.

Table 4-3 The Unemployment Insurance Weekly Claims Report

Release Schedule	*Agency*	*Web Address*	*Sensitivity*
Weekly: Every Thursday, 8:30 a.m. ET	Employment and Training Administration, Department of Labor	`www.dol.gov/opa/media/press/eta/ui/current.htm`	High

The following sections overview what you can find in this report and how you can use it in your investments.

Keeping track of unemployment insurance claims

The unemployment insurance claims that newly unemployed workers file are collected and reported in the Unemployment Insurance Weekly Claims Report. The report delivers this timely information so that the prior week's new claims are reported in the current week's report.

The actual claims data that the local unemployment offices collect make up the weekly claims report. The local offices forward that information to the state unemployment offices, which, in turn, forward the aggregate data to the Department of Labor. The Department of Labor then issues the newly collected weekly claims data every Thursday.

Because the Department of Labor issues the Unemployment Insurance Weekly Claims Report every week, the report coincides with the BLS Employment Situation report once every month (see the earlier section "Tracking the BLS Employment Situation Report" for details). Given that the claims report is released one day before the Employment Situation report, you can be sure that stock and bond traders, but especially bond traders, use the weekly claims report to try and foretell the next day's Employment Situation report. Sometimes they're successful, and sometimes they aren't.

The Unemployment Insurance Weekly Claims Report also lists the states with the largest increase and decrease in insurance claims. The report provides an estimate for the total U.S. unemployment, but this number isn't considered as reliable as the one that the BLS Employment Situation surveys provide. Too many categories of unemployed workers that are ineligible for unemployment insurance exist and aren't included in the category of insured employees.

Figure 4-3 shows an excerpt from the Unemployment Insurance Weekly Claims Report. In this excerpt, you can see the initial claims and the continuing claims. The continuing claims are labeled *Insured Unemployment* (abbreviated as *Ins. Unemployment*). Both sets of data are adjusted for seasonality. However, both the seasonally adjusted (SA) and the not seasonally adjusted (NSA) data are reported. The data used in the continuing claims reports lag initial claims by one week.

UNEMPLOYMENT INSURANCE DATA FOR REGULAR STATE PROGRAMS

WEEK ENDING	Advance Dec. 11	Dec. 4	Change	Nov. 27	Prior Year[1]
Initial Claims (SA)	420,000	423,000	-3,000	438,000	490,000
Initial Claims (NSA)	486,284	585,509	-99,225	412,922	555,383
4-Wk Moving Average (SA)	422,750	428,000	-5,250	431,500	481,250
WEEK ENDING	Advance Dec. 4	Nov. 27	Change	Nov. 20	Prior Year[1]
Ins. Unemployment (SA)	4,135,000	4,113,000	+22,000	4,277,000	5,320,000
Ins. Unemployment (NSA)	4,031,909	4,215,511	-183,602	3,665,773	5,192,075
4-Wk Moving Average (SA)	4,185,500	4,232,750	-47,250	4,290,250	5,412,750
Ins. Unemployment Rate (SA)[2]	3.3%	3.3%	0.0	3.4%	4.0%
Ins. Unemployment Rate (NSA)[2]	3.2%	3.3%	-0.1	2.9%	3.9%

Figure 4-3: Excerpt from the Unemployment Insurance Weekly Claims Report.

You may find that comparing continuing claims from one year to another, or even comparing one state to another, is troublesome. Most states typically offer up to 26 weeks of unemployment benefits. Some states occasionally provide longer periods of unemployment insurance on their own, and the federal government occasionally extends unemployment insurance benefits as it did during the 2009–2010 recession. During this time, 25 states provided unemployment benefits for up to 99 weeks, and others provided them for 60 weeks.

Smoothing jobless claim fluctuations

When reviewing jobless claims with the Unemployment Insurance Weekly Claims Report, make sure that you take into consideration some ups and downs. For instance, holiday-shortened workweeks often see fewer unemployment claims. After all, newly unemployed workers have one fewer day for filing claims. Applicants tend to catch up with filing during the week following the holiday. As a result, the report from the four-day workweek shows fewer claims than expected, and the report for the following week indicates a big jump in claims. This factor (among others) makes for erratic week-to-week changes in the weekly claims report.

To help smooth this irregularity, the weekly claims report provides a four-week moving average of unemployment claims (see Chapter 2 for the lowdown on moving averages). Figure 4-3 shows a seasonally adjusted four-week moving average. This number is the one that most analysts regularly follow.

Unemployment insurance eligibility requirements

Only those who are laid off from work are eligible for unemployment insurance. A layoff can be due to a variety of factors, including a reduction in force, a plant closing, a failed business, a business consolidation, or a buyout. Employees who have been fired for something they did or didn't do (dismissed for cause) aren't eligible for unemployment insurance.

Further, those who are self-employed (including many agricultural workers) are ineligible for unemployment insurance. Because only those who have held a job for some period of time are eligible, recent high school or college graduates are typically ineligible as well. Eligibility differences vary from state to state, but all require a one-week waiting period to confirm eligibility before insurance claims are paid.

When someone loses a job and applies for unemployment insurance, the application is reported as a claim regardless of the applicant's eligibility. This is why the new claims from one week don't always match the following week's change in continuing claims data.

Analyzing the claims numbers

Historically, when the Unemployment Insurance Weekly Claims Report shows an initial four-week moving average of more than 400,000 claims, investors typically take that statistic as a sign of economic weakness. They don't expect a recovery in the job market until the initial claims four-week moving average remains consistently less than 375,000.

Analysts consider a continuing claims value greater than 3 million to be quite troublesome for the economy. However, in 2010, unemployed workers had been eligible for unemployment benefits for up to 99 weeks, which makes comparisons with earlier recessions difficult. You can see in Figure 4-3 that the number is greater than 5 million. Regardless of whether unemployment benefits had been extended, 5 million unemployment benefit recipients are troublesome for the economy, not to mention for the unemployed workers themselves.

Determining how the market may react to increased claims

A strong correlation links increases in the weekly claims four-week moving average with deteriorating economic performance. Increases in new claims over a period of a couple of months are often followed by decreases in the economy. Although the reverse is also true, it's rarely a leading indicator. Economic activity often picks up long before that positive activity shows up in a jobs report.

The following list shows how the Unemployment Insurance Weekly Claims Report can affect the different markets:

- **Bond markets:** Bond traders are especially sensitive to changes in the weekly claims report. As I note earlier in this chapter, what's good for the economy is bad for bonds, and vice versa. When employees start filing for unemployment insurance, bond traders anticipate weakness in the economy and bid bond prices higher, which pushes interest rates lower.

  Longer-term bond investors may not be as quick as bond traders to move when the weekly claims report suggests economic weakness, but they should still consider changes to their portfolios. As the economy weakens, lengthening the average duration of their bond holdings, especially as they take new positions, makes sense. Doing so may allow bond investors to capture capital gains as prices rise, while locking in relatively attractive yields as interest rates fall.
- **Stock markets:** Stocks tend to fare poorly when an economy falters. So stock traders and investors are wise to consider rotating into stocks of less economically sensitive companies as unemployment claims rise. Historically, stocks of food and pharmaceutical companies hold their value better during an economic downturn compared to tech and finance companies.
- **Currency markets:** The U.S. dollar tends to be strong when interest rates are high (unless high interest rates are caused by a high inflation rate). However, it isn't a certainty that this relationship will hold during every period of economic strength or weakness. The relative strength of the U.S. economy compared to other countries is likely to have a greater impact on the dollar's price than bond prices.
- **Commodity markets:** If a linkage exists between unemployment claims and the commodity markets, it's that commodities used in manufacturing and construction tend to fall in price during periods of economic weakness and rise during periods of economic strength. Increasing unemployment insurance claims may trigger price changes in these industrial commodities.

Eyeing the ADP National Employment Report®

In 2006, Macroeconomic Advisers, LLC℠, brought a new economic indicator to life and released it into the wild. They engineered this indicator, which is referred to as the *ADP National Employment Report®,* to anticipate and improve upon the BLS Employment Situation report. (Flip to the earlier section "Tracking the BLS Employment Situation Report" for more information on this important indicator.) Although it's not as widely followed or as influential as the Employment Situation report, traders and investors use the ADP National Employment Report® to help estimate the coming Employment Situation data and the report's market impact.

Table 4-4 provides some general information about the ADP National Employment Report®.

Table 4-4 ADP National Employment Report®

Release Schedule	*Agency*	*Web Address*	*Sensitivity*
Monthly: Published schedule; usually 8:15 a.m. ET on the Wednesday two days before the BLS Employment Situation report is released	ADP and Macroeconomic Advisers, LLC℠	`adpemploymentreport.com`	High

In the following sections, I explain what this report is all about and how to use its information in your investments.

ADP® is a data-processing firm that provides payroll processing and other business services to a large population of U.S. businesses. Macroeconomic Advisers℠ uses anonymous ADP® payroll data to try and anticipate the BLS Employment Situation survey sampling results. Macroeconomic Advisers℠ looks at the same week as the BLS Establishment Survey, employs similar seasonal adjustments, and uses a similar cross section of employers when creating its employment report.

Reviewing key parts of ADP's jobs report

The ADP National Employment Report® provides the following payroll-based employment information for U.S. businesses:

- Total U.S. employment
- Employment for U.S. goods-producing industries (aggregate value for manufacturing, mining, and construction)
- Employment for U.S. service industries (transportation, retail, utilities, warehousing, and so on)
- Employment for the U.S. manufacturing industries (segregated from the goods-producing value)
- Employment for small (1–49 employees), medium (50–499 employees), and large (more than 499 employees) U.S. companies

ADP® adjusts the data it provides for seasonality. Revisions are usually minor. Figure 4-4 shows a sample of the ADP National Employment Report®. It shows total employment and the month-to-month change from the previous report.

DERIVED FROM ADP PAYROLL DATA

Table 1. Employees on nonfarm private payrolls by selected industry sector and size*
(In thousands)

Industry / Size of Payroll	Seasonally Adjusted						
	Jun. 2010	Jul. 2010	Aug. 2010	Sep. 2010	Oct. 2010	Nov. 2010	Change from: Oct. 2010 - Nov. 2010p
Total nonfarm private	106,936	106,978	107,015	107,044	107,126	107,219	93
Small (1-49)	48,237	48,260	48,276	48,297	48,337	48,391	54
Medium (50-499)	41,194	41,215	41,230	41,241	41,279	41,316	37
Large (> 499)	17,505	17,503	17,509	17,506	17,510	17,512	2
Goods-producing	17,545	17,517	17,499	17,472	17,450	17,464	14
Small (1-49)	6,404	6,394	6,383	6,373	6,362	6,367	5
Medium (50-499)	7,671	7,665	7,662	7,657	7,655	7,668	13
Large (> 499)	3,470	3,458	3,454	3,442	3,433	3,429	-4
Service-providing	89,391	89,461	89,516	89,572	89,676	89,755	79
Small (1-49)	41,833	41,866	41,893	41,924	41,975	42,024	49
Medium (50-499)	33,523	33,550	33,568	33,584	33,624	33,648	24
Large (> 499)	14,035	14,045	14,055	14,064	14,077	14,083	6
Addendum:							
Manufacturing	11,504	11,492	11,497	11,491	11,486	11,502	16

p = preliminary

Source: ADP® and Macroeconomic Advisers[SM]. Used with permission.

Figure 4-4: The ADP National Employment Report®.

Comparing the ADP® and BLS reports

The ADP® report differs from the BLS Employment Situation report in several significant ways:

- **The ADP® uses only private industry data.** The report doesn't include any government agency payroll data. This exclusion is usually of little consequence because government employment tends to be more stable than in the public sector. However, state and local governments were forced to reduce employment during the 2009–2010 recession. The ADP® report didn't capture this reduction.
- **Nothing like the Household Survey is included in the ADP® report.** In other words, only employers are surveyed, not employees, which means that some workers, including agricultural (farm) workers, domestic workers, and self-employed individuals, aren't counted. (Head to the earlier section "Surveying households: The Household Survey" for more on that survey.)
- **The ADP® report isn't as detailed as the BLS report.** The ADP® report typically runs 5 pages long compared to a recent Employment Situation report that was 38 pages long. Although it may lack detail, the ADP® report still provides a good summary preview of the upcoming BLS Employment Situation report. Plus, ADP® says its estimates are a bit better than the BLS estimates because they're based on real payroll data rather than surveys.
- **The ADP® collects data from fewer businesses.** The ADP® collects data from approximately 340,000 businesses; the BLS collects data from 400,000 businesses. Both samples are very large, so the impact of this difference is generally small.

Although the ADP® report doesn't exactly match the BLS report, ADP® describes its report as showing the true levels of employment. It claims that its preliminary report is closer to the final revisions of the BLS Employment Situation report when compared to the preliminary BLS survey data.

According to the ADP®, a very high correlation exists between the preliminary ADP® report and the final revisions of the BLS Employment Situation report. The actual correlation varies, but it hovers around 0.95 correlation, where 1.0 is perfect correlation.

Figuring out how the market will react to the ADP® report

The ADP National Employment Report® can help economic analysts anticipate the BLS Employment Situation report. As a result, investors, traders, and business managers all use the ADP® report to make important financial decisions. When these folks make these decisions, they can impact both the bond market and the stock market. I show you how in the following sections.

Taking a look at the bond market reaction

Bond traders are most interested in employment reports for the quick trade. They can use the ADP National Employment Report® to improve their positions leading into the release of the BLS Employment Situation report. Analysts also use the ADP® report to adjust their forecasts and consensus forecasts as the BLS release nears. Longer-term bond investors are more likely to use these reports to plan for changes to their portfolio over time.

When the job market shows strength, bond prices typically fall and interest rates rise. The reverse is equally true. In a tough job market, bond prices rise and interest rates fall. As always, markets are more likely to react to surprising results than to the reported data itself. Remember that a single report is only one of many considerations for traders and investors.

If you're a bond investor, you would be wise to use the ADP® report with the BLS Employment Situation report to make portfolio adjustments. When the economy shows signs of deterioration, the maturity dates in bond portfolios should lengthen to lock in higher yields and possibly capture some capital gains. As the economy improves, look to shorter maturity dates to avoid capital losses and to make capital available as yields rise.

Forecasting the stock market reaction

Stock traders, like bond traders, are likely to view the ADP® report as an opportunity to make a quick trade. Investors are more concerned with what the report means for the economy down the road.

Weakness in the job market typically leads to stock weakness. Early signs of job weakness tell stock investors to make plans to rotate out of high-growth businesses and into stocks that are less sensitive to the economy. When jobs are strong, stocks are, too.

Different stock sectors react differently to the ADP® and other employment reports. People still need food and medicine even in challenging economic times. So pharmaceutical and food stocks often perform better than tech and finance stocks during an economic downturn. During this time, customers may like an extra beer or two, but they're likely to choose a lower-cost brew rather than a craft beer or high-quality wine.

Advertising for Jobs: The Conference Board Help Wanted Online Index

For more than 50 years, the Conference Board published a well-regarded indicator known as the *Help Wanted index*. In it, they tallied the aggregate number of help wanted ads published in newspapers across the country. As the Internet became the preferred job-searching forum, the old Help Wanted index fell out of favor.

In 2008, the Conference Board retired the newspaper-based indicator and replaced it with the relatively new Internet-based help wanted index, referred to as the *Help Wanted Online index*.

Table 4-5 shows a quick rundown of this index.

Table 4-5 Help Wanted Online Index

Release Schedule	*Agency*	*Web Address*	*Sensitivity*
Monthly: Published schedule, near the 1st of the month, 10:00 a.m. ET	The Conference Board	`www.conference-board.org/data/helpwantedonline.cfm`	Too new to know

The Conference Board Help Wanted Online index is released near the first of each month, making it among the earliest job-market indicators available. Releases aren't on a fixed schedule, but the release dates are published and available on the Conference Board website and as part of each report. The Help Wanted Online index covers a period similar to that of the BLS Employment Situation report. The following sections explain how you can use this index.

Measuring the availability of jobs online

The Help Wanted Online index reports the total online ads and the number of new online ads each month. In addition, the Conference Board estimates the number of unemployed workers available for each advertised job; it calls this statistic the *supply/demand rate*.

The Conference Board collects data from a large variety of Internet job boards, including online newspaper advertising and major Internet sites. The Conference Board updates the list of source websites each month. Small regional job boards may also be included, but those with a limited number of ads are likely to be excluded.

Companies posting available jobs on their own websites aren't directly included in the Conference Board index. However, some job boards and forums do harvest available jobs from corporate websites, so these postings can make it into the Online Help Wanted index. The Conference Board tries to distinguish new ads from existing ads. It also attempts to remove ads duplicated on multiple job boards.

For the purposes of the Help Wanted Online index, an ad is counted as a single ad regardless of the level of the position or the number of jobs being advertised. In other words, a posting for an entry-level job counts the same as a posting for a vice-president position. And a listing for 20 clerical jobs counts as one ad just like any other job ad.

The board reports job vacancies by region, by state, and by select cities, along with month-to-month changes and changes to the supply/demand rate. The section of the Help Wanted Online index called *Occupational Highlights* reports the types of jobs available in each geographic area. The index shows aggregate U.S. vacancies and the availability of specific occupations in select regions and cities in the United States.

Predicting how the market will react

Although the information in the Help Wanted Online index is useful to business leaders and economic analysts, it's typically delivered too late to be interesting to stock or bond traders. The BLS Employment Situation report provides similar information and is released several weeks earlier.

Even though this index has little predictive ability as a leading indicator, it's worth monitoring as a confirming indicator. The Help Wanted Online index should move in tandem with the BLS Employment Situation report, the ADP National Employment Report®, and the Unemployment Insurance Weekly Claims Report. (You can read about all three of these reports earlier in the chapter.) As long as it does, it acts as a confirming indicator. If you find that it's out of step, dig deeper to understand why it differs.

Collecting the BLS Mass Layoff Statistics Report

Another report that's useful to business leaders and economic analysts is the BLS *Mass Layoff Statistics (MLS) report.* The MLS report is really a combination of two reports:

- Mass Layoffs report, which is published monthly
- Extended Mass Layoffs report, which is published quarterly

These reports scrub unemployment data collected from state and local agencies to find and report large-scale layoffs. To be included in either report, a mass layoff must affect 50 or more employees at a single location during a five-week period. These reports include layoffs at publicly and privately owned businesses and layoffs at all levels of government.

Table 4-6 gives you an overview of the MLS report.

Table 4-6 BLS Mass Layoff Statistics Report

Release Schedule	*Agency*	*Web Address*	*Sensitivity*
Monthly and quarterly: Published schedule	U.S. Bureau of Labor Statistics (BLS), Department of Labor	`www.bls.gov/mls`	Low

If a large company like Ford Motor Company were to lay off 50 workers at one facility and 50 workers at a second facility, these layoffs would count as two events in the Mass Layoffs report. If those same workers remained out of work for 31 or more days, they would become part of the Extended Mass Layoffs report. The BLS reports only actual layoffs; it doesn't consider or report planned layoffs. Therefore, if a company announces layoff plans but doesn't implement them, those plans don't become part of the MLS report.

Mass layoff events can occur at any time, regardless of the state of the economy. As a result, these reports are poor economic predictors; in other words, they're not useful as leading indicators. But although investment markets rarely react to the MLS report, the report sometimes affects individual stocks and sectors. Plus, it can provide excellent information about the strength of specific industries and geographic regions throughout the United States. And corporate managers may watch for supply-chain disruptions and competitive pressures in the MLS report.

The MLS data can be difficult to find on the main MLS webpage. Use these links to directly access the data:

- Mass Layoffs report: www.bls.gov/news.release/mmls.toc.htm
- Extended Mass Layoffs report: www.bls.gov/news.release/mslo.toc.htm

The BLS seasonally adjusts the layoff statistics, but it also provides the unadjusted data. It reports information regionally, by state, and by industry.

Surfing Monster Employment Indexes

Monster Worldwide, Inc., is the parent of Monster.com, the employment firm and Internet jobs board. The company describes itself as a full-service recruiting firm, but it's mostly known for its website that provides a place to post resumes and review help wanted ads. The company also issues monthly (quarterly in Canada) employment indexes known as the *Monster Employment Indexes*. Table 4-7 provides a rundown of the Monster Employment Indexes.

Table 4-7 Monster Employment Indexes

Release Schedule	*Agency*	*Web Address*	*Sensitivity*
Monthly: Generally the first Thursday of each month, 10:00 a.m. ET, for U.S.; second Tuesday of each month for Europe; published schedule for India	Monster Worldwide, Inc.	about-monster.com/employment-index	Low
Quarterly: Published schedule for Canada			

Monster publishes employment indexes for the United States, Canada, Europe, and India. The U.S. Monster Employment Index is published on the day before the BLS Employment Situation report. Typically, this day is the first Thursday of the month. However, if the BLS Employment Situation report is released on the first day of the month, the Monster Employment Index comes out on the last day of the previous month.

The Monster Employment Indexes are published for Europe (Belgium, France, Germany, Italy, Netherlands, Sweden, and United Kingdom) on the second Tuesday of each month. The Monster Employment Index Canada is released quarterly. You can view the publishing schedule for the Monster Employment Index India at `about-monster.com/employment/schedule/164`.

The Monster Employment Indexes show information from Monster.com, along with data from other major job boards and career sites. In the United States, the report is segregated by industry, occupation, city, and region. The indexes also show the top-growth industries and top-growth occupations as well as the lowest-growth industries and occupations. Reports for select U.S. cities, called the U.S. Monster Local Index, are also available. (Visit `about-monster.com/employment/index/16` for more information.)

Help wanted ads are a precursor to hiring, and in that sense, these indexes are billed by Monster.com as leading indicators to anticipate job growth or decline. However, the real value of the Monster Employment Indexes comes from their being released just a day before the BLS Employment Situation report. Because of this release date, investors, business leaders, and analysts watch these indexes for significant changes that may find their way into the Employment Situation report. Even so, the Monster Employment Indexes rarely move markets on their own.

Chapter 5

Survey Says: Considering Consumer Sentiment, Confidence, and Comfort

In This Chapter

- Using surveys to get the lowdown on how consumers feel
- Becoming familiar with consumer sentiment
- Interpreting consumer confidence
- Finding out what makes consumers comfortable

Pop quiz, question one: Who's more likely to spend freely — a customer who's feeling hopeful about the future or one who's feeling anxious? The answer seems obvious. Optimistic consumers probably buy most of the things they need and some of the stuff they want. People who are concerned about their economic future, on the other hand, may scrimp on even the necessities.

Pop quiz, question two: What makes people feel good about their future? Your intuition may tell you that having a good job, being able to pay bills, or having little debt makes people feel comfortable about their future. Or you may guess that low interest rates, a strong job market, or even world peace affects the way people feel about the economy.

If your answers to the pop quiz questions look like these, you're in good company. Academics and analysts have been trying for decades to figure out how regular people feel about their current economic situation. Researchers want to understand what emotional states consumers are in and how those states will affect their future spending. Investors and business leaders care about the way everyday consumers feel because many of them believe confident consumers buy a lot more stuff — from soap to cereal and TVs to iPads. And those buyers drive the global economy.

Unfortunately, figuring out just how much consumers contribute to the economy isn't as simple as you may think. (I tackle this question in my discussion about the U.S. gross domestic product, or GDP, in Chapter 7.) But for the moment, just know that consumers are directly or indirectly responsible for the majority of economic activity in the United States. If you include all spending for healthcare, including Medicare, consumer spending accounts for as much as 70 percent of the U.S. economy. This chapter looks at some surveys that try to figure out consumers by asking them how they feel about the economy.

Trying to Figure Out Consumers

The most direct way to find out how consumers feel about the economy is to ask them:

- How do you feel about the economy?
- How do you feel about your job?
- Are you feeling insecure or confident about the future?

Of course, not everyone will be completely forthcoming (or rational) when you ask these questions. After all, you're asking people how they feel. Some may be defensive or guarded in their answers. Others may respond more pessimistically than they really feel based on the fact that they've had a bad day at work or have just seen a particularly troubling clip from the nightly news. The reverse is equally true. Still, if you ask enough people, you're likely to get a pretty good idea about how regular Joes and Josephines feel about their economic future — which is where surveys come into play.

Many surveys ask questions like the ones I pose at the beginning of this section to try to gauge how consumers feel about the economy, about their jobs, and about the future. This chapter looks at three prominent U.S. consumer surveys in the order of their market influence (I discuss international consumer surveys in Chapter 17). Each one takes a different approach to surveying and gets varying results, but ultimately they're all trying to figure out how people feel right now and how their feelings may affect their spending or investing in the coming months and years.

Private research firms provide these three surveys. The complete survey results are available by subscription, but, lucky for you, you can get excerpts of them at no charge.

In the general media, you may see the terms *survey* and *index* used interchangeably. But they really mean two different things. Organizations use *surveys* to collect information from consumers. They then perform calculations on the survey results and report those calculations as an *index*. (See Chapter 2 for more information about how surveys and indexes are created and used.)

Surveying UM's Consumer Sentiment Index

Without a doubt, the winner of the Wall Street popularity contest is the University of Michigan's (UM's) *Consumer Sentiment Index.* The University of Michigan first published this index in 1946. It was among the first consumer surveys done anywhere, and it's still the benchmark by which analysts evaluate all other consumer surveys. In fact, this survey asks many of the same questions today that it asked in 1946. Although the Consumer Sentiment Index began as an annual indicator, it became a monthly indicator in 1978.

The Consumer Sentiment Index is part of the University of Michigan's Surveys of Consumers report, which the school releases in conjunction with Thomson Reuters, a large research and investment data vendor. The index tries to measure how consumers feel about national economic conditions and tries to gauge their future purchasing plans. It plays a big part in the news and occasionally causes big moves in the investment markets.

Table 5-1 lists the information you need to know to follow the Consumer Sentiment Index.

Table 5-1 Consumer Sentiment Index

Release Schedule	***Agency***	***Web Address***	***Sensitivity***
Monthly: Last Friday of each month, 9:45 a.m. ET	University of Michigan's Survey Research Center	`www.customers.reuters.com/community/university/`	Occasionally high

The following sections give you a more in-depth look at this index, including what it measures, how it utilizes the data, and how you can use this information in your investing.

Eyeing the importance of this index

One reason for the popularity of the Consumer Sentiment Index is its remarkable ability to track the U.S. economy. Couple that with its long history, and you have an indicator that provides valuable insight into consumers' feelings and purchasing plans. As an added bonus, this survey gives data-crunching subscribers plenty of historical information to analyze. (Find historical Consumer Sentiment data at `www.sca.isr.umich.edu/`. ***Note:*** This data becomes available to the general public several months after its original release date.)

The University of Michigan and Thomson Reuters release the Surveys of Consumers report twice each month. The early midmonth release is just a preliminary report, available only to subscribers. The final report comes out two weeks later, typically the last Friday of the month. A press release summarizing the final Consumer Sentiment Index is available at no charge from a variety of media sources, including the main website listed in Table 5-1. This website also includes links to previous press releases going back the better part of a year.

The Consumer Sentiment Index isn't adjusted for seasonality. Except for the changes from the preliminary to the final report, there are few revisions to the data or the benchmark used for this index. (See Chapter 2 for more information about the types of adjustments made to some indicators.)

Considering the consumer's expectations

The Consumer Sentiment Index is actually just one part of three indexes in the Surveys of Consumers report, but the Consumer Sentiment Index is the headline index and essentially combines the results of the other two indexes in the report. The other two indexes are

- **Current Conditions Index:** Provides a look at consumers' current financial situation and purchasing plans
- **Consumer Expectations Index:** Provides a look at consumers' future outlook

To create the three Surveys of Consumers indexes, researchers at the University of Michigan Survey Research Center survey approximately 500 U.S. households via the telephone each month. About 60 percent of respondents are new to each survey; the remaining 40 percent are previous participants. Researchers reinterview people within six months of their original survey in an attempt to improve the continuity of the survey's results.

The official survey questionnaire asks about a wide range of topics, but it always includes the following five questions. I include them just as the researchers ask them.

1. We are interested in how people are getting along financially these days. Would you say that you (and your family living there) are better off or worse off financially than you were a year ago?
2. Now looking ahead — do you think that a year from now you (and your family living there) will be better off financially, or worse off, or just about the same as now?
3. Now turning to business conditions in the country as a whole — do you think that during the next twelve months we'll have good times financially, or bad times, or what?

4. Which would you say is more likely — that the country as a whole will have continuous good times during the next five years or so or that it will have periods of widespread unemployment or depression?
5. Generally speaking, do you think now is a good or bad time for people to buy major household items, such as furniture, refrigerators, stoves, televisions, and so on?

Researchers use the responses to Questions 1 and 5 to calculate the Current Conditions Index, the responses to Questions 2, 3, and 4 to calculate the Consumer Expectations Index, and the responses to all five questions to calculate the Consumer Sentiment Index. (How exactly do analysts calculate the Consumer Sentiment Index? Check out the sidebar "Calculating the Consumer Sentiment Index" to find out.)

One controversial feature of this survey has to do with Question 4, which asks about continuous good times during the next five years. Although this question has been a part of the survey since the beginning, its time frame is so far into the future that some analysts believe people have a hard time imagining that far ahead. The concern is that few even try; instead, they give an answer based on the way they feel about current conditions.

Correlating consumer sentiment and spending: What the data mean

The Consumer Sentiment Index typically ranges from 70 to 100, but it occasionally shows much lower and modestly higher readings. As a general rule, readings below 80 correspond with poor economic performance and readings over 90 signal prosperity. However, the level of the index matters less than its changes. A rising indicator shows an improving economy while a falling indicator corresponds with future economic problems.

Of course, this indicator isn't perfect, and it doesn't announce every recession or recovery. For example, when the job market lags behind the economic expansion, as is common, consumers are slow to feel the effects of new business prosperity. In such cases, the Consumer Sentiment Index is sometimes late to identify improving economic conditions, at least too late for most investors and traders.

Because of this delay in announcing some recessions and recoveries and because of the Consumer Sentiment Index's somewhat erratic nature, some analysts question the index's predictive capabilities. However, analysts can't ignore the relatively strong correlation between the long-term average of this index and the broad economic cycles. To see this connection yourself, compare a 12-month moving average of the Consumer Sentiment Index to a broad measure of the economy, like the GDP (see Chapter 2 for details about moving averages and Chapter 7 for more on the GDP). Figure 5-1 shows a graphic representation of the Consumer Sentiment Index along with a 12-month moving average. Notice that the index turned higher before the end of every recession.

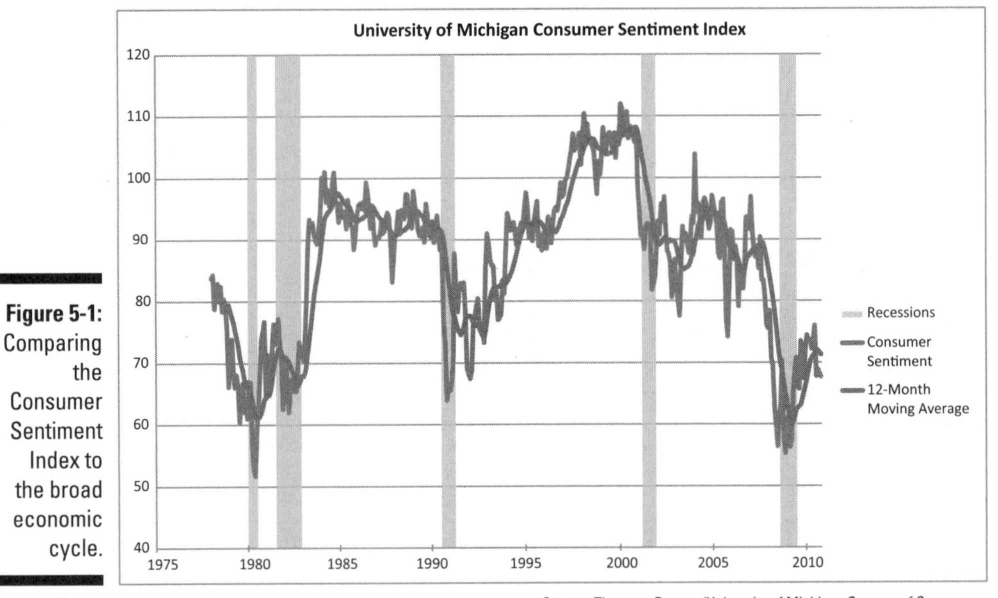

Figure 5-1: Comparing the Consumer Sentiment Index to the broad economic cycle.

Source: Thomson Reuters/University of Michigan Surveys of Consumers.

Moving averages for the Consumer Sentiment Index and the Current Conditions Index show a strong correlation to the current economy and are fairly good predictors of future economic slowdowns. After all, consumer spending often declines before a recession, and that decline usually shows up in the survey results.

On the other hand, the job market almost always recovers later than the general business market. For this reason, consumers don't see the signs of prosperity as quickly as they do the omens of recession. That's where the Consumer Expectations Index comes into play.

Although the Consumer Expectations Index isn't as well known as the Consumer Sentiment Index and rarely appears in the news, it's a better gauge for finding future recoveries. In fact, the Consumer Expectations Index plays a role in computing another highly regarded forecasting tool called the *Index of Leading Economic Indicators* (also called the LEI). The LEI is published by the Conference Board, which is also the publisher of the competing Consumer Confidence Index that I discuss later in this chapter. (See Chapter 10 for more information on the LEI.)

Calculating the Consumer Sentiment Index

To calculate the Consumer Sentiment Index (CSI), follow these steps (Q1, Q2, Q3, Q4, and Q5 represent the five survey questions):

1. **For each question, subtract the percentage of negative responses from the percentage of positive responses and then add 100.**

   Here's what this step looks like for each question:

   Sum for Q1 = (percentage of positive answers from Q1 – percentage of negative answers from Q1) + 100

2. **Add the sums from all the questions together, divide by the constant 6.7558 to scale the index to the original base month of January 1966, and then add 2 to the result to compensate for some changes to the survey that happened in the 1950s.**

   CSI = ((Sum for Q1 + Q2 + Q3 + Q4 + Q5) ÷ 6.7558) + 2

Now for a simple example. Say that 75 percent of consumers answered the first question by saying that they're better off and 25 percent said that they're worse off. Step 1 looks like this:

Sum for Q1 = (75 – 25) + 100 = 150

This is a simple example, so just assume that all the people surveyed answered the remaining questions exactly the same as they did the first. So Step 2 looks like this:

CSI = ((150 + 150 + 150 + 150 + 150) ÷ 6.7558) + 2 = 113

The resulting index value of 113 is wildly optimistic. The real-life index hasn't shown that level of optimism in more than a decade.

Large manufacturing companies pay close attention to the Surveys of Consumers report because a strong correlation exists between the movements of the Consumer Expectations Index and purchases of big-ticket items like cars, TV sets, and washers and dryers. Some manufacturers even use the Consumer Expectations Index as a forecasting tool to help adjust production in advance of an economic recession.

Looking for unexpected changes

You can use the Consumer Sentiment Index in several different ways. As with many economic indicators, the unexpected changes create the most interest. Investment analysts, for example, look for changes in the trend of the Consumer Sentiment Index rather than for specific values or percentage changes. The best way to see these trend changes is to use a moving average of 9 to 12 months (see Chapter 2 for more about moving averages).

Refer to Figure 5-1 for an example. It's a graph of the Consumer Sentiment Index, a 12-month moving average, and a shaded area showing recessions.

Notice how erratic the Consumer Sentiment Index is and how the 12-month moving average smoothes out its erratic nature. (If you want more details on how to use moving averages for decision making, check out the latest edition of *Trading For Dummies,* which I coauthored with Lita Epstein, or *Technical Analysis For Dummies* by Barbara Rockefeller.)

Knowing how the markets will react

The three indexes in the Surveys of Consumers report occasionally have a significant impact on stock and bond markets. You most often see this impact after periods of economic expansion and, to a lesser extent, after long periods of economic decline.

Unfortunately, these indexes tell investors little about the magnitude of any coming change in the economy, so only the most aggressive stock and bond traders react to it without first receiving confirmation from other indicators that the economy is changing.

Bond markets are usually the first to react to signs of deterioration in the economy. What's bad for the economy is often good for bonds. Investors with a relatively long-term investment horizon see hints that the economy may be cooling (as shown in the Consumer Sentiment and Current Situation Indexes) as less of a signal to act than a warning to start looking for other signs that confirm the weakness. They often use the job reports that I discuss in Chapter 4 as confirming indicators.

If the economy is, in fact, cooling and you're a bond investor, try to reallocate assets into longer-term bonds as shorter-duration bonds mature. If you're a stock investor, begin reallocating assets away from economically sensitive companies and, possibly, equities to long-maturity bonds.

Understanding the Consumer Confidence Index

The *Consumer Confidence Index* comes out of a widely regarded survey called, very creatively, the Consumer Confidence Survey. The Conference Board, a worldwide not-for-profit organization, creates this particular report each month; the organization provides the whole report to its members and passes on some limited excerpts at no charge to everyone else.

Table 5-2 provides the information you need to know to follow the Consumer Confidence Index.

Table 5-2 Consumer Confidence Index

Release Schedule	*Agency*	*Web Address*	*Sensitivity*
Monthly: Last Tuesday of each month, 10:00 a.m. ET	The Conference Board	www.conference-board.org/data/ConsumerConfidence.cfm	Occasionally high

With its Consumer Confidence Survey, the Conference Board attempts to gather insight into the consumer's thoughts about local job markets and local business conditions. Any hint that people are becoming pessimistic about their job situation or about the economy may signal that an economic slowdown is coming.

Although the data are adjusted for seasonality, seasonality doesn't appear to affect consumer confidence much.

This report, which was first published in 1967, doesn't have the longevity of the University of Michigan's Consumer Sentiment Index, and it doesn't have quite the same market or business impact. Nonetheless, it's a valuable resource for investors, business leaders, economists, and researchers because it keeps them abreast of changing economic conditions. The following sections explain what this report measures, how it comes up with the data, and how you can use the information.

Seeing how people feel about the economy

Every month the Conference Board mails approximately 5,000 questionnaires to ask consumers about their job situations and their expectations for the future. Only a portion of those consumers return the survey — usually between 2,500 to 3,000.

Each survey asks the following five questions; two questions refer to current conditions and three refer to future expectations:

1. How would you rate the present general business conditions in your area? Good, normal, or bad?

2. Six months from now, do you think they will be better, the same, or worse?
3. What would you say about available jobs in your area right now? Plenty, not so many, or hard to get?
4. Six months from now, do you think there will be more, the same, or fewer jobs available in your area?
5. How would you guess your total family income to be six months from now? Higher, the same, or lower?

The survey also asks questions about spending plans and other economic factors. For example, the survey asks about big-ticket purchases planned for the next six months, such as new or used automobiles, new or existing homes, and consumer durables, such as refrigerators, TVs, kitchen appliances, and air conditioners. It also asks about vacation plans and expectations for inflation, stock prices, and interest rates.

The detailed data, including the planned-purchases data, are available only to subscribers. Subscription reports include 12 months of data for each index, including details about the raw data collected during the surveys. Analysts tabulate the data according to the respondents' age and income level and by geographic region. Subscribers also have access to an archive of historical data. Subscriptions probably make the most sense for business leaders and well-heeled investors.

Based on the survey answers, the Conference Board creates and reports these three indexes:

- **Present Situation Index:** Based on Questions 1 and 3, this index represents the consumer's current outlook. It's also called the *Appraisal of the Present Situation*.
- **Expectations Index:** Based on Questions 2, 4 and 5, this index represents the consumer's expectations for the next six months. It's also called the *Expectations for Six Months Hence.*
- **Consumer Confidence Index:** This index is a combination of the Present Situation and Expectations Indexes; it's weighted 40 percent for the Present Situation and 60 percent for the Expectation Index. The Consumer Confidence Index is the headline index, and it's also called the *Composite Series*.

The Conference Board website (which I list in Table 5-2) provides a summary of the three indexes at no charge, along with a paragraph or two summarizing the changes behind the indexes.

Looking for happy consumers

Both the Consumer Confidence Index and the Present Situation Index do an admirable job of mirroring current economic conditions. This section shows how these two indexes, along with the Consumer Expectations Index, are reported and how you can use the information when making your investing and business decisions.

Figure 5-2 shows a sample of the Consumer Confidence Index report. Notice that the Composite Series goes from November 2009 through November 2010. The *(p)* next to the November 2010 column indicates that the data in that column are preliminary. The *(r)* next to the October 2010 column indicates that the calculations in that column are final. The report also includes a year's worth of data for the Present Situation and Expectations Indexes, along with breakouts for each question.

As a general rule, a moving average of the Consumer Confidence Index that's above 100 typically indicates future economic expansion. A moving average that's below 80 usually coincides with an economic slowdown.

Figure 5-3 shows one of the charts included in the Conference Board report. It overlays the Consumer Expectations Index onto changes in the GDP.

Comparing and contrasting surveys

Although similarities exist between the Conference Board and the University of Michigan surveys, they do have significant differences in methodology. The main differences between the two consumer surveys are

- **The number of participants:** The Consumer Sentiment Index is based on telephone surveys of 500 people, while the Consumer Confidence Index is based on surveys sent to 5,000 people. You may think more is better, and statisticians agree that the larger group improves the statistical significance of the survey. However, the Conference Board doesn't include previous respondents in its survey. Some analysts argue that this lack of repeat respondents makes the Consumer Confidence Index more erratic compared to the Consumer Sentiment Index, but it doesn't seem to be more erratic in practice. In fact, the University of Michigan's smaller sample size may cause its index to exhibit more volatility; the narrower range of values and the techniques used to construct the index mask that volatility.
- **The survey's general focus:** The Consumer Confidence Index focuses on local conditions rather than national conditions and on employment rather than spending plans. Yes, the Conference Board asks about spending in its survey, but those responses aren't part of the Consumer Confidence Index. Data about planned purchases are available only to subscribers.

THE CONFERENCE BOARD **CONSUMER CONFIDENCE SURVEY®** DECEMBER 2010 www.conferenceboard.org

Consumer Confidence and Buying Plans
Based on surveys conducted by TNS
Percentage of households = 100%

All series seasonally adjusted	2009 Nov.	Dec.	2010 Jan.	Feb.	Mar.	Apr.	May	June	July	Aug.	Sep.	Oct.(r)	Nov.(p)
Composite Series: Index Numbers, 1985=100													
Consumer Confidence Index®	50.6	53.6	56.5	46.4	52.3	57.7	62.7	54.3	51.0	53.2	48.6	49.9	54.1
Present Situation	21.2	20.2	25.2	21.7	25.2	28.2	29.8	26.8	26.4	24.9	23.3	23.5	24.0
Expectations	70.3	75.9	77.3	62.9	70.4	77.4	84.6	72.7	67.5	72.0	65.5	67.5	74.2
Appraisal of Present Situation: Percent													
Business Conditions													
Good	8.1	7.5	8.5	6.8	8.5	8.9	9.7	8.4	8.8	8.4	8.2	8.3	8.1
Bad	44.5	45.7	44.7	45.1	42.1	40.0	39.5	41.0	43.3	42.3	46.0	42.3	43.6
Normal	47.4	46.8	46.8	48.1	49.4	51.1	50.8	50.6	47.9	49.3	45.8	49.4	48.3
Employment													
Jobs plentiful	3.1	3.1	4.4	4.0	4.0	4.7	4.6	4.3	4.4	4.0	3.8	3.5	4.0
Jobs not so plentiful	47.7	48.8	49.1	48.7	49.7	50.5	51.5	52.2	50.5	50.5	50.4	50.2	49.5
Jobs hard to get	49.2	48.1	46.5	47.3	46.3	44.8	43.9	43.5	45.1	45.5	45.8	46.3	46.5
Expectations for Six Months Hence: Percent													
Business Conditions													
Better	19.7	21.2	20.7	16.1	18.0	19.7	22.8	17.1	15.8	16.9	15.0	15.8	16.7
Worse	14.6	11.8	12.7	15.9	13.6	12.4	11.9	13.9	15.3	13.4	16.6	14.4	12.1
Same	65.7	67.0	66.6	68.0	68.4	67.9	65.3	69.0	68.9	69.7	68.4	69.8	71.2
Employment													
More jobs	15.8	16.4	15.8	13.2	14.1	17.7	20.2	16.2	14.2	14.7	14.5	14.5	15.5
Fewer jobs	23.1	20.6	18.9	24.7	21.4	19.9	17.8	20.1	20.9	19.6	22.6	22.3	18.8
Same	61.1	63.0	65.3	62.1	64.5	62.4	62.0	63.7	64.9	65.7	62.9	63.2	65.7
Income													
Increase	10.9	10.4	11.0	10.1	10.8	10.5	11.4	10.6	10.6	10.6	10.3	9.7	10.6
Decrease	18.9	18.4	16.3	17.8	17.4	16.7	16.4	16.8	17.7	16.7	16.3	16.0	17.3
Same	70.2	71.2	72.7	72.1	71.8	72.8	72.2	72.6	71.7	72.7	73.4	74.3	72.1
Plans to Buy Within Six Months: Percent													
Automobile													
Yes	4.5	3.9	5.2	5.3	3.9	5.4	6.0	4.1	4.7	4.7	5.0	5.2	5.4
New	1.9	1.5	2.2	1.9	1.3	2.4	2.7	1.4	1.7	1.8	2.2	2.2	1.9
Used	2.0	1.8	2.5	2.6	2.1	2.1	2.7	2.0	2.4	2.5	2.0	2.2	2.9
Uncertain	0.6	0.6	0.5	0.8	0.5	0.9	0.6	0.7	0.6	0.4	0.8	0.8	0.6
Home													
Yes	2.1	1.7	2.4	2.7	2.8	2.1	2.1	2.0	1.9	2.1	2.0	2.2	1.7
New	0.4	0.4	0.7	0.6	0.7	0.4	0.3	0.2	0.3	0.4	0.4	0.4	0.4
Lived in	1.3	1.0	1.2	1.3	1.3	1.4	1.2	1.1	1.2	1.2	1.2	1.0	1.1
Uncertain	0.4	0.3	0.5	0.8	0.8	0.3	0.6	0.7	0.4	0.5	0.4	0.8	0.2
Major appliances													
Total plans	23.7	23.6	26.3	27.8	25.5	27.8	26.0	23.7	28.3	24.6	27.7	25.4	24.4
Refrigerator	3.5	3.7	4.8	4.6	4.1	5.2	4.6	3.6	3.6	3.7	3.6	3.6	3.7
Washing machine	2.8	3.4	3.6	3.7	3.2	3.5	3.1	3.1	3.9	2.8	3.8	3.7	3.0
TV Set	7.8	7.4	7.3	9.0	8.1	7.7	7.3	7.5	9.1	7.7	8.2	8.0	8.2
Vacuum Cleaner	3.6	3.2	3.7	3.6	4.0	3.9	3.8	3.6	4.5	4.7	4.3	3.6	3.5
Range	2.0	2.0	2.5	2.2	2.1	3.0	2.7	1.8	2.4	1.8	2.6	2.4	2.1
Clothes dryer	2.7	2.9	2.8	3.4	3.0	3.0	3.3	2.9	2.9	2.1	2.9	2.5	2.2
Air conditioner	1.3	1.0	1.6	1.3	1.0	1.5	1.2	1.2	1.9	1.8	2.3	1.6	1.7
Carpet	3.7	3.3	3.7	2.7	3.6	3.1	3.6	3.2	3.2	3.3	3.4	2.8	3.4
Vacation Intended Within Six Months: Percent													
Vacation Intended		37.0		36.9		38.3		36.5		38.0		39.3	
Destination													
U.S.		30.6		31.1		32.0		31.0		31.6		32.6	
Foreign country		7.1		7.7		7.9		7.1		7.3		8.0	
Means of Travel													
Automobile		18.7		19.8		20.7		19.5		19.6		22.8	
Airplane		14.6		16.0		17.8		17.8		16.6		13.4	
Other		3.4		3.2		3.2		2.8		3.2		3.8	

(p) - preliminary (r) - revised

A monthly report from The Consumer Research Center

ISSN 1046-1876

The Conference Board www.conferenceboard.org
The Americas 845 Third Avenue, New York, NY 10022-6600, United States / Tel +1 212 759 0900 / Fax +1 212 980 7014
Asia CHINA Beijing Representative Office, 7-2-72 Qijiayuan, 9 Jianwai Street, Beijing 100600 P.R. China / Tel +86 10 8532 4688 / Fax +86 10 8532 5332 / www.conferenceboard.cn
HONG KONG Suite No. 2-3, 18/F, Queen's Place, 74 Queen's Road Central, Hong Kong SAR / Tel +852 2804 1000 / Fax +852 2869 1403
INDIA A-701 Mahalaxmi Heights, Keshavrao Khadye Marg, Mahalaxmi (East), Mumbai 400 011 India / Tel +91 22 23051402
SINGAPORE 8 Eu Tong Sen Street #22-81, The Central, Singapore 059818
Europe Chaussée de La Hulpe 130, box 11, B-1000 Brussels, Belgium / Tel +32 2 675 54 05 / Fax +32 2 675 03 95

Figure 5-2: Sample Consumer Confidence Index report.

Source: The Conference Board.

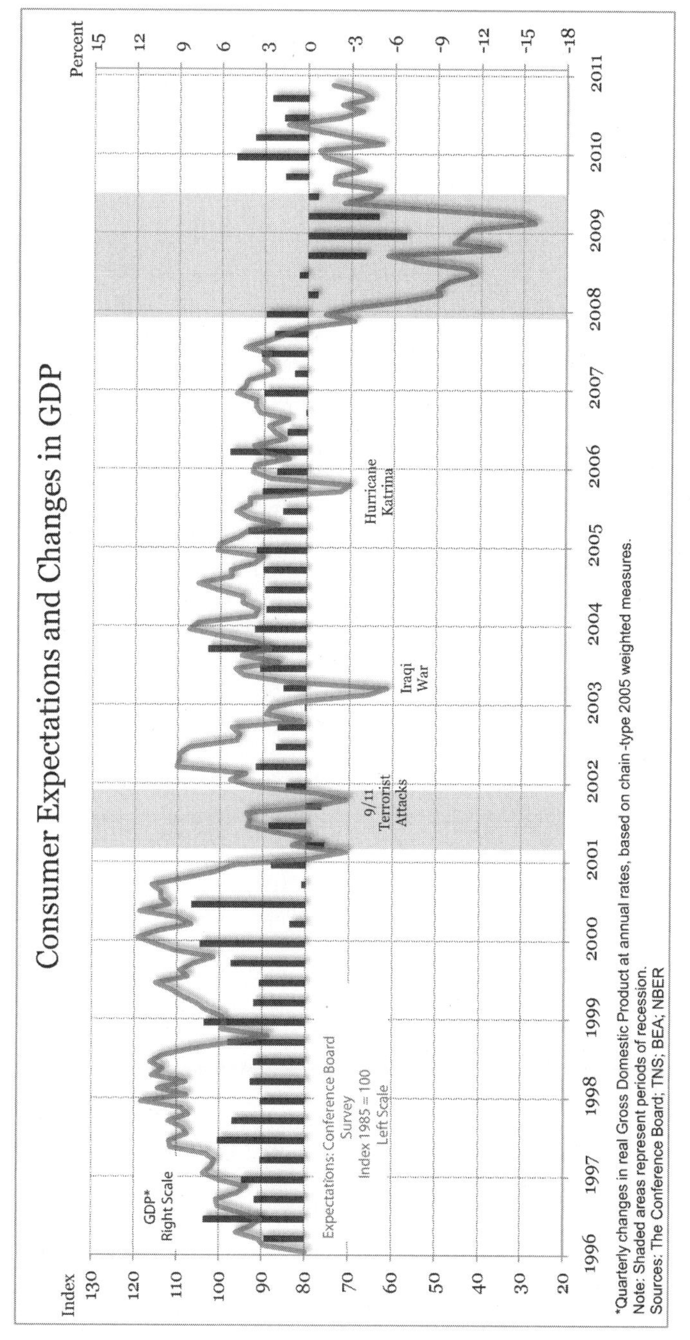

Source: The Conference Board.

Figure 5-3: Comparing the Consumer Expectations Index to changes in the GDP.

- **The look-ahead period for the Expectations Index:** This may be the most significant difference. You may recall that one of the questions in the University of Michigan survey asks consumers how they think the economy will look five years from now. In contrast, the Conference Board asks consumers to look ahead six months. The shorter time horizon appears to give the Conference Board's Expectations Index a small advantage for anticipating future spending plans and economic conditions.

Surprisingly, given the differences in methodology, questions, and time frames, the results between the two surveys are often very similar. Differences sometimes show up in month-to-month reports, but they're often due to differences in the timing of the data collection rather than substantive differences in the indexes themselves.

The timing issue affects both the Conference Board and the University of Michigan reports. If anything newsworthy happens after analysts collect the survey data, it doesn't show up in the current report. If the newsworthy event has sufficient staying power, it will likely show up in subsequent reports. Otherwise, people will forget about the event by the time the next survey goes out, and it will never be in the index; this is actually the better problem to have. After all, if a newsworthy event affects the survey result but doesn't have any long-term effect on the economy, it just amplifies the erratic nature of the index.

Finding surprises in the confidence survey

Ideally, a consumer survey would forecast how customers will actually spend money. Unfortunately, too many outside factors influence respondents to the Conference Board's survey to perfectly gauge future consumer spending. People tend to get wrapped up in the news of the day or to be influenced by their own momentary fears, but those transient concerns don't necessarily affect people's economic situation. This gap between consumer feelings and reality makes for an imperfect look into consumers' future spending.

Still, if you smooth out the erratic nature of the Consumer Confidence Index, you can turn it into a pretty good indicator of future economic activity. In fact, all the Consumer Board indexes benefit from smoothing out the month-to-month fluctuations. You can use a relatively long-term moving average of 9 to 12 months for this smoothing (see Chapter 2 for more about moving averages). These moving averages are a little slow to react, but they appear to improve the predictive capability of the Conference Board indexes.

Calculating the Consumer Confidence Index

The Conference Board's Consumer Confidence Index arbitrarily uses 1985 as the base year and assigns it a value of 100 (refer to Chapter 2 for more information about baseline indexes).

To calculate the Consumer Confidence Index (CCI), follow these steps (Q1, Q2, Q3, Q4, and Q5 represent the five main survey questions):

1. **For each question, divide the sum of the positive and negative percentages into the positive percentage.**

   Q1 = positive % ÷ (positive % + negative %)

2. **Divide the result for each question by a constant to represent the 1985 base year value and then multiply by 100.**

   Q1 = (positive % ÷ (positive % + negative %)) ÷ (base year value) × 100

3. **Average the resulting values from each question to find the index.**

   CCI = (Q1 + Q2 + Q3 + Q4 + Q5) ÷ 5

You calculate the other Conference Board indexes (Present Situation and Expectations Indexes) in the same manner.

The 12-month moving averages for both the Consumer Confidence Index and the Present Situation Index show current economic conditions well and telegraph early signs of an economic downturn. A 12-month moving average for the Expectations Index does a better job of anticipating recoveries.

If you have access to the Consumer Confidence Survey's subscription reports, you can eke out another good predictor from the rough data. In the *Employment* section of the report shown in Figure 5-2, under the *Appraisal of Present Situation* heading, you see the responses to the question of whether people think jobs are plentiful, not so plentiful, or hard to get. If you create a ratio of those who think jobs are plentiful divided by those who think jobs are hard to get, you get a handy homemade indicator that's often very useful. For example, using the data from the sample report shown in Figure 5-2, you get a ratio of 0.08 (4.0 ÷ 46.5 = 0.08). In other words, only 8 percent of all respondents think jobs are plentiful. Until that number starts trending higher, for at least several months, you can't have much confidence that the economy is on stable footing.

Adjusting your portfolio strategy

Investment markets are most concerned about unexpected changes. During an economic expansion, you can expect people to be optimistic. But when fewer people are optimistic than the previous month or, more important, when a significant turn in a 6- to 12-month moving average occurs, investors start to notice.

Although market reaction to the Consumer Confidence Index is often muted, unexpected changes can trigger both stock and bond traders to react. However, this indicator rarely causes investors to make a permanent shift in their strategy or allocation of assets.

Unless you measure your investment horizon in hours or days, look for other signs of an economic change before taking any major action. For example, if the Consumer Confidence Index shows unexpected weakness, look to the Bureau of Labor Statistics Employment Situation report or the Unemployment Insurance Weekly Claims Report before making substantive changes to your investment strategy.

Reviewing the Bloomberg Consumer Comfort Index

If you're too impatient to wait for the monthly releases of the Consumer Sentiment and Consumer Confidence Indexes, perhaps the weekly Bloomberg Consumer Comfort Index is more to your liking.

The report has had several sponsors and names since it first began in 1985, but the index is now formally called the *Bloomberg Consumer Comfort Index,* though you sometimes see it referred to as the *Bloomberg Confidence Survey* or the *Bloomberg Confidence surveys.*

Table 5-3 provides the information you need to know to follow this weekly report.

Table 5-3 Bloomberg Consumer Comfort Index

Release Schedule	*Agency*	*Web Address*	*Sensitivity*
Weekly: Every Thursday, 9:45 a.m. ET	Bloomberg	`www.bloomberg.com/consumer-comfort-index/`	Low

The following sections give you the lowdown on this survey and use its formal name (the Consumer Comfort Index) to avoid any confusion with the University of Michigan and Conference Board indicators.

Justifying another consumer survey: What makes this one unique

Given that two well-regarded consumer surveys already existed when the Consumer Comfort Index began, you may wonder why anyone would chose to start yet another one. But investors, analysts, and business leaders all benefit from its creation. The survey's weekly format offers a more frequent look into the consumers' views of current economic conditions and their personal finances. Plus, it addresses the timing issue that afflicts the two monthly surveys.

Bloomberg's partner in this project is Langer Research Associates. Langer Research randomly surveys 250 people by telephone each week to ask them about their financial condition and their willingness to spend money. This survey's primary concern is to gauge the U.S. economy's current conditions. It asks its responders three questions about current conditions and only one question about their expectations for the future (compared to the three each for the other two surveys I describe in this chapter). But only the three current-condition questions go into calculating the Consumer Comfort Index. Here are the four questions that appear on the survey:

1. Would you describe the state of the nation's economy these days as excellent, good, not so good, or poor?
2. Would you describe the state of your own personal finances these days as excellent, good, not so good, or poor?
3. Considering the cost of things today and your own personal finances, would you say now is an excellent time, a good time, a not so good time, or a poor time to buy the things you want and need?
4. Do you think the nation's economy is getting better, getting worse, or staying the same?

Correlating comfort, recovery, and recession

Survey results for the Bloomberg Consumer Comfort Index are published weekly. However, single-week results aren't reported. Instead, results for the current week's survey are added to the results from the previous three weeks and reported as a single index value. This calculation method effectively turns the index into a four-week moving average of consumer comfort (see Chapter 2 for more about moving averages). This approach helps to overcome some of the data-collection timing issues that occasionally affect the monthly surveys from the University of Michigan and the Conference Board. Results aren't adjusted for seasonality.

The Bloomberg website (which I list in Table 5-3) reports on the survey results each week. This weekly report includes the headline index value (that is, the Bloomberg Consumer Comfort Index) and a summary of the survey's findings. Survey results and the weekly index value are also available to other news outlets and are occasionally reported elsewhere.

Figure 5-4 shows an excerpt from the first table of a recent Consumer Comfort Index data summary. It shows details from the past six weeks for the Overall index, the Personal Finances index, and the Buying Climate index. It also shows individual measures for the questions that make up the index.

The second page of the Consumer Comfort data summary shows survey demographics tabulated by age, sex, income, region, race, political identification, and marital and employment status. Figure 5-5 shows a long-term graph that plots the value of the Consumer Comfort Index and shows corresponding periods of economic recession.

Bloomberg Weekly Consumer Comfort Index (Table)

Following is a table with the latest survey results:

	May 29 2011	May 22 2011	May 15 2011	May 8 2011	May 1 2011	April 24 2011
Overall index	-47.1	-48.4	-49.4	-46.9	-46.2	-45.1
State of Economy	-74.6	-75.7	-75.6	-75.0	-75.8	-74.3
Positive Net	13	12	12	13	12	13
Excellent	1	1	1	0	0	0
Good	12	11	12	12	12	13
Negative Net	87	88	88	88	88	87
Not-so Good	44	43	40	42	41	40
Poor	44	45	48	46	47	47

	May 29 2011	May 22 2011	May 15 2011	May 8 2011	May 1 2011	April 24 2011
Personal Finances	-13.4	-13.7	-16.5	-10.6	-6.9	-9.2
Positive Net	43	43	42	45	47	45
Excellent	4	5	4	5	5	4
Good	39	38	37	40	42	42
Negative	57	57	58	55	54	55
Not-so Good	36	35	36	34	34	35
Poor	21	22	23	21	19	19
Buying Climate	-53.1	-55.8	-56.1	-54.9	-56.0	-51.8
Positive Net	24	22	22	23	22	24
Excellent	4	3	2	1	1	1
Good	20	20	20	21	21	23
Negative	77	78	78	77	78	76
Not-so Good	45	46	45	46	47	46
Poor	31	32	33	32	31	30

Figure 5-4: An example of a Bloomberg Consumer Comfort Index data summary.

Source: Bloomberg Consumer Comfort Index produced by Langer Research Associates.

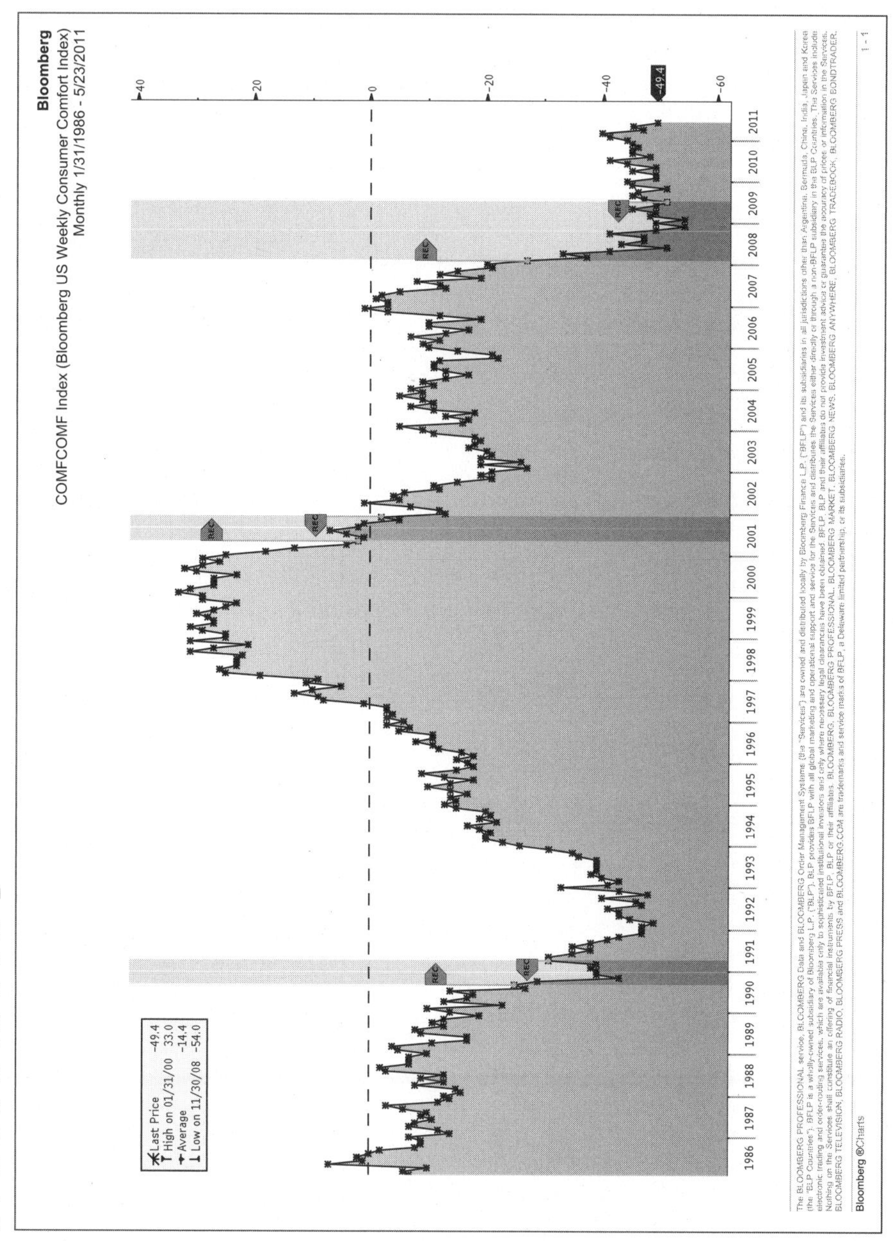

Figure 5-5: A sample graph showing Consumer Comfort Index weekly tracking results.

Source: Bloomberg Consumer Comfort Index produced by Langer Research Associates.

Calculating the Consumer Comfort Index

Calculating the Consumer Comfort Index involves the most straightforward process of all the surveys I discuss in this chapter.

To calculate the Consumer Comfort Index (CCI), Bloomberg's partner, Langer Research Associates, follows these steps (Q1, Q2, and Q3 represent the three main survey questions):

1. **For each question, add together the results for the excellent and good responses and then subtract the results for the not-so-good and poor responses.**

   Q1 = (excellent %) + (good %) – (not so good %) – (poor %)

2. **Add the results for all three questions and divide by 3.**

   CCI = (Q1 + Q2 + Q3) ÷ 3

3. **Take the average index of all three questions to get the Consumer Comfort Index.**

Correlation is very high between the Consumer Comfort Index, the Consumer Sentiment Index, and the Consumer Confidence Index. At the very least, this correlation allows investors and business leaders to use the Consumer Comfort Index as an early look into consumers' emotional state, which they can then use to forecast the results of the more prominent surveys.

Modifying your portfolio strategy

The best use for the Consumer Comfort Index, like other current condition indexes, is to identify economic peaks. When the Consumer Comfort Index begins to fall, it often coincides with falling income and wages, leading to a drop in spending. The job market and consumer spending often lag behind when the economy starts to recover from a recession, which is why the Consumer Comfort Index usually lags behind economic expansions.

The weekly format of this report has its advantages. The three consumer surveys usually don't differ in direction, so some analysts use the Consumer Comfort Index to anticipate the results from the monthly release of the Consumer Sentiment and Consumer Confidence Indexes. However, the Consumer Comfort Index is too erratic for all but the most aggressive traders to use as a timing tool. Most traders use the Consumer Comfort Index as a signal to begin looking for other signs of economic change.

Chapter 6

Spreading the Wealth: Consumer Spending and the Economy

In This Chapter

- Understanding the most influential reports on consumer dollars
- Tracking consumer income, spending, and saving
- Following retail sales volumes, including e-commerce sales
- Finding out how much debt consumers owe

Spending may not make the world go 'round, but it's absolutely essential to the economy. In fact, the amount of money people spend — and what they spend it on — determines the strength of the economy. Likewise, the amount of money people earn influences how much they spend and how much they borrow so they can spend even more.

Wouldn't you like to see how much money people are spending right now and identify where that money is coming from? And while you're wishing for nice things, wouldn't you like to know what people are buying?

Fortunately, all this information is readily available. This chapter looks at some of the most prominent reports about consumer income, spending, and borrowing. Although many reports cover this arena, the focus of this chapter is on the most reliable reports and the ones that move the investment markets the most.

Making and Spending: The BEA's Personal Income and Outlays Report

Every time you buy something, you contribute to the economy. Over the long run, it's better for the economy if you spend money you've earned rather than money you've borrowed, but both types of spending are important. They're so important, in fact, that investors, economists, and business leaders all want to know exactly how much you and your fellow consumers are spending.

Several places track all the details of consumer money making and spending, but the most authoritative and reliable source is the monthly report from the Bureau of Economic Analysis (BEA) called *Personal Income and Outlays.* Table 6-1 lists the information you need to know to find and follow this report.

Table 6-1 Personal Income and Outlays Report

Release Schedule	*Agency*	*Web Address*	*Sensitivity*
Monthly: Published schedule, 8:30 a.m. ET	U.S. Bureau of Economic Analysis, Department of Commerce	`www.bea.gov/national/index.htm#personal`	Moderate

Although this report has a moderate market impact, its impact would be even greater if it didn't take so long to compile. Unfortunately, the data in the report is one month old by the time the BEA releases it; for example, August income and spending data are reported at the end of September. To see the monthly release schedule for this report, go to the BEA website: `www.bea.gov/newsreleases/news_release_sort_national.htm`. (Check out the nearby sidebar "Why isn't the BEA's report more current?" for details on why this report takes so long to compile.)

Despite its long compilation time, this report is an excellent preview of things to come. For one thing, personal income and spending show a very strong correlation to the economy's strength. In addition, the BEA uses information taken directly from this monthly report to calculate the quarterly gross domestic product (GDP; see Chapter 7 for details on this important indicator), and both investors and the Federal Reserve keep a close eye on this report for its insight into inflation. These facts alone are more than enough reason for investors, analysts, and business leaders to keep tabs on this report. The report's effect on the markets, especially when the results are unexpected, is added incentive to watch this one carefully.

In the following sections, I explain how wages, savings, and purchases are reported, and I show you how a phenomenon called the wealth effect affects personal spending. I also cover the relationship between spending and income and explain their economic impact. Finally, I show how the Federal Reserve and investors use the Personal Income and Outlays report.

Tracking personal wages, savings, and purchases

Consumer spending on products and services is responsible for the majority of all economic activity in the United States. When wages fall, consumer appetites for new products, especially expensive products like automobiles and kitchen appliances, slow down dramatically. When consumer spending slows, so does the economy.

To keep tabs on consumer spending, the BEA collects income and spending data from many sources (for examples, see the sidebar "Why isn't the BEA's report more current?" later in this chapter) and then publishes the data in the Personal Income and Outlays report each month. This report comes in two formats:

- **A brief press release:** This press release summarizes the report's findings and includes a chart or two. The press release provides a good overview, but if you really want to understand what's happening with consumers, I suggest that you dig into the data tables in the detailed analysis.
- **A detailed analysis:** The detailed analysis provides — go figure — a lot more details, including a remarkable set of data tables. I discuss the in-depth analysis in the following paragraphs.

The detailed Personal Income and Outlays report includes 11 data tables. The first six tables cover income, spending, and savings. The remaining tables dig deeper into spending. All 11 tables adjust personal income and spending for seasonality and present them in both current and chained dollars. Recall that chained dollars are indexed for inflation (see Chapter 2 for more on adjusting data for seasonality and inflation).

Tables 1 through 6 show different views of income, spending, and savings. Each one tabulates the information over a different time frame or provides a comparison to previous periods:

- **Table 1:** Personal Income and Its Disposition (Months)
- **Table 2:** Personal Income and Its Disposition (Years and Quarters)
- **Table 3:** Change from Preceding Period (Months)
- **Table 4:** Change from Preceding Period (Years and Quarters)
- **Table 5:** Percent Change from Preceding Period (Months)
- **Table 6:** Percent Change from Preceding Period (Years and Quarters)

Figure 6-1 shows you what Table 1 looks like. It's a representative example of the first six tables and provides a very good overview of the report as a whole.

Table 1. Personal Income and Its Disposition (Months)
[Billions of dollars]

		Seasonally adjusted at annual rates					
		2010					
		May	June	"July-Sept" have been removed	October r	November r	December p
Personal income	**Personal income**	**12,532.8**	**12,540.0**		**12,673.0**	**12,717.9**	**12,772.4**
	Compensation of employees, received	**7,985.8**	**7,984.8**		**8,088.2**	**8,098.6**	**8,119.5**
	Wage and salary disbursements	**6,403.7**	**6,400.4**		**6,487.3**	**6,494.6**	**6,511.7**
	Private industries	5,207.8	5,207.0		5,303.8	5,309.7	5,325.2
	Goods-producing industries	1,062.9	1,054.2		1,071.5	1,069.0	1,070.5
	Manufacturing	679.6	673.1		683.1	680.6	680.8
	Services-producing industries	4,144.9	4,152.9		4,232.3	4,240.7	4,254.7
	Trade, transportation, and utilities	1,007.2	1,006.2		1,025.3	1,025.5	1,028.0
	Other services-producing industries	3,137.7	3,146.6		3,206.9	3,215.1	3,226.6
	Government	1,195.9	1,193.4		1,183.6	1,184.9	1,186.5
	Supplements to wages and salaries	**1,582.1**	**1,584.4**		**1,600.9**	**1,604.0**	**1,607.8**
	Employer contributions for employee pension and insurance funds	1,103.1	1,105.5		1,115.6	1,118.1	1,121.0
	Employer contributions for government social insurance	479.0	479.0		485.2	485.9	486.9
	Proprietors' income with inventory valuation and capital consumption adjustments	**1,051.7**	**1,048.3**		**1,075.3**	**1,083.2**	**1,091.3**
	Farm	38.9	40.3		55.4	58.1	60.9
	Nonfarm	1,012.7	1,008.0		1,019.9	1,025.1	1,030.3
	Rental income of persons with capital consumption adjustment	**298.8**	**299.6**		**308.2**	**309.9**	**311.8**
	Personal income receipts on assets	**1,915.0**	**1,917.3**		**1,891.7**	**1,909.0**	**1,930.9**
	Personal interest income	1,205.3	1,205.6		1,172.9	1,186.5	1,200.1
	Personal dividend income	709.7	711.8		718.9	722.5	730.8
	Personal current transfer receipts	**2,285.4**	**2,293.8**		**2,325.9**	**2,334.6**	**2,338.4**
	Government social benefits to persons	2,248.4	2,256.5		2,286.6	2,296.0	2,300.0
	Old-age, survivors, disability, and health insurance benefits	1,207.9	1,208.6		1,229.8	1,228.9	1,239.2
	Government unemployment insurance benefits	137.1	136.1		128.7	131.1	125.1
	Other	903.4	911.9		928.1	936.0	935.8
	Other current transfer receipts, from business (net)	37.0	37.2		39.3	38.6	38.4
	Less: Contributions for government social insurance, domestic	**1,003.9**	**1,003.9**		**1,016.3**	**1,017.4**	**1,019.5**
	Less: Personal current taxes	**1,151.8**	**1,152.0**		**1,200.1**	**1,206.0**	**1,213.1**
DPI	**Equals: Disposable personal income**	**11,381.0**	**11,388.0**		**11,472.9**	**11,511.9**	**11,559.2**
Personal outlays	**Less: Personal outlays**	**10,670.4**	**10,668.1**		**10,844.0**	**10,877.6**	**10,945.1**
	Personal consumption expenditures	10,292.1	10,288.8		10,478.4	10,513.8	10,583.3
	Goods	3,374.8	3,361.2		3,512.3	3,522.4	3,565.3
	Durable goods	1,074.6	1,069.5		1,136.2	1,131.5	1,139.2
	Nondurable goods	2,300.1	2,291.7		2,376.1	2,390.9	2,426.1
	Services	6,917.3	6,927.6		6,966.1	6,991.5	7,018.0
	Personal interest payments [1]	206.0	206.5		189.9	187.3	184.7
	Personal current transfer payments	172.3	172.8		175.8	176.4	177.1
	To government	100.1	100.6		103.0	103.6	104.3
	To the rest of the world (net)	72.2	72.2		72.8	72.8	72.8
Personal savings	**Equals: Personal saving**	**710.6**	**719.8**		**628.8**	**634.4**	**614.1**
	Personal saving as a percentage of disposable personal income	**6.2**	**6.3**		**5.5**	**5.5**	**5.3**
	Addenda:						
Real DPI	**Personal income excluding current transfer receipts, billions of chained (2005) dollars [2]**	**9,240.2**	**9,250.8**		**9,287.3**	**9,310.6**	**9,327.2**
	Disposable personal income:						
	Total, billions of chained (2005) dollars [2]	10,262.4	10,281.6		10,297.8	10,322.7	10,333.1
	Per capita:						
	Current dollars	36,746	36,742		36,899	36,997	37,122
	Chained (2005) dollars	33,135	33,172		33,120	33,175	33,185
	Population (midperiod, thousands) [3]	309,718	309,946		310,927	311,157	311,381

p Preliminary
r Revised
1. Consists of nonmortgage interest paid by households.
2. The current-dollar measure is deflated by the implicit price deflator for personal consumption expenditures.
3. Population is the total population of the United States, including the Armed Forces overseas and the institutionalized population.
The monthly estimate is the average of estimates for the first of the month and the first of the following month; the annual and quarterly estimates are averages of the monthly estimates.

Figure 6-1: Table 1 provides an overview of the Personal Income and Outlays report as a whole.

In the following sections, I explain Table 1 in greater depth and point out the relevant information you can pull from the table's data to help with your investments.

Personal income

The first component in Table 1 of the Personal Income and Outlays report is *personal income,* which is income that individuals earn from a variety of sources. Personal income is the source of most consumer spending (the rest comes from credit). Table 1 breaks personal income into the following categories:

- **Wages and salaries:** Includes wages and salaries paid to individuals by private industry and government employers

Why isn't the BEA's report more current?

The reason why the Personal Income and Outlays report takes so long to be published is that the BEA collects data from more than a dozen sources and combines them into its monthly report. For example, the BEA compiles income data from the monthly Employment Situation report (see Chapter 4), as well as directly from government agencies like the Social Security Administration, the Internal Revenue Service (IRS), and the Federal Reserve. Information about consumer spending also comes from a variety of sources, including the retail-sales-related reports that I discuss later in this chapter, private trade associations like the National Automobile Dealers Association, as well as reports from other government indexes like the Consumer Price Index and the Producer Price Index (see Chapter 12 for information on the CPI and PPI).

The BEA makes limited revisions to the monthly data for up to several months after the initial release, as well as annually. Changes in methodology occur, and additional data sources are occasionally added. You can expect to see changes to the benchmark index every three to five years. (See Chapter 2 for more on periodic revisions and changes to benchmark indexes.)

- **Supplements to wages and salaries:** Includes employer contributions for employee benefits, such as private pension and profit-sharing plans, private unemployment insurance, healthcare insurance, life insurance, and temporary disability insurance
- **Proprietor's income:** Includes income from sole proprietorships, partnerships, and tax-exempt corporations
- **Rental income:** Includes income from rental property and also royalties from patents, copyrights, and natural-resource rights
- **Personal income receipts on assets:** Includes the following two subcategories:
    - **Interest income:** Generally includes interest paid to consumers on bank deposits, corporate bonds, and government bills and bonds
    - **Dividend income:** Includes all dividends paid to consumers by corporations
- **Transfer payments:** Includes payments to individuals from Social Security, hospital or supplemental medical insurance, unemployment insurance, food stamps, and temporary disability insurance

Proceeds or profits from any asset sales (including the sale of real estate, bonds, or stocks), monetary gifts from friends and families, and charitable contributions don't go into the personal income calculation. From a global perspective, these exclusions are expected. After all, the proceeds of the sale of your home or some stocks don't represent income in the traditional sense. (The IRS accounts for profits from asset sales as capital gains rather than income.) From the BEA's point of view, charitable contributions shuffle income earned by one person to someone else, so it doesn't want to count that income twice (once as your income and once as the charity recipient's income).

You may be surprised by the BEA's definition of *personal* in the phrase *personal income.* The report excludes corporate and most business income, which makes sense. But it includes income earned by private welfare funds and private trust funds as well as income earned by some not-for-profit organizations, specifically those that serve households. The BEA's thinking is that individuals ultimately use this earned income, so it affects their spending.

Disposable personal income

Investors and business leaders want to know how much money people have available that they can actually spend on goods and services. The Personal Income and Outlays report refers to this money as *disposable personal income,* or DPI.

The BEA calculates DPI by subtracting the following amounts from the total personal income:

- Income and property taxes
- Individual contributions to Social Security
- User fees and other nontax payments paid by individuals to governments or government agencies

The amount left over is the DPI, or the amount of income remaining that consumers can spend on things they want and need.

Table 1 of the Personal Income and Outlays report, which appears in Figure 6-1, represents DPI in current dollars. The table also shows *real DPI,* which is the DPI in chained (or inflation-indexed) 2005 dollars. (For details on chaining and inflation indexing, see Chapter 2). The BEA adjusts the year used as the baseline for the chaining index every four to five years.

Indexing disposable income is important to investors and business leaders because they need to understand how income growth compares to changes in the general level of prices to understand consumers' actual purchasing power. Indexing provides that comparison. (The Personal Income and Outlays report also indexes spending calculations. I discuss these calculations in the section on personal spending.)

Think of the relationship between income and inflation like this: If consumers' income rises but inflation rises by an equal amount, then consumers' real purchasing power hasn't changed at all. If inflation rises faster than personal income, then consumers' real purchasing power has fallen. In short, people can't buy as much when inflation outpaces income.

Real DPI is calculated by using the *PCE price deflator*, which is one of several ways to measure inflation (*PCE* stands for personal consumption expenditures; see the next section). Although the PCE price deflator isn't as widely followed as the Consumer Price Index, or CPI (see Chapter 12), knowledgeable investors and business leaders watch it carefully because it is arguably a closer estimate of real inflation and is somewhat less volatile than CPI. In addition, the PCE price deflator offers a reasonably good monthly estimate of the Federal Reserve's favorite inflation estimate, the GDP deflator (see Chapter 7), which is released quarterly.

Personal spending

Another important component of the Personal Income and Outlays report is personal spending. *Personal spending* shows how much money people actually spend and where they spend it. Table 1 in Figure 6-1 lists personal spending as *personal outlays*. Personal spending breaks down into the following subcategories:

- **Personal consumption expenditures**: The first subcategory, personal consumption expenditures (PCE), is BEA's shorthand for the summation of durable goods, nondurable goods, and services. The PCE is important because it's used to calculate the quarterly GDP. In fact, PCE is the largest individual component in the GDP calculation (see Chapter 7 for details). Here's what you need to know about the components of PCE:
  - **Durable goods:** *Durable goods* are big-ticket items that are supposed to last for at least three years; they include items like cars, trucks, television sets, computers, kitchen appliances, and furniture.

    Durable goods spending is the most economically sensitive of the spending categories, which is why so many people pay attention to it. Any increase or decrease in durable goods spending often precedes a change in the economy, so it's a good economic barometer all by itself.
  - **Nondurable goods:** Sometimes called *consumable goods*, this category includes this book, for example (in either e-book or paper format), food, medicine, gasoline, shoes, and clothes.
  - **Services:** If someone does something for you, that something is a *service*. This spending category includes haircuts, legal advice, healthcare, air transportation, and household utilities like phone service and electricity.

    You may be surprised to discover that spending on services is the largest of the personal spending categories. Recently, spending on services averaged almost 65 percent of total personal spending, followed by spending on nondurable and durable goods, which made up 21 percent and 10 percent of personal spending, respectively.
- **Personal interest payments:** This subcategory includes all interest payments made to businesses (such as credit card interest and interest paid

on bank or auto loans), but it doesn't include your mortgage interest. Oddly enough, the BEA accounts for your mortgage interest expense as part of a category they call rental income in the personal income section.

- **Personal transfer payments:** This subcategory includes fees, fines, and donations that you paid to any government or government agency. It also includes any money that individuals in the United States transfer to people out of the country.

In addition to being listed in Tables 1 through 6 of the Personal Income and Outlays report, personal spending (particularly PCE, or spending on goods and services, which is what interests the BEA the most) appears in more detail in Tables 7 through 11. The BEA tabulates this spending-related info in the following ways:

- **Table 7:** Personal Spending by Type of Product (Months)
- **Table 8:** Personal Spending by Type of Product (Years and Quarters)
- **Table 9:** Spending Change from Preceding Period (Months)
- **Table 10:** Percent Change from Month One Year Ago
- **Table 11:** Price Indexes Percent Change from Month One Year Ago

These tables show seasonally adjusted, chained (inflation-indexed) spending data. Table 7, for example, shows total expenditures in chained dollars and percentage changes from previous periods. (See Chapter 2 for details on seasonal adjustments.)

The price indexes found in Tables 9, 10, and 11 may provide the most useful data in the whole report. I discuss why the Federal Reserve carefully watches these indexes (as you should, too) later in this chapter in the section "Reacting to surprising results." Figure 6-2 shows Table 11, one of the widely used PCE price indexes.

Table 11. Price Indexes for Personal Consumption Expenditures: Percent Change From Month One Year Ago

	2010							
	May	June	July	August	September	October r	November r	December p
Personal consumption expenditures (PCE)	**2.1**	**1.4**	**1.5**	**1.4**	**1.3**	**1.2**	**1.1**	**1.2**
Goods	2.2	0.3	0.8	0.6	0.5	0.8	0.6	1.1
Durable goods	−1.3	−1.7	−1.4	−1.0	−1.4	−1.9	−2.1	−2.2
Nondurable goods	3.8	1.2	1.8	1.4	1.4	2.0	1.8	2.7
Services	2.0	1.9	1.9	1.7	1.7	1.4	1.3	1.2
Addenda:								
PCE excluding food and energy	1.5	1.4	1.3	1.2	1.1	0.8	0.8	0.7
Food [1]	0.4	0.2	0.7	0.7	1.3	1.3	1.3	1.3
Energy goods and services [2]	15.3	3.4	5.6	4.0	4.2	6.4	4.1	8.2
Market-based PCE [3]	1.8	1.1	1.3	1.2	1.2	1.2	1.1	1.3
Market-based PCE excluding food and energy [3]	1.1	1.1	1.1	1.1	1.0	0.8	0.8	0.8

p Preliminary
r Revised
1. Food consists of food and beverages purchased for off-premises consumption; food services, which include purchased meals and beverages, are not classified as food.
2. Consists of gasoline and other energy goods and of electricity and gas services.
3. Market-based PCE is a supplemental measure that is based on household expenditures for which there are observable price measures. It excludes most imputed transactions (for example, financial services furnished without payment) and the final consumption expenditures of nonprofit institutions serving households.

Figure 6-2: Table 11 shows a PCE price index.

Personal savings

The difference between personal income and personal spending is *personal savings.* If any income remains after you and your fellow consumers spend your money on purchases and services, the BEA has savings to report.

The BEA doesn't actually use any data sources to calculate personal savings; it simply infers it from the income and spending data. Consumers can store their savings almost anywhere — in stocks, bonds, savings accounts, certificates of deposit, money markets, or 401(k)s. They can also use their savings to pay down credit card debt or pay off a second mortgage. As far as the BEA is concerned, any income left over after spending is considered personal savings. You can see this calculation in Table 1 (refer to Figure 6-1).

Table 1 has one more statistic worth noting. It's called the *personal savings rate* and appears just below the personal savings data. The BEA calculates personal savings as a percentage of disposable income to come up with the personal savings rate.

Figure 6-3 shows a graphic representation of the personal savings rate from 2004 to 2010. Increases in the personal savings rate mean that consumers were spending and borrowing less, relative to DPI. Spikes in the savings rate often coincide with consumers' feeling anxious about the economy. In Figure 6-3, you can see that the personal savings rate hovered around 5.3 percent in 2010 after falling below 2 percent in 2005 and rising above 7 percent early in 2009.

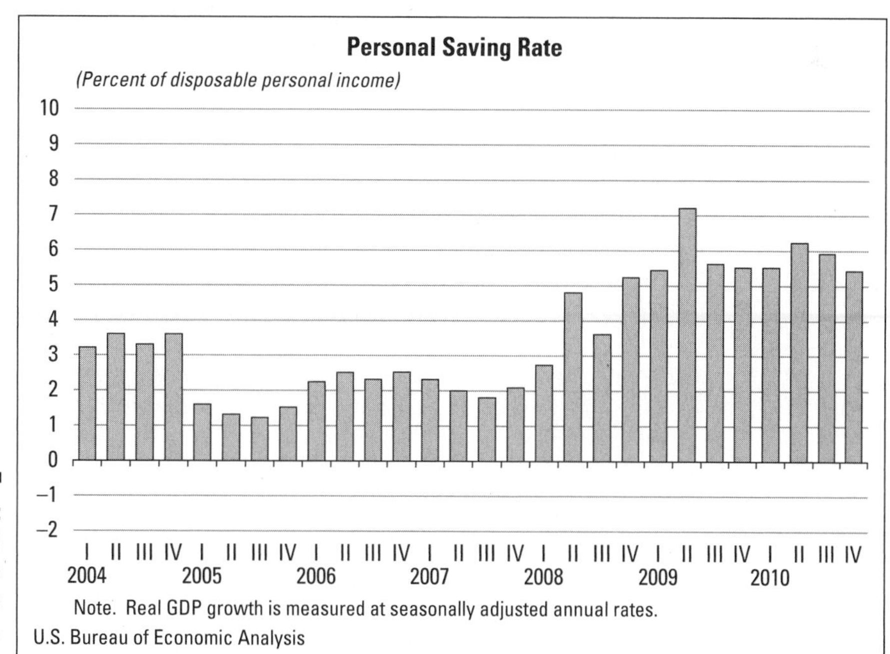

Figure 6-3: Personal savings rate from 2004 to 2010.

You can find an updated chart similar to the one shown in Figure 6-3 at `research.stlouisfed.org/fred2/series/PSAVERT`.

Highlighting consumers' economic impact: The wealth effect

A clear link exists between income and spending; after all, spending growth often coincides with income growth. The correlation between spending and DPI is even stronger. However, income doesn't always have to support spending (that is, an increase in spending doesn't necessarily have to coincide with an increase in income). One dramatic example of this slightly backward relationship occurred as housing prices rose throughout the 1990s into the first few years of the 21st century. People were feeling exceptionally flush because they were able to use the equity in their homes — as well as other sources of inexpensive credit — to fuel spending. Economists call situations like this one the *wealth effect.*

When people feel wealthy, whether or not they're actually earning more money, they're more likely to spend. The wealth effect isn't dependent on home prices alone. Increases in the value of any valuable asset can trigger wealth-effect spending. In fact, the wealth effect often coincides with solid gains in the stock market.

The wealth effect works the other way, too. When the value of a major asset falls, the negative wealth effect kicks in, leading people to spend less in total and less as a percentage of income. For example, when home or stock assets fall in value, people feel less wealthy, if not downright poor. Again, this poor feeling has nothing to do with people's actual income, but it affects spending nonetheless.

Identifying the relationship between spending, income, and the economy

Increased spending almost always coincides with a strong, growing economy. Conversely, decreased spending usually indicates a slow or slowing economy. However, this relationship is more of a coincident indicator rather than a predictive or leading indicator (see Chapter 2 for the lowdown on coincident and leading indicators).

The same relationship exists on the income side, but it isn't quite as strong. In other words, spending, not income, drives the economy. Even so, income growth does have some predictive ability to forecast future spending and future economic growth (or lack thereof): Increased income typically indicates future economic strength, and decreased income often leads to a slowing economy.

You must be circumspect when examining income reports. Many factors influence how and when income levels change. For example, the government regularly adjusts payments for Social Security and other transfer payments to compensate for inflation. These so-called COLA payments (*cost-of-living adjustments* or sometimes *cost-of-living allowances*) can raise income levels, but they represent a single change, not sustainable growth in income. You see a similar effect at the end of the year when businesses pay bonuses. The BEA tries to compensate for seasonal variations like these, but it can't remove 100 percent of the effect they have on the data.

Reacting to surprising results

Knowledgeable investors, business leaders, economists, and government officials keep close tabs on the Personal Income and Outlays report. Stock analysts, for example, use this report to estimate earnings growth for consumer product companies. Depending on the industry, decreases in consumer spending can lead analysts to reduce earnings estimates, which can depress a stock's price.

The PCE price indexes shown in Tables 9, 10, and 11 are another important reason why investors and business leaders keep track of this report. The Federal Reserve uses these price indexes as one of their target indicators to keep inflation under control, which is why the indexes have an outsized influence on the economy's future.

Growth in the PCE price indexes can harm investors in both stocks and bonds:

- Bond investors do best when the economy is in decline and prices for consumer products and services are relatively stable. When the economy is growing, as shown by growing income and spending, interest rates are likely to rise, bond prices are likely to fall, and bond investors are likely to suffer. If the PCE price indexes start showing inflationary pressure, bond investors can expect trouble because the Federal Reserve is likely to raise the federal funds interest rate as a result, causing bond prices to fall farther.
- Stock investors thrive when income and spending grow. However, stock investors don't like inflation any more than their counterparts in the bond markets because it impacts corporate profits and generally reduces a stocks' total return. During periods of high inflation, equity portfolios have a hard time maintaining purchasing power, much less offering an attractive return on the investment. Stock prices generally also suffer during periods of low consumer spending. When interest rates are high and consumer spending is low, stocks have a hard time outperforming the total return from a bond portfolio.

Surveying Retail Sales: The Census Bureau's Retail Trade Report

Consumer spending has a direct impact on retailers' total revenues and earnings. When consumers spend freely, many retailers thrive. When spending slows, retailers that sell consumer staples may slow a bit, but those retailers that sell expensive durable goods, like kitchen appliances, or discretionary services, like vacation travel, feel the brunt of the spending slowdown.

For better or worse, investors closely follow the Census Bureau's *Retail Trade report.* This report can move markets, sometimes for good reason, so keeping track of retail sales makes sense. However, the Retail Trade report is prone to significant revisions, so investors must be cautious about acting on this report.

Technically, the Retail Trade report is a collection of three separate reports:

- **Advance Monthly Sales for Retail and Food Services report**: This report contains early estimates of monthly sales in the retail trade and food service sectors.

  This report is the most interesting of the three for investors because it provides the very first look at consumer spending estimates. It also gives investors a glimpse at the data used to calculate personal consumption expenditures (PCE) in the Personal Income and Outlays report (see the section "Tracking personal wages, savings, and purchases" for details).
- **Monthly Retail Trade report**: This report contains current estimates of retail and food service sales and inventories.
- **Annual Retail Trade report**: This report contains sales, inventory, purchases, accounts receivable, and expenses data from retail, accommodation, and food service companies.

Every month the Census Bureau sends surveys to about 5,000 retailers that sell products used primarily by consumers rather than businesses. The bureau asks these retailers to reply by the sixth business day of the month and then uses their responses to calculate and publish the advance report (results from 8,000 additional surveys are used to produce the Monthly Retail Trade report). Significant revisions are common.

Generally, the Retail Trade report excludes sales by service providers with the exception of some product installation services and services that further product sales. But because services account for the largest portion of consumer spending and this report doesn't include common services like auto insurance or air transportation, it clearly gives an incomplete picture of consumer spending.

Because the Advance Monthly Sales for Retail and Food Services report is the most interesting for investors, I focus on that report in the following sections. For simplicity's sake, I call it by its more common name, the *Monthly Retail Sales report,* or just the *Retail Sales report,* for short. Table 6-2 provides the information you need to stay current with this report. The monthly publication schedule is available on the Census Bureau website at `www.census.gov/retail/marts/www/martsdates.pdf`.

Table 6-2 Monthly Retail Sales Report

Release Schedule	***Agency***	***Web Address***	***Sensitivity***
Monthly: Published schedule, 8:30 a.m. ET	U.S. Census Bureau, Department of Commerce	`www.census.gov/retail/`	High

In the following sections, I show you how to interpret this report and explain how stock and bond investors use the information in it to make portfolio adjustments.

Highlighting product purchases

The Monthly Retail Sales report presents retail sales data in two tables. These tables show how much people bought and what types of retailers they bought from:

- **Table 1:** Shows estimated monthly sales in seasonally adjusted and nonadjusted dollars (see Chapter 2 for info on seasonal adjustments). Reported results aren't indexed for inflation.
- **Table 2:** Shows percentage changes from the previous year and the previous month. These percentage values are typically more useful for investors than the dollar amounts presented in Table 1. Adjustments are made for seasonality, and both adjusted and nonadjusted data are shown. Figure 6-4 shows an example of Table 2.

The Monthly Retail Sales report presents its data by type of retailer rather than by type of product. Although this method makes data collection and reporting simpler, it makes comparing this report to the Personal Income and Outlays report very difficult because that report categorizes spending into subcomponents of PCE, durable goods, nondurable goods, and service spending (see the section "Making and Spending: The BEA's Personal Income and Outlays Report" for more info).

Table 2. Estimated Change in Monthly Sales for Retail and Food Services, by Kind of Business

(Estimates are shown as percents and are based on data from the Advance Monthly Retail Trade Survey, Monthly Retail Trade Survey, and administrative records.)

NAICS code	Kind of Business	Percent Change[1]					
		Dec. 2010 Advance from --		Nov. 2010 Preliminary from –		Oct. 2010 through Dec. 2010 from –	
		Nov. 2010 (p)	Dec. 2009 (r)	Oct. 2010 (r)	Nov. 2009 (r)	Jul. 2010 through Sep. 2010	Oct. 2009 through Dec. 2009
	Retail & food services, total	0.6	7.9	0.8	7.5	3.3	7.8
	Total (excl. motor vehicle & parts)	0.5	6.7	1.0	6.4	2.6	6.5
	Retail	0.7	8.2	0.9	7.8	3.6	8.1
441	Motor vehicle & parts dealers	1.1	14.2	0.2	13.0	7.1	13.9
4411, 4412	Auto & other motor veh. dealers	1.1	14.7	0.1	13.4	7.7	14.5
442	Furniture & home furn. stores	1.0	1.4	-0.1	1.4	-0.4	1.8
443	Electronics & appliance stores	-0.6	1.8	-1.2	-0.4	-1.6	1.6
444	Building material & garden eq. & supplies dealers	2.0	13.1	-1.1	11.2	5.3	13.2
445	Food & beverage stores	-0.6	2.7	0.6	2.8	1.5	2.8
4451	Grocery stores	-0.5	2.7	0.6	2.8	1.5	2.7
446	Health & personal care stores	1.6	6.5	0.3	4.2	1.9	5.1
447	Gasoline stations	1.6	10.3	3.8	8.9	6.2	10.6
448	Clothing & clothing accessories stores	-0.2	7.4	2.0	7.6	2.6	6.4
451	Sporting goods, hobby, book & music stores	0.4	7.1	1.4	10.4	3.3	8.0
452	General merchandise stores	-0.7	2.8	1.1	4.7	1.0	3.0
4521	Department stores (ex. L.D.)	-1.9	-1.3	2.8	1.5	0.2	-1.0
453	Miscellaneous store retailers	-1.3	6.2	-2.0	8.3	1.4	8.8
454	Nonstore retailers	2.6	15.0	1.9	13.7	4.8	14.1
722	Food services & drinking places	0.2	5.3	0.5	4.5	1.3	4.8

(p) Preliminary estimate (r) Revised estimate

(1) Estimates shown in this table are derived from adjusted estimates provided in Table 1 of this report.

Note: Table 3 provides estimated measures of sampling variability. Additional information on confidentiality protection, sampling error, nonsampling error, sample design, and definitions may be found at http://www.census.gov/retail.

Source: U.S. Census Bureau

Figure 6-4: Table 2 of the Monthly Retail Sales report shows the percentage change in retail sales.

Monitoring spending trends

You can also use the Monthly Retail Sales report to identify changes in consumer spending patterns and anticipate economic changes. Because the information in this report is used to compute PCE, which I discuss in the earlier section "Personal spending," it has a direct impact on future GDP reports (see Chapter 7).

To use this report to monitor spending trends, look at the first two lines of data in Table 2 in Figure 6-4. The first line shows total spending for all product retailers. The second line subtracts out motor vehicle and automobile part sales.

Why does the report subtract these sales? Even in the worst economic climate, sales of motor vehicles and automobile parts represent a very large portion of total retail sales. However, sales of these long-lasting durable goods vary with the business cycle: Automakers sell more cars when people feel better about their economic situation. Auto sales are also subject to large month-to-month fluctuations. Often, you can attribute these changes to marketing promotions, but sometimes these changes defy explanation, making seasonal or other periodic adjustments less helpful.

By breaking out this volatile spending component, the Monthly Retail Sales report allows investors and business leaders to more easily track core product spending — that is, spending for products that people generally buy regularly. So if you follow this report, be sure to pay closer attention to the total minus auto sales; it's a better representation of consumer spending patterns.

Investing based on the survey results

The Monthly Retail Sales report has been known to move the market as a whole, as well as specific retail sectors. When retail sales are up, stocks of retailers often follow. Likewise, when retail sales are down, the whole market often follows.

Traders and investors closely follow the top two lines of Table 2 in the Monthly Retail Sales report, which show the following (refer to Figure 6-4):

- Percentage change in total retail and food service sales
- Percentage change in total sales, excluding motor vehicles and parts

Percentage changes from one period to the next are more useful than actual dollar changes, especially when you're comparing current periods to those from several years or decades ago. However, the report's month-to-month percentage changes can be very volatile, so focus on the report's three-month changes, which help smooth out some of this volatility.

Unfortunately, the Monthly Retail Sales report doesn't compensate for inflation, which affects both month-to-month and year-over-year spending changes. As a result, you can't tell whether consumers are actually buying more or they're simply spending more due to increasing prices.

Some investors and analysts try to compensate for this deficiency by using a measure like the Consumer Price Index (CPI) to create their own indexed data (see Chapter 12 for details about the CPI), but that approach isn't ideal. The composition of CPI data is very different from the data used in the Monthly Retail Sales report, making the CPI an imperfect tool to index retail sales for inflation. Careful traders and investors watch the retail sales numbers, while keeping in mind that the data don't compensate for inflation.

Although this report is usually most interesting to stock investors and traders, the bond market sometimes gets in on the action, too. For example, if retail sales are trending higher, bond investors can expect bad news for the bond market because bonds are most profitable when the economy isn't doing all that well.

How Much Consumers Borrow: The Consumer Credit Outstanding Report

When consumers don't have quite enough income to cover expenses, they use credit instead. To cover everyday purchases, people use credit cards issued by banks, gas stations, and retailers. For bigger-ticket purchases, like cars, new kitchen appliances, or even school tuition, consumers sometimes take out loans.

Although credit can be used to fuel spending and economic growth, it has a dark side. Credit-driven spending isn't sustainable. When consumers rack up too much debt or when interest rates grow too high, spending comes to a halt. Investors keep a wary watch for signs of overextended consumer credit because it will soon cause economic growth to stall.

The U.S. Federal Reserve tracks consumer borrowing (including credit card debt and personal loans) and reports it in the monthly Consumer Credit Outstanding report. Each report provides a very brief summary of the monthly findings and tells how much outstanding credit has grown throughout the month. The only debts excluded from the Consumer Credit Outstanding report are home mortgages and home equity loans.

Take a look at Table 6-3 to find out how to keep track of this monthly report and Figure 6-5 to see an example of the report.

Table 6-3 Consumer Credit Outstanding Report

Release Schedule	*Agency*	*Web Address*	*Sensitivity*
Monthly: Typically the fifth business day of each month, 3:00 p.m. ET	Federal Reserve	`federalreserve.gov/releases/g19/`	Low

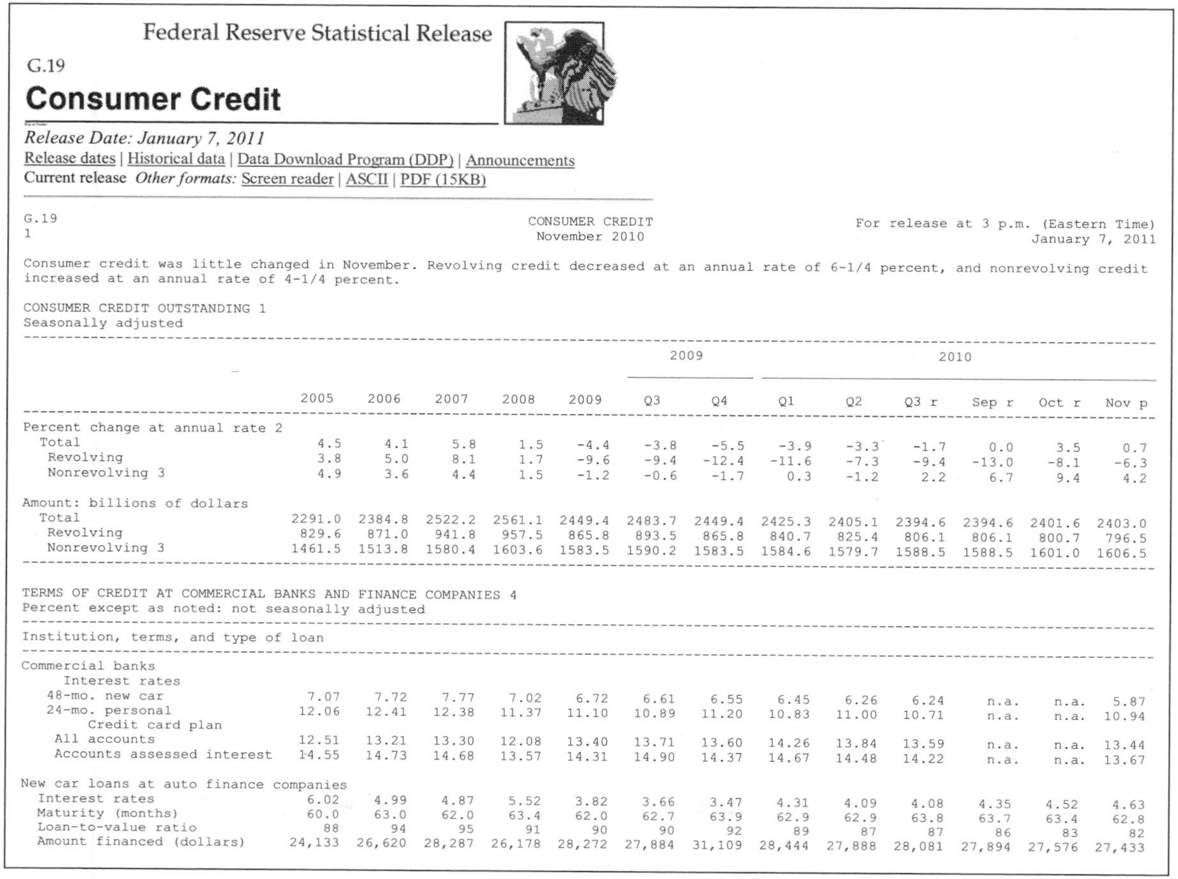

Federal Reserve Statistical Release

G.19

Consumer Credit

Release Date: January 7, 2011

Release dates | Historical data | Data Download Program (DDP) | Announcements

Current release *Other formats:* Screen reader | ASCII | PDF (15KB)

G.19
1

CONSUMER CREDIT
November 2010

For release at 3 p.m. (Eastern Time)
January 7, 2011

Consumer credit was little changed in November. Revolving credit decreased at an annual rate of 6-1/4 percent, and nonrevolving credit increased at an annual rate of 4-1/4 percent.

CONSUMER CREDIT OUTSTANDING 1
Seasonally adjusted

						2009		2010					
	2005	2006	2007	2008	2009	Q3	Q4	Q1	Q2	Q3 r	Sep r	Oct r	Nov p
Percent change at annual rate 2													
Total	4.5	4.1	5.8	1.5	-4.4	-3.8	-5.5	-3.9	-3.3	-1.7	0.0	3.5	0.7
Revolving	3.8	5.0	8.1	1.7	-9.6	-9.4	-12.4	-11.6	-7.3	-9.4	-13.0	-8.1	-6.3
Nonrevolving 3	4.9	3.6	4.4	1.5	-1.2	-0.6	-1.7	0.3	-1.2	2.2	6.7	9.4	4.2
Amount: billions of dollars													
Total	2291.0	2384.8	2522.2	2561.1	2449.4	2483.7	2449.4	2425.3	2405.1	2394.6	2394.6	2401.6	2403.0
Revolving	829.6	871.0	941.8	957.5	865.8	893.5	865.8	840.7	825.4	806.1	806.1	800.7	796.5
Nonrevolving 3	1461.5	1513.8	1580.4	1603.6	1583.5	1590.2	1583.5	1584.6	1579.7	1588.5	1588.5	1601.0	1606.5

TERMS OF CREDIT AT COMMERCIAL BANKS AND FINANCE COMPANIES 4
Percent except as noted: not seasonally adjusted

Institution, terms, and type of loan													
Commercial banks													
Interest rates													
48-mo. new car	7.07	7.72	7.77	7.02	6.72	6.61	6.55	6.45	6.26	6.24	n.a.	n.a.	5.87
24-mo. personal	12.06	12.41	12.38	11.37	11.10	10.89	11.20	10.83	11.00	10.71	n.a.	n.a.	10.94
Credit card plan													
All accounts	12.51	13.21	13.30	12.08	13.40	13.71	13.60	14.26	13.84	13.59	n.a.	n.a.	13.44
Accounts assessed interest	14.55	14.73	14.68	13.57	14.31	14.90	14.37	14.67	14.48	14.22	n.a.	n.a.	13.67
New car loans at auto finance companies													
Interest rates	6.02	4.99	4.87	5.52	3.82	3.66	3.47	4.31	4.09	4.08	4.35	4.52	4.63
Maturity (months)	60.0	63.0	62.0	63.4	62.0	62.7	63.9	62.9	62.9	63.8	63.7	63.4	62.8
Loan-to-value ratio	88	94	95	91	90	90	92	89	87	87	86	83	82
Amount financed (dollars)	24,133	26,620	28,287	26,178	28,272	27,884	31,109	28,444	27,888	28,081	27,894	27,576	27,433

Figure 6-5: Example of the Consumer Credit Outstanding report.

The report breaks outstanding credit into two broad categories:

- **Revolving credit:** Revolving loans don't have a fixed number of payments. They include personal lines of credit and credit card accounts. Note that every credit card transaction counts as a type of revolving credit even if you pay off your statement every month.
- **Nonrevolving credit:** Nonrevolving loans (also called installment credit) have a fixed number of payments. Examples include auto loans, student loans, personal mobile-home loans, and vacation loans. Loans may be secured or unsecured. (Keep in mind that loans secured by real estate, such as mortgages and home equity loans, aren't included in this report.)

The report shows the amount of credit outstanding and then shows the average interest rates charged for new car and personal loans and the annualized percentage change from recent months, quarters, and years. The data are adjusted for seasonality.

Of course, borrowing causes a bit of a conundrum because it allows people to spend more today to buy things that they have to pay for later (along with interest). Credit-fueled spending has the perverse effect of eventually slowing future economic growth. When too many borrowers are unable to repay their loans, the effect is serious economic harm. You don't have to look too far to find an example in the recent mortgage and housing crisis.

One way to determine whether consumers are taking on too much debt is to look at historical trends. For example, you can compare consumer debt as a percentage of disposable personal income (DPI, from the BEA's Personal Income and Outlays report that I discuss earlier in this chapter). This ratio typically averages between 15 and 17 percent. When the ratio climbs above 20 percent, you can expect to see consumers struggle to keep up with their debt payments.

People use this report more frequently as a business-management and policy-planning tool than as an investment-planning tool. In rare instances, however, this report can affect investment markets. For instance, if consumer borrowing rises significantly or unexpectedly, bond markets are likely to react. In this case, interest rates are likely to rise as bond prices fall.

Tracking Online Sales: The Quarterly Retail E-Commerce Sales Report

Even if you're living alone on top of a mountain, sitting cross-legged as you wait to enlighten brave wisdom seekers, you almost certainly know that

Amazon.com upended the bookselling business in the first years of the 21st century. Of course, they've since branched out and now sell an almost indescribably broad selection of products.

Amazon is not alone, of course. The Internet has had a profound impact on retail in the United States and throughout the world. Although the Monthly Retail Sales report includes Internet sales, it doesn't segregate them in any meaningful way. The U.S. Census Bureau saw the writing on the (Facebook) wall and began publishing a quarterly report to track Internet retail sales.

The *Quarterly Retail E-Commerce Sales report* is still relatively new and currently has little impact on the investment markets. However, as Internet retailing grows, you can expect the influence of this report to grow as well. Down the line, you'll be glad you kept abreast of trends in Internet spending.

Table 6-4 shows you what you need to know to follow the Quarterly Retail E-Commerce Sales report.

Table 6-4 Quarterly Retail E-Commerce Sales Report

Release Schedule	*Agency*	*Web Address*	*Sensitivity*
Quarterly: Published schedule, 10:00 a.m. ET	U.S. Census Bureau, Department of Commerce	`www.census.gov/retail/`	Low

To be included in this e-commerce report, orders for goods and services just have to be placed over the Internet. In other words, the report includes almost any form of online transaction, including those initiated by e-mail, EDI (electronic data interchange) networks, and corporate extranets. Consumers can make their payments online, but a sale's inclusion in this report doesn't require online payment.

Many Internet transactions are beyond the reach of the Census Bureau's sampling methods. For example, the Census Bureau uses the same survey it uses to collect data for the Retail Trade report to collect data for the Quarterly Retail E-Commerce Sales report. Because only companies participate in the Retail Trade survey, transactions that occur between private individuals, even if they found each other on an online forum like Craigslist, aren't included in the e-commerce report.

The Quarterly Retail E-Commerce Sales report uses a format similar to that of the Advance Monthly Sales for Retail and Food Services report that I discuss in the section "Surveying Retail Sales: The Census Bureau's Retail Trade Report." The data are adjusted for seasonal variations but not for inflation or other price changes. Although the report includes four data tables, only the first is of interest for our purposes. (Table 2 is interesting only to statisticians and Tables 3 and 4 provide a longer history of the data in Table 1.)

Table 1, shown in Figure 6-6, shows adjusted and nonadjusted data in the following four broad categories:

- Total retail sales compared to e-commerce sales
- E-commerce sales as a percentage of the total
- The percentage change from prior quarters for both total retail sales and e-commerce sales
- The percentage change from the same quarter a year ago

Table 1. Estimated Quarterly U.S. Retail Sales: Total and E-commerce[1]
(Estimates are based on data from the Monthly Retail Trade Survey and administrative records.)

Quarter	Retail Sales (millions of dollars)		E-commerce as a Percent of	Percent Change From Prior Quarter		Percent Change From Same Quarter A Year Ago	
	Total	E-commerce	Total	Total	E-commerce	Total	E-commerce
Adjusted							
3rd quarter 2010(p)	978,731	41,525	4.2	0.8	4.0	6.0	13.6
2nd quarter 2010(r)	971,384	39,941	4.1	1.1	3.2	7.5	14.7
1st quarter 2010	960,469	38,719	4.0	2.1	1.5	6.3	14.3
4th quarter 2009	940,708	38,141	4.1	1.9	4.4	2.1	14.6
3rd quarter 2009(r)	923,211	36,540	4.0	2.1	4.9	-7.8	1.6
Not Adjusted							
3rd quarter 2010(p)	980,226	38,843	4.0	-0.9	3.9	5.8	14.1
2nd quarter 2010(r)	989,229	37,385	3.8	10.3	1.9	7.6	14.1
1st quarter 2010	896,741	36,680	4.1	-9.0	-18.8	6.8	14.2
4th quarter 2009	985,649	45,199	4.6	6.4	32.8	2.0	15.0
3rd quarter 2009	926,265	34,031	3.7	0.7	3.9	-8.0	1.6

(p) Preliminary estimate. (r) Revised estimate.

[1] E-commerce sales are sales of goods and services where an order is placed by the buyer or price and terms of sale are negotiated over an Internet, extranet, Electronic Data Interchange (EDI) network, electronic mail, or other online system. Payment may or may not be made online.

[2] Estimates are adjusted for seasonal variation, but not for price changes. Total sales estimates are also adjusted for trading-day differences and moving holidays.

Note: Table 2 provides estimated measures of sampling variability. For information on confidentiality protection, sampling error, nonsampling error, sample design, and definitions, see http://www.census.gov/retail/mrts/how_surveys_are_collected.html.

Figure 6-6: Table 1 of the Quarterly Retail E-Commerce Sales report.

Part III
The Essence of Business: Product and Service Indicators

"Business here is good, but the weak dollar is killing my overseas markets!"

In this part . . .

In this part, you get to see the economy from the business point of view. You get an inside look into what companies are making and how much they're making. You also find out how to tell whether business is booming or starting to slow down. And you discover which products are the best indicators of economic health. (Here's a hint: Toothpaste isn't one of them.)

Part III also includes the Big Kahuna of all economic indicators, the Gross Domestic Product (GDP) report. You get an overview of what this mammoth report includes, how investors and business leaders use the information in it, and how you can use that information in your investment planning. You also find out about the U.S. Federal Reserve and its role in keeping the economy growing and inflation-free.

Chapter 7

GDP: The Whole Enchilada

In This Chapter

- Surveying the GDP report and the information it contains
- Seeing how businesses, investors, and the government use the GDP report
- Understanding how to calculate GDP
- Tweaking GDP for inflation

Ancient Egyptian hieroglyphics were all but undecipherable until the French rediscovered the Rosetta stone. Although economic reports aren't quite as impenetrable as those ancient hieroglyphic scripts, divining their full meaning is sometimes very difficult for the uninitiated observer. Nowhere is this truer than the Gross Domestic Product (GDP) report. Fortunately, this chapter serves as your personal Rosetta stone, allowing you to translate GDP from its dense economic shorthand into something useful for your business and investment planning. It outlines what the GDP report is, how it's created, and how you can use it.

Although this chapter focuses on U.S. GDP, the methods for calculating GDP are more or less standardized throughout the industrialized world. So you can easily apply the concepts that I discuss in this chapter to GDP reports from most industrialized countries.

Grasping What the GDP Report Is

The *GDP report* is a quarterly report from the U.S. Bureau of Economic Analysis (BEA). In essence, the GDP report tries to concentrate everything the nation does into a single quarterly report. It measures the country's economic output and shows how much the economy is growing or contracting. To do so, the report sums up total dollar values of everything made or sold in the United States and puts them into a series of tables to quantify the health of the country's economy.

The data in the GDP includes details about

- Personal income and spending
- National income and spending
- Corporate spending and production
- Inflation

Table 7-1 provides what you need to stay up-to-date with this report.

Table 7-1 Gross Domestic Product Report

Release Schedule	*Agency*	*Web Address*	*Sensitivity*
Quarterly with monthly revisions: Published schedule, 8:30 a.m. ET	U.S. Bureau of Economic Analysis, Department of Commerce	`www.bea.gov/newsreleases/national/gdp/gdpnewsrelease.htm`	Moderate to high

The following sections clarify when the BEA releases the GDP data, what place the economy's growth rate has in the GDP report, and how the BEA counts up U.S. products and services to calculate GDP.

Breaking down the GDP schedule

The BEA releases the GDP report quarterly with intermittent dates for revised reports. Having a strong understanding of these releases allows you to know what information is being released and how to interpret it.

Each quarter the BEA releases the GDP in three stages:

- **Advance estimate:** The first release of a quarter's GDP report happens about one month after the end of the quarter. It begins with a brief summary of that quarter's economic performance and ends with a warning. The summary tells the *headline number* — the annual rate of growth for the current quarter's real GDP. (*Real* means that the value has been adjusted for inflation; in this case, the adjustment is based on the dollar-chaining technique. See Chapter 2 for details about inflation adjustments.) The warning emphasizes that the estimates released in the report are based on incomplete information and are likely to change.
- **Preliminary report:** The first revision is released one month after the advance estimate.
- **Final report:** The second revision is released one month after the preliminary report.

Table 7-2 illustrates the GDP report's release schedule.

Table 7-2 GDP Release Schedule

Quarter	*Advance Estimate*	*Preliminary Report*	*Final Report*
Q1 (January–March)	April	May	June
Q2 (April–June)	July	August	September
Q3 (July–September)	October	November	December
Q4 (October–December)	January	February	March

Although calling the second revision the *final report* implies that the BEA is done with its revisions, you can expect to see more of them. Some of the data required for the report, such as information about state and local government purchases, are available only once a year. The BEA estimates this data each quarter, but it makes annual revisions to the GDP report as the actual data become available. Previously issued GDP reports are subject to these annual revisions for up to 3 years, or more precisely, 12 quarters after the final report.

The BEA also makes periodic *benchmark revisions* (in which the BEA adjusts the GDP report for new products, especially new types of products that didn't previously exist).These benchmark changes are substantially different from the traditional quarterly and annual revisions in which only data values are revised. During benchmark revisions, the BEA can change definitions, concepts, and statistical methods used to collect and tabulate the data. As a result, these benchmark changes can affect data series going back years and sometimes even decades. The BEA may also rearrange the layout of the report to provide new ways to view the data or to reclassify existing sections of the report. (See Chapter 2 for more on benchmark revisions.)

Historically, benchmark revisions were made every five years or so. But in 2010 the BEA introduced a new approach called *flexible annual benchmark revisions*. The goal of the new flexible annual revisions is to make future benchmark change a little less disruptive; however, this new approach means that business leaders and investors have more revisions to consider.

Finding the economy's growth rate

The first item mentioned in all versions of the GDP report summary is the *economic real growth rate* for the current quarter. It's the headline number in the report — in other words, the one everyone fixates on — and it shows the change in the economy from one period to the next in percentage terms.

(*Real* means the percentage value is adjusted for inflation, but it's also annualized and adjusted for seasonality. See Chapter 2 for more about seasonal adjustments and annualizing data.)

You also find the economic growth rate, along with more detailed information, in the report's attached tables. For example, Figure 7-1 shows a sample Table 1 from the GDP report, which presents the headline GDP growth rate for the most recent quarter along with data for the previous 16 quarters and annual data for the past 3 years.

Table 1 also shows the annualized growth rate for each of the data components that makes up the GDP. The data are adjusted for seasonality and are indexed for inflation. I address these GDP components and the method for calculating them in the section "Knowing How the GDP Is Calculated."

Table 1 in Figure 7-1 comes from the January 2011 GDP report, which means it's an advance estimate of the last quarter of 2010. So you can expect to see at least two more revisions to that quarter's data before the report is declared final.

To find out the details behind the GDP rates shown in Table 1 of the GDP report (refer to Figure 7-1), take a look at Table 2 in Figure 7-2. While Table 1 shows the percentage change from preceding periods, Table 2 shows which GDP components account for these changes. In other words, Table 2 shows the relative economic contributions of consumers, businesses, and the government so that you can see which economic sectors are growing and which ones are not.

For example, look at the values for *Gross private domestic investment* in Figure 7-2. I explain private domestic investment in the section "Knowing How the GDP Is Calculated" later in this chapter, but for now, notice that *Gross private domestic investment* was the biggest drag on GDP for both 2008 and 2009 and that things would've been much worse without the category *Net exports of goods and services*.

Keep in mind that the values in Figure 7-2 are percentage point changes rather than percentages, which are what Figure 7-1 shows (see Chapter 2 for more about this distinction). Regardless of whether the economy is growing or is in recession, businesses still make products and sell services and governments and consumers still buy them.

Figure 7-1: Table 1 shows the real GDP percentage change from the preceding period.

Table 1. Real Gross Domestic Product and Related Measures: Percent Change From Preceding Period

	2008	2009	2010	Seasonally adjusted at annual rates															
				2007				2008				2009				2010			
				I	II	III	IV	I	II	III	IV	I	II	III	IV	I	II	III	IV
Gross domestic product (GDP)	**0.0**	**–2.6**	**2.9**	**0.9**	**3.2**	**2.3**	**2.9**	**–0.7**	**0.6**	**–4.0**	**–6.8**	**–4.9**	**–0.7**	**1.6**	**5.0**	**3.7**	**1.7**	**2.6**	**3.2**
Personal consumption expenditures	**–0.3**	**–1.2**	**1.8**	**2.4**	**1.5**	**1.7**	**1.4**	**–0.8**	**0.1**	**–3.5**	**–3.3**	**–0.5**	**–1.6**	**2.0**	**0.9**	**1.9**	**2.2**	**2.4**	**4.4**
Goods	–2.5	–2.0	4.3	2.3	1.4	2.4	1.1	–5.8	0.3	–7.7	–10.8	1.8	–1.5	7.2	1.7	5.7	3.4	4.1	10.1
Durable goods	–5.2	–3.7	7.7	4.6	4.6	3.8	2.4	–10.8	–2.9	–12.0	–22.3	4.8	–3.1	20.1	–1.1	8.8	6.8	7.6	21.6
Nondurable goods	–1.1	–1.2	2.8	1.1	–0.2	1.7	0.5	–3.0	2.0	–5.5	–4.9	0.4	–0.7	1.7	3.1	4.2	1.9	2.5	5.0
Services	0.9	–0.8	0.5	2.4	1.6	1.4	1.5	1.9	0.0	–1.3	0.6	–1.6	–1.7	–0.5	0.5	0.1	1.6	1.6	1.7
Gross private domestic investment	**–9.5**	**–22.6**	**16.7**	**–3.6**	**9.5**	**–2.9**	**–9.4**	**–9.4**	**–7.6**	**–12.5**	**–36.8**	**–42.2**	**–18.5**	**11.8**	**26.7**	**29.1**	**26.2**	**15.0**	**–22.5**
Fixed investment	–6.4	–18.3	3.8	–1.0	3.7	–1.2	–4.8	–6.2	–4.6	–11.9	–24.9	–35.4	–10.1	0.7	–1.3	3.3	18.9	1.5	4.2
Nonresidential	0.3	–17.1	5.5	6.8	11.1	9.4	5.7	2.0	–1.6	–8.6	–22.7	–35.2	–7.5	–1.7	–1.4	7.8	17.2	10.0	4.4
Structures	5.9	–20.4	–14.0	10.7	28.0	24.3	7.4	–0.1	7.5	–3.6	–8.9	–41.0	–20.2	–12.4	–29.2	–17.8	–0.5	–3.5	0.8
Equipment and software	–2.4	–15.3	15.1	5.1	4.3	2.9	4.8	3.0	–6.0	–11.1	–29.5	–31.6	0.2	4.2	14.6	20.4	24.8	15.4	5.8
Residential	–24.0	–22.9	–3.0	–16.4	–12.0	–24.1	–29.3	–27.9	–14.0	–22.6	–32.6	–36.2	–19.7	10.6	–0.8	–12.3	25.7	–27.3	3.4
Change in private inventories	....	....	....	....	....	....	....	....	....	....	....	....	....	....	....	....	....	....	....
Net exports of goods and services	....	....	....	....	....	....	....	....	....	....	....	....	....	....	....	....	....	....	....
Exports	6.0	–9.5	11.7	6.4	6.8	15.8	11.6	5.7	13.2	–5.0	–21.9	–27.8	–1.0	12.2	24.4	11.4	9.1	6.8	8.5
Goods	6.3	–12.0	14.6	12.9	7.6	12.8	9.9	9.6	14.5	–4.3	–26.6	–34.1	–3.7	18.7	31.7	14.0	11.5	5.8	10.0
Services	5.3	–3.9	5.8	–6.9	4.9	23.0	15.7	–2.8	10.2	–6.6	–9.8	–12.3	4.7	0.1	10.2	5.8	3.9	8.9	5.1
Imports	–2.6	–13.8	12.6	4.6	4.6	5.0	–10.6	–1.4	2.9	–0.1	–22.9	–35.3	–10.6	21.9	4.9	11.2	33.5	16.8	–13.6
Goods	–3.5	–15.8	14.6	6.8	4.8	5.1	–11.8	–3.3	4.6	–1.0	–28.3	–38.9	–10.6	27.4	6.2	12.0	40.5	17.4	–15.5
Services	2.4	–4.2	3.5	–6.3	3.6	4.4	–4.0	9.4	–6.0	5.0	11.7	–16.8	–10.9	1.5	–0.5	7.8	4.3	14.2	–3.8
Government consumption expenditures and gross investment	**2.8**	**1.6**	**1.1**	**–0.5**	**3.4**	**3.5**	**1.2**	**2.3**	**3.3**	**5.3**	**1.5**	**–3.0**	**6.1**	**1.6**	**–1.4**	**–1.6**	**3.9**	**3.9**	**–0.6**
Federal	7.3	5.7	4.8	–4.8	7.1	9.6	1.1	6.9	7.8	14.2	8.1	–5.0	14.9	5.7	0.0	1.8	9.1	8.8	–0.2
National defense	7.5	5.4	3.9	–7.2	8.3	10.2	0.0	6.8	6.9	19.7	5.2	–8.4	16.8	9.0	–2.5	0.4	7.4	8.5	–2.0
Nondefense	6.7	6.5	6.6	0.5	4.7	8.2	3.4	6.9	9.6	3.0	14.8	2.6	10.9	–0.9	5.6	5.0	12.8	9.5	3.7
State and local	0.3	–0.9	–1.3	2.1	1.3	0.2	1.3	–0.3	0.8	0.3	–2.4	–1.7	1.0	–1.0	–2.3	–3.8	0.6	0.7	–0.9
Addenda:																			
Final sales of domestic product	0.5	–2.1	1.4	1.3	2.3	2.6	3.7	–0.2	1.1	–3.9	–4.6	–3.9	0.2	0.4	2.1	1.1	0.9	0.9	7.1
Gross domestic purchases	–1.1	–3.6	3.2	0.9	3.1	1.3	–0.4	–1.6	–0.5	–3.2	–7.7	–7.2	–2.1	3.0	3.0	3.9	5.1	4.2	–0.3
Final sales to domestic purchasers	–0.6	–3.1	1.9	1.3	2.2	1.6	0.4	–1.1	0.0	–3.1	–5.7	–6.3	–1.2	1.8	0.2	1.3	4.3	2.6	3.4
Gross national product (GNP)	0.3	–2.8	....	0.8	3.5	4.1	4.4	–0.9	0.1	–3.2	–8.6	–4.9	–0.5	2.6	4.9	4.4	1.8	2.3	....
Disposable personal income	1.7	0.6	1.4	1.8	0.6	1.5	2.2	1.4	9.2	–8.4	2.7	0.4	5.9	–4.4	0.0	1.3	5.6	0.9	1.7
Current-dollar measures:																			
GDP	2.2	–1.7	3.8	5.3	6.5	4.4	3.8	1.0	4.1	0.4	–7.9	–3.9	–0.4	2.3	4.7	4.8	3.7	4.6	3.4
Final sales of domestic product	2.7	–1.1	2.4	5.8	5.6	4.6	4.6	1.8	4.3	0.5	–6.1	–2.7	0.6	1.2	1.8	2.1	2.9	3.0	7.3
Gross domestic purchases	2.1	–3.8	4.6	5.4	6.3	3.4	3.4	2.1	4.2	0.6	–11.7	–9.2	–1.5	4.3	5.1	6.2	5.2	4.8	1.8
Final sales to domestic purchasers	2.5	–3.2	3.2	5.8	5.5	3.6	4.1	2.9	4.5	0.8	–10.1	–8.1	–0.5	3.3	2.2	3.5	4.4	3.2	5.4
GNP	2.5	–1.9	....	5.3	6.7	6.3	5.3	0.9	3.5	1.1	–9.8	–4.0	–0.2	3.4	4.6	5.5	3.8	4.4	....
Disposable personal income	5.1	0.7	3.1	5.8	4.1	3.9	6.5	5.4	14.3	–4.4	–3.3	–1.2	8.0	–1.6	2.7	3.4	5.5	1.7	3.5

See "Explanatory Note" at the end of the tables.

Table 2. Contributions to Percent Change in Real Gross Domestic Product

				Seasonally adjusted at annual rates															
	2008	2009	2010	2007				2008				2009				2010			
				I	II	III	IV	I	II	III	IV	I	II	III	IV	I	II	III	IV
Percent change at annual rate:																			
Gross domestic product	**0.0**	**–2.6**	**2.9**	**0.9**	**3.2**	**2.3**	**2.9**	**–0.7**	**0.6**	**–4.0**	**–6.8**	**–4.9**	**–0.7**	**1.6**	**5.0**	**3.7**	**1.7**	**2.6**	**3.2**
Percentage points at annual rates:																			
Personal consumption expenditures	**–0.18**	**–0.84**	**1.27**	**1.64**	**1.08**	**1.20**	**0.98**	**–0.54**	**0.08**	**–2.46**	**–2.26**	**–0.34**	**–1.12**	**1.41**	**0.69**	**1.33**	**1.54**	**1.67**	**3.04**
Goods	**–0.60**	**–0.46**	**1.00**	**0.56**	**0.34**	**0.57**	**0.27**	**–1.42**	**0.08**	**–1.86**	**–2.57**	**0.41**	**–0.32**	**1.62**	**0.42**	**1.29**	**0.79**	**0.94**	**2.26**
Durable goods	–0.42	–0.27	0.56	0.38	0.38	0.31	0.20	–0.92	–0.23	–0.95	–1.79	0.35	–0.21	1.35	–0.07	0.62	0.49	0.54	1.48
Motor vehicles and parts	–0.39	–0.17	0.08	0.06	0.17	–0.08	–0.07	–0.53	–0.57	–0.60	–0.85	0.26	–0.10	0.83	–0.56	–0.06	0.15	0.12	0.90
Furnishings and durable household equipment	–0.07	–0.12	0.15	0.10	–0.07	0.04	0.02	–0.18	0.09	–0.20	–0.33	–0.15	–0.12	0.12	0.16	0.23	0.15	0.10	0.19
Recreational goods and vehicles	0.08	0.03	0.27	0.21	0.20	0.32	0.23	–0.13	0.28	–0.09	–0.39	0.19	–0.05	0.36	0.34	0.28	0.20	0.26	0.34
Other durable goods	–0.04	–0.02	0.06	0.01	0.07	0.03	0.01	–0.09	–0.02	–0.06	–0.22	0.06	0.05	0.05	–0.01	0.18	–0.02	0.07	0.05
Nondurable goods	–0.18	–0.18	0.45	0.17	–0.03	0.27	0.07	–0.50	0.31	–0.91	–0.78	0.06	–0.11	0.27	0.49	0.67	0.31	0.39	0.78
Food and beverages purchased for off-premises consumption	–0.04	–0.05	0.15	–0.01	–0.11	0.09	0.19	–0.07	–0.01	–0.26	–0.50	0.01	0.20	0.22	0.28	0.20	–0.16	0.17	0.26
Clothing and footwear	–0.01	–0.10	0.13	0.12	0.04	0.08	–0.02	–0.05	0.23	–0.27	–0.28	–0.07	–0.10	0.01	0.13	0.26	0.14	–0.03	0.31
Gasoline and other energy goods	–0.13	0.03	0.00	–0.05	–0.07	–0.01	–0.12	–0.22	–0.13	–0.41	0.30	0.14	–0.01	–0.04	–0.05	0.02	0.07	0.00	–0.08
Other nondurable goods	0.01	–0.06	0.17	0.11	0.11	0.11	0.02	–0.15	0.22	0.03	–0.29	–0.02	–0.20	0.08	0.14	0.18	0.25	0.25	0.29
Services	**0.41**	**–0.38**	**0.27**	**1.08**	**0.74**	**0.62**	**0.71**	**0.88**	**0.00**	**–0.59**	**0.30**	**–0.75**	**–0.79**	**–0.21**	**0.27**	**0.03**	**0.75**	**0.74**	**0.78**
Household consumption expenditures (for services)	0.25	–0.30	0.22	1.16	0.84	0.36	0.42	0.74	–0.04	–0.79	0.08	–0.29	–0.46	–0.37	0.12	0.01	0.69	0.72	0.76
Housing and utilities	0.09	0.14	0.15	0.10	–0.03	0.12	–0.07	0.31	0.04	–0.20	0.60	0.01	0.06	0.24	0.23	–0.06	0.14	0.44	0.08
Health care	0.29	0.23	0.16	0.47	0.16	0.14	0.29	0.58	0.29	–0.02	0.23	0.40	0.38	–0.01	0.21	–0.04	0.35	0.14	0.33
Transportation services	–0.12	–0.18	0.03	0.05	0.00	–0.04	–0.06	–0.11	–0.15	–0.18	–0.31	–0.23	–0.10	–0.07	–0.02	0.07	0.08	0.08	0.04
Recreation services	–0.01	–0.06	–0.01	0.05	0.10	0.11	0.00	–0.01	–0.03	–0.12	–0.09	0.02	–0.08	–0.12	–0.03	0.00	–0.01	0.11	–0.01
Food services and accommodations	–0.03	–0.16	0.11	–0.01	0.15	0.12	0.16	–0.23	0.06	–0.15	–0.30	–0.19	–0.16	–0.06	0.02	0.29	0.11	0.12	0.17
Financial services and insurance	0.03	–0.21	–0.13	0.21	0.30	0.13	0.14	0.02	–0.08	0.03	–0.26	–0.30	–0.23	–0.21	–0.21	–0.16	0.07	–0.27	0.16
Other services	–0.02	–0.07	–0.07	0.28	0.15	–0.22	–0.04	0.18	–0.16	–0.14	0.22	0.00	–0.34	–0.14	–0.08	–0.08	–0.05	0.11	–0.01
Final consumption expenditures of nonprofit institutions serving households	0.16	–0.08	0.05	–0.08	–0.10	0.27	0.29	0.14	0.04	0.20	0.22	–0.46	–0.34	0.16	0.15	0.02	0.06	0.02	0.02
Gross output of nonprofit institutions	0.18	0.04	0.07	0.29	0.00	0.07	0.27	0.30	0.11	0.08	0.32	–0.11	–0.05	–0.02	0.12	–0.07	0.25	0.09	0.24
Less: Receipts from sales of goods and services by nonprofit institutions	0.02	0.12	0.02	0.37	0.10	–0.20	–0.02	0.17	0.07	–0.11	0.10	0.34	0.28	–0.18	–0.03	–0.09	0.18	0.07	0.21
Gross private domestic investment	**–1.53**	**–3.24**	**1.84**	**–0.65**	**1.51**	**–0.46**	**–1.53**	**–1.47**	**–1.17**	**–1.95**	**–6.32**	**–6.80**	**–2.30**	**1.22**	**2.70**	**3.04**	**2.88**	**1.80**	**–3.20**
Fixed investment	**–1.02**	**–2.69**	**0.46**	**–0.15**	**0.62**	**–0.18**	**–0.76**	**–0.98**	**–0.69**	**–1.83**	**–4.01**	**–5.71**	**–1.26**	**0.12**	**–0.12**	**0.39**	**2.06**	**0.18**	**0.50**
Nonresidential	0.03	–1.96	0.53	0.75	1.23	1.06	0.67	0.25	–0.16	–1.00	–2.84	–4.49	–0.72	–0.13	–0.10	0.71	1.51	0.93	0.43
Structures	0.22	–0.81	–0.43	0.35	0.88	0.82	0.28	0.00	0.30	–0.14	–0.36	–1.99	–0.76	–0.41	–1.01	–0.53	–0.01	–0.09	0.02
Equipment and software	–0.19	–1.15	0.97	0.40	0.35	0.24	0.39	0.25	–0.46	–0.86	–2.47	–2.50	0.04	0.28	0.91	1.24	1.52	1.02	0.41
Information processing equipment and software	0.23	0.01	0.50	0.64	0.11	0.32	0.61	0.38	0.25	–0.19	–0.52	–0.25	0.36	0.52	0.79	0.32	0.57	0.34	0.49
Computers and peripheral equipment	0.08	–0.01	0.15	0.15	–0.03	0.11	0.15	0.19	0.11	–0.12	–0.19	–0.07	0.09	0.12	0.36	0.03	0.24	0.01	0.18
Software	0.10	0.03	0.18	0.18	0.01	0.06	0.09	0.26	0.04	0.04	–0.04	–0.12	0.16	0.13	0.25	0.17	0.15	0.18	0.16
Other	0.05	–0.02	0.17	0.30	0.13	0.15	0.38	–0.07	0.10	–0.11	–0.30	–0.07	0.12	0.27	0.18	0.12	0.17	0.15	0.15
Industrial equipment	–0.06	–0.31	0.06	–0.09	0.38	0.01	–0.27	0.04	–0.04	–0.11	–0.30	–0.78	–0.17	–0.11	–0.03	0.00	0.39	0.07	0.13
Transportation equipment	–0.31	–0.54	0.31	–0.01	–0.32	–0.08	0.04	–0.02	–0.67	–0.59	–1.16	–0.92	0.22	–0.05	0.20	0.62	0.40	0.40	–0.25
Other equipment	–0.05	–0.30	0.10	–0.13	0.18	–0.01	0.00	–0.14	0.01	0.04	–0.50	–0.55	–0.38	–0.07	–0.05	0.30	0.17	0.20	0.04
Residential	–1.05	–0.74	–0.07	–0.91	–0.62	–1.24	–1.43	–1.23	–0.53	–0.84	–1.18	–1.22	–0.54	0.25	–0.02	–0.32	0.55	–0.75	0.08
Change in private inventories	**–0.51**	**–0.55**	**1.38**	**–0.49**	**0.90**	**–0.28**	**–0.77**	**–0.49**	**–0.48**	**–0.12**	**–2.31**	**–1.09**	**–1.03**	**1.10**	**2.83**	**2.64**	**0.82**	**1.61**	**–3.70**
Farm	0.01	0.02	0.03	0.25	–0.31	0.08	0.06	–0.19	0.37	–0.08	0.13	–0.11	0.12	–0.19	0.21	0.07	0.02	–0.09	–0.06
Nonfarm	–0.53	–0.57	1.35	–0.74	1.21	–0.36	–0.82	–0.30	–0.85	–0.04	–2.44	–0.97	–1.15	1.29	2.62	2.57	0.80	1.71	–3.64
Net exports of goods and services	**1.18**	**1.13**	**–0.48**	**–0.02**	**0.01**	**0.87**	**3.21**	**0.84**	**1.04**	**–0.63**	**1.50**	**2.88**	**1.47**	**–1.37**	**1.90**	**–0.31**	**–3.50**	**–1.70**	**3.44**
Exports	**0.72**	**–1.18**	**1.34**	**0.71**	**0.76**	**1.71**	**1.32**	**0.67**	**1.61**	**–0.66**	**–3.03**	**–3.61**	**–0.08**	**1.30**	**2.56**	**1.30**	**1.08**	**0.82**	**1.04**
Goods	0.53	–1.04	1.12	0.95	0.58	0.98	0.78	0.78	1.24	–0.41	–2.65	–3.14	–0.26	1.29	2.19	1.09	0.93	0.49	0.85
Services	0.19	–0.15	0.22	–0.24	0.17	0.74	0.54	–0.11	0.37	–0.25	–0.38	–0.47	0.18	0.01	0.37	0.21	0.15	0.33	0.19
Imports	**0.46**	**2.32**	**–1.82**	**–0.73**	**–0.75**	**–0.84**	**1.89**	**0.18**	**–0.57**	**0.03**	**4.53**	**6.48**	**1.55**	**–2.67**	**–0.66**	**–1.61**	**–4.58**	**–2.53**	**2.40**
Goods	0.52	2.20	–1.72	–0.89	–0.65	–0.72	1.78	0.42	–0.75	0.15	4.82	5.95	1.23	–2.64	–0.68	–1.41	–4.46	–2.16	2.29
Services	–0.07	0.12	–0.09	0.16	–0.10	–0.12	0.11	–0.24	0.18	–0.12	–0.29	0.53	0.33	–0.03	0.02	–0.20	–0.12	–0.37	0.11
Government consumption expenditures and gross investment	**0.54**	**0.32**	**0.23**	**–0.09**	**0.64**	**0.66**	**0.24**	**0.44**	**0.65**	**1.04**	**0.31**	**–0.61**	**1.24**	**0.33**	**–0.28**	**–0.32**	**0.80**	**0.79**	**–0.11**
Federal	**0.51**	**0.43**	**0.39**	**–0.33**	**0.48**	**0.64**	**0.08**	**0.47**	**0.55**	**1.00**	**0.61**	**–0.40**	**1.11**	**0.45**	**0.01**	**0.15**	**0.72**	**0.71**	**–0.01**
National defense	0.36	0.27	0.22	–0.34	0.38	0.47	0.01	0.32	0.34	0.93	0.28	–0.45	0.85	0.48	–0.13	0.02	0.40	0.46	–0.11
Consumption expenditures	0.27	0.23	0.14	–0.27	0.20	0.45	0.01	0.31	0.02	0.81	0.26	–0.29	0.67	0.37	–0.17	0.02	0.25	0.41	–0.32
Gross investment	0.09	0.04	0.08	–0.08	0.17	0.01	0.00	0.01	0.32	0.12	0.02	–0.17	0.17	0.12	0.04	0.01	0.15	0.05	0.21
Nondefense	0.15	0.16	0.17	0.01	0.10	0.18	0.07	0.15	0.21	0.07	0.33	0.06	0.26	–0.03	0.14	0.13	0.32	0.25	0.10
Consumption expenditures	0.13	0.14	0.12	0.02	0.08	0.15	0.08	0.13	0.17	0.04	0.30	0.09	0.25	–0.07	0.12	0.07	0.27	0.18	0.04
Gross investment	0.02	0.01	0.05	–0.01	0.03	0.02	–0.01	0.02	0.04	0.03	0.03	–0.03	0.01	0.04	0.02	0.06	0.05	0.06	0.06
State and local	**0.04**	**–0.11**	**–0.16**	**0.25**	**0.16**	**0.02**	**0.16**	**–0.04**	**0.10**	**0.04**	**–0.30**	**–0.21**	**0.13**	**–0.12**	**–0.29**	**–0.48**	**0.08**	**0.09**	**–0.10**
Consumption expenditures	0.00	–0.07	–0.10	0.17	0.14	0.02	0.09	–0.06	–0.05	0.04	–0.11	–0.07	–0.03	–0.17	–0.03	–0.11	–0.09	–0.14	–0.08
Gross investment	0.03	–0.05	–0.07	0.07	0.02	0.00	0.07	0.02	0.14	0.00	–0.19	–0.15	0.16	0.05	–0.25	–0.36	0.17	0.23	–0.02
Addenda:																			
Goods	–0.13	–0.99	2.85	0.55	1.69	0.89	2.52	–0.36	–0.09	–3.01	–5.19	–0.62	–0.17	1.67	5.74	4.90	–0.20	1.99	2.31
Services	0.94	–0.10	0.55	0.92	1.23	1.87	1.53	0.92	0.69	–0.08	0.08	–0.95	0.61	–0.10	0.57	0.02	1.21	1.15	0.72
Structures	–0.81	–1.54	–0.54	–0.59	0.32	–0.49	–1.16	–1.28	–0.01	–0.91	–1.66	–3.30	–1.14	0.02	–1.30	–1.18	0.71	–0.58	0.14
Motor vehicle output	–0.53	–0.56	0.46	0.29	0.13	–0.06	–0.45	–0.23	–1.09	–0.53	–1.72	–1.18	–0.04	1.56	0.25	0.74	–0.06	0.49	–0.34
Final sales of computers	0.14	0.03	0.10	0.02	0.07	0.26	0.19	0.11	0.19	0.04	0.08	0.05	–0.06	–0.02	0.09	0.10	0.03	0.29	0.31

See "Explanatory Note" at the end of the tables.

Gross private domestic investment

Net exports of goods and services

Figure 7-2: Table 2 shows the contributions to percent change in real GDP.

Counting products and services in the GDP

To tabulate the GDP, the BEA must first add up the values of everything produced in the United States. Unfortunately, the accounting for all these goods and services can get really complicated. The overall goal is to count each product or service only once. But doing so can be difficult because some products are used in more than one capacity — as the end product itself or as a component to produce another end product.

The BEA addresses this issue in its definition of GDP: *GDP* is the market value of final goods and services produced by labor and property located in the United States. In this definition, the word *final* distinguishes products that are in their final form from those that are used as components of another product. The phrase *produced by labor and property in the United States* excludes all transactions where a product is sold through an intermediary like a wholesaler, as well as all products produced outside the United States. However, the definition includes durable goods like machine tools and factory control equipment that are used to create other goods, as well as products like lubricants and fertilizer that are consumed during the production of other goods.

To illustrate the GDP concept of *final good,* consider a tomato. Many factors go into producing a tomato: The farmer needs seeds, fertilizer, weed control, and labor to produce a single tomato. If the BEA's GDP includes only final products, is the tomato a final product according to the BEA definition? To answer this question, you need to know how the tomato will be used.

If the farmer sells the tomato at a roadside stand to a customer who plans to eat it, that sale makes it a final good and it's included in GDP. If, however, the farmer sells the tomato to a restaurant owner who uses it to prepare a salad, the final good is the salad, not the tomato. The value of the salad is included in the GDP, but the value of the tomato is not.

Similarly, if the farmer sells the tomato to a wholesaler, who then sells it to a chain of grocery stores, neither the sale to the wholesaler nor the sale to the grocery stores is included in GDP. Only when the grocery store sells the tomato to a consumer does it become a final good that's included in the GDP.

You may argue that the GDP should include the sale of the tomato when the farmer sold it to the restaurant owner because it's a final product regardless of the use of the tomato. After all, the restaurant may use only a portion of the tomato in the salad. But if you took that approach and then also counted the value of the restaurant salad in the GDP, you'd be counting the tomato's value twice. Remember that the idea is to count each product only once.

Finally, consider the situation where the farmer has more than one type of customer. Perhaps the farmer sells some tomatoes at the farmers' market, some to the restaurant owner, and some to the wholesaler. This situation is common, so the BEA tries to compensate for it. The GDP tries to account for the aggregate transactions for all products and to distinguish between those product components that can be purchased alone or as part of another product.

The one exception to this rule is that the BEA always treats new goods sold to the government as final goods — even if the government uses them as inputs for other products. So going back to the tomato example, if the farmer sells the tomato to a federal, state, or local government, the BEA considers it a final good even if it's turned into a salad and sold to a student in a high school cafeteria.

Other activities have economic value but aren't included in GDP. For example, the GDP doesn't include unpaid charity work or the work you do for your own home or children. In addition, the GDP doesn't include illegal or black-market activities. These large-dollar activities are hard to estimate and almost impossible to measure. So although the illegal drug trade in the United States is roughly estimated to be billions of dollars per year (production of marijuana may be the largest cash crop in as many as ten states), none of that economic activity goes into the GDP.

Highlighting the GDP's Importance

To most economic analysts, the GDP report is the most useful economic report. Although it may not move the investment markets to the degree that a weekly or monthly indicator can, the GDP report is packed with so much information about the state of the economy that you need to study it carefully to understand the economy's current and future trends.

The GDP generally tends to grow over time. Although this growth doesn't demonstrate perpetual upward motion, the number of months of economic growth often dwarf the number of months in recession.

As businesses grow, they hire new workers, invest in new machinery, and build new factories. Employment levels go up, unemployment goes down, and personal income rises. Growth feeds on itself, and the economic expansion continues until some shock occurs. The shock may be something dramatic — a war, terror attack (like 9/11), or pestilence — but it may also be something rooted in the economy itself, like excessive price inflation or a pricing bubble. The U.S. economy experienced this type of economic shock twice in the first decade of the 21st century, the first starting with the Internet stock price bubble and then again during the run up in housing prices. Both pricing bubbles ended in economic recession and falling prices, for Internet stocks in the first case and real estate in the second.

Economic recessions are terribly uncomfortable for everyone except possibly bondholders and can be terribly disruptive for individuals and business owners. However, the cycle of creative destruction does encourage the reallocation of underused or underpriced assets into more productive pursuits. This reallocation of labor and capital is ultimately better for the economy and the country as a whole and often offers an investment opportunity to patient and savvy investors.

The following sections walk you through how the GDP is used and why it's the most important economic indicator you can follow in your investing.

Declaring recessions and recoveries

The GDP provides valuable economic information. When the economy turns south, the GDP can help you identify when the economy is in a recession or, worse yet, a depression and when it's in recovery mode.

The most severe economic downturn is a *depression.* People used to call any economic downturn a *depression,* but since the Great Depression in the 1930s, most have abandoned that use of the term. Today, the popular definition of a *depression* is any time the GDP falls by 10 percent or more, although some economists adjust the definition to account for inflation (saying that a depression is when the real GDP falls by 10 percent or more). In either case, the United States hasn't seen economic performance this bad since 1937–1938 when the GDP declined by more than 18 percent.

Meanwhile, a *recession* is any economic decline that falls short of a depression. To make this term a little more precise, the popular and business media define a recession as being two consecutive quarters of GDP decline. The worst recession since the Great Depression occurred when the GDP fell by 4.9 percent during the period between the end of 1973 and early 1975.

Although this definition has become popular, it's not the one that most economists and analysts use. Instead, they look to the Business Cycle Dating Committee (BCDC) of the National Bureau of Economic Research for a more inclusive definition. The BCDC's approach evaluates real GDP along with employment, income statistics, and the Federal Reserve's Industrial Production index (see Chapter 4 for employment indicators, Chapter 6 for income statistics, and Chapter 8 for industrial production data). This approach allows the BCDC to pinpoint the start and end of a recession or contraction better than if it were to use the quarterly GDP report alone.

As the economy starts to improve, a recovery happens. During this economic expansion, consumer demand for products and services grows. The market for durable goods helps drive industrial output higher. Eventually, jobs become more plentiful, providing more money for consumers to spend.

The BCDC publishes a list of all recessions and recoveries dating back to 1854; check out this list at the National Bureau of Economic Research website: `www.nber.org/cycles/US_Business_Cycle_Expansions_and_Contractions_20100920.pdf`. Note that the BCDC calls recessions *contractions* and recoveries *expansions* and that the BCDC doesn't use the term *depression,* even during the Great Depression.

Surveying how businesses use the GDP

Businesses are very sensitive to economic cycles. So it makes sense that business leaders incorporate the GDP report in developing business plans, making and adjusting hiring decisions, planning capital expenditures, and fine-tuning sales and production quotas.

Whenever businesses experience a drop in sales, inventories tend to grow and businesses quickly respond by cutting back production. Management questions every expense and curtails spending for things like office equipment, travel, and sometimes even office supplies. If things get bad enough, management may idle workers and production facilities. Only when sales increase enough to bring inventory levels back to target levels do managers begin hiring workers and redeploying idled equipment or facilities.

Being able to anticipate future ups and downs in sales helps business leaders plan ahead and take advantage of any economic situation. GDP forecasts, while far from perfect, are useful planning tools. One source of these forecasts is the Federal Reserve's *FOMC Statement* (see Chapter 8). Another is the Philadelphia Federal Reserve's Survey of Professional Forecasters, which you can find at `www.philadelphiafed.org/research-and-data/real-time-center/survey-of-professional-forecasters`.

Understanding how the government uses the GDP

The White House and Congress use the GDP report to prepare the federal budget, and the Federal Reserve uses it to help formulate monetary policy. The GDP also provides feedback for the success or failure of policy decisions.

For example, the Federal Reserve carefully follows PCE (personal consumption expenditures) price indexes, and these indexes appear in Table 4 of the GDP report (check out Figure 7-4 later in this chapter). The GDP report also presents the core rate of inflation, or the *PCE excluding food and energy,* a statistic that's extremely important to the Federal Reserve. You find this stat in the GDP Appendix.

Perhaps the most compelling reason for you to keep track of the PCE price indexes, especially the core prices, is the Federal Reserve's publicly stated preference for it over the Consumer Price Index, or CPI (see Chapter 12 for more about inflation and CPI).

Eyeing how investors use the GDP

Money managers use the GDP report for investment planning. However, from a trader's point of view, the GDP is often old news. The data used to compile the report are already available, so savvy investors and traders can estimate the report's value before it's actually released. Still, any surprise that differs from the consensus GDP estimate is likely to kick off a flurry of trading activity and repositioning of investment assets. (You can find the latest consensus GDP estimate on the Philadelphia Federal Reserve website at `www.philadelphiafed.org/research-and-data/real-time-center/survey-of-professional-forecasters` and find out more about consensus forecasts in Chapter 2.).

You can use several areas of the GDP report to help you with your investment planning. The areas of the report that show strength or weakness in specific sectors are particularly interesting to those investors who tend to follow the Sector Rotation Model, which helps them identify the current stage of the business cycle. Check out Chapter 3 for a brief introduction to the Sector Rotation Model and my book *Trading For Dummies,* coauthored with Lita Epstein (John Wiley & Sons, Inc.), for even more details. The following sections point out how bond, stock, currency, and commodities investors can use the GDP report.

Watching bond market reactions

Bond investors prefer a slow and steady economy, or even a declining economy, over rapid growth. Any hint that the economy is racing ahead, especially if the reported growth rate is unexpected, is likely to hit bond prices hard and drive up long-term interest rates.

Bond investors need to keep a close watch on the GDP reports. During periods when the GDP is showing economic growth, prices for long-term bonds tend to fall faster than shorter-term bonds, so investors should keep the duration of their portfolios relatively short. When the GDP shows that the economy is reaching its peak, bond investors should lock in longer-term rates. When bond prices are rising and interest rates are falling, the prices of long-term bonds appreciate faster than shorter-term bonds. Bond investors can benefit from the high interest rate and the potential for capital gains due to price appreciation.

I recommend that bond investors also keep a close eye on the GDP's PCE price indexes for signs of growing inflationary pressures. Inflation generally harms the value of bond interest payments and drives bond prices lower. Bond portfolios don't do well in the face of inflation. The only exception may be bondholders who own inflation-indexed bonds. The U.S. Treasury offers inflation-indexed bonds called *Treasury Inflation-Protected Securities* (TIPS) that may hold up better than their traditional counterparts in the face of inflation, but they haven't really been tested in a high-inflation economy. So no one really knows whether they offer the protection bond buyers hope they're buying when they pay higher prices for TIPS.

To find out how much TIPS bonds cost, follow the TIPS spread (you can see a chart of the TIPS spread at `bit.ly/TipsSpread`). In other words, find out the difference in yield between traditional Treasury bonds and TIPS bonds. The spread shows how fearful bond investors are about the risk of future inflation. The TIPS spread is interpreted as an inflation forecast over the term of the bond. The higher the spread, the more worried bond investors are. (For more on the TIPS spread, see Chapter 14.)

Observing stock market reactions

Stock investors are most interested in corporate profitability, specifically the earnings growth rate. However, equity investors also need to carefully watch the GDP's PCE indexes because the Federal Reserve will react to inflation pressures by raising interest rates to keep inflation in check. Few stocks perform well in a high-inflation environment, but stocks of cyclical consumer product companies are likely to be hurt the worst. Financial firms and some real-estate developers and managers may hold up better in this environment.

If you're a stock investor, consider the old Wall Street axiom about three steps and a stumble. Oldtimers in the market expect stock prices to correct (or fall) after the Federal Reserve raises interest rates three times. The market doesn't always work out that way, but it happens with enough frequency that you should keep a careful watch.

Because the stock market tends to anticipate economic changes, you can't use the GDP report itself as a leading indicator. However, you can use it to validate that your portfolio is positioned correctly. When the GDP shows that the economy is expanding, investors should favor stocks in growth sectors like technology, communications, basic materials (steel and chemical companies), and durable goods manufacturers. During an economic contraction, few stocks will perform well, but stocks of companies that sell consumer staples, like food and beverages, pharmaceuticals, and household products, tend to hold their value better than most.

Tracking the value of U.S. currency

The value of the U.S. dollar is very sensitive to the state of the economy and the rate of inflation. That's why currency traders and foreign investors keep a close watch on the GDP report. Overseas investors prefer strong economic growth, a rising stock market, low inflation, and relatively high bond yields. When one or more of these elements are out of whack, the value of the U.S. dollar may decline.

When the GDP report shows that the economy is growing, you know that many businesses are profitable and growing, and that growth fuels rising stock prices. Interest rates also tend to rise and stay higher when the economy is doing well. As long as inflation stays in check, overseas investors will continue to invest in the United States, thus increasing the demand for dollars. This helps prop up the value and the price of the dollar. Although many factors affect currency trading, all things being equal, traders prefer to own U.S. dollars while U.S. GDP is reporting economic growth.

However, foreign investors face a double-whammy when the GDP shows that the U.S. economy is slowing. Stock prices fall simultaneously with the demand for U.S. dollars. Even overseas bond investors can suffer. Although U.S. bond prices are likely to rise as the economy slows, if the U.S. dollar falls, so does the overseas investor's total return.

Following commodities

Some commodity prices are very sensitive to the state of the economy, while others are mostly unaffected. If you invest in commodities, the GDP can help you identify periods of growth and contraction, which, in turn, can help you identify potential areas of strength and weakness in the commodities markets. When the GDP shows that the economy is expanding, commodities like building materials and industrial metals tend to increase in price. When the economy is contracting, these same commodities often fall in value. Similarly, energy prices tend to rise as the GDP shows a growing economy because of an increased demand for fuel for transportation and electricity. In contrast, prices for grains, pork bellies, and orange juice are less sensitive to economic changes.

Knowing How the GDP Is Calculated

The basic formula for calculating GDP is relatively simple. It adds up the value of all purchases for final goods and services produced and purchased in the United States. The basic GDP equation looks like this:

$$GDP = C + I + G + (X - M)$$

Here's what the variables on the right side of the equation mean:

- **C:** Personal consumption expenditures (PCE)
- **I:** Gross private domestic investments
- **G:** Government consumption expenditures and gross investments
- **(X – M):** Net export value of goods and services (exports – imports)

Although this equation seems simple enough, assembling the GDP report requires a lot more attention to detail. To get a sense of the complexity involved, take a look at Table 3 from the GDP report in Figure 7-3. It illustrates each of the GDP components. I discuss the variables in the GDP equation in the following sections.

Although you'll never need to calculate GDP for yourself, understanding the basic formula can shed light on what's included and what's excluded from the GDP numbers. For example, recall that only final goods and services produced in the United States are included in the GDP. Because the GDP uses PCE to calculate the value of goods and services, all imported products must be subtracted from GDP. Why? Because PCE includes imported goods that consumers purchase and imported products aren't produced in the United States.

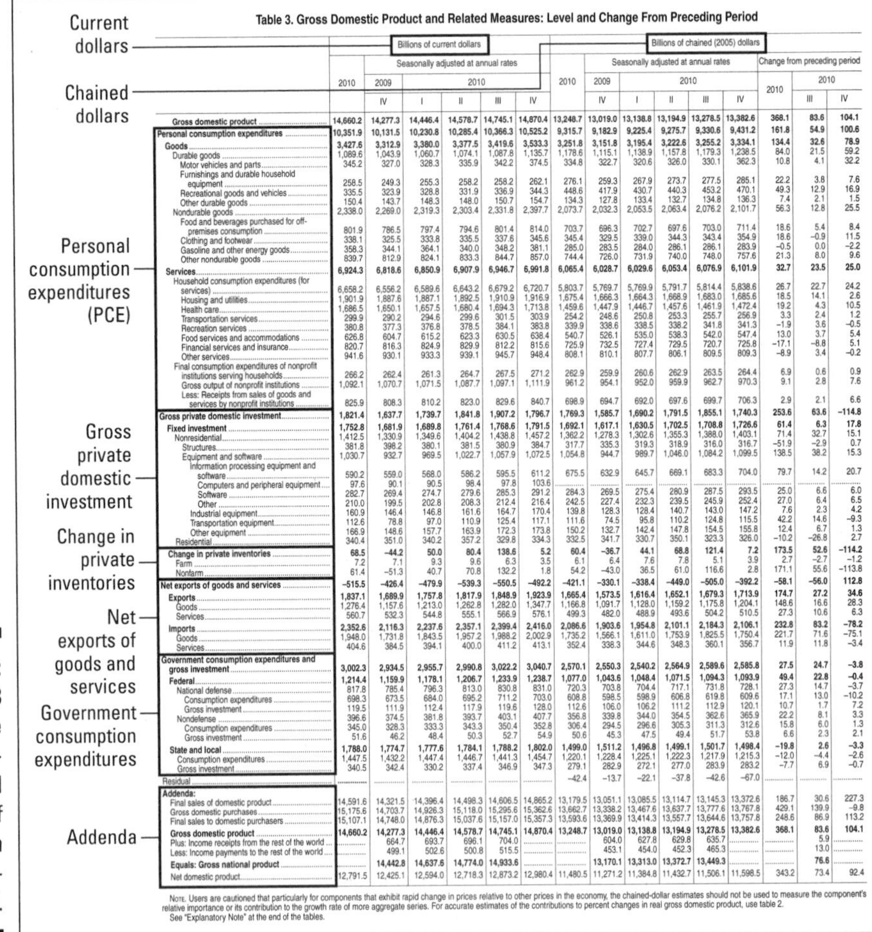

Table 3. Gross Domestic Product and Related Measures: Level and Change From Preceding Period

	Billions of current dollars						Billions of chained (2005) dollars						Change from preceding period		
	Seasonally adjusted at annual rates						Seasonally adjusted at annual rates								
	2010	2009	2010				2010	2009	2010				2010	2010	
		IV	I	II	III	IV		IV	I	II	III	IV		III	IV
Gross domestic product	14,660.2	14,277.3	14,446.4	14,578.7	14,745.1	14,870.4	13,248.7	13,019.0	13,138.8	13,194.9	13,278.5	13,382.6	368.1	83.6	104.1
Personal consumption expenditures	10,351.9	10,131.5	10,230.8	10,285.4	10,366.3	10,525.2	9,315.7	9,182.9	9,225.4	9,275.7	9,330.6	9,431.2	161.8	54.9	100.6
Goods	3,427.6	3,312.9	3,380.0	3,377.5	3,419.6	3,533.3	3,251.8	3,151.8	3,195.4	3,222.6	3,255.2	3,334.1	134.4	32.6	78.9
Durable goods	1,089.6	1,043.9	1,060.7	1,074.1	1,087.8	1,135.7	1,178.6	1,115.1	1,138.9	1,157.8	1,179.3	1,238.5	84.0	21.5	59.2
Motor vehicles and parts	345.2	327.0	328.3	335.9	342.2	374.5	334.8	322.7	320.6	326.0	330.1	362.3	10.8	4.1	32.2
Furnishings and durable household equipment	258.5	249.3	255.3	258.2	258.2	262.1	276.1	259.3	267.9	273.7	277.5	285.1	22.2	3.8	7.6
Recreational goods and vehicles	335.5	323.9	328.8	331.9	336.9	344.3	448.6	417.9	430.7	440.3	453.2	470.1	49.3	12.9	16.9
Other durable goods	150.4	143.7	148.3	148.0	150.7	154.7	134.3	127.8	133.4	132.7	134.8	136.3	7.4	2.1	1.5
Nondurable goods	2,338.0	2,269.0	2,319.3	2,303.4	2,331.8	2,397.7	2,073.7	2,032.3	2,053.5	2,063.4	2,076.2	2,101.7	56.3	12.8	25.5
Food and beverages purchased for off-premises consumption	801.9	786.5	797.4	794.6	801.4	814.0	703.7	696.3	702.7	697.6	703.0	711.4	18.6	5.4	8.4
Clothing and footwear	338.1	325.5	333.8	335.5	337.6	345.6	345.4	329.5	339.0	344.3	343.4	354.9	18.6	–0.9	11.5
Gasoline and other energy goods	358.3	344.1	364.1	340.0	348.2	381.1	285.0	283.5	284.0	286.1	286.1	283.9	–0.5	0.0	–2.2
Other nondurable goods	839.7	812.9	824.1	833.3	844.7	857.0	744.4	726.0	731.9	740.0	748.0	757.6	21.3	8.0	9.6
Services	6,924.3	6,818.6	6,850.9	6,907.9	6,946.7	6,991.8	6,065.4	6,028.7	6,029.6	6,053.4	6,076.9	6,101.9	32.7	23.5	25.0
Household consumption expenditures (for services)	6,658.2	6,556.2	6,589.6	6,643.2	6,679.2	6,720.7	5,803.7	5,769.7	5,769.9	5,791.7	5,814.4	5,838.6	26.7	22.7	24.2
Housing and utilities	1,901.9	1,887.6	1,887.1	1,892.5	1,910.9	1,916.9	1,675.4	1,666.3	1,664.3	1,668.9	1,683.0	1,685.6	18.5	14.1	2.6
Health care	1,686.5	1,650.1	1,657.5	1,680.4	1,694.3	1,713.8	1,459.6	1,447.9	1,446.7	1,457.6	1,461.9	1,472.4	19.2	4.3	10.5
Transportation services	299.9	290.2	294.6	299.6	301.5	303.9	254.2	248.6	250.8	253.3	255.7	256.9	3.3	2.4	1.2
Recreation services	380.8	377.3	376.8	378.5	384.1	383.8	339.9	338.6	338.5	338.2	341.8	341.3	–1.9	3.6	–0.5
Food services and accommodations	626.8	604.7	615.2	623.3	630.5	638.4	540.7	526.1	535.0	538.3	542.0	547.4	13.0	3.7	5.4
Financial services and insurance	820.7	816.3	824.9	829.9	812.2	815.6	725.9	732.5	727.4	729.5	720.7	725.8	–17.1	–8.8	5.1
Other services	941.6	930.1	933.3	939.1	945.7	948.4	808.1	810.1	807.7	806.1	809.5	809.3	–8.9	3.4	–0.2
Final consumption expenditures of nonprofit institutions serving households	266.2	262.4	261.3	264.7	267.5	271.2	262.9	259.9	260.6	262.9	263.5	264.4	6.9	0.6	0.9
Gross output of nonprofit institutions	1,092.1	1,070.7	1,071.5	1,087.7	1,097.1	1,111.9	961.2	954.1	952.0	959.9	962.7	970.3	9.1	2.8	7.6
Less: Receipts from sales of goods and services by nonprofit institutions	825.9	808.3	810.2	823.0	829.6	840.7	698.9	694.7	692.0	697.6	699.7	706.3	2.9	2.1	6.6
Gross private domestic investment	1,821.4	1,637.7	1,739.7	1,841.8	1,907.2	1,796.7	1,769.3	1,585.7	1,690.2	1,791.5	1,855.1	1,740.3	253.6	63.6	–114.8
Fixed investment	1,752.8	1,681.9	1,689.8	1,761.4	1,768.6	1,791.5	1,692.1	1,617.1	1,630.5	1,702.5	1,708.8	1,726.6	61.4	6.3	17.8
Nonresidential	1,412.5	1,330.9	1,349.6	1,404.2	1,438.8	1,457.2	1,362.2	1,278.3	1,302.6	1,355.3	1,388.0	1,403.1	71.4	32.7	15.1
Structures	381.8	398.2	380.1	381.5	380.9	384.7	317.7	335.3	319.3	318.9	316.0	316.7	–51.9	–2.9	0.7
Equipment and software	1,030.7	932.7	969.5	1,022.7	1,057.9	1,072.5	1,054.8	944.7	989.7	1,046.0	1,084.2	1,099.5	138.5	38.2	15.3
Information processing equipment and software	590.2	559.0	568.0	586.2	595.5	611.2	675.5	632.9	645.7	669.1	683.3	704.0	79.7	14.2	20.7
Computers and peripheral equipment	97.6	90.1	90.5	98.4	97.8	103.6	....	....	....	....	....	....	....	....	....
Software	282.7	269.4	274.7	279.6	285.3	291.2	284.3	269.5	275.4	280.9	287.5	293.5	25.0	6.6	6.0
Other	210.0	199.5	202.8	208.3	212.4	216.4	242.5	227.4	232.3	239.5	245.9	252.4	27.0	6.4	6.5
Industrial equipment	160.9	146.4	146.8	161.6	164.7	170.4	139.8	128.3	128.4	140.7	143.0	147.2	7.6	2.3	4.2
Transportation equipment	112.6	78.8	97.0	110.9	125.4	117.1	111.6	74.5	95.8	110.2	124.8	115.5	42.2	14.6	–9.3
Other equipment	166.9	148.6	157.7	163.9	172.3	173.8	150.2	132.7	142.4	147.8	154.5	155.8	12.4	6.7	1.3
Residential	340.4	351.0	340.2	357.2	329.8	334.3	332.5	341.7	330.7	350.1	323.3	326.0	–10.2	–26.8	2.7
Change in private inventories	68.5	–44.2	50.0	80.4	138.6	5.2	60.4	–36.7	44.1	68.8	121.4	7.2	173.5	52.6	–114.2
Farm	7.2	7.1	9.3	9.6	6.3	3.5	6.1	6.4	7.6	7.8	5.1	3.9	2.7	–2.7	–1.2
Nonfarm	61.4	–51.3	40.7	70.8	132.2	1.8	54.2	–43.0	36.5	61.0	116.6	2.8	171.1	55.6	–113.8
Net exports of goods and services	–515.5	–426.4	–479.9	–539.3	–550.5	–492.2	–421.1	–330.1	–338.4	–449.0	–505.0	–392.2	–58.1	–56.0	112.8
Exports	1,837.1	1,689.9	1,757.8	1,817.9	1,848.9	1,923.9	1,665.4	1,573.5	1,616.4	1,652.1	1,679.3	1,713.9	174.7	27.2	34.6
Goods	1,276.4	1,157.6	1,213.0	1,262.8	1,282.0	1,347.7	1,166.8	1,091.7	1,128.0	1,159.2	1,175.8	1,204.1	148.6	16.6	28.3
Services	560.7	532.3	544.8	555.1	566.9	576.1	499.3	482.0	488.9	493.6	504.2	510.5	27.3	10.6	6.3
Imports	2,352.6	2,116.3	2,237.6	2,357.1	2,399.4	2,416.0	2,086.6	1,903.6	1,954.8	2,101.1	2,184.3	2,106.1	232.8	83.2	–78.2
Goods	1,948.0	1,731.8	1,843.5	1,957.2	1,988.2	2,002.9	1,735.2	1,566.1	1,611.0	1,753.9	1,825.5	1,750.4	221.7	71.6	–75.1
Services	404.6	384.5	394.1	400.0	411.2	413.1	352.4	338.3	344.6	348.3	360.1	356.7	11.9	11.8	–3.4
Government consumption expenditures and gross investment	3,002.3	2,934.5	2,955.7	2,990.8	3,022.2	3,040.7	2,570.1	2,550.3	2,540.2	2,564.9	2,589.6	2,585.8	27.5	24.7	–3.8
Federal	1,214.4	1,159.9	1,178.1	1,206.7	1,233.9	1,238.7	1,077.0	1,043.6	1,048.4	1,071.5	1,094.3	1,093.9	49.4	22.8	–0.4
National defense	817.8	785.4	796.3	813.0	830.8	831.0	720.3	703.8	704.4	717.1	731.8	728.1	27.3	14.7	–3.7
Consumption expenditures	698.3	673.5	684.0	695.2	711.2	703.0	608.8	598.5	598.9	606.8	619.8	609.6	17.1	13.0	–10.2
Gross investment	119.5	111.9	112.4	117.9	119.6	128.0	112.6	106.0	106.2	111.2	112.9	120.1	10.7	1.7	7.2
Nondefense	396.6	374.5	381.8	393.7	403.1	407.7	356.8	339.8	344.0	354.5	362.6	365.9	22.2	8.1	3.3
Consumption expenditures	345.0	328.3	333.3	343.3	350.4	352.8	306.4	294.5	296.6	305.3	311.3	312.6	15.8	6.0	1.3
Gross investment	51.6	46.2	48.4	50.3	52.7	54.9	50.6	45.3	47.5	49.4	51.7	53.8	6.6	2.3	2.1
State and local	1,788.0	1,774.7	1,777.6	1,784.1	1,788.2	1,802.0	1,499.0	1,511.2	1,496.8	1,499.1	1,501.7	1,498.4	–19.8	2.6	–3.3
Consumption expenditures	1,447.5	1,432.2	1,447.4	1,446.7	1,441.3	1,454.7	1,220.1	1,228.4	1,225.1	1,222.3	1,217.9	1,215.3	–12.0	–4.4	–2.6
Gross investment	340.5	342.4	330.2	337.4	346.9	347.3	279.1	282.9	272.1	277.0	283.9	283.2	–7.7	6.9	–0.7
Residual	....	....	....	....	....	....	–42.4	–13.7	–22.1	–37.8	–42.6	–67.0	....	....	....
Addenda:															
Final sales of domestic product	14,591.6	14,321.5	14,396.4	14,498.3	14,606.5	14,865.2	13,179.5	13,051.1	13,085.5	13,114.7	13,145.3	13,372.6	186.7	30.6	227.3
Gross domestic purchases	15,175.6	14,703.7	14,926.3	15,118.0	15,295.6	15,362.6	13,662.7	13,338.2	13,467.6	13,637.7	13,777.6	13,767.8	429.1	139.9	–9.8
Final sales to domestic purchasers	15,107.1	14,748.0	14,876.3	15,037.6	15,157.0	15,357.3	13,593.6	13,369.9	13,414.3	13,557.7	13,644.6	13,757.8	248.6	86.9	113.2
Gross domestic product	14,660.2	14,277.3	14,446.4	14,578.7	14,745.1	14,870.4	13,248.7	13,019.0	13,138.8	13,194.9	13,278.5	13,382.6	368.1	83.6	104.1
Plus: Income receipts from the rest of the world	....	664.7	693.7	696.1	704.0	....	....	604.0	627.8	629.8	635.7	....	....	5.9	....
Less: Income payments to the rest of the world	....	499.1	502.6	500.8	515.5	....	....	453.1	454.0	452.3	465.3	....	....	13.0	....
Equals: Gross national product	....	14,442.8	14,637.6	14,774.0	14,933.6	....	....	13,170.1	13,313.0	13,372.7	13,449.3	....	....	76.6	....
Net domestic product	12,791.5	12,425.1	12,594.0	12,718.3	12,873.2	12,980.4	11,480.5	11,271.2	11,384.8	11,432.7	11,506.1	11,598.5	343.2	73.4	92.4

NOTE. Users are cautioned that particularly for components that exhibit rapid change in prices relative to other prices in the economy, the chained-dollar estimates should not be used to measure the component's relative importance or its contribution to the growth rate of more aggregate series. For accurate estimates of the contributions to percent changes in real gross domestic product, use table 2.
See "Explanatory Note" at the end of the tables.

Figure 7-3: Table 3 shows the GDP components and their level of change from the preceding period.

Checking the books: GDP's accounting system

The system of accounting that the BEA uses to keep track of GDP is called the *U.S. National Income and Product Accounts* (NIPA). A variety of U.S. economic reports, including the BEA's Personal Income and Outlays report (see Chapter 6), use the NIPA. The NIPA structure follows the format recommended by the United Nations, called the *U.N. System of National Accounts.* Many industrial countries use a similar accounting structure.

The NIPA approach is similar to a traditional double-entry accounting journal. For the national accounts, one side of the ledger shows income from producers and the other side shows purchases by consumers. After all, every transaction has a buyer and a seller. Accounting for all purchases from the buyer's point of view is called the *expenditure approach*; accounting from the seller's point of view is called the *income approach.*

One way that the NIPA differs from traditional accounting practices is that it uses a third way to track GDP: the *value-added* or *production approach.* In this method, the value added at every step of the manufacturing process is added to create GDP. For example, if a miller buys $100 worth of wheat from a farmer, grinds it into flour, and sells it to a baker for $150, then the miller has added $50 worth of value to the product. That $50 is added to the GDP in the value-added approach. In a similar manner, you can count the farmer's value added by subtracting the cost of seed and fertilizer from the $100 value of the wheat.

All three accounting approaches should arrive at the same answer, and except for small discrepancies, they usually do. However, most Wall Street analysts rely on the expenditure approach, which is why I focus on that approach throughout this chapter.

More information about the structure and use of the NIPA is available at the BEA website: `www.bea.gov/national/pdf/nipa_primer.pdf`.

Measuring personal consumption

Consumer spending, or *personal consumption expenditures* (PCE) as it's known in the GDP report, is the single-largest component in the GDP. Figure 7-3 shows PCE's value to be about $10.3 trillion and a little more than 70 percent of the total GDP. The PCE data in the GDP comes directly from the PCE statistic in the BEA's Personal Income and Outlays report (see Chapter 6 for details). However, because the GDP report is a quarterly report while the Personal Income and Outlays report is a monthly report, the BEA has to average the monthly PCE data for the quarterly GDP.

PCE classifies personal consumption into three broad categories, and the GDP report preserves these categories:

- **Durable goods:** This category includes big-ticket items that are intended to last at least three years. Although this is the smallest PCE category (historically ranging from 10 to 15 percent of total consumer spending), it's the most economically sensitive and, thus, the most watched. It tends to be lower in slow economic times and higher when the economy is doing well.

- **Nondurable goods:** This category includes clothing, shoes, food, pharmaceuticals, or any products that are intended to last less than three years. The percentage spent on nondurable goods is currently less than 25 percent of total PCE, and that percentage has been falling for decades.
- **Services:** This broad category includes healthcare, legal services, mortgages, insurance, spa treatments, and air travel. In short, a service is anything that someone does for you. Spending on services as a percentage of total PCE has been steadily rising for years. It currently represents more than 65 percent of all consumer spending.

If you divide PCE by the GDP, you get an answer suggesting that consumer spending represents roughly 70 percent of all GDP. Although factual, this number is a bit misleading. PCE includes money spent on consumers' behalf for government programs like Medicare and Medicaid, which makes the ratio larger than you may have expected if you were counting only consumers' direct purchases. Also, imported products make up some percentage of consumers' purchases and are included in PCE, but they're not part of GDP. Although this difference is small, it does distort the actual ratio of consumer spending relative to GDP.

Tracking private investments

Spending by businesses, formally titled *Gross private domestic investment*, represents about 15 percent of the total GDP (refer to Figure 7-3 to see this category in Table 3 of the GDP report). Business spending is very sensitive to the economic cycle. As the economy grows, businesses invest in the facilities and machinery required to increase profits. At the first sign of economic trouble, management carefully examines every business expense, and as a result, business spending often drops dramatically as the economy slows.

Gross private domestic investment measures the production of capital goods in the United States. In this case, the word *gross* means that it includes the market value of depreciation. This statistic measures expenditures for capital goods. If you were to subtract capital depreciation (also called the *capital consumption adjustment*) from the gross private domestic investment, the result would be *net private domestic investment*, the amount of capital used to actually expand the stock of capital equipment. Check out the latest edition of *Accounting For Dummies* by John A. Tracy (John Wiley & Sons, Inc.) for a refresher on depreciation.

The GDP tracks two broad categories of gross private domestic investment: fixed investments and change in private inventory.

Investing in fixed assets

Fixed investment, also called *capital spending,* is the larger of the two gross private domestic investment categories. It includes nonresidential investments, such as office and warehouse facilities, computers and software, industrial equipment, transportation equipment, and residential construction of single-family homes and multiunit apartments.

The purpose of GDP is to measure current production of final goods, not sales. In other words, GDP includes products when they're produced, not when they're sold (although their value is determined by the sales price). So whether newly produced computers are in use or recently built warehouses are occupied doesn't matter. The GDP's only concern is that they were produced or built.

Accounting for business inventories

At this point, you may be asking yourself: What about houses that are built but not sold? What about the computers that are still sitting on some retailer's shelf? The GDP accounts for these unsold products through the category called *Change in private inventories* (refer to Figure 7-3). So basically, the GDP is the total of all products sold plus the change in inventories. This change may be positive or negative. If inventories grew, the amount is added to the GDP; if inventories shrank, the value is subtracted.

To see how this GDP category works, consider this example. If a home builder builds 12 homes this quarter but sells only 10, there are 2 unsold homes. These two homes are placed into inventory. The ten homes sold are included as part of the GDP because of the sales transaction. But the GDP also needs to count the value of the two unsold homes. They were produced, after all. The value of those two homes — the change in inventory value — is added to the GDP. (An estimated value for the sales price of the home is used to add this value to the GDP.)

To continue the example, during the next quarter, the home builder builds 12 more homes and sells 13. One home now remains in inventory. The GDP includes the 13 home sales. To account for the fact that the home builder produced only 12 of the homes in the current quarter, the GDP uses the change in private inventory calculation. The home builder's inventory has dropped from two homes to one. Because the home builder sold 13 homes, the value of all 13 homes is added to the GDP; because the home builder sold one home from inventory, its value is subtracted from the GDP.

The home builder in my example is obviously a small business, building fewer than 50 homes a year, and must pay careful attention to inventory levels. As sales slow, inventories grow. Too many unsold homes is a huge problem for any home builder, large or small, just like rising inventory levels is a problem for any business.

The home builder must react to growing inventories by slowing production. If things get bad enough, the business may begin laying off workers or stopping production altogether. In that situation, the home builder will resume production only after the inventory of unsold homes is manageable again. As this common scenario plays out on the larger economic stage, you can see how changes in the economy easily affect jobs, personal income, and consumer spending.

Counting government consumption

The GDP report includes federal, state, and local government spending under the heading *Government consumption expenditures and gross investment* (refer to Figure 7-3).

Federal spending breaks down into two more categories, one for defense items and one for nondefense items. The defense category includes spending for military hardware and the armed forces payroll. Nondefense spending includes payroll for government employees, equipment purchases, construction of interstate highways, and maintenance of national parks and federal buildings.

The GDP report combines state and local spending into one category. All government spending is subdivided into subcategories for *gross investment,* which includes structures and equipment, and *consumption expenditures*, which include nondurable goods and services used by the government.

Combined, federal, state, and local government spending for goods and services represents about 20 percent of the total GDP. But keep in mind that the government component of GDP doesn't directly account for all government spending in this section. For example, the GDP accounts for transfer payments from Social Security and Medicare to citizens in the PCE section when consumers actually spend the money.

Monitoring imports and exports

The United States is among the largest exporters in the world, currently ranked number three behind China and Germany, and is the world's largest importer. China is the second-largest importer and Germany is number three. The GDP accounts for the value of exports and imports by adding the value of all exports and subtracting the value of all imports.

Exported products and services are produced in the United States, so, of course, the GDP adds in their value. But what about imports from other countries? When considering the value of imports, remember that the GDP is calculated by adding expenditures and changes to inventory. When consumers buy retail products that were produced in a foreign country, those transactions are included in PCE. However, because the products weren't produced in the United States, their value must be subtracted from the total GDP.

In Figure 7-3, you can see that the GDP combines exports and imports under the heading *Net exports of goods and services*. In this case, the word *net* means that the value of total imports is subtracted from the total value of exports. The United States typically imports more than it exports, so the net value is usually negative.

Purchasing and selling domestic products

Several additional GDP categories merit a quick mention. You see these categories listed under the heading *Addenda* in Figure 7-3:

- **Final sales of domestic product:** This statistic is identical to the overall GDP calculation except that it excludes the calculation for change in private inventories. This category shows how many U.S. products were actually sold during any quarter, making it a good gauge of demand for U.S. products and services (from both foreign and domestic customers).
- **Gross domestic purchases:** This category measures purchases made by U.S. consumers, businesses, and governments of all products and services, including imported products and services. It's identical to the standard GDP calculation except that it excludes the calculation for net exports of goods and services.
- **Final sales to domestic purchasers:** This category gauges demand for all products and services, including imports, from all consumers, businesses, and governments. It measures gross domestic purchases minus the change in inventories.
- **Gross national product (GNP):** GNP is GDP's predecessor. Its value is still a part of the GDP report. (See the nearby sidebar "Comparing GDP and GNP" for the difference between the two calculations.)

Comparing GDP and GNP

Gross domestic product (GDP) is the reporting standard used today, but before 1991, the United States used the gross national product (GNP) instead. These measures are similar but not identical. The United States made the change to make the U.S. GDP report more consistent with the United Nations System of National Accounts. As a result, comparing U.S. economic output with that of other nations is a whole lot easier.

The difference between the two statistics is the net income value from foreign sources. GNP includes foreign income sources; GDP doesn't. Typically, this difference affects the information about large multinational corporations. For example, if a company like General Motors manufacturers an automobile in Canada, at least a portion of that car's value is included in GNP but not in GDP. Automobiles manufactured in the United States by foreign-owned car companies are included in GDP but not in GNP. (In practice, the math is more complicated than this simple example, but you get the idea.)

The change from GNP to GDP has made the advance estimate report somewhat more reliable because net income from foreign sources is rarely available at the time the GDP advance estimate report is released. Although the GNP value is included in the GDP report, it isn't published until the first revision when more reliable data about income from foreign sources is available.

You can derive GNP from GDP by following the calculations shown in the following table. The difference between the GDP and GNP is small, at least relative to the GDP as a whole. Still, a billion here and a billion there adds up to a pretty big number.

Statistic	Calculation	Amount
U.S. GDP		$xx,xxx billion
	Add income from the rest of the world	+ $xxx billion
	Subtract payments to the rest of the world	– $xxx billion
U.S. GNP		= $xx,xxx billion

Seeing How GDP Is Adjusted for Inflation

That consumer product prices rise regularly is about as surprising as the sun rising in the east or Democrats and Republicans disagreeing about tax policy and almost everything else. Only a few industries buck this trend — think computers that keep getting smaller and faster while prices stay relatively consistent. For everything else, prices just seem to keep going up. But prices don't determine your standard of living. Rather, the quantity and quality of the goods and services you consume determine how well you live.

GDP measures the economy by tabulating the prices of the products and services you buy. As the GDP rises, you need to figure out whether that rise is the result of people buying more products or whether the price of that product is simply rising. Knowing the difference is important because rising prices may make the economy appear to be growing when, in reality, prices are just going up.

To get a clearer picture of this concept, consider modern-day movies. Box office reports often declare that the latest summer blockbuster brought in more money than any other movie before it. The question that those reports don't answer, however, is whether people bought more tickets for that record-breaking movie than for any other movie before it or whether movie tickets just cost more today than they used to.

In terms of the number of tickets ever sold, *Gone with the Wind* likely wins the biggest-blockbuster-ever award, followed by *Star Wars* and *The Sound of Music*. Sure, James Cameron's movies *Avatar* and *Titanic* both brought in tons of cash, a lot more than *Gone with the Wind*. But when you adjust for ticket-price inflation, neither of Cameron's movies is in the top-five ticket sales-a-thon.

A rising GDP is good for almost everyone as long as more products are actually being made available. However, if GDP is rising because of price inflation and not an increase in the production of products, very few people benefit. Inflation hurts both stock and bond investors, and it ultimately impacts business profitability and consumers' purchasing power, as well. Fortunately, the GDP report makes it easy to see when inflation is occurring. The following sections take a closer look at why adjusting GDP for inflation is important and what you need to consider when comparing GDP price indexes over time.

Chaining dollars to inflation

GDP uses the *chained-dollar* technique to adjust for inflation, which means that a constantly changing basket of goods and services is used to measure and adjust for inflation. Notice that Table 3 of the GDP report, shown in Figure 7-3, contains two broad columns:

- Billions of current dollars
- Billions of chained (2005) dollars

The BEA first calculates the GDP by using the current dollar value (sometimes called the *nominal dollar value*) of all goods and services. In other words, the BEA uses current prices to determine the value of everything produced in the United States. The BEA then uses chained-dollar values (which I discuss in Chapter 2) to index the GDP statistics for inflation. In Figure 7-3, the baseline value is that of a 2005 dollar, but you can expect that to change every five years or so.

Chained-dollar indexing tries to be smarter about inflation indexing compared to the static basket-of-goods approach used in more well-known inflation indexes like the Consumer Price Index, or CPI (see Chapter 12 for details about that index). The chained-dollar technique looks at more than prices alone. If, for example, prices in one widely used product rise dramatically, consumers will either use less of that product or substitute a similar product. Say the price of corn flakes skyrockets. Consumers are likely to switch to a substitute breakfast cereal, perhaps shredded wheat. The chained-dollar index attempts to recognize product switches like this one and to factor them into the inflation index.

No inflation-indexing technique is perfect. The GDP-based chained-dollar technique may understate inflation's impact just as CPI may overstate it. Details about how well the chained-dollar index actually accomplishes its task are complicated and well beyond the scope of this book. However, if you're interested, check out the BEA's lucid discussion about chaining dollars on its website at `www.bea.gov/scb/pdf/2003/11November/1103%20Chain-dollar.pdf`.

When analyzing the GDP report, tracking both the current and chained-dollar statistics is important. Values in current dollars show the strength of one industry compared to another and the relative size of the U.S. economy compared to that of other countries. However, chained-dollar values allow you to evaluate U.S. GDP over time because they help you determine whether total U.S. production is really rising or whether price increases alone make it appear that GDP is growing.

Comparing GDP price indexes over time

In addition to the chained-dollar values you see in Table 3 (refer to Figure 7-3), the GDP report provides a number of indexes that measure price changes and inflation over time. These indexes are important because they can show you where inflation is having the largest impact on consumers and the economy.

Figure 7-4 shows Table 4 of the GDP report, which provides the percentage change of the price indexes from previous periods. (Although not shown here, Tables 5 and 6 present the real and current-dollar GDP price indexes and their major components; go to `http://1.usa.gov/iZEdJ2` to see these tables in the final 2010 GDP report.)

Figure 7-4: Table 4 shows the GDP price indexes.

Table 4. Price Indexes for Gross Domestic Product and Related Measures: Percent Change From Preceding Period

	2008	2009	2010	Seasonally adjusted at annual rates															
				2007				2008				2009				2010			
				I	II	III	IV	I	II	III	IV	I	II	III	IV	I	II	III	IV
Gross domestic product (GDP)	**2.2**	**0.9**	**1.0**	**4.4**	**3.2**	**2.0**	**0.9**	**1.9**	**3.2**	**4.5**	**−1.2**	**1.1**	**0.3**	**0.7**	**−0.2**	**1.0**	**1.9**	**2.1**	**0.3**
Personal consumption expenditures	**3.3**	**0.2**	**1.7**	**4.0**	**3.5**	**2.3**	**4.2**	**3.9**	**4.6**	**4.4**	**−5.8**	**−1.6**	**1.9**	**2.9**	**2.7**	**2.1**	**0.0**	**0.8**	**1.8**
Goods	3.2	−2.5	1.7	3.2	4.7	0.8	5.4	5.1	4.9	7.2	−17.7	−6.0	3.7	5.7	2.8	2.6	−3.6	0.9	3.6
Durable goods	−1.4	−1.6	−1.4	−1.8	−1.4	−2.1	−1.4	−0.7	−2.0	−0.7	−3.4	−2.1	0.1	−2.5	0.7	−2.0	−1.6	−2.2	−2.4
Nondurable goods	5.6	−2.9	3.2	6.1	8.1	2.3	9.1	8.1	8.3	11.0	−23.5	−7.9	5.4	9.7	3.8	4.7	−4.6	2.4	6.5
Services	3.4	1.5	1.7	4.4	2.9	3.1	3.7	3.3	4.5	3.0	0.7	0.5	1.1	1.7	2.7	1.8	1.8	0.7	0.9
Gross private domestic investment	**0.7**	**−2.0**	**−1.8**	**2.1**	**0.1**	**−0.2**	**0.4**	**−0.2**	**1.0**	**1.9**	**4.8**	**−4.1**	**−6.7**	**−6.0**	**−0.7**	**−2.0**	**−0.7**	**0.5**	**2.3**
Fixed investment	0.8	−1.7	−1.6	2.1	0.2	−0.2	0.2	0.0	1.3	2.8	2.2	−3.0	−5.7	−4.8	−1.0	−1.4	−0.7	0.1	1.0
Nonresidential	1.4	−1.2	−1.9	2.0	0.7	−0.3	0.2	0.6	2.1	4.5	4.3	−3.1	−5.7	−5.1	−2.4	−1.9	0.0	0.2	0.8
Structures	4.7	−2.6	−1.5	5.0	1.8	3.3	4.8	3.5	4.9	8.1	8.1	−5.6	−12.2	−10.5	−2.1	0.9	2.0	2.9	3.2
Equipment and software	−0.2	−0.5	−1.9	0.7	0.3	−2.0	−2.1	−0.9	0.8	2.6	2.2	−1.6	−2.0	−2.4	−2.5	−3.1	−0.8	−0.8	−0.1
Residential	−1.2	−3.4	−0.4	2.2	−1.2	0.1	0.7	−1.4	−1.1	−2.8	−5.2	−2.9	−6.0	−3.3	4.3	0.6	−3.2	−0.1	2.1
Change in private inventories	...	...	...	...	...	...	...	...	...	...	...	...	...	...	...	...	...	...	...
Net exports of goods and services	...	...	...	...	...	...	...	...	...	...	...	...	...	...	...	...	...	...	...
Exports	4.7	−5.4	4.2	3.4	4.4	2.6	5.8	7.8	10.6	5.7	−22.3	−11.5	0.7	4.6	4.6	5.1	4.8	0.2	8.1
Goods	4.8	−6.8	4.8	2.7	4.5	2.2	6.1	8.6	13.2	5.4	−27.5	−13.8	2.7	4.8	4.6	5.8	5.3	0.4	11.0
Services	4.2	−2.2	2.9	5.1	4.2	3.7	5.1	5.8	4.8	6.4	−9.0	−6.6	−3.2	4.0	4.7	3.7	3.7	−0.2	1.6
Imports	10.4	−10.7	6.5	3.9	4.0	2.8	24.3	19.4	16.6	2.2	−32.1	−27.3	2.3	8.6	21.8	12.4	−7.7	−8.1	18.9
Goods	11.3	−12.3	7.1	4.1	3.5	2.1	28.0	22.0	17.3	1.7	−34.6	−30.7	2.0	9.2	24.8	14.6	−9.6	−9.2	21.8
Services	5.7	−2.8	3.7	2.8	6.8	6.6	5.9	6.2	13.4	4.8	−17.2	−10.2	3.8	6.2	9.2	2.5	1.6	−2.2	5.9
Government consumption expenditures and gross investment	**4.7**	**−0.3**	**1.9**	**8.4**	**4.6**	**2.9**	**4.7**	**7.3**	**6.5**	**3.9**	**−5.2**	**−1.7**	**0.6**	**0.4**	**1.5**	**4.6**	**0.9**	**0.3**	**3.1**
Federal	3.1	−0.2	1.7	8.7	3.5	0.4	2.3	6.5	4.7	1.6	−4.2	0.7	−0.8	−0.1	1.5	4.5	0.9	0.5	1.7
National defense	3.6	−0.7	2.0	8.4	4.1	0.9	3.1	6.4	6.3	2.0	−5.9	0.1	−1.8	0.3	1.6	5.3	1.2	0.5	2.1
Nondefense	2.2	0.8	1.1	9.3	2.3	−0.6	0.8	6.6	1.6	0.6	−0.4	2.2	1.1	−1.0	1.5	2.8	0.2	0.4	0.9
State and local	5.6	−0.4	2.0	8.3	5.3	4.4	6.2	7.7	7.5	5.3	−5.8	−3.2	1.5	0.8	1.5	4.6	0.9	0.2	4.0
Addenda:																			
Final sales of domestic product	2.2	1.0	1.0	4.4	3.2	2.0	0.8	2.0	3.2	4.6	−1.5	1.3	0.4	0.8	−0.3	1.0	1.9	2.1	0.2
Gross domestic purchases	3.2	−0.2	1.3	4.4	3.2	2.0	3.8	4.0	4.5	3.9	−4.4	−2.0	0.6	1.4	2.1	2.1	0.1	0.7	2.1
Final sales to domestic purchasers	3.2	−0.2	1.4	4.5	3.2	2.0	3.7	4.0	4.5	4.1	−4.6	−1.9	0.7	1.5	2.0	2.2	0.1	0.6	2.0
Gross national product (GNP)	2.2	0.9	...	4.4	3.1	2.0	0.9	2.0	3.2	4.5	−1.3	1.1	0.3	0.8	−0.2	1.0	1.9	2.1	...
Implicit price deflators:																			
GDP	2.2	0.9	0.9	4.4	3.2	2.0	0.9	1.8	3.4	4.5	−1.2	1.0	0.3	0.7	−0.3	1.1	2.0	2.0	0.3
Gross domestic purchases	3.2	−0.2	1.3	4.4	3.1	2.1	3.8	3.8	4.7	4.0	−4.3	−2.2	0.5	1.3	2.0	2.2	0.1	0.6	2.1
GNP	2.2	0.9	...	4.4	3.1	2.0	0.9	1.8	3.4	4.5	−1.2	1.0	0.3	0.7	−0.3	1.0	1.9	2.0	...

See "Explanatory Note" at the end of the tables.

Implicit price deflators

Using price indexes as price deflators

A *price index,* which I describe in Chapter 2, shows a data series on a common scale, usually starting at 100, relative to a base year. Currently the GDP uses 2005 as the base year. In other words, the index value for 2005 is 100. Subsequent years are indexed to that base year, so a year's price index value is proportionally larger than 100 if the GDP for that year is larger than that of the base year and proportionally smaller than 100 if the year's GDP is smaller than that of the base year.

One of the uses of a price index is as a *price deflator.* Using a price index as a price deflator allows you to convert current-dollar values into approximate real (inflation-adjusted) dollars. An *implicit price deflator,* like those shown in Figure 7-4, is the ratio of the current-dollar value of a series, such as GDP, to its corresponding chained-dollar value, multiplied by 100.

GDP Implicit price deflator = (Current-dollar GDP ÷ Chained-dollar GDP) × 100

Working in the other direction, if you divide the current-dollar GDP by the GDP deflator and then multiple by 100, you get the value for real GDP. In other words, you *deflate* current-dollar GDP into real-dollar GDP.

Real (chained-dollar) GDP = (Current-dollar GDP ÷ GDP implicit price deflator) × 100

This approach works for subcomponents of GDP, such as PCE, as well.

Each of the indexes shown in Figure 7-4 shows year-over-year changes for three years, followed by the quarterly changes for those same three years. (The example shown in Figure 7-4 is from the 2010 advance estimate report, so the data reported for 2010 would have been adjusted in future reports.)

In Figure 7-4, you can see that the GDP price index, or total GDP price inflation (the top line in the report), is 2.2 percent in 2008, 0.9 percent in 2009, and 1.0 percent in 2010. The Federal Reserve's target for inflation is between 1 and 2 percent.

In addition to the top-line GDP price index, another set of useful statistics are the *Implicit price deflators*, which you can see at the bottom of Table 4 in Figure 7-4. The first of these price deflators is for the GDP index as a whole. The others correspond to the GDP derivatives shown in Table 3 of the GDP report (refer to Figure 7-3).

Although useful, both the GDP price deflator and the top-line GDP price index include the price of exports but exclude imports. In other words, they don't index price inflation perfectly for all U.S. purchases. To find the price index inflation including imports, look at the *Gross domestic purchases* heading under the *Implicit price deflators* category. Like its counterpart in Table 3 (refer to Figure 7-3), the gross domestic purchases price deflator excludes exports but includes imports.

The implicit price deflator for gross domestic purchases is most useful when import prices rise or fall significantly. For instance, import prices may rise when the value of the U.S. currency falls or when the worldwide price for a commodity like oil rises dramatically. In the case of rising oil prices, consumers feel the effects directly at the gas pump and in terms of the cost of almost every transportation product.

Chapter 8

Following the Fed

In This Chapter

- Reviewing how the Fed affects the economy
- Setting the federal funds rate
- Finding beauty in the Beige Book
- Watching the Fed track manufacturing and industrial production
- Leveraging the expertise of the regional Fed banks

The *Federal Reserve System* is the United States' central bank. It's sometimes called the *Federal Reserve* or simply the *Fed.* Whatever you call it, the U.S. central bank is a very powerful part of the U.S. economy and a reliable source of economic information.

The Fed's actions have a direct impact on U.S. businesses, investors, and consumers. For example, the Fed influences the general availability of credit and can exert pressure to affect the level of interest rates charged by banks and mortgage lenders. It's also responsible for regulating national banks and managing the amount of money sloshing around in the banking system. In addition, the Fed creates and publishes its own economic surveys, forecasts, economic research, and reports to the U.S. Congress.

In this chapter, I discuss the role of the Federal Reserve and the decisions it makes, and I explain how those decisions impact the economy, businesses, investment markets, and you. In addition, I discuss several of the Fed's most influential pronouncements and reports.

Understanding the Fed's Role

To better grasp economic indicators and the data you get from them, you need a firm comprehension of the Federal Reserve and its role in the U.S. economy. Unfortunately, who the Fed is isn't always crystal clear. The good news: I'm here to help make sense of the fogginess. Although the Fed seems cloaked in mystery (it's an independent organization, neither owned nor directly controlled by the U.S. Government), it's generally considered to have a beneficial and stabilizing influence on the U.S. economy. The Fed's basic roles are as follows:

- It makes and enforces U.S. banking regulations.
- It controls the U.S. money supply to try and keep inflation under control by influencing interest rates and the availability of credit.

The following sections give you the ins and outs of the Fed and explain these basic roles in greater depth.

Outlining the Fed's basic structure

Before digging into the Fed's actions and reports, allow me to uncloak the mystery surrounding the Fed by explaining what makes it up.

In 1913, the U.S. Congress passed the Federal Reserve Act, which created the Federal Reserve to minimize political influence over the nation's monetary and financial systems. Although Congress doesn't directly control the Fed, it does oversee the Fed's actions and has the power to revise (or even repeal) the Federal Reserve Act. Here's how the Fed is structured:

- **Board of Governors:** Also known as the *Federal Reserve Board,* this is the Fed's governing body. The seven-member Board of Governors is appointed by the U.S. president and confirmed by Congress to staggered 14-year terms. Openings occur every two years, so a U.S. president can appoint only two governors to the board in any four-year presidential term.
- **Regional Federal Reserve banks:** Twelve regional Federal Reserve banks provide banking services, such as cash and check processing, for federally chartered banks. They also provide special banking services to the U.S. Government.
- **Federal Open Market Committee (FOMC):** The FOMC is responsible for determining the Fed's monetary policy (which I discuss later in the section "Digging into monetary policy"). FOMC voting members include the 7 members of the Board of Governors, the president of the New York Federal Reserve Bank, and 4 of the remaining 11 regional Federal Reserve bank presidents. Although all the regional presidents attend and participate in FOMC meetings, the 11 remaining regional presidents take one-year turns in the voting positions.

- **Member banks:** Every federally chartered bank in the United States must be a member of the Federal Reserve System. State-chartered banks may join the system but they don't have to do so.

The Fed's decisions don't require the approval of the U.S. president or anyone else in the executive or legislative branches of government. Although its governing body is subject to congressional oversight and its chairman regularly reports to Congress, neither Congress nor the president can override or veto decisions made by the Fed.

Understanding central banking

Most countries have a central bank, and, for the most part, central banking responsibilities are similar from one country to another. Like most central banks, the U.S. Federal Reserve is responsible for the following:

- **Setting and implementing the U.S. monetary policy:** The Fed has to balance the often-conflicting goals of minimizing the damaging effects of currency inflation and simultaneously encouraging full employment. I discuss monetary policy and its economic impact in detail in the next section.
- **Regulating banking institutions:** The Fed is responsible for ensuring the financial safety of the nation's banks. It works with other federal and state regulators, such as the Federal Deposit Insurance Corporation (FDIC) and the Office of Thrift Supervision (OTS), to audit and supervise the nation's banks. Banks must be financially sound, they must be in compliance with laws and regulations, and they must take only manageable risks.
- **Maintaining the stability of the financial system:** The Fed must contain or mitigate any risks that may harm the banking system. This generally means that the Fed must be prepared to provide short-term liquidity (credit) when banks experience unexpected withdrawals during a financial panic.
- **Providing specialized financial services:** The Fed provides clearing services for the nation's payment systems. Clearing services include processing paper-check payments between member banks and processing electronic-funds transfers, like payroll direct deposits, Social Security benefit payments, and tax refunds. The Fed also distributes coin and currency to member banks.

This list shows the Fed's primary responsibilities, but it provides only a glimpse of the Fed's expansive role in the U.S. economy. For example, the Fed also holds some of the U.S. foreign exchange reserves and manages currency exchange rates. It also has an anti-money-laundering program and a broad community affairs and educational outreach program. For more on the Fed's structure and responsibilities, go to http://federalreserve.gov/pf/pf.htm.

The Fed is an important and influential player in the U.S. economy. Its actions have a direct impact on interest rates and the availability of credit, both of which have important implications for investors, business leaders, and consumers. So you can see why keeping track of the Fed's activities is well worth your time.

Digging into monetary policy

Of all the Fed's responsibilities, setting and implementing the U.S. monetary policy is the one that most affects businesses, investors, and the economy. *Monetary policy* is a set of tools that the Fed uses to influence interest rates and manage the availability of credit and money.

The Fed does the following three things to implement monetary policy:

- **Buys and sells U.S. securities:** The Fed can influence bond prices and interest rates by buying and selling U.S. Treasury securities and other federal agency securities in the open market. In Fed terminology, these actions are called *open-market operations*.

  The Fed doesn't directly control interest rates. Instead, it tries to influence interest rates by buying and selling U.S. Government securities in the open market. It's a simple function of supply and demand. If the Fed buys enough U.S. Treasury bonds, it tends to drive all bond prices higher and all interest rates lower. Lower interest rates generally stimulate the economy. The reverse is also true. If the Fed wants to slow the economy, it can sell bonds to bring prices down and drive interest rates up.

  The interest rate charged for loans between member banks — called the *federal funds rate* or just the *fed funds rate* — is of particular importance to the Fed because it sets a target range for this rate. Find out more about this interest rate in the section "Reading the Fed's FOMC Statement."

- **Lends to member banks:** The Fed can lend money to member banks to help them meet short-term liquidity needs. The Fed's lending facility is called the *discount window,* and loans to member banks are called *discount window loans.* Discount rates are published on the Fed website at www.frbdiscountwindow.org/index.cfm.

Lending to member banks was once the Fed's primary monetary policy tool, and member banks still use it to manage liquidity. However, its role in monetary policy is now overshadowed by open-market operations.

- **Sets reserve requirements:** Member banks have to hold a minimum amount of customer deposits in reserve. Each bank can hold its reserves in the bank's cash vault or on deposit at the Federal Reserve. The Fed's Board of Governors sets the reserve requirements.

So what does all this have to do with the U.S. economy and your personal investments? Banks take in deposits in the form of checking accounts, savings accounts, and certificates of deposit. In turn, they make loans to fellow banks and other customers, using these deposits. For example, sometimes member banks need short-term loans from other banks so they can meet their reserve requirements. The rate charged between member banks (the federal funds rate) is subject to market pressures just like every other interest rate. The Fed uses open-market operations to keep this rate within its stated targets. And the Fed's reserve requirements limit how much individual banks can loan at any one time.

Although the management of the federal funds rate seems esoteric, it's important. Changes to the federal funds rate can cause cascading changes to other interest rates, including the rates charged for consumer credit cards, business loans, and mortgages. These cascading changes affect the availability of credit in the economy and the money supply, and, over time, they can even affect the employment situation and the prices of consumer products and services.

When the Fed believes that the risk of inflation is very low or that unemployment is unacceptably high, it's likely to set a low target for the federal funds rate in the hope of stimulating the economy. Conversely, if the Fed thinks that inflation is likely to rise, it'll raise the federal funds rate target.

Unfortunately, changes to the federal funds rate don't cause instantaneous changes to the economy. For example, in January 2009, the Fed set the federal funds target rate very low — to 0.25 percent — to stimulate the economy. Although the economy did improve somewhat by the third quarter of 2009, economic growth remained anemic and the federal funds rate remained unchanged through 2010 and into 2011.

The Fed's target funds rate is actually a range of rates. For example, in January 2009, the target range set by the Fed was 0 to 0.25 percent. Rates change daily but tend to fluctuate within the range set by the Fed. The regional Federal Reserve banks can influence the day-to-day federal funds rate within the target zone by adjusting the discount rate, which is the interest rate the Fed charges when it loans to member banks.

Managing — not printing — the money supply

Unlike the central banks of most other countries, the U.S. Federal Reserve doesn't print the U.S. currency. The U.S. Treasury's Bureau of Engraving and Printing does that. But the Fed does control the quantity of currency issued and manages the country's money supply. If this distinction seems too small to make a difference, consider this: The value of all the U.S. currency in circulation is only a tiny fraction of the U.S. money supply.

The Fed is more interested in bank deposits than currency or coins. One measure of total money supply is called *M2;* it includes all currency in circulation, plus checking-account deposits, savings accounts, money market accounts, and certificates of deposit. As of February 2011, M2 was $8.8 trillion. In contrast, a recent Fed estimate for the total value of all U.S. currency in circulation was about $830 billion. In other words, the M2 is more than ten times the amount of currency and coins in circulation.

M2 is a component in the Leading Economic Index (see Chapter 10 for details), and the Fed watches the money supply statistics to gauge economic and financial conditions.

Of course, this is an oversimplification of a very complicated topic. For those of you interested in the fascinating details about money supply, check out the most recent edition of *Economics For Dummies* by Sean Flynn (John Wiley & Sons, Inc.). You can follow the M2 money supply aggregate for yourself on the Federal Reserve website: `www.federalreserve.gov/releases/h6/hist/h6hist7.htm`.

Reading the Fed's FOMC Statement

The Federal Open Market Committee (FOMC) is responsible for setting the Fed's monetary policy and the federal funds target rate. The FOMC announces any changes to the federal funds rate in its report, which is called the *FOMC Statement.* This economic report may be the single-most influential document produced by the Federal Reserve. The FOMC Statement is short — rarely longer than a single page — but its impact is huge. Table 8-1 gives a quick overview of this report.

Table 8-1 Federal Open Market Committee (FOMC) Statement

Release Schedule	*Agency*	*Web Address*	*Sensitivity*
Eight releases per year: Published schedule, 2:15 p.m. ET	Federal Open Market Committee (FOMC) of the Federal Reserve	`www.federalreserve.gov/monetarypolicy/default.htm`	Very high

The following sections give you a more in-depth explanation of the FOMC Statement, including why you want to keep an eye on it, what it includes, and how you can react to the data.

Eyeing why this report is important

One of the FOMC's main responsibilities is to evaluate current economic conditions and make economic forecasts based on them. Then it has to decide whether the Fed needs to make changes to the federal funds rate. A long lag exists between Fed actions and their impact on future economic activity, which makes the timing of the FOMC's decisions difficult but crucial. I can't overstate the importance of the FOMC report to businesses, investors, and the economy. Any change to the federal funds target rate (or even the Fed's economic outlook) can instantly move investment markets and can eventually change the economy's rate of growth.

The FOMC meets eight times each year. Following each meeting, the FOMC provides a carefully worded press release (that is, the FOMC Statement), outlining its monetary policy objectives and any changes to its views about the current or future economic situation. You can find the dates for the FOMC meetings and the release dates for the FOMC Statement on the Federal Reserve website at `www.federalreserve.gov/monetarypolicy/fomccalendars.htm`.

A decline in the federal funds rate normally stimulates economic activity. But the trade-off is that overly exuberant economic activity can lead to inflation. The Fed must balance the desire for economic growth with its mandate to control inflation. Raising the federal funds rate slows economic growth and reduces inflationary pressures.

Forecasting the future with the FOMC

The FOMC Statement includes more than changes to the federal funds rate. It covers a lot of carefully worded ground, and investors, economists, and analysts carefully parse it for subtle shifts in the Fed's thinking. In addition to changes to the federal funds rate, the FOMC Statement also includes

- **A review of the current economic situation:** Based on the Fed's reading of economic indicators, as well as the FOMC's own business surveys and analysis, the FOMC Statement briefly describes the current economic climate and the job situation, along with the reasoning behind its conclusions.

- **Expectations for the future:** The FOMC Statement describes any actions that the FOMC plans to take to support its monetary policy and the results that it expects from these actions.
- **Future threats to the economy:** The FOMC describes what aspects of the economic situation it plans to monitor during the period between the current and next FOMC meetings.
- **Voting results**: When drafting monetary policy, the FOMC tries to reach a consensus. The voting results show whether any voting members disagreed with the announced monetary policy.

Three weeks following the release of the FOMC Statement, the FOMC releases the complete minutes and actual transcripts of the most recent regularly scheduled FOMC meeting to the public. You can find these transcripts on the Federal Reserve website at `www.federalreserve.gov/monetarypolicy/fomccalendars.htm`.

Reacting to the FOMC Statement

Release of the FOMC Statement often triggers a flurry of investment and trading activity. Any change in the federal funds target rate usually causes instantaneous reactions in stock, bond, and currency markets, though those knee-jerk reactions may be short lived. Increases in the federal funds rate ultimately raise the cost of borrowing for both businesses and consumers. Conversely, decreases in the federal funds rate should make borrowing easier and cheaper for both businesses and consumers.

Although investors may react instantly to an FOMC release, a lag exists between the FOMC's actions and any economic impact. How so? Investors have an old axiom about the Fed and interest rates: three steps and a stumble. Sounds like a bad dance move, right? As you may already know, the economy is hard to slow down and takes a long time to change directions. For this reason, the economy usually doesn't show any signs of a slowdown immediately following the first increase of the federal funds rate. You can expect two, three, or more interest rate hikes before the economy starts to slow in reaction to the higher rates.

The investment markets tend to react to the FOMC Statement based on their prior expectations for the report. If traders have correctly anticipated an increase in the federal funds rate, then reactions may be muted. However, if the FOMC surprises the investment community by announcing a larger-than-expected change to the federal funds rate, you can expect fireworks in the investment markets, as I explain in the following sections.

Positioning your bond portfolio

Bond investors are most concerned with the effects of inflation and its effect on their portfolios. Rising inflation hurts bond returns. Therefore, bondholders pay careful attention to the FOMC for any hint that the Fed is struggling to maintain its inflation targets. Raising the federal funds rate is certainly a clue that the FOMC is worried about inflation. However, the FOMC is likely to explicitly state any concerns about the risk of inflation or an overheated economy in the FOMC Statement.

Some long-maturity bondholders sell in response to the Fed's raising the federal funds rate, causing interest rates to rise for these bonds as well. Only when investors are convinced that the Fed has inflation under control or when bond prices are low enough — and interest rates are high enough — to compensate for the inflation risk will they show interest in long-maturity bonds again.

Seeing how equity investors react to the FOMC

High interest rates are bad news for stocks because high borrowing costs hurt profitability. Increases in the federal funds rate eventually slow the economy, and an economic slowdown further harms equity investments. The first sign of FOMC interest rate action may not warrant an immediate reallocation of your equity portfolio, but it's a clear sign that you need to start planning how to handle an economic slowdown. Keep the three-steps-and-a-stumble axiom in mind. As rates rise, especially after the Fed has made two or three rate-hike announcements, plan to move away from high-growth stocks into more stable, income-producing investments.

Of course, the reverse is equally true. After the FOMC begins to reduce the federal funds rate, businesses can start to take advantage of lower borrowing costs and improving market conditions. That's when equity investors need to start moving back into growth stocks.

Following the currency markets

High federal funds rates tend to make the U.S. dollar and U.S. bonds more attractive to foreign investors. As the FOMC raises the federal funds rate, you can expect the value of the dollar to rise. From a trader's perspective, the immediate move in the price of the dollar depends on the trader's expectations and whether the FOMC met those expectations or surprised currency traders by making a larger or smaller move. Regardless of the timing, however, higher federal funds rates ultimately correspond with a stronger dollar.

Boring into the Beige Book

If you think beige is boring, you haven't read the Fed's Beige Book economic report. Formally known as the *Summary of Commentary on Current Economic Conditions by Federal Reserve District*, the *Beige Book* describes business conditions in each of the Fed's 12 districts. The regional Federal Reserve banks compile the information in this report from interviews with local business leaders and then distribute it to the FOMC participants before each FOMC meeting.

This report is a surprisingly good read — not as much fun as a *For Dummies* book, of course, but for a Fed report, it's rather engaging. It doesn't have any charts, numbers, or in-depth data to analyze. Instead, it's a succinct summary of business leaders' current experiences and expectations for their own businesses. Table 8-2 provides a brief overview of the Beige Book.

Table 8-2 The Beige Book

Release Schedule	*Agency*	*Web Address*	*Sensitivity*
Eight releases per year: Two weeks before the FOMC meeting, 2:15 p.m. ET	The Federal Reserve	`www.federalreserve.gov/FOMC/BeigeBook/`	Moderate

The rainbow of book covers

The Beige Book isn't the only Fed book known by the color of its cover.

- The *Green Book* provides a forecast of the U.S. economy.
- The *Blue Book* describes monetary policy alternatives and their implications.

The Federal Reserve Board's staff compiles both of these books and then distributes them, along with the Beige Book, to FOMC members before each meeting. Unlike the Beige Book, however, the Green Book and Blue Book aren't released to the public.

An archive of Beige Books is available on the Minneapolis Federal Reserve Bank website at `www.minneapolisfed.org/bb/`. The Green Book's data is eventually made available to the public, but long after its original publication. To see this book's very old data sets, visit `www.philadelphiafed.org/research-and-data/real-time-center/greenbook-data/`. Blue Book data is never made public.

You may be wondering, why beige? Well, *Summary of Commentary on Current Economic Conditions by Federal Reserve District* is just a mouthful. And the color of the report's cover is a light tan, which is kind of beige-y. (It used to be red, but apparently that was too flashy for the Fed.)

Although the Beige Book probably won't help you predict the FOMC's federal funds rate, it does do an adequate job of predicting growth in the current quarter. The Fed releases the Beige Book two weeks before each FOMC meeting and simultaneously makes it available to the general public. As an investor or business leader, you need to at least keep up with the Beige Book report for an early look into current and future business conditions for both bonds and stocks:

- **Bonds:** Bonds perform best during a weak economy. Economic strength causes bond investors to sell long-dated maturities and to take positions in shorter-term investments. The reason for this is that increases in interest rates tend to produce larger declines in long-term bond prices than in short-term bond prices. The Beige Book's anecdotes offer an early look into what's really happening in the economy. As the economy strengthens, bond investors usually start to lock in the higher yields from longer-dated bonds.
- **Stocks:** Stock investors prefer to see economic strength. Equity investors look to the Beige Book for signs that the economy is growing and will continue to grow. Late in an economic expansion, however, continued strength may raise fears that the Fed will begin raising the federal funds to slow the economy. When the economy shows signs of deterioration, stock investors need to move away from growth stocks and into less volatile equity investments or short-term fixed-income vehicles.

Monitoring Manufacturing with the Industrial Production and Capacity Utilization Report

The Fed's *Industrial Production and Capacity Utilization report* is widely followed by investors, economists, and policymakers. Investors like this report because it provides an in-depth look into a broad cross section of manufacturing industries. Economists monitor it for early signs of inflationary pressures. And the National Bureau of Economic Research (NBER) uses it to help peg when a recession officially begins and ends. (See Chapter 7 for details on the NBER.)

You may wonder why a report that covers the manufacturing sectors, which represent only 20 percent of the U.S. economy, generates so much attention. After all, the service sectors make up by far the largest percentage of the U.S. economy. But when you compare the impact that the business cycle has on the manufacturing versus service industries, it makes sense that a manufacturing report would create more fuss than a service one.

Manufacturing companies are more sensitive than service industries to interest rate changes and to changes in consumer purchasing patterns. Although service providers aren't immune to the effects of the business cycle, their growth is relatively consistent from quarter to quarter and year to year. Even during a recession, people still go to the doctor, buy homeowner's insurance, and take their cars in for repair.

Table 8-3 provides a snapshot of the Industrial Production and Capacity Utilization report.

Table 8-3 Industrial Production and Capacity Utilization Report

Release Schedule	*Agency*	*Web Address*	*Sensitivity*
Monthly: Published schedule, 9:15 a.m. ET	The Federal Reserve	`federalreserve.gov/releases/g17/current/`	Moderate

Keep reading for more information about this report, including what the report measures, what kind of data it shows, and how you can use it in your planning.

Seeing what the report measures

The Fed's monthly Industrial Production and Capacity Utilization report covers manufacturing, mining, and electric and gas utilities. The report is made up of two indexes, which show real and potential output for these industrial sectors. These indexes are expressed as volume of output, not value.

Revisions to the Industrial Production and Capacity Utilization report are common. The current month's estimate is preliminary and may be revised for up to five months as new source data become available. Annual revisions can affect data for five years or more. Base year updates occur every five years or so and may require the reindexing of many years of previous data. Data in this report are seasonally adjusted.

For a variety of reasons, the data takes several months to filter into the Industrial Production and Capacity Utilization report. In fact, only about 70 percent of the total information you see in the final report is part of the preliminary release. However, the early estimates are usually very good because revisions to the report tend to be small.

Be aware that disruptions in the supply chain can cause fluctuations in the report's data that aren't rooted in the economic cycle or consumer purchasing patterns. For example, a labor strike or severe weather can affect output across several industries.

Release dates for the Industrial Production and Capacity Utilization report, along with files containing the data shown in the report and more detailed data series, are available on the Federal Reserve website: `www.federalreserve.gov/releases/g17/`.

The following two sections take a closer look at the two indexes in this report.

How much is being made: Industrial production

The Industrial Production index tells how much is being produced in the United States. It includes everything manufactured, mined, assembled, or generated regardless of whether the production facility is owned by a U.S. or foreign company. In other words, it converts into an index the tons of coal, gallons of petrochemicals, and numbers of automobiles, refrigerators, tubes of toothpaste, fishing poles, machine tools, computer chips, and everything else made in the United States each month.

Price isn't a factor in computing this index because it's all about the number being produced, not the value. The index expresses industrial production volume as a percentage of the output in the base year, which is currently 2007. The biggest percentage changes in economic output occur in the old smokestack industries and their modern high-tech counterparts.

Manufacturing businesses are very sensitive to the business cycle. A strong correlation exists between movements in the Industrial Production index and changes in the Gross Domestic Product (GDP) report (see Chapter 7), as well as changes in the Employment Situation report (see Chapter 4) and the Personal Income and Outlays report (see Chapter 6).

How much could be made: Capacity utilization

While the Industrial Production index details how much is being made, the Capacity Utilization index tells how much could be made. It answers this question: How much could the United States produce if every mine, every power plant, every manufacturing facility, and every piece of manufacturing equipment were running at full capacity? In other words, this index shows how much of the nation's industrial capacity is actually in use. Like the Industrial Production index, it expresses this capacity as a percentage of the base year, which is currently 2007.

To put together the Capacity Utilization index, the Fed needs to answer the following questions about every production facility in the country:

- Does it operate five or seven days a week?
- Does it operate on a single shift, or does it operate 24 hours every day?
- Are some production lines idle, or is every piece of equipment being used to its fullest capacity?

Of course, companies rarely operate any facility at 100 percent capacity. They always need some downtime for maintaining equipment. Even facilities that operate 24 hours a day 7 days a week vary output to meet demand and still require periodic maintenance. Plus, the availability of raw materials or labor sometimes limits production in one way or another.

The Fed's Capacity Utilization index defines *fullest capacity* as *sustainable maximum output,* or the level of output a facility can sustain after factoring in downtime for maintenance and the continuous availability of labor and materials required for production. Total industry capacity utilization typically averages about 80 percent. This index has never shown 100 percent utilization.

Some issues make it difficult to definitively determine total capacity utilization. Consider that many U.S. companies operate offshore facilities. As domestic demand ramps up, companies can easily import products from their offshore facilities or purchase the needed products from offshore vendors to satisfy consumer desires without actually raising domestic production. The Capacity Utilization index doesn't include these foreign manufacturing capacities even though they're clearly available.

Correlating output, capacity, and growth

A direct correlation exists between economic growth and the performance of U.S. manufacturers, especially durable goods manufacturing. As long as the manufacturing sector is healthy and growing and has the capacity to grow, you can expect the economy to remain healthy. However, as manufacturing becomes constrained by capacity limitations, the risk of inflation grows. The Fed's Industrial Production and Capacity Utilization report can help you stay informed about the health of U.S. manufacturing and its relationship to the overall economy.

Figure 8-1 shows the summary table from the February 2011 Industrial Production and Capacity Utilization report.

INDUSTRIAL PRODUCTION AND CAPACITY UTILIZATION: SUMMARY
Seasonally adjusted

	2007=100						Percent change						
Industrial production	2010 Aug.[r]	Sept.[r]	Oct.[r]	Nov.[r]	Dec.[r]	2011 Jan.[p]	2010 Aug.[r]	Sept.[r]	Oct.[r]	Nov.[r]	Dec.[r]	2011 Jan.[p]	Jan. '10 to Jan. '11
Total index	93.6	93.9	93.8	94.1	95.2	95.1	.1	.3	.0	.3	1.2	-.1	5.2
Previous estimates	93.7	94.0	93.8	94.1	94.9		.2	.3	-.1	.3	.8		
Major market groups													
Final Products	95.4	95.4	95.6	95.5	96.4	96.8	-.1	.0	.2	-.1	1.0	.4	4.7
Consumer goods	95.3	95.1	94.9	94.7	95.7	95.8	-.3	-.2	-.2	-.3	1.0	.1	2.2
Business equipment	94.6	95.2	96.4	96.8	97.8	98.7	.3	.6	1.3	.3	1.0	.9	11.4
Nonindustrial supplies	85.4	85.2	84.9	85.7	86.2	86.0	.0	-.1	-.4	1.0	.6	-.3	3.1
Construction	79.1	79.0	79.4	80.4	80.3	80.2	.3	-.2	.4	1.3	.0	-.2	7.2
Materials	94.8	95.5	95.4	95.8	97.2	96.9	.4	.8	-.2	.4	1.5	-.4	6.2
Major industry groups													
Manufacturing (see note below)	90.8	90.9	91.3	91.6	92.3	92.6	.0	.1	.4	.3	.9	.3	5.5
Previous estimates	90.9	91.0	91.4	91.6	92.0		.1	.1	.4	.3	.4		
Mining	103.0	104.2	104.9	103.9	104.4	103.7	1.9	1.2	.7	-1.0	.5	-.7	7.5
Utilities	101.4	101.9	97.7	99.7	103.8	102.2	-1.2	.5	-4.1	2.1	4.1	-1.6	.1

	Percent of capacity												Capacity growth
Capacity utilization	Average 1972-2010	1988-89 high	1990-91 low	1994-95 high	2008-09 low	2010 Jan.	2010 Aug.[r]	Sept.[r]	Oct.[r]	Nov.[r]	Dec.[r]	2011 Jan.[p]	Jan. '10 to Jan. '11
Total industry	80.5	85.2	78.7	85.1	68.2	72.3	75.0	75.2	75.2	75.4	76.2	76.1	.0
Previous estimates							75.1	75.3	75.2	75.4	76.0		
Manufacturing (see note below)	79.1	85.6	77.2	84.6	65.4	69.8	72.3	72.4	72.7	72.9	73.5	73.7	.0
Previous estimates							72.4	72.5	72.8	72.9	73.2		
Mining	87.4	86.4	83.6	88.9	79.6	82.2	87.9	88.9	89.5	88.5	88.8	88.1	.3
Utilities	86.5	92.9	84.3	93.3	77.6	82.4	81.2	81.5	78.1	79.6	82.8	81.2	1.5
Stage-of-process groups													
Crude	86.4	87.8	84.2	90.0	78.3	82.6	87.0	88.2	88.6	88.3	89.4	88.6	-.5
Primary and semifinished	81.3	86.6	77.9	87.9	65.7	69.7	72.0	72.0	71.3	72.3	73.5	73.2	-.4
Finished	77.4	83.4	77.3	80.5	67.5	72.0	74.0	74.1	74.6	74.1	74.4	74.7	1.2

r Revised. p Preliminary.
Note. The statistics in this release cover output, capacity, and capacity utilization in the U.S. industrial sector, which is defined by the Federal Reserve to comprise manufacturing, mining, and electric and gas utilities. Mining is defined as all industries in sector 21 of the North American Industry Classification System (NAICS); electric and gas utilities are those in NAICS sectors 2211 and 2212. Manufacturing comprises NAICS manufacturing industries (sector 31-33) plus the logging industry and the newspaper, periodical, book, and directory publishing industries. Logging and publishing are classified elsewhere in NAICS (under agriculture and information respectively), but historically they were considered to be manufacturing and were included in the industrial sector under the Standard Industrial Classification (SIC) system. In December 2002 the Federal Reserve reclassified all its industrial output data from the SIC system to NAICS.

Figure 8-1: Industrial Production and Capacity Utilization summary.

As you can see in Figure 8-1, the report expresses industrial production in the following ways:

- **Total index:** This category shows the previous six months of industrial production data as a percentage of the base year in 2007. The values for all but the current month are revised from previous estimates. You can see the previous estimates in the second line of the data summary.

  For example, the reported industrial production for January 2011 was 95.1, meaning that total industrial production in that month was 95.1 percent of what it was in January 2007.

- **Major market groups**: This category shows the output of finished products as well as the materials and equipment necessary to manufacture products.

- **Major industry groups**: This category shows output by major industry classification, as defined by the widely used North American Industry Classification System (NAICS) industry codes. The primary NAICS classifications include durable and nondurable manufacturing, mining, and utilities. Manufacturing is by far the largest component of the three.

The Industrial Production and Capacity Utilization report expresses capacity utilization in the following ways (refer to Figure 8-1):

- **Total industry**: This category shows the high and low capacity utilization values, average capacity, and month-to-month and year-over-year changes.
- **Manufacturing, mining, and utilities**: This category shows the total industry utilization broken down into manufacturing, mining, and utilities. The layout is the same as for total industry.
- **Stage-of-process groups:** This category shows the utilization of various steps in manufacturing processes. The crude processing stage includes raw materials like lumber or mined metals. The primary and semifinished processing stage includes output from the crude processing stage. And the finished processing stage includes output from the primary and semifinished processing stage. The purpose of this particular summary is to show any steps in the manufacturing chain that may slow or constrain a later stage of production.

A complete description of the major market groups and major industry groups, including details regarding series classification, relative weights, and data sources, is available on the Fed's website at `www.federalreserve.gov/releases/g17/about.htm`. For more about the NAICS industry codes, go to `www.census.gov/naics/`.

Although the reported industrial production figures don't consider price — only output — you can use them to calculate a monthly estimate for the GDP growth rate. Your estimate won't be perfect, but it'll be close. If you figure out the annualized three-month percentage change in industrial output and multiply it by the annualized three-month percentage change in consumer inflation, the result is a very good approximation of the annualized real (inflation-adjusted) GDP growth rate.

Repositioning your portfolio

Although traders may not jump when the Industrial Production and Capacity Utilization report is released, it provides a great deal of information for thoughtful investors and business leaders. In addition to the summary shown in Figure 8-1, the Industrial Production and Capacity Utilization report shows a dozen charts and more than a dozen data tables. Investors and business leaders can find useful information in both.

The charts show the relationship between total production and total capacity over time, as well as the relationship between outputs of various industries. Periods of weak production and utilization may offer an opportunity to buy investment assets or business properties at attractive prices. Periods of strong utilization may highlight opportunities for machinery manufacturers and construction firms.

Beyond the total industrial production information, stock investors are most interested in the breakout of specific industries provided in several of the report's data tables. I discuss these tables in the following sections.

Industrial production: Market and industry group summary

Table 1 of the Industrial Production and Capacity Utilization report shows the month-to-month, quarter-to-quarter, and year-over-year production percentage changes for categories such as consumer durable and nondurable goods, business equipment, and construction supplies. This table is important to investors and business leaders because it shows them the relative performance of market and industry groups, including consumer and business durable goods, nondurable goods, and energy utilities. Figure 8-2 shows an example of Table 1.

Table 4 of the report has the same layout and covers the same categories as Table 1, but it shows the data as an index rather than a percentage change in production.

Industrial production: Special aggregates

Table 2 shows the month-to-month and year-over-year percentage change in production for selected subcategories, such as high-tech products, motor vehicles and parts, and energy products. Investors should pay close attention to the category *Selected high-technology industries*. Rising values mean that manufacturers are investing in modernization and efficiency improvements.

Table 5 covers the same categories as Table 2, but it shows the data as an index rather than a percentage change in production.

Motor vehicle assemblies

Table 3 shows the total output for autos and trucks. The investment community pays close attention to auto manufacturing because it still represents a significant portion of total U.S. manufacturing capacity and represents about 4 percent of total U.S. GDP.

Table 1
INDUSTRIAL PRODUCTION: MARKET AND INDUSTRY GROUP SUMMARY
Percent change, seasonally adjusted

Item	NAICS	2010 proportion[1]	Fourth quarter to fourth quarter 2008	2009	2010	Annual rate 2010 Q2	Q3[r]	Q4[r]	Monthly rate 2010 Aug.[r]	Dec.[r]	2011 Jan.[p]	Jan. '10 to Jan. '11
Total IP		100.00	-7.6	-3.8	5.9	7.2	6.2	3.2	.1	1.2	-.1	5.2
MARKET GROUPS												
Final products and nonindustrial supplies		55.09	-7.2	-4.2	5.0	6.9	5.7	1.5	-.1	.9	.2	4.3
Consumer goods		28.48	-6.1	-.9	3.0	1.3	7.3	-1.1	-.3	1.0	.1	2.2
Durable		6.09	-18.3	-2.1	5.4	10.9	13.4	-8.0	-3.4	-.2	1.4	4.3
Automotive products		2.99	-24.1	6.0	6.2	4.8	27.3	-16.8	-5.8	-.3	3.0	2.9
Home electronics		.29	-3.4	2.4	-2.3	10.0	28.6	1.1	1.8	-.4	-.8	5.9
Appliances, furniture, carpeting		.89	-18.8	-10.5	1.8	13.5	-8.5	.4	-1.8	-1.9	-1.0	1.1
Miscellaneous goods		1.92	-11.1	-9.9	7.3	20.3	2.2	2.0	-1.0	.9	.6	7.8
Nondurable		22.39	-2.0	-.5	2.4	-1.2	5.7	.9	.6	1.4	-.3	1.6
Non-energy		17.45	-3.0	-.4	1.9	2.1	.9	2.8	.9	.2	.2	1.3
Foods and tobacco		9.47	-3.6	.5	5.0	8.3	5.0	1.8	1.2	.2	-.2	3.5
Clothing		.26	-6.1	-13.6	8.4	.3	-5.4	11.9	2.4	2.2	1.3	4.4
Chemical products		5.51	-1.7	.1	-1.3	-6.2	-2.7	4.3	.8	.4	.9	-1.1
Paper products		1.67	-5.2	-5.2	-4.1	-2.8	-6.6	2.0	-.4	-.4	.7	-2.3
Energy		4.94	1.6	-.9	3.9	-12.3	24.2	-5.1	-.7	5.4	-2.0	2.6
Business equipment		9.64	-8.3	-6.4	11.7	18.7	9.3	9.9	.3	1.0	.9	11.4
Transit		1.72	-27.1	11.1	3.3	3.9	23.1	-.1	1.2	.2	1.2	6.3
Information processing		2.90	.7	-.9	13.6	21.9	11.2	9.1	-.3	.8	.6	12.8
Industrial and other		5.02	-6.4	-14.3	13.6	22.3	3.9	14.1	.3	1.5	1.0	12.4
Defense and space equipment		2.13	-1.9	1.8	3.1	6.5	3.0	-2.6	.2	-.3	1.2	3.7
Construction supplies		4.39	-14.2	-11.8	7.8	25.2	-2.1	5.2	.3	.0	-.2	7.2
Business supplies		9.86	-7.6	-6.0	1.8	3.3	2.4	-.3	-.2	.8	-.3	1.4
Materials		44.91	-8.2	-3.2	7.1	7.5	6.8	5.3	.4	1.5	-.4	6.2
Non-energy		27.22	-12.6	-4.8	8.2	10.3	4.9	7.1	.1	1.7	.1	7.4
Durable		16.13	-12.1	-9.1	10.8	17.1	5.0	7.0	-.4	1.4	.5	9.6
Consumer parts		2.24	-23.6	-7.7	10.0	19.9	12.0	.9	-4.8	-.2	.7	9.5
Equipment parts		5.94	-5.7	-8.1	12.0	14.6	6.7	9.7	.7	1.7	.7	11.2
Other		7.95	-13.1	-10.4	10.2	18.4	1.9	6.8	.1	1.7	.2	8.4
Nondurable		11.09	-13.5	2.1	4.5	.9	4.8	7.2	.7	2.1	-.6	4.3
Textile		.43	-16.4	-2.2	7.4	13.0	12.0	.0	-.7	2.2	-.6	8.0
Paper		2.08	-11.3	-5.6	.2	4.8	-2.7	-2.6	-1.3	1.0	-.3	.7
Chemical		5.35	-18.0	9.5	6.8	-1.0	7.6	13.9	.3	3.2	-.9	6.4
Energy		17.69	-.6	-.9	5.4	3.3	9.8	2.6	.9	1.2	-1.0	4.5
INDUSTRY GROUPS												
Manufacturing		74.58	-10.0	-4.1	6.0	9.4	4.3	4.0	.0	.9	.3	5.5
Manufacturing (NAICS)	**31–33**	71.24	-10.0	-3.7	6.5	9.9	4.7	4.4	.0	.9	.3	6.0
Durable manufacturing		37.50	-11.3	-6.3	8.9	15.4	6.5	4.7	-.5	.8	.6	8.2
Wood products	321	.93	-20.9	-10.7	1.2	21.3	-18.2	3.8	-.8	.2	-1.3	-1.6
Nonmetallic mineral products	327	1.73	-15.9	-11.8	5.0	22.2	4.1	-2.3	.0	-3.3	-1.0	.7
Primary metal	331	2.50	-23.2	-3.1	11.7	18.7	-18.3	20.1	-.7	4.7	-.9	9.3
Fabricated metal products	332	5.79	-7.1	-11.7	11.7	18.1	15.7	6.5	1.2	.8	.3	11.7
Machinery	333	4.91	-8.2	-19.1	18.1	28.8	6.4	17.5	.0	2.0	1.3	16.5
Computer and electronic products	334	7.04	-2.6	1.7	12.7	19.9	8.9	7.8	.2	1.5	.9	13.0
Electrical equip., appliances, and components	335	1.93	-5.6	-10.4	8.8	12.9	.6	10.7	1.2	-.9	-1.0	4.5
Motor vehicles and parts	3361–3	4.00	-27.5	1.4	8.2	9.2	29.7	-14.8	-6.1	.2	3.2	5.3
Aerospace and miscellaneous transportation equipment	3364–9	4.19	-13.2	2.6	-1.2	-1.8	4.6	-2.9	.9	-.5	.7	.3
Furniture and related products	337	1.19	-16.3	-15.2	3.9	16.1	-1.0	2.7	-.9	.2	.4	6.8
Miscellaneous	339	3.31	-.2	-2.9	2.4	8.0	-.1	4.1	-.7	.2	.2	3.0
Nondurable manufacturing		33.73	-8.5	-.6	3.9	4.0	2.7	4.0	.6	1.0	-.1	3.5
Food, beverage, and tobacco products	311,2	11.25	-3.3	.0	5.0	6.4	6.2	2.2	1.7	.2	-.3	3.4
Textile and product mills	313,4	.73	-15.1	-5.5	3.3	6.4	5.1	-2.2	-1.5	1.1	-.4	2.6
Apparel and leather	315,6	.32	-14.9	-13.9	8.1	-3.3	-1.7	14.4	2.1	2.5	1.2	4.6
Paper	322	2.46	-13.2	-.3	1.6	3.0	-2.1	-.9	-.9	1.2	.1	2.3
Printing and support	323	1.60	-9.2	-14.0	-3.2	6.3	-3.4	-7.7	1.0	-.7	-.8	-3.9
Petroleum and coal products	324	2.51	-4.4	-1.5	5.3	26.8	5.4	-1.1	-1.2	.2	-1.0	10.9
Chemical	325	12.15	-10.4	3.9	2.9	-4.7	1.4	9.8	.5	2.0	.1	2.6
Plastics and rubber products	326	2.72	-15.0	-8.8	8.5	17.0	.3	4.2	-.2	1.4	.6	7.7
Other manufacturing (non-NAICS)	**1133,5111**	3.34	-9.1	-11.3	-5.1	-.2	-5.6	-4.1	-.5	.1	.3	-3.2
Mining	**21**	14.02	-.3	-4.5	8.9	11.0	10.7	6.4	1.9	.5	-.7	7.5
Utilities	**2211,2**	11.40	-.3	-1.4	2.0	-9.7	14.0	-6.0	-1.2	4.1	-1.6	.1
Electric	2211	9.84	-1.4	-1.7	1.7	-6.2	10.6	-9.4	-1.7	4.7	-1.6	-.4
Natural gas	2212	1.56	4.9	.6	4.0	-29.1	38.4	18.8	1.9	.9	-1.4	3.4

r Revised. p Preliminary.

Figure 8-2: Table 1 shows the percentage changes for different industry categories.

Table 7
CAPACITY UTILIZATION
Percent of capacity, seasonally adjusted

Item		2010 proportion	1972-2010 ave.	1994-95 high	2008-09 low	2010 Q2	Q3[r]	Q4[r]	2010 Aug.[r]	Dec.[r]	2011 Jan.[p]
Total industry		100.00	80.5	85.1	68.2	73.9	75.0	75.6	75.0	76.2	76.1
Manufacturing[1]		77.79	79.1	84.6	65.4	71.6	72.4	73.0	72.3	73.5	73.7
Manufacturing (NAICS)	31–33	74.10	78.9	84.8	65.2	71.8	72.6	73.4	72.6	73.9	74.0
Durable manufacturing		40.68	77.2	83.7	61.0	69.4	70.4	71.0	70.2	71.5	71.9
Wood products	321	1.14	78.1	87.2	53.4	62.9	60.8	62.5	60.8	63.0	62.4
Nonmetallic mineral products	327	2.30	76.5	82.6	52.0	56.7	57.5	57.4	57.6	56.2	55.8
Primary metal	331	2.70	79.4	94.1	46.8	70.2	66.4	69.0	65.8	72.2	71.5
Fabricated metal products	332	5.84	77.3	85.7	65.1	72.6	75.6	77.1	75.8	77.9	78.2
Machinery	333	5.09	78.1	87.2	61.1	71.5	73.0	76.2	72.9	77.7	78.8
Computer and electronic products	334	7.49	78.1	84.7	68.0	73.6	73.7	73.7	73.7	74.2	74.6
Electrical equip., appliances, and components	335	1.87	82.8	93.0	70.4	76.9	77.1	79.1	77.6	78.9	78.1
Motor vehicles and parts	3361–3	5.03	75.4	87.6	35.8	59.4	63.6	61.3	62.1	60.4	62.1
Aerospace and miscellaneous transportation equipment	3364–9	4.40	72.9	68.8	66.3	70.8	71.2	70.3	71.5	69.8	70.3
Furniture and related products	337	1.28	77.8	82.6	64.6	69.7	70.3	71.6	70.1	72.3	72.6
Miscellaneous	339	3.55	76.0	80.7	68.4	70.2	69.6	69.6	69.4	69.7	69.9
Nondurable manufacturing		33.42	81.1	86.1	70.1	74.7	75.3	76.2	75.4	76.8	76.6
Food, beverage, and tobacco products	311,2	10.65	81.3	85.8	73.6	78.0	79.0	79.3	79.5	78.9	78.4
Textile and product mills	313,4	.81	80.7	92.5	57.3	66.8	68.4	68.7	68.1	69.4	69.0
Apparel and leather	315,6	.31	78.6	87.3	65.8	75.5	76.7	80.9	77.5	83.0	83.9
Paper	322	2.36	87.0	92.6	69.7	78.0	78.0	78.2	77.7	79.2	79.2
Printing and support	323	1.87	82.3	85.7	63.4	65.0	64.9	64.1	65.5	63.9	63.3
Petroleum and coal products	324	2.25	86.0	91.0	74.8	84.5	86.0	86.1	85.8	86.7	85.8
Chemical	325	12.05	78.0	81.9	67.5	73.8	74.3	76.2	74.1	77.6	77.6
Plastics and rubber products	326	3.12	82.1	92.7	57.3	65.9	65.9	66.5	66.0	67.2	67.7
Other manufacturing (non-NAICS)	1133,5111	3.69	83.4	83.2	68.0	68.4	67.4	66.5	67.7	66.7	66.9
Mining	21	11.79	87.4	88.9	79.6	85.5	87.7	88.9	87.9	88.8	88.1
Utilities	2211,2	10.41	86.5	93.3	77.6	79.2	81.6	80.2	81.2	82.8	81.2
Selected high-technology industries		4.09	78.1	86.8	67.0	73.9	73.2	73.0	73.2	73.8	74.5
Computers and peripheral equipment	3341	.85	78.0	87.0	67.7	77.4	79.6	78.2	79.6	77.8	78.0
Communications equipment	3342	.95	76.5	83.6	73.4	81.5	79.7	81.7	78.9	82.1	81.8
Semiconductors and related electronic components	334412–9	2.29	80.2	92.4	61.8	69.9	68.7	68.3	69.0	69.7	71.0
Measures excluding selected high-technology industries											
Total industry		95.91	80.6	85.0	68.1	73.8	75.1	75.6	75.0	76.3	76.1
Manufacturing[1]		73.70	79.1	84.5	65.2	71.4	72.3	73.0	72.2	73.4	73.6
STAGE-OF-PROCESS GROUPS											
Crude		15.45	86.4	90.0	78.3	84.9	87.0	88.8	87.0	89.4	88.6
Primary and semifinished		45.46	81.3	87.9	65.7	71.2	72.1	72.4	72.0	73.5	73.2
Finished		39.09	77.4	80.5	67.5	73.1	74.0	74.4	74.0	74.4	74.7

r Revised. p Preliminary.
1. Refer to note on cover page.

Figure 8-3: Table 7 shows the percentage change in capacity utilization for different manufacturing sectors.

Capacity utilization

Table 7 shows the month-to-month and year-over-year percentage change in capacity utilization for manufacturers of durable and nondurable goods, mining utilities, and high-tech industries. The table includes average capacity utilization, as well as high- and low-utilization periods. You can use this table, which is shown in Figure 8-3, to help pinpoint when industries are approaching full capacity and will soon need to expand production facilities.

Reviewing Regional Fed Reports

In addition to the reports generated by the Fed's Board of Governors and the FOMC, the regional Federal Reserve banks also conduct surveys, analyze economic sectors, and publish a remarkable quantity of reports. Each of the regional Federal Reserve banks specializes in a different part of the economy, based at least in part on the distribution of industries throughout the country. For investors, these areas of specialization provide useful insight into the state of individual business sectors. This section briefly reviews a couple of the most prominent regional Federal Reserve bank reports.

Surveying business outlook

Each month the Federal Reserve Bank of Philadelphia publishes the *Business Outlook Survey,* which looks at manufacturing throughout the Philadelphia Federal Reserve District. To generate this report, the Fed asks manufacturing companies in the district about employment, working hours, new orders, shipments, and inventories. Table 8-4 offers a quick glance at this report.

Table 8-4 Business Outlook Survey

Release Schedule	*Agency*	*Web Address*	*Sensitivity*
Monthly: Third Thursday of the month,12:00 p.m. ET	Federal Reserve Bank of Philadelphia	`www.phil.frb.org/research-and-data/regional-economy/business-outlook-survey/`	Moderate

First published in 1968, this survey was the first manufacturing survey conducted by any of the regional Federal Reserve banks. Investors and business leaders widely follow this report, which is issued during the same month that the survey is taken, making it very timely. A strong correlation exists between the Business Outlook Survey and the well-known and widely followed Manufacturing ISM Report On Business® (see Chapter 10 for details).

Although the Business Outlook Survey surveys only manufacturers within the Fed's Philadelphia district, it turns out to be a good indicator for the nation as a whole. The Philadelphia district covers a very populous section of the country and has a broad variety of manufacturers.

The survey report is only two pages long. It includes a summary of the manufacturing climate and a table showing the survey's responses. Figure 8-4 shows an example of the questionnaire response table.

BUSINESS OUTLOOK SURVEY February 2011	February vs. January					Six Months from Now vs. February				
	Previous Diffusion Index	Increase	No Change	Decrease	Diffusion Index	Previous Diffusion Index	Increase	No Change	Decrease	Diffusion Index
What is your evaluation of the level of general business activity?	19.3	45.5	41.6	9.6	35.9	49.8	55.8	30.9	9.0	46.8
Company Business Indicators										
New Orders	23.6	42.4	36.3	18.7	23.7	43.3	48.8	37.7	6.7	42.1
Shipments	13.4	44.3	46.5	9.1	35.2	42.7	56.7	29.4	5.5	51.2
Unfilled Orders	8.7	23.5	66.4	8.5	14.9	11.8	29.4	55.9	7.2	22.2
Delivery Times	2.3	13.0	80.6	3.0	10.0	13.5	12.4	72.2	7.8	4.7
Inventories	6.8	24.8	51.1	22.7	2.1	13.9	25.1	51.3	15.7	9.4
Prices Paid	54.3	67.2	32.8	0.0	67.2	66.4	74.7	15.2	1.6	73.1
Prices Received	17.1	28.5	60.7	7.6	21.0	38.2	45.0	43.7	4.9	40.1
Number of Employees	17.6	29.0	64.5	5.4	23.6	31.0	32.4	54.6	8.0	24.4
Average Employee Workweek	10.6	23.3	62.1	10.4	12.8	22.9	24.2	53.1	10.3	13.9
Capital Expenditures	--	--	--	--	--	29.0	24.4	61.7	8.2	16.2

NOTES:
(1) Items may not add up to 100 percent because of omission by respondents.
(2) All data are seasonally adjusted.
(3) Diffusion indexes represent the percentage indicating an increase minus the percentage indicating a decrease.
(4) Survey results reflect data received through February 14, 2011.

Figure 8-4: The questionnaire response table from the Business Outlook Survey.

The questionnaire response table shows whether manufacturers expect an increase, decrease, or no change for each of the survey questions. The Fed then uses the responses to compile a diffusion index for each of the questions by subtracting the number of negative responses from the positive responses. A positive number indicates that more manufacturers expect improvement in their businesses. A negative number indicates the reverse. You can see the diffusion indexes in Figure 8-4. Focus on the diffusion index for general business activity (in the first line of the table) because it offers a timely peek into the state of the economy as a whole.

The Philadelphia Fed shows off its social media credibility by posting a video summary of the Business Outlook Survey to YouTube. The video is short and to the point. You can find it at the website listed in Table 8-4.

Don't be surprised if you see the results of the Business Outlook Survey show up in the FOMC's Beige Book. The Philadelphia Fed relies on this survey for a portion of its Beige Book submission.

Indexing national activity

Each month the Federal Reserve Bank of Chicago publishes the *National Activity Index.* The index combines the information from 85 existing monthly indicators (including production and income data, employment and unemployment statistics, personal consumption information, and housing reports) into a single value. The goal of the report is to gauge overall U.S. economic activity. Use the information in Table 8-5 to follow the National Activity Index.

Table 8-5 National Activity Index

Release Schedule	*Agency*	*Web Address*	*Sensitivity*
Monthly: Published schedule, 8:30 a.m. ET	Federal Reserve Bank of Chicago	www.chicagofed.org/webpages/publications/cfnai/index.cfm	Low

The index is designed to have an average value of zero. When the index is at zero, the national economy is expanding at its long-term average rate of growth. A positive number indicates above-average growth, and a negative number indicates below-average growth.

The indicator is also published as a three-month moving average (see Chapter 2 for the skinny on moving averages). A three-month moving average below –0.7 indicates an economic contraction. A moving average above –0.7 indicates that a recession has likely ended.

Figure 8-5 shows a chart of the three-month moving average for the National Activity Index from 1997 through 2010.

The National Activity Index isn't a leading indicator. At best, it coincides with the current economic environment, so its predictive ability is low. However, it has a good track record of identifying the beginning and ending of recessions, and you can use it to confirm the results seen in other economic indicators.

Surfing the net regional bank style

Each of the regional Federal Reserve banks maintains its own website, on which it posts a wealth of interesting economic information. Check out these sites for details:

- **District 1 — Boston:** www.bos.frb.org/
- **District 2 — New York:** www.newyorkfed.org/
- **District 3 — Philadelphia:** www.philadelphiafed.org/
- **District 4 — Cleveland:** www.clevelandfed.org/
- **District 5 — Richmond:** www.richmondfed.org/
- **District 6 — Atlanta:** www.frbatlanta.org/
- **District 7 — Chicago:** www.chicagofed.org/

- **District 8 — St. Louis:** www.stlouisfed.org/
- **District 9 — Minneapolis:** www.minneapolisfed.org/
- **District 10 — Kansas City:** www.kansascityfed.org/
- **District 11 — Dallas:** www.dallasfed.org/
- **District 12 — San Francisco:** www.frbsf.org/

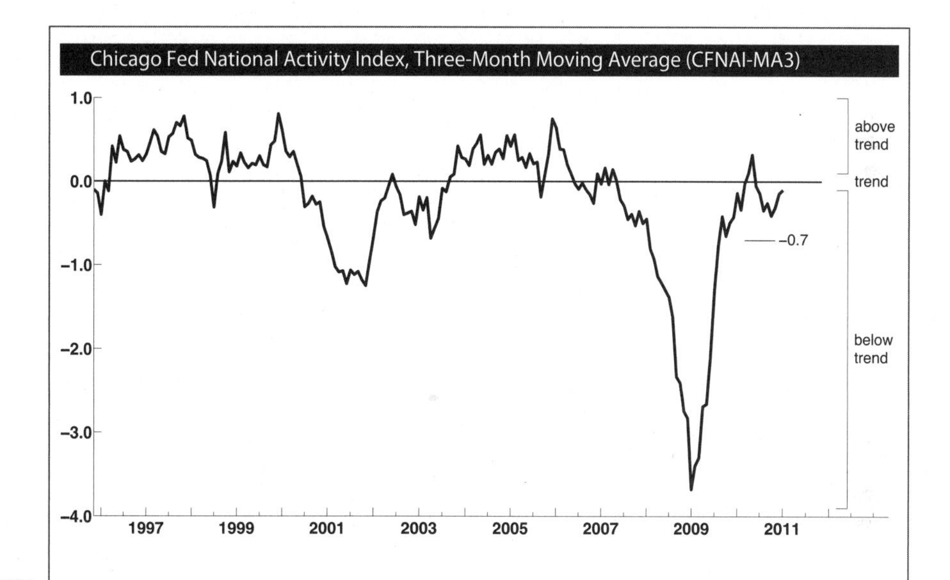

CFNAI and CFNAI-MA3 for the latest six months and year-ago month

	Jan '11	Dec '10	Nov '10	Oct '10	Sep '10	Aug '10	Jan '10
CFNAI							
Current	−0.16	+0.18	−0.33	−0.29	−0.32	−0.62	+0.05
Previous	N/A	+0.03	−0.40	−0.30	−0.37	−0.49	+0.14
CFNAI-MA3							
Current	−0.10	−0.14	−0.31	−0.41	−0.26	−0.35	−0.14
Previous	N/A	−0.22	−0.36	−0.39	−0.23	−0.29	−0.08

Current and Previous values reflect index values as of the February 24, 2011, release and January 27, 2011, release, respectively. N/A indicates not applicable.

Figure 8-5: The National Activity Index from the Federal Reserve Bank of Chicago.

Chapter 9

Profiling Manufacturing: New Orders and Shipments

In This Chapter

- Keeping track of orders for durable goods
- Reviewing factory orders, back orders, and shipments
- Understanding why inventories matter

U.S. manufacturers are very sensitive to changes in the economy, more so than any other economic sector. In fact, even small changes in consumer and business purchasing behavior have a huge impact on manufacturers. One easy way to track this purchasing behavior is to watch the flow of new orders to manufacturers and their product shipments.

If you've ever thought that economic forecasting would be a whole lot easier if you could actually see into the future, you're going to like the indicators I discuss in this chapter. While most economic indicators report what has already happened, this chapter showcases a few economic indicators that turn this model upside down by foretelling what is about to happen. They monitor the manufacturing sectors and provide economic insight that you simply can't find anywhere else.

Filling Orders for Durable Goods: The Advance Report on Durable Goods

To tell the economy's future, you need a great fortuneteller. The *Advance Report on Durable Goods,* short for the *Advance Report on Durable Goods Manufacturers' Shipments, Inventories, and Orders,* is the best substitute for a crystal ball that anyone could ask for.

The Advance Report on Durable Goods actually can tell the future. After all, companies report actual sales orders they've received for products that they'll soon have to manufacture. As a business leader or investor, you won't find a better manufacturing forecast than seeing actual sales orders in hand.

Note: As the name implies, the Advance Report on Durable Goods precedes a second report called the *Full Report on Manufacturers' Shipments, Inventories, and Orders*. The full report, which is commonly called the *Factory Orders report,* includes more extensive information about durable goods manufacturing and introduces information about nondurable product manufacturers as well. I discuss the Factory Orders report more fully in the section "Monitoring Factory Orders and Sales: The Factory Orders Report."

Table 9-1 provides what you need to know to follow the Advance Report on Durable Goods. For a copy of the release schedule, go to the website listed in the table and click on the link for Release Schedule, which is located in the right-hand column near the bottom of the page.

Table 9-1 Advance Report on Durable Goods

Release Schedule	*Agency*	*Web Address*	*Sensitivity*
Monthly: Published schedule, 8:30 a.m. ET	U.S. Census Bureau, Department of Commerce	`www.census.gov/manufacturing/m3/`	High

The following sections outline how the advance report is generated, why the information in it is important, and how you can use it in your investment portfolio.

Knowing where the data come from

Both the Advance Report on Durable Goods and the full Factory Orders report are based on the same Census Bureau survey. But the advance report generates most of the attention because the data collected for it are fresh and the report itself is timely. Both reports cover the calendar month just completed. The advance report covers orders and shipments of durable goods and is released four weeks or so after the end of each month. The more thorough full report also covers nondurable goods and is released a week later.

Looking for historical info

The Census Bureau provides historical data series for both the Advance Report on Durable Goods and the full Factory Orders report. It also offers directions on how to decipher the data files. Here's where to go for the data series and the directions for reading them:

- **Historical data series:** www.census.gov/manufacturing/m3/historical_data/index.html
- **Directions for reading historic data series:** www.census.gov/manufacturing/m3/historical_data/naicshist.pdf

Although the Census Bureau takes pains to clarify that it doesn't take the survey it uses to generate the advance and full reports from a statistically random sample and that the survey may not accurately represent the entire U.S. manufacturing base, the reports have nonetheless proved their value. They're exceptionally good forecasting tools.

The advance report and the full report show three months of new order and total shipment data, along with corresponding month-to-month percentage changes. They also provide seasonal adjustments alongside the unadjusted data. The current month's data may be revised both in the full report and in subsequent issues of the advance report. No adjustments are made for inflation, and the data are not annualized. (See Chapter 2 for a refresher on inflation indexing and annualizing data.)

Tracking new factory orders: Why these stats are important

Although the full Factory Orders report is more thorough, the Advanced Report on Durable Goods creates the biggest investment market fireworks because business leaders and investors are interested in the early data, particularly the new order durable goods statistics, provided in the advance report. This focus on new order durable goods stats makes sense because new orders drive production. Without customer orders, durable goods manufacturers have little reason to keep their factories turned on.

In case you're wondering, *durable goods* are products that are intended to last three years or longer. Consumer durable goods include things like trucks, automobiles, household appliances, television sets, personal computers, and furniture. Business durable goods include computer systems, communication gear, farming machinery, factory machine tools, and transportation equipment, like heavy-duty trucks, ships, and airplanes. The U.S. Government also buys durable goods from U.S. manufacturers; government durable goods include office equipment and specialized equipment for the military, like submarines, tanks, and fighter jets.

Nondurable goods, on the other hand, are things you use or consume regularly. Consumer nondurables are sometimes called *consumer staples* and include food, beverages, pharmaceuticals, clothing, soap, laundry detergent, and other household products. In the business world, office supplies like paper, pens, and paper clips are nondurables, as are manufacturing supplies like lubricants, paperboard containers, pesticides, fertilizers, and most petrochemical products.

New orders for manufactured goods, especially durable goods, offer an excellent forecast for future manufacturing activity, which, in turn, offers a general forecast of where the economy is heading. Companies buy durable goods only when they're confident that their businesses can justify the expense based on their prospects for future growth. That's why the new order stats in the Advance Report on Durable Goods are so compelling to investors and business leaders. An increase in the value of new orders is usually a sign that businesses and consumers are feeling more confident about the economy. Conversely, a decrease in the value of new orders is often a sign that the economy is heading for a slowdown.

Now, I'm not saying that nondurable goods are unimportant. They're actually quite important. In fact, nondurable goods represent about half of the U.S. manufacturing output. However, the purchase and production of durable goods are much more sensitive to the economic climate (and, thus, are much better economic indicators). Consumers need to regularly buy nondurable products like food, medicine, and clothing, regardless of the current business cycle. Although they may substitute less-expensive nondurables during times of economic stress, consumers can completely forgo durable goods purchases whenever they're anxious about the economy.

Figuring out what the data mean

The Advance Report on Durable Goods provides valuable information that you can use as an investor. However, you can't take full advantage of the report if you don't have a firm understanding of what the different categories in the report mean. This section explains the different sections of the report.

Figure 9-1 shows an excerpt from the advance report. Specifically, the excerpt shows Table 1 of the report, which provides the new order and total shipment data.

Table 1. Durable Goods Manufacturers' Shipments and New Orders [1]

[Estimates are shown in millions of dollars and are based on data from the Manufacturers' Shipments, Inventories, and Orders Survey.]

Item	Seasonally Adjusted						Not Seasonally Adjusted		
	Monthly			Percent Change			Year to Date		
	Jan 2011 [2]	Dec 2010 [r]	Nov 2010	Dec - Jan [2]	Nov - Dec [r]	Oct - Nov	2011	2010	Change 11/10
DURABLE GOODS									
Total:									
Shipments	202,873	202,243	197,633	0.3	2.3	0.5	182,369	172,452	5.8
New Orders [4]	200,547	195,206	196,053	2.7	-0.4	-0.1	184,947	170,890	8.2
Excluding transportation:									
Shipments	154,700	153,974	150,907	0.5	2.0	1.6	140,400	128,088	9.6
New Orders [4]	150,092	155,678	151,196	-3.6	3.0	4.6	139,037	123,803	12.3
Excluding defense:									
Shipments	192,212	190,980	186,268	0.6	2.5	0.5	173,732	160,466	8.3
New Orders [4]	187,452	183,908	184,347	1.9	-0.2	-1.0	171,713	156,353	9.8
Manufacturing with unfilled orders:									
Shipments	148,177	148,537	144,541	-0.2	2.8	1.1	131,881	122,838	7.4
New Orders	152,526	147,223	148,860	3.6	-1.1	0.2	142,601	129,311	10.3
Primary metals:									
Shipments	22,960	22,068	21,020	4.0	5.0	4.6	21,535	17,124	25.8
New Orders	23,172	22,915	23,162	1.1	-1.1	13.9	22,928	18,412	24.5
Fabricated metal products:									
Shipments	28,049	28,007	27,577	0.1	1.6	1.1	25,161	23,580	6.7
New Orders	28,144	27,934	27,770	0.8	0.6	3.0	25,788	23,930	7.8
Machinery:									
Shipments	25,746	27,325	25,418	-5.8	7.5	2.6	23,430	20,194	16.0
New Orders	27,752	31,911	27,362	-13.0	16.6	0.4	27,317	21,347	28.0
Computers and electronic products [4]:									
Shipments	33,853	33,176	33,817	2.0	-1.9	0.2	31,480	30,808	2.2
New Orders	26,760	28,706	28,616	-6.8	0.3	6.7	23,202	22,424	3.5
Computers and related products:									
Shipments	6,042	6,175	6,461	-2.2	-4.4	-0.1	5,238	4,899	6.9
New Orders	5,521	6,109	6,783	-9.6	-9.9	7.3	4,717	4,393	7.4
Communications equipment:									
Shipments	3,210	3,400	3,492	-5.6	-2.6	4.7	2,438	2,859	-14.7
New Orders	3,414	3,988	3,555	-14.4	12.2	13.3	2,799	3,016	-7.2
Electrical equipment, appliances, and components:									
Shipments	10,150	10,033	9,857	1.2	1.8	1.7	8,950	7,945	12.6
New Orders	10,298	10,829	10,760	-4.9	0.6	8.7	9,915	8,912	11.3
Transportation equipment:									
Shipments	48,173	48,269	46,726	-0.2	3.3	-2.8	41,969	44,364	-5.4
New Orders	50,455	39,528	44,857	27.6	-11.9	-13.3	45,910	47,087	-2.5
Motor vehicles and parts:									
Shipments	30,720	30,306	29,447	1.4	2.9	-2.1	28,494	28,595	-0.4
New Orders	30,517	30,384	29,611	0.4	2.6	-2.4	28,466	28,747	-1.0
Nondefense aircraft and parts:									
Shipments	7,056	7,506	6,659	-6.0	12.7	-7.3	5,194	4,950	4.9
New Orders	7,400	148	5,019	4,900.0	-97.1	-59.6	4,981	4,904	1.6
Defense aircraft and parts:									
Shipments	4,517	4,687	4,870	-3.6	-3.8	1.5	3,483	4,776	-27.1
New Orders	5,408	4,486	5,043	20.6	-11.0	6.4	5,548	6,598	-15.9
All other durable goods:									
Shipments	33,942	33,365	33,218	1.7	0.4	0.8	29,844	28,437	4.9
New Orders	33,966	33,383	33,526	1.7	-0.4	0.9	29,887	28,778	3.9
Capital goods [3]:									
Shipments	73,894	76,552	74,018	-3.5	3.4	0.2	64,561	62,119	3.9
New Orders	77,233	71,714	74,365	7.7	-3.6	-5.8	70,892	64,476	10.0
Nondefense capital goods:									
Shipments	65,655	67,589	65,280	-2.9	3.5	0.5	57,787	52,266	10.6
New Orders	66,318	63,411	65,647	4.6	-3.4	-7.9	59,770	53,169	12.4
Excluding aircraft:									
Shipments	61,829	63,113	61,576	-2.0	2.5	1.5	55,505	49,736	11.6
New Orders	62,323	66,967	64,221	-6.9	4.3	3.3	58,184	50,639	14.9
Defense capital goods:									
Shipments	8,239	8,963	8,738	-8.1	2.6	-1.5	6,774	9,853	-31.2
New Orders	10,915	8,303	8,718	31.5	-4.8	14.2	11,122	11,307	-1.6

Figure 9-1: Table 1 of the Advance Report on Durable Goods.

As you can see in the figure, Table 1 subdivides manufacturers into broad categories like electrical equipment manufacturers, transportation equipment manufacturers, and machinery manufacturers. Each of these broad categories shows both new orders and shipments for the current month and the two previous months. Here's what these two terms mean:

- **New orders:** For the current month, the new order data includes all orders received during the month minus any cancellations. When the order is scheduled to ship doesn't matter; it could ship in the current month or any future month.
- **Shipments:** The shipment data is the total value of all completed sales of durable goods during the reporting month. Generally, companies report actual product shipments to customers or distributors. However, in the case of some very large products, like aircraft or military equipment, the report is based on manufacturer-provided estimates of the completed work instead.

Most of the categories shown in Figure 9-1 are self-explanatory. However, several of them may require a little clarification:

- **Total new orders:** The headline number for this report is the total value of all durable goods orders received during the month minus any order cancellations. (It doesn't include the capital goods categories, which I discuss later in this list.)

  Because month-to-month percentage changes can be very large, figuring out the underlying trend may be a little difficult. Check out the next section for several ways to deal with this volatility.
- **Total new orders excluding transportation:** Although all durable goods components exhibit some volatility, the transportation sector exhibits very large swings in the value of new orders. This instability isn't surprising. After all, commercial airlines don't order new airplanes every day. When an airline enters an order for jumbo jets, you see a very obvious change in the total value of new orders. So to give you a more stable picture of new order totals, this category on the report subtracts civilian transportation equipment (and nondefense government transportation equipment) from the total new orders.
- **Total new orders excluding defense:** Government defense equipment also causes some pretty big swings in the value of new orders. The Pentagon doesn't order new submarines or fighter jets every day. When it does, you see large spikes in the total value of new orders. This category on the report removes these spikes from the total new orders calculation.

- **Capital goods:** The capital goods category, which you see near the bottom of Figure 9-1, shows data that have been recategorized from other sections of the report. The total value of new orders that you see at the top of the table in Figure 9-1 doesn't include the data shown in this category. If it did, the data would be counted twice.

  In case you're curious, *capital goods* are those goods that businesses use to manufacture other products or services. Examples include factory machine tools, mining and oil drilling equipment, power distribution equipment, and transportation gear, such as automobiles, airplanes, and railroad equipment.

- **Nondefense capital goods:** This subcategory of capital goods is also called *core capital goods*. It removes all defense production from its data. Nondefense capital goods data are an excellent business-spending indicator. Historically, this indicator begins to slip months before the economy shows signs of slowing.

Table 2 from the advance report follows the same format as shown in Figure 9-1, but it lists order backlogs and inventories. Here's what these two terms mean:

- **Unfilled orders:** Also known as the *order backlog*, unfilled orders consist of all orders that the manufacturers haven't been able to produce yet. When factories are so busy that they can't produce enough to meet all the orders they've received, look for future economic growth. Large backlogs lead to job growth and eventually to companies' increasing production capacity. However, delivery delays for manufacturing components cause production bottlenecks at other manufacturing facilities. Delays can also lead to price increases and eventually to inflation.

- **Total inventories:** Finished goods inventories grow when manufacturing facilities produce more product than what they sell. Growth in total inventories often precedes an economic contraction.

Correlating manufacturing and future growth

The new orders section of the Advance Report on Durable Goods offers an exceptionally good look into the economic future. Even better, its forecasting ability isn't limited to durable goods manufacturers alone; it also does an admirable job of forecasting the economy as a whole.

Calculating total new orders minus defense and transportation

The Advance Report on Durable Goods contains all the data you need to calculate the total value of new orders without defense and transportation spending, but you have to perform the calculations yourself. Use Table 1 of the advance report and follow these steps to calculate this new statistic:

1. **Subtract the *excluding defense new orders* value from the *total new orders* value to figure out how much was spent on total defense.**

   Total new orders – Excluding defense new orders = Total new orders for defense (TD)

2. **Subtract the *excluding transportation new orders* value from the *total new orders* value to figure out how much was spent on total transportation.**

   Total new orders – Excluding transportation new orders = Total new orders for transportation (TT)

3. **Subtract the *total new orders for defense* (TD) and *total new orders for transportation* (TT) from the *total new orders* to calculate the value for new orders of *core durable goods* — that is, all durable goods except defense and transportation.**

   Total new orders – (TD) – (TT) = Total value of new orders for core durable goods

Keep a running total of this statistic to help you monitor the core new order values without the volatile defense and transportation sectors.

Unfortunately, the month-to-month changes in the new orders statistics are often volatile. Due to the limited number of orders and huge costs associated with some large durable goods, like aircraft orders and defense equipment, the total new orders value can change dramatically from one month to the next. This section offers several techniques for dealing with this volatility and for figuring out the underlying trend of the new orders value.

Figure 9-2 shows just how volatile new order statistics can be. The spiky up and down lines on this chart represent the month-to-month percentage changes of the total value of new orders. Readings above the centerline mean that the value of new orders increased from the previous month. Readings below the centerline mean that the value of orders decreased.

Obviously, you need to smooth out this data to see whether new orders are actually trending higher or lower. You can use several techniques to do so:

- **Use a moving average.** You can remove some of the month-to-month volatility by using a moving average (see Chapter 2 for a refresher on how to construct a moving average). A three- or six-month moving average allows you to more easily see which way the value of new orders is trending. Figure 9-2 shows a six-month moving average. As long as this moving average is above the centerline, the average value of new orders is increasing.

- **Take a yearly analysis.** You can also look at the year-over-year changes in new orders instead of focusing on the month-to-month changes. Fortunately, the Advance Report on Durable Goods includes year-to-year comparisons as part of the data that isn't seasonally adjusted, as shown in Figure 9-1.
- **Exclude defense and transportation.** You can also remove some of the volatility by removing the most volatile components from the new order statistics. Doing so isn't difficult, but you do need to sharpen your pencil a bit to perform the necessary calculations (see the nearby sidebar "Calculating total new orders minus defense and transportation" for details). You can also combine this technique with either a moving average or a year-over-year comparison to get an even better sense of the trend for new orders.

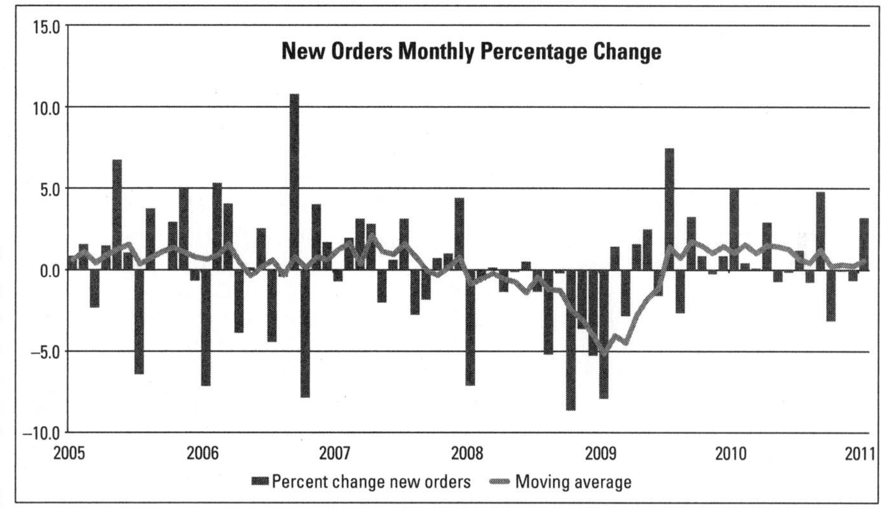

Figure 9-2: Monthly percentage change in the total value of new orders.

Manufacturing your portfolio response

Increases in new orders for durable goods are generally favorable for stocks and unfavorable for bonds. Conversely, decreases in new orders for durable goods are often greeted with selling by stock investors and with enthusiasm by bond investors. The following sections break down how different investors can use the Advance Report on Durable Goods.

Because month-to-month changes in the advance report can be extremely volatile, investors often have a hard time figuring out what's actually happening. So make sure that you find the underlying trend, as I discuss in the preceding section, before you make any rash investment decisions. Looking at moving averages is helpful, but the best way to find the underlying trend is to look at the core changes in new orders excluding transportation and defense orders.

Watching the bond market's reaction

Bond market investors often worry about the effects of inflation on their bond portfolio because rising inflation harms the total return on fixed-income investments. Bond prices fall, interest rates rise, and inflation diminishes the value of the future payments. Likewise, bond market investors worry when the total value of new orders for durable goods rises because rising new orders may presage rising inflation. On the other hand, bond investors generally relax when new orders fall.

When the value of new orders persistently rises, shorten the average maturity of your bond portfolios. When the value of new orders shows a sustained downward trend, lock in lower-priced bonds with higher yields.

Seeing how stocks react

Stock investors like to see the value of new orders for durable goods increase. They interpret a decreasing value of new orders for durable goods as a sign of poor economic health because it will ultimately harm corporate profits. Stocks of manufacturing companies are usually the hardest hit as new orders trend lower, but you can expect the effect to quickly cascade into unrelated industries.

The health of the manufacturing sectors is usually a good barometer for the economy and the stock market as a whole. As the value of new orders for durable goods begins to trend higher, start moving out of lower-risk, fixed-income investments into growth stocks. When the trend reverses, start paring back your exposure to growth stocks and begin moving to a more conservative investment position.

Knowing how to react if you invest in commodities

Industrial metal traders carefully watch the primary metals sector in the Advance Report on Durable Goods. The advance report shows an aggregate value for new orders for iron and steel mills, aluminum and nonferrous metal foundries, and ferrous metal foundries.

Futures contracts exist for many of these metals, including aluminum, nickel, copper, uranium, and steel. (A *futures contract* is a standardized buy/sell agreement specifying the product, quantity, quality, delivery date, and delivery location. See Chapter 15 for details.) Of course, precious metals like gold, silver, platinum, and palladium are also used in manufacturing electronics and automobiles and are actively traded in the *commodities markets* (the exchanges where futures contracts are bought and sold).

Rising new orders for durable goods often drive commodity prices higher. For people who invest in commodities, a trend toward higher new order values marks a good time for long positions in these commodity markets. Conversely, a trend toward falling values may depress the prices of industrial metals and may represent a good time to sell (or short) the product. (In trader's lingo, a *long* position means that you take an ownership position in the product in the hope of selling it later for a higher price. A *short* position is the opposite of a long position. Traders short a commodity by selling first, in the hope of buying it back at a lower price.)

Observing the effect on currency

The value of the U.S. dollar is directly related to the strength of the U.S. economy and U.S. interest rates. Rising values of durable goods orders often precede strength in the U.S. dollar; falling values often precede weakness.

Monitoring Factory Orders and Sales: The Factory Orders Report

The Factory Orders report follows one week behind the Advance Report on Durable Goods. It reports similar information — new orders, shipments, back orders, and inventory — but in much more detail and for a broader base of U.S. manufacturers.

Formally called the *Full Report on Manufacturers' Shipments, Inventories, and Orders,* this report includes revisions to the advance report along with more extensive information about durable goods manufacturers. In addition, it also provides information about nondurable manufacturers. Table 9-2 gives you the info you need to follow this report.

Table 9-2 Factory Orders Report

Release Schedule	*Agency*	*Web Address*	*Sensitivity*
Monthly: Published schedule, 10:00 a.m. ET	U.S. Census Bureau, Department of Commerce	www.census.gov/manufacturing/m3/	Low

The Factory Orders report doesn't move investment markets like the advance report does. However, the detail you get from reviewing this report is well worth your time. The following sections take a closer look at this report and highlight what you need to know about it.

The U.S. Bureau of Economic Analysis (BEA) uses the Factory Orders report data when compiling the gross domestic product (GDP) report (see Chapter 7 for more about the BEA and GDP). Also, the Conference Board includes new orders values from this report when calculating its Index of Leading Economic Indicators, or LEI (see Chapter 10 for more details).

Comparing the full and advance versions

Figure 9-3 shows Table 1 from the Factory Orders report. This table shows the value of manufacturers' shipments by industry groups. To get a sense of the detail provided by the Factory Orders report, compare Figure 9-3 with Figure 9-1 from the advance report earlier in this chapter. Instead of including only a single entry for shipments under each broad manufacturing category, the Factory Orders report shown in Figure 9-3 provides a lot more detail.

For example, where the advance report shows a single value for machinery shipments, the Factory Orders report expands the machinery category into nine subcomponents. (Check out the nine subcategories in Figure 9-3.)

Table 1. Value of Manufacturers' Shipments for Industry Groups[1]

[Estimates are shown in millions of dollars and are based on data from the Manufacturers' Shipments, Inventories, and Orders Survey.]

Industry	Seasonally Adjusted						Not Seasonally Adjusted						
	Monthly			Percent Change			Monthly				Year to date		
	Jan. 2011[p]	Dec. 2010[r]	Nov. 2010	Dec. - Jan.	Nov. - Dec.	Oct. - Nov.	Jan. 2011[p]	Dec. 2010[r]	Nov. 2010	Jan. 2010	2011[p]	2010	Percent 2011/ 2010
All manufacturing industries	447,440	439,364	427,630	1.8	2.7	1.6	409,142	431,950	419,394	373,302	409,142	373,302	9.6
Excluding transportation	399,386	391,132	380,904	2.1	2.7	2.1	367,361	380,984	372,934	328,938	367,361	328,938	11.7
Excluding defense	436,748	428,113	416,265	2.0	2.8	1.6	400,476	419,552	408,023	361,316	400,476	361,316	10.8
With unfilled orders	148,251	148,556	144,541	- 0.2	2.8	1.1	131,890	150,019	140,329	122,838	131,890	122,838	7.4
Durable goods industries	202,838	202,140	197,633	0.3	2.3	0.5	182,253	202,382	192,493	172,452	182,253	172,452	5.7
Wood products	6,559	6,594	6,455	- 0.5	2.2	0.9	5,435	5,880	6,115	5,484	5,435	5,484	- 0.9
Nonmetallic mineral products	8,296	8,094	8,097	2.5	0.0	- 0.7	6,972	6,940	7,928	6,616	6,972	6,616	5.4
Primary metals	23,075	22,111	21,020	4.4	5.2	4.6	21,646	18,865	19,587	17,124	21,646	17,124	26.4
Iron and steel mills	11,364	10,569	9,905	7.5	6.7	6.1	10,487	9,055	9,073	7,853	10,487	7,853	33.5
Aluminum and nonferrous metals	10,319	10,186	9,813	1.3	3.8	3.3	9,872	8,621	9,298	8,265	9,872	8,265	19.4
Ferrous metal foundries	1,392	1,356	1,302	2.7	4.1	2.7	1,287	1,189	1,216	1,006	1,287	1,006	27.9
Fabricated metal products	28,052	28,012	27,577	0.1	1.6	1.1	25,162	25,835	26,495	23,580	25,162	23,580	6.7
Machinery	25,528	27,286	25,418	- 6.4	7.3	2.6	23,169	28,320	23,638	20,194	23,169	20,194	14.7
Farm machinery	1,916	2,154	2,152	- 11.0	0.1	- 0.9	1,688	1,813	1,649	1,661	1,688	1,661	1.6
Construction machinery	3,111	2,928	2,795	6.3	4.8	0.5	2,743	3,044	2,794	1,684	2,743	1,684	62.9
Mining, oil field, and gas field machinery	1,378	1,381	1,354	- 0.2	2.0	3.4	1,376	1,600	1,343	1,480	1,376	1,480	- 7.0
Industrial machinery	2,846	3,209	3,098	- 11.3	3.6	15.3	2,800	3,978	2,581	2,181	2,800	2,181	28.4
Photographic equipment	788	714	703	10.4	1.6	- 2.4	627	816	756	610	627	610	2.8
Ventilation, heating, air- conditioning, and refrigeration equipment	2,397	2,381	2,361	0.7	0.8	0.6	1,927	2,400	2,185	2,111	1,927	2,111	- 8.7
Metalworking machinery	1,775	1,874	1,775	- 5.3	5.6	5.7	1,581	2,003	1,706	1,485	1,581	1,485	6.5
Turbines, generators, and other power transmission equipment	3,143	4,356	3,128	- 27.8	39.3	0.5	3,061	4,441	3,134	2,266	3,061	2,266	35.1
Material handling equipment	1,765	1,741	1,710	1.4	1.8	2.4	1,617	1,784	1,640	1,371	1,617	1,371	17.9

Machinery category's nine subcomponents

Figure 9-3: The Factory Orders report goes into a lot more detail than the advance report.

You find the same expansive detail for all the categories shown in the advance report. In addition to the shipments data, the full Factory Orders report details new orders (Table 2), back orders (Table 3), inventories (Table 4), and a whole lot more. Additional tables from the Factory Orders report include

- **Table 5 — Topical series:** *Topical series* are regroupings of the separate industry categories shown in Tables 1 through 4. Table 5 regroups shipments, new orders, inventory, and back orders. The most important value in these topical series is the regrouping called *new orders nondefense capital goods excluding aircraft.* A strong correlation exists between the *new orders nondefense capital goods excluding aircraft* topical series and the future economy. A decline in this new orders topical series usually precedes an economic downturn, while an increase often precedes economic expansion. The *shipments* topical series is also worth a quick look because the BEA uses it to calculate the capital investment component of GDP.
- **Table 6 — Inventory valuation by stage of fabrication:** This table categorizes inventories as being raw materials and supplies, works in process, or finished goods. Changes in inventory levels can help you spot economic changes. Inventory buildups often precede economic downturns; declines often lead to future growth.
- **Table 7 — Ratio of shipments to inventories and unfilled orders:** Table 7 clarifies the relationship between backlogs, shipments, and inventories by showing two ratios. The first, the inventory to shipment ratio, shows the relationship between current inventory levels and completed orders. The second shows the ratio between back orders and shipments. I discuss the inventory to shipment ratio more fully in the section "Counting Business Inventories: The Manufacturing and Trade Inventories and Sales Report."
- **Table 8 — Revisions to previously published monthly changes:** This table shows revisions made to shipments, inventories, new orders, and backlogs from previous releases of the full Factory Orders report. This table tends to show very small changes from release to release.

Investing in the full report

Although the Factory Orders report rarely moves investment markets, neither business leaders nor equity investors should ignore it. Careful analysis can provide insight into early trends for the whole economy, as well as for specific industries.

Information in this report can help pinpoint trouble — or opportunity — in manufacturing industries well before other reports. For example, a fall in new orders is a clear sign that customers may be losing their appetite for a company's products. You can make the same conclusion as inventories start to rise. Conversely, rising new orders, rising back orders, and falling inventories correspond with growing business.

Counting Business Inventories: The Manufacturing and Trade Inventories and Sales Report

Although information about manufacturers' inventories is available in the Factory Orders report that I discuss in the preceding section, that report is missing one crucial piece of data: the inventory positions of the manufacturers' customers (usually retailers and wholesalers).

The only insights into the manufacturers' customers that the Factory Orders report provides are the new orders statistics. While those stats are useful to an extent, knowing how the manufacturers' distributors and retailers are handling their inventories is also important because their inventories have a direct impact on manufacturers' future business.

Although computerized ordering systems and just-in-time manufacturing have helped companies better manage inventory levels, inventory problems still confound business management and regularly impact the economy. When consumers feel anxious about their financial well-being, they buy less. Inventories pile up in distribution centers and on retailers' shelves.

That's where the *Manufacturing and Trade Inventories and Sales report,* also known as the *Business Inventories report,* comes into play. This report looks at inventories across a wide business spectrum and shows inventory levels for manufacturers, wholesalers, and retailers. Table 9-3 provides more insight into this report.

Table 9-3 Manufacturing and Trade Inventories and Sales Report

Release Schedule	*Agency*	*Web Address*	*Sensitivity*
Monthly: Published schedule, 10:00 a.m. ET	U.S. Census Bureau, Department of Commerce	`www.census.gov/mtis/`	Low

The Business Inventories report is only three pages long, and some of its information is dated by the time the report is released. For example, the Factory Orders report (which I discuss in the preceding section) provides the same manufacturers' inventories as the Business Inventories report, and that report is released two weeks before the Business Inventories report.

However, the Business Inventories report does provide some important new information about retail inventories, including the essential inventory-to-sales (I/S) ratio.

The *I/S ratio* tells you how long businesses would take to sell all their inventory. For example, if the ratio is 1.25, businesses would take 1.25 months at the current sales pace to sell everything they have in inventory. Figure 9-4 shows the aggregate I/S ratio for U.S. businesses.

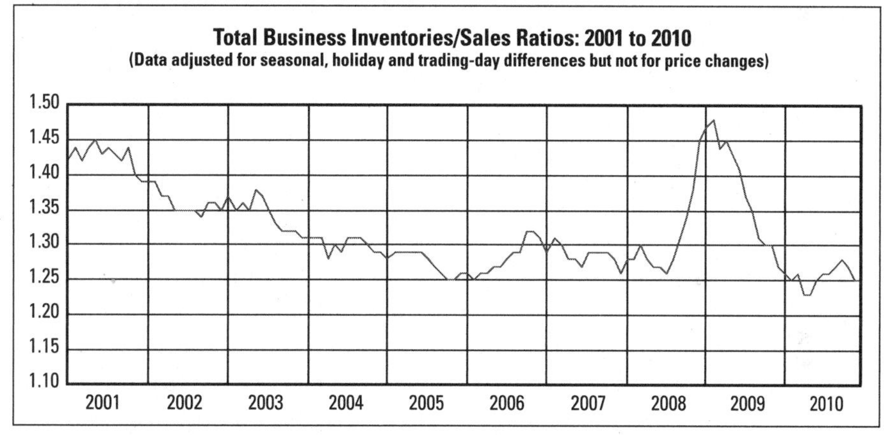

Figure 9-4: Total I/S ratios for U.S. businesses.

Before 2001, the I/S ratio for all businesses averaged about 1.45 months. As you can see from Figure 9-4, the ratio in 2010 stayed below the 1.30 level. Notice that the I/S ratio spiked to 1.54 months in 2008; recall the very large recession that coincided with that inventory peak. It took more than a year for businesses to work through that inventory increase.

The Business Inventories report also includes I/S ratios for manufacturing, wholesale, and retail sectors and shows I/S ratios for different kinds of businesses, such as food and beverage stores, department stores, and durable goods retailers, like motor vehicle and parts dealers and furniture dealers.

The I/S ratios provide a very early look into problem areas within the economy, sometimes before these problems show themselves in the Factory Orders or Advance Durable Goods reports. Even though the Business Inventories report is a low-profile indicator with little investment market impact, both investors and business leaders are wise to monitor it.

Chapter 10

Grappling with Economic Indexes

In This Chapter

- Surveying purchasing managers
- Looking into service industries
- Indexing leading economic indicators

This chapter wrestles with three economic reports that try to represent monthly economic conditions by using a single, easy-to-understand index value. Surveys of purchasing managers form the basis of two of the three reports. These survey-based reports show the current state of the manufacturing and service sectors, respectively, and provide near-term business activity forecasts.

The third report consolidates economic information from existing indicators to create a new way to look at the current state of the business cycle. These business and economic indexes provide a quick and easy way to track the current state of the economy and get a glimpse into its future course.

Measuring ISM's Manufacturing Survey

If you've ever worked in a large company, you know that purchasing managers make formidable adversaries at the negotiating table. Even if you don't have that firsthand experience, you may know that purchasing managers are important people. They have a unique vantage from which to grasp the current condition of their companies' business and supply chain, a viewpoint that helps them forecast the economy.

The purchasing department orders everything a company needs, from office supplies to manufacturing equipment and the raw materials necessary for production. Purchasing agents keep up with new customer orders. They make sure that the facility has a sufficient inventory of production material to keep the facilities operating on schedule. And purchasing agents are knowledgeable about commodity pricing, the availability of manufacturing supplies, and delivery times for all the raw materials used in production.

Each month, the Institute for Supply Management (ISM) surveys purchasing managers about the current condition of their businesses and their experiences in the marketplace and publishes two reports. Economists, business leaders (including purchasing managers), and investors widely follow the first report, the *Manufacturing ISM Report On Business®* (ROB), which I discuss in greater detail in the following sections. (The second survey-based report is the *Non-Manufacturing ISM Report On Business®,* which I discuss later in this chapter.) The reports are easy to interpret and timely, and they provide more insight than production reports alone.

Table 10-1 gives a quick overview of the Manufacturing ISM Report On Business®.

Table 10-1 Manufacturing ISM Report On Business®

Release Schedule	*Agency*	*Web Address*	*Sensitivity*
Monthly: First business day of each month, 10:00 a.m. ET	Institute for Supply Management	`ism.ws/ismreport/index.cfm`	High

Understanding how the ISM surveys purchasing agents

The Manufacturing ISM Report On Business® is a collection of information about manufacturers and their supply chains. Each report provides a performance summary by industry, anecdotal reports from the survey's respondents, a section about commodity pricing and availability, and indexes for a variety of business measures. The indexes get all the attention, and one specific index — the *PMI* (which used to be called the Purchasing Managers Index, but is now known only by its initials) — is the most attractive of all.

The ISM selects companies that represent the industry and geographic distribution of U.S. manufacturers for its surveys. This selection process means that large industries, such as auto manufacturing and its supply chain, have more representation in the survey than smaller industries.

The survey questions that form the basis of the indexes all take the same form and call for respondents to answer in one of the following ways: either "better, worse, or the same" or "increase, decrease, or no change." The ISM converts the responses to each question into a *diffusion index* (an index that shows how far responses spread away from the center; see Chapter 2 for a primer on diffusion indexes).

ISM diffusion indexes, including the PMI, are reported on a scale that ranges from 0 to 100. The diffusion indexes show 50 as their midpoint. If an index is above 50, more respondents answered the survey question with a response of "better" or "increasing," compared to those who answered with "worse" or "decreasing." A value below 50 means that more people answered by saying "worse" or "decreasing."

Checking the health of manufacturers

The ISM indexes that appear in the Manufacturing ISM Report On Business® are good indicators to foresee changes in the gross domestic product (GDP) and to identify changes in the business cycle. Each index identifies the direction of the current trend and any change to the trend. Unfortunately, these indexes provide little information to help you identify the magnitude of the trend or trend change.

Here's a brief description of each index:

- **PMI (the former Purchasing Managers Index):** Serves as the headline index for the Manufacturing ISM Report on Business® and provides a good overview of the manufacturing sectors. It's an aggregate of five ISM indexes. I discuss the PMI index more fully in the next section.
- **New Orders Index:** Measures the change in order quantities from the preceding month but doesn't measure differences in prices paid by the customer. Rising values for the New Orders Index generally indicate that rising production and a growing economy will follow.
- **Production Index:** Reports production levels compared to the preceding month. As with the New Orders Index, rising values in the Production Index usually precede increases in the economy as a whole.
- **Employment Index:** Reports the rate of increase or decrease of overall employment levels compared to the preceding month. The Employment Index may foretell changes in the Employment Situation report (see Chapter 4), but it's linked more closely to manufacturing industries than to the general economy.

- **Supplier Deliveries Index:** Shows whether suppliers are delivering production materials more quickly or slowly compared to the preceding month. An index above 50 represents increasing delivery times. If delivery issues are due to increased demand and tight supplies, the situation may lead to higher prices and eventually to inflation. The Supplier Deliveries Index is part of the Conference Board Leading Economic Index, which I discuss later in this chapter.
- **Inventories Index:** Measures increases or decreases in manufacturers' inventory levels compared to the preceding month. Increasing inventory levels often signal slowing sales.
- **Customers' Inventories Index:** Measures the inventory levels of manufacturing customers. Lower values often lead to an increase in new orders and a future pickup in production.
- **Prices Index:** Reports rising or falling prices for raw materials and other inputs to the manufacturing processes. Increases in this indicator may lead to consumer-product price increases, which can eventually lead to inflationary pressures. (This index may also be useful for identifying deflationary scenarios; however, that has yet to be confirmed in the real economy.)
- **Backlog of Orders Index:** Reports whether order backlogs are growing or declining. Rising backlogs usually precede production growth and growth in the general economy.
- **New Export Orders Index:** Measures the level of orders or services to be provided outside of the United States compared to the preceding month. Export growth is often a sign of a growing economy, but it can also be driven by a weak U.S. dollar.
- **Imports Index:** Measures the rate of change for raw material imports compared to the preceding month. Normally, import growth occurs during periods of strong economic growth. A strong U.S. dollar may make prices of imported products more attractive than domestically produced materials.

The Report On Business® provides additional details about each index, including a short summary that tells which industries reported growth or declines, along with a chart showing the recent history for each index (see Figure 10-1). The summaries help business leaders, policy analysts, and investors pinpoint areas of strength and weakness in the U.S. economy.

ISM Report On Business® FEBRUARY 2011 — MANUFACTURING

‡Miscellaneous Manufacturing (products such as medical equipment and supplies, jewelry, sporting goods, toys and office supplies).

PRODUCTION

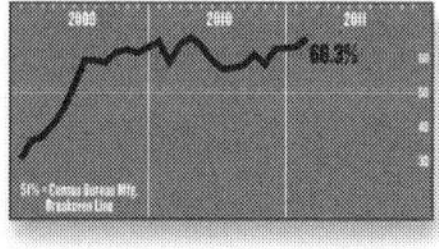

ISM's Production Index registered 66.3 percent in February. The 12 industries reporting growth in production during the month of February — listed in order — are: Apparel, Leather & Allied Products; Petroleum & Coal Products; Machinery; Transportation Equipment; Paper Products; Electrical Equipment, Appliances & Components; Chemical Products; Fabricated Metal Products; Miscellaneous Manufacturing‡; Food, Beverage & Tobacco Products; Printing & Related Support Activities; and Computer & Electronic Products.

NEW ORDERS

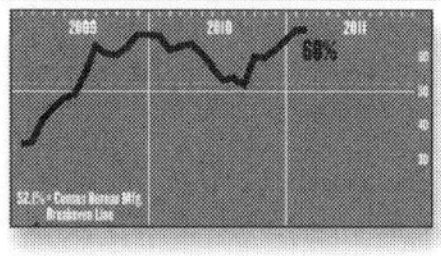

ISM's New Orders Index registered 68 percent in February. The 13 industries reporting growth in new orders in February — listed in order — are: Apparel, Leather & Allied Products; Petroleum & Coal Products; Electrical Equipment, Appliances & Components; Wood Products; Printing & Related Support Activities; Machinery; Transportation Equipment; Chemical Products; Paper Products; Fabricated Metal Products; Food, Beverage & Tobacco Products; Computer & Electronic Products; and Miscellaneous Manufacturing‡.

EMPLOYMENT

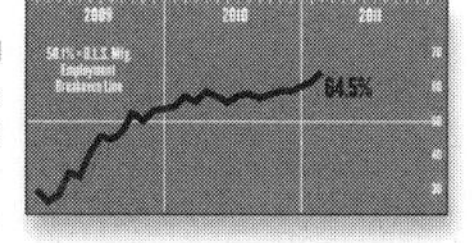

ISM's Employment Index registered 64.5 percent in February. Fourteen manufacturing industries reported growth in employment in February in the following order: Textile Mills; Petroleum & Coal Products; Transportation Equipment; Apparel, Leather & Allied Products; Computer & Electronic Products; Machinery; Food, Beverage & Tobacco Products; Electrical Equipment, Appliances & Components; Printing & Related Support Activities; Nonmetallic Mineral Products; Paper Products; Fabricated Metal Products; Chemical Products; and Miscellaneous Manufacturing‡.

SUPPLIER DELIVERIES

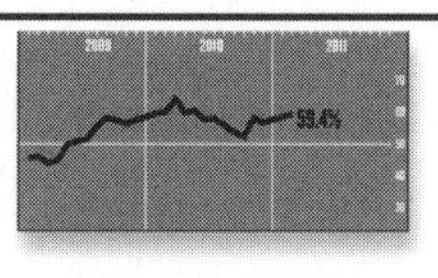

The delivery performance of suppliers to manufacturing organizations was slower in February as the Supplier Deliveries Index registered 59.4 percent. The seven industries reporting slower supplier deliveries in February — listed in order — are: Machinery; Chemical Products; Transportation Equipment; Fabricated Metal Products; Electrical Equipment, Appliances & Components; Food, Beverage & Tobacco Products; and Computer & Electronic Products.

INVENTORIES

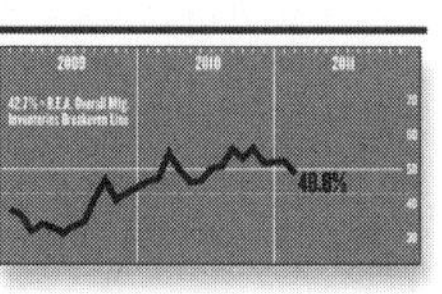

Manufacturers' inventories declined in February following seven consecutive months of growth. The Inventories Index registered 48.8 percent, 3.6 percentage points less than the 52.4 percent recorded for January. The four industries reporting higher inventories in February are: Apparel, Leather & Allied Products; Chemical Products; Electrical Equipment, Appliances & Components; and Computer & Electronic Products.

CUSTOMERS' INVENTORIES

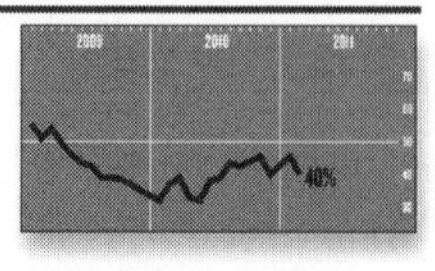

ISM's Customers' Inventories Index registered 40 percent in February, 5.5 percentage points lower than in January when the index registered 45.5 percent. This is the 23rd consecutive month the Customers' Inventories Index has been below 50 percent, indicating that respondents believe their customers' inventories are too low at this time. Two manufacturing industries reported customers' inventories as being too high during February: Primary Metals; and Food, Beverage & Tobacco Products.

PRICES

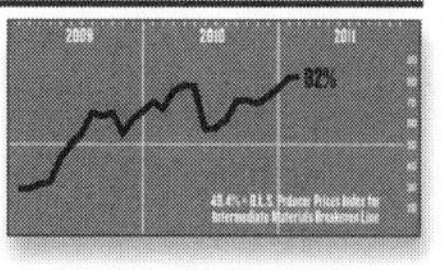

The ISM Prices Index registered 82 percent in February. The 13 industries reporting paying increased prices during the month of February — listed in order — are: Fabricated Metal Products; Food, Beverage & Tobacco Products; Machinery; Chemical Products; Electrical Equipment, Appliances & Components; Plastics & Rubber Products; Paper Products; Transportation Equipment; Apparel, Leather & Allied Products; Nonmetallic Mineral Products; Primary Metals; Computer & Electronic Products; and Miscellaneous Manufacturing‡.

BACKLOG OF ORDERS

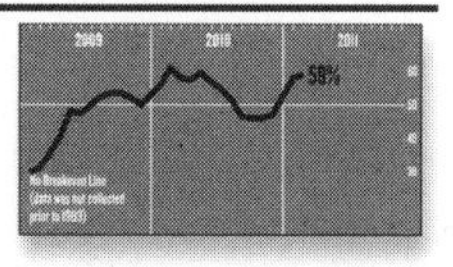

ISM's Backlog of Orders Index registered 59 percent in February. The 10 industries reporting increased order backlogs in February — listed in order — are: Electrical Equipment, Appliances & Components; Apparel, Leather & Allied Products; Paper Products; Printing & Related Support Activities; Fabricated Metal Products; Machinery; Miscellaneous Manufacturing‡; Transportation Equipment; Chemical Products; and Computer & Electronic Products.

NEW EXPORT ORDERS

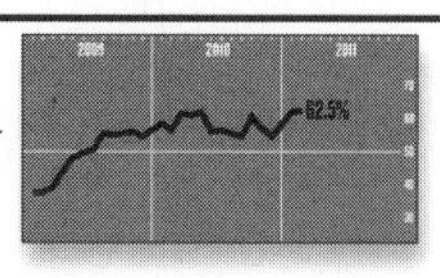

ISM's New Export Orders Index registered 62.5 percent in February. The 12 industries reporting growth in new export orders in February — listed in order — are: Petroleum & Coal Products; Furniture & Related Products; Apparel, Leather & Allied Products; Printing & Related Support Activities; Machinery; Chemical Products; Transportation Equipment; Fabricated Metal Products; Electrical Equipment, Appliances & Components; Paper Products; Computer & Electronic Products; and Food, Beverage & Tobacco Products.

IMPORTS

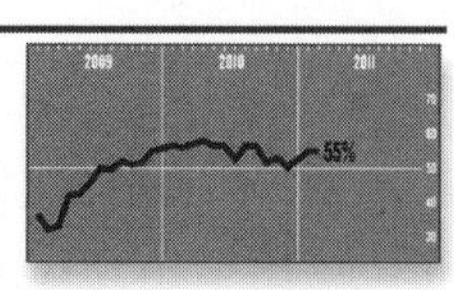

Imports of materials by manufacturers continued to expand in February as the Imports Index registered 55 percent, the same as reported in January. The nine industries reporting growth in imports during the month of February — listed in order — are: Apparel, Leather & Allied Products; Nonmetallic Mineral Products; Primary Metals; Miscellaneous Manufacturing‡; Printing & Related Support Activities; Transportation Equipment; Machinery; Chemical Products; and Electrical Equipment, Appliances & Components.

Source: Institute for Supply Management™. Used with permission.

Figure 10-1: Index summaries from the ISM Manufacturers' Report On Business®.

Surveying purchasing managers' insights for the PMI

The PMI is ISM's headline index. Its predecessor, the Purchasing Mangers Index, was first created by the Department of Commerce. The PMI has become a widely used and reported economic indicator because it has a strong history of anticipating manufacturers' profits well before other economic reports. You can rely on the PMI to foretell the economy's turning points.

The PMI is a composite index, made up of five of the ISM Report On Business® indexes. Equally weighted and seasonally adjusted, the five indexes are as follows:

- The New Orders Index
- The Production Index
- The Employment Index
- The Supplier Deliveries Index
- The Inventories Index

When manufacturing represented a larger percentage of the U.S. economy, a PMI reading of below 50 meant that the U.S. economy was heading for a recession. Although that reading still indicates that the manufacturing portion of the U.S. economy is declining, ISM now estimates that a PMI value below 42.5 corresponds to a contraction of the whole economy.

Still, a strong correlation remains between the PMI, the U.S. GDP (see Chapter 7), and the business cycle. Figure 10-2 illustrates this relationship by showing the value of the PMI over time, with periods of economic contraction shaded in gray.

In addition to the PMI for U.S. manufacturing, ISM also provides a PMI for global manufacturing. It's published in conjunction with JPMorgan, and you can find it on the ISM website listed in Table 10-1. I discuss this global PMI more fully in Chapter 17.

Monitoring market movement

Investment markets are very sensitive to changes in the Manufacturing ISM Report On Business®. Although equities markets, bond markets, and commodities markets may focus on different aspects of this report, they all share an affinity for these purchasing manager surveys. The following sections explain how the different markets react to the Report On Business®.

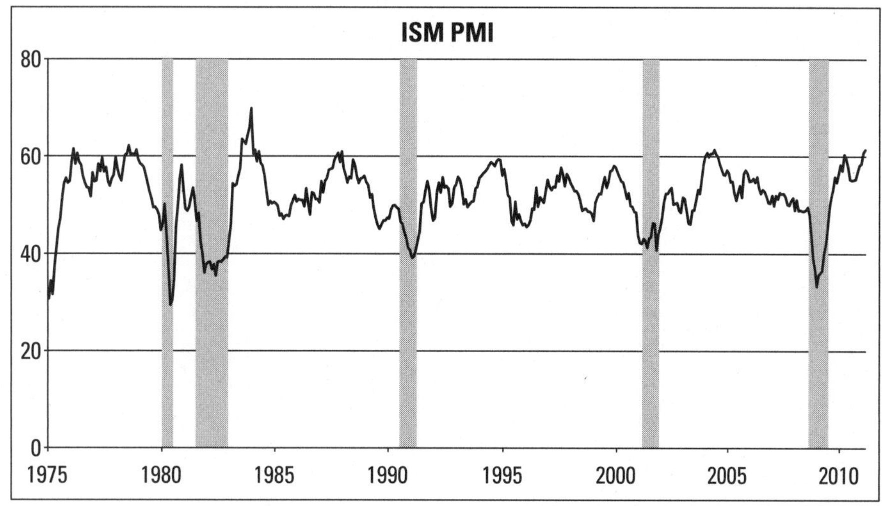

Figure 10-2: The PMI and economic contractions.

Source: Institute for Supply Management™. Used with permission.

Seeing stock market reactions to the PMI

Unexpected PMI changes trigger immediate trading activity in the stocks of both manufacturing-sector companies and the market as a whole. However, investors are equally interested in the industries that reported growth or decline in specific indexes (see Figure 10-1), as well as the overall "Performance by Industry" summary at the beginning of the report.

Broad-based indexes like the PMI rarely represent the condition of every industry or sector. Some industries lead during an economic expansion, while others decline during the same period. For example, falling oil prices are rarely good news for oil refineries and gasoline retailers. But they're great news for the transportation industry or any sector that incurs high transportation costs when moving its products to market. Falling oil prices also favor industries with high energy requirements, such as steel mills or aluminum foundries.

If you're an equity investor, you need to pay close attention to both the PMI and the subindexes. A trend of rising PMI values usually corresponds with a growing economy, which is usually good for equities. The strength of specific manufacturing sectors can help you identify investment opportunities and the current state of the business cycle as well.

Detailing bond reactions to manufacturing expansion

The way bond investors react to manufacturing sector growth is almost always exactly the opposite of the way equity investors react. Economic growth leads to rising interest rates, lower bond prices, and, sometimes, inflation. Inflation is never good news for bondholders because it makes interest payments less valuable.

Bond investors track both the PMI and the subindexes that can indicate either current or future price increases because they offer an early hint that inflation may become an issue. As prices rise, bond investors need to shorten the duration of their portfolios. Long-term bonds are much more sensitive to inflationary pressures than short-term bonds. The Prices Index is obviously the first place to look for insight into future price increases, but bond investors also monitor the Backlog of Orders Index, the Supplier Deliveries Index, and the New Orders Index.

Digging for insight into the commodities markets

ISM surveys of purchasing managers help commodities traders identify manufacturing materials that are in short supply and provide some insight into current and future demand. Although futures markets often have a good handle on current and future supply for traded commodities, the ISM reports help identify the actual demand for primary metals and other raw materials used in manufacturing.

Gauging Non-Manufacturing Companies

Manufacturing represents about 20 percent of the U.S. economy, so the creation of an economic indicator to measure the remaining 80 percent seems reasonable. The ISM has done just that with the *Non-Manufacturing ISM Report on Business®.*

This report is commonly called the *ISM services report,* or just *the services report.* It was first published in 1998 and, like its manufacturing counterpart, is based on surveys of purchasing managers in non-manufacturing industries throughout the United States. Also like the manufacturer's report, it creates diffusion indexes (see Chapter 2 for more about diffusion indexes) to report changes in the current month's data compared to the preceding month's data.

Table 10-2 gives a quick overview of this report.

Table 10-2 Non-Manufacturing ISM Report On Business®

Release Schedule	*Agency*	*Web Address*	*Sensitivity*
Monthly: Third business day of each month, 10:10 a.m. ET	Institute for Supply Management	`ism.ws/ismreport/index.cfm`	Low but growing

Like the manufacturing ISM report, the services report provides a performance summary by industry, anecdotal reports from the survey's respondents, a section about commodity pricing and availability, and indexes for a variety of business measures.

Most of the subindexes are the same for both reports. However, the service report doesn't include the Production Index or the PMI, and it contains several indexes not included in the manufacturing report. Here's a brief explanation of the additional indexes:

- **Non-Manufacturing Index:** Known as the NMI, this new composite index was first introduced in 2008. It serves as an indicator of the overall economic condition for the non-manufacturing sectors and is the service report's counterpart to the PMI. The NMI is an equally weighted composite of the following non-manufacturing diffusion indexes: the Business Activity Index, the New Orders Index, the Employment Index, and the Supplier Deliveries Index. The NMI doesn't have a long track record, but I expect it to gain more influence as investors become more comfortable with it. Of course, service industries aren't as economically sensitive as manufacturing industries. Still, the NMI offers investors a tool to monitor the health of this large business segment.
- **Business Activity Index:** Prior to 2008, this index was the headline index for the service report. It measures the change in business activity of service-sector businesses.
- **Inventory Sentiment Index:** This index measures whether survey respondents believe that their inventory levels are too high or too low. An index of above 50 indicates that respondents believe that their inventories are too high, below 50 indicates that inventories are too low, and a reading of 50 means that inventories are just right.

The commodity pricing section of the services report also differs from its manufacturing counterpart. Few of the listed products are traditionally considered commodities, but they do impact pricing and profitability in the non-manufacturing industries. A few examples of the listed commodities include airfares, beef, cable products, capital equipment, coffee, consulting services, dairy products, and electrical and energy supplies, among many others.

The Non-Manufacturing ISM Report On Business® receives little attention in the markets. One reason for investors' ho-hum response is that services aren't as sensitive as manufacturing companies to changes in the business cycle. Nevertheless, investors can benefit from the details in the Non-Manufacturing ISM Report On Business®, including the NMI composite. It's likely to become a more important index as traders, investors, and business leaders become comfortable with it.

Looking At the Leading Economic Index

With a name like the *Leading Economic Index* (LEI), you may expect this indicator to be the perfect economic forecasting tool. It's not, of course; there's no such thing. However, it does consolidate a great deal of existing economic data into a single, easy-to-understand index.

If you're looking for a quick shortcut to analyze the current state of the business cycle and the general economy or to confirm the analysis you've already done, consider giving the LEI a look. The report is freely available, and Table 10-3 gives you an overview.

Table 10-3 The Conference Board Leading Economic Index

Release Schedule	*Agency*	*Web Address*	*Sensitivity*
Monthly: Published schedule, 10:10 a.m. ET	The Conference Board	www.conference-board.org/data/bcicountry.cfm?cid=1	Low

You can find the publication date for the next release of the Leading Economic Index in the Technical Notes of the current release. The Technical Notes are linked in the upper right-hand corner of the website listed in Table 10-3.

The idea to create an all-encompassing index has been around for a while. The LEI was first published by the U.S. Department of Commerce but was privatized in 1995 and transferred to the Conference Board.

The LEI is one index in a trio of simultaneously published indexes. In addition to the Leading Economic Index, the Conference Board also publishes the Coincident Economic Index (CEI) and the Lagging Economic Index. All three are composites of existing economic indicators, but the LEI is the one that interests investors and business leaders the most.

The composition of indexes that the Conference Board uses to calculate the LEI is periodically updated. Currently, the LEI is a composite of the following economic indicators:

- **Average weekly hours, manufacturing:** From the Employment Situation report (see Chapter 4)
- **Average weekly initial claims for unemployment insurance:** From the Unemployment Insurance Weekly Claims Report (see Chapter 4)

- **Manufacturers' new orders, consumer goods and materials:** From the Full Report on Manufacturers' Shipments, Inventories, and Orders (see Chapter 9)
- **Index of supplier deliveries–vendor performance:** From the Manufacturing ISM Report On Business®, reviewed earlier in this chapter
- **Manufacturers' new orders, nondefense capital goods:** From the Full Report on Manufacturers' Shipments, Inventories, and Orders (see Chapter 9)
- **Building permits, new private housing units:** From the Housing Starts report (see Chapter 11)
- **Stock prices, 500 common stocks:** The Standard & Poor's (S&P) 500 Index of large company stocks
- **Real money supply:** From the Federal Reserve's money supply reports (see Chapter 8)
- **Interest rate spread, 10-year Treasury bonds less federal funds:** The difference between the market rate for 10-year Treasury bonds and the federal funds rate (Check out Chapter 8 for information about the federal funds rate; see Chapter 14 for more about the yield curve and interest rate spreads.)
- **Index of Consumer Expectations:** From the University of Michigan Consumer Sentiment Index (see Chapter 5)

You can see the performance of the Leading Economic Index and the Coincident Economic Index in Figure 10-3.

As you can see, the LEI turned down well in advance of the two recessions shown in Figure 10-3 and turned up before the two recessions were complete. The CEI showed similar movements, but the timing of the motion coincided more closely with the start and finish of the economic contraction.

Although these indexes do what they're intended to do, they don't get a lot of attention from investors. The problem is that most of the data used to calculate the LEI is already known before the composite indexes are released.

From Wall Street's perspective, this lack of timeliness makes the LEI announcement anticlimactic. Another problem is that not all the data used to calculate the composite are available when the index is published. The Conference Board must estimate several of the indicators used in the report, which doesn't improve LEI's attractiveness for investors. In short, investors don't pay close attention to the LEI release.

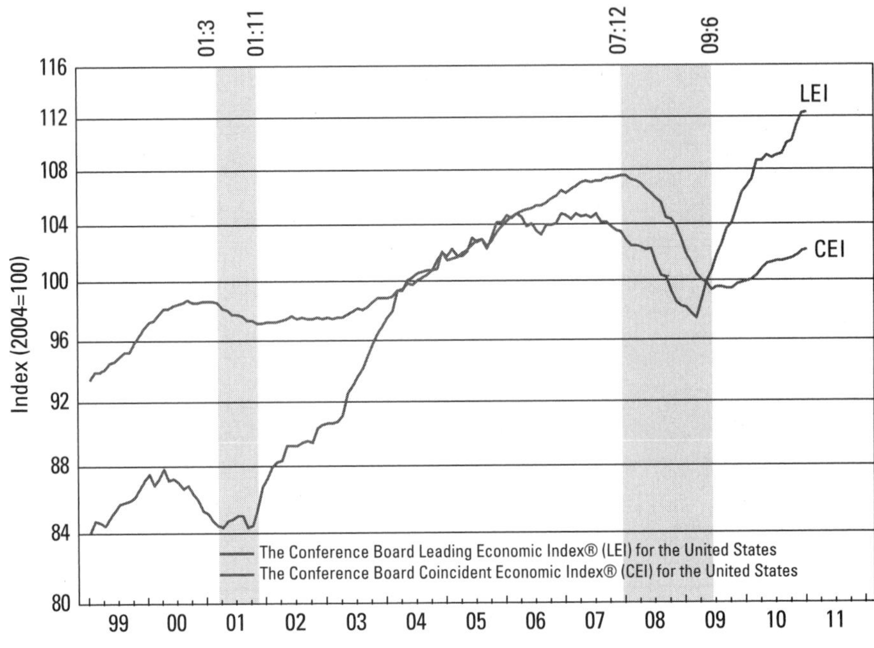

Figure 10-3: The Conference Board's LEI and CEI.

Nevertheless, the LEI has a pretty good track record, and it may be a useful tool for you. Taken together, the Leading, Coincident, and Lagging Indexes provide a useful look at the economic situation and the current business cycle. As long as you don't expect perfection — or market-shaking results — these indexes are worth a look.

Chapter 11

Spending on Housing and Residential Construction

In This Chapter

- Understanding how the housing market affects the economy
- Building and selling new homes
- Buying and selling existing homes
- Delving into the mortgage market
- Following home prices with the S&P/Case-Shiller Indices

Homeownership may not be the original American Dream, but it has become a modern symbol of abundance and prosperity. Owning the home you live in satisfies a basic need for shelter, but it also serves as a status symbol, a huge expense, a long-term investment, and recently for some homeowners, a personal piggy bank. After all, a house is the largest purchase most people will ever make — until they buy another one.

Housing is also one of the largest components in the U.S. economy. New-home construction has an outsized effect on business and the business cycle. Although existing-home sales also play a role, the recurring expenditures for maintenance, repair, insurance, and mortgage interest or rent have the biggest impact of all.

Given housing's huge effect on the economy, you probably aren't surprised to know that many economic reports and indicators track this important sector. This chapter reviews the most prominent indicators that track the sales of new and existing homes, building permits and new housing starts, mortgage applications, foreclosures, and housing prices.

Growing the Economy One House at a Time

The economic impact of new-home construction is quite significant. In fact, grasping the housing market's full economic impact can be eye-opening; it's more than just the cost of some lumber and roofing tiles. A newly constructed home drives the purchase of both building materials and consumer durables.

To illustrate, most new homes contain lumber, concrete, flooring substrates and surfaces, roofing, insulation, air ducts, air-conditioning equipment, drywall, windows, kitchen cabinets, bathroom cabinets, interior doors, exterior doors, closet doors, garage doors, plumbing fixtures, and kitchen appliances. Furthermore, new homeowners are usually in the market for new furniture, floor coverings, window coverings, consumer electronics, and landscaping materials.

Many diverse businesses feel the effects of new-home building:

- The construction industry directly employs plumbers, carpenters, electricians, painters, roofers, and day laborers.
- New-home builders keep building-material factories humming and factory workers gainfully employed.
- Builders and new homeowners involve the banking, finance, and insurance industries when they apply for construction loans, buy title insurance and property insurance, and, of course, apply for new mortgages.

In short, new residential construction is responsible for jobs and wages across a huge swath of industries. Rising demand for new homes has a stimulative effect on the economy, while falling demand can lead to an economic slowdown. In the following sections, I cover the relationship between housing and the economy, as well as the factors that influence demand for housing.

Realizing the relationship between housing and GDP

Housing's multiplier effect — where the construction of a new residence impacts so many businesses — has an outsized impact on the U.S. economy. On average, new-home construction directly accounts for about 5 percent of gross domestic product, or GDP (see Chapter 7 for details on GDP). But that's not all. Housing-related services, such as maintenance, repairs, remodeling, and mortgage interest, add another 12 to 13 percent to GDP, making housing's total GDP impact about 18 percent per year.

Accounting for housing in GDP

The value of housing is found in two places in GDP: residential fixed investment and housing services. The value of new-home construction is recognized in the *residential fixed investment* GDP category (which also includes improvements to existing homes and even the value of new mobile homes). Housing services are reported as personal consumption expenditures (PCE) in GDP (see Chapter 6 for details about PCE). However, the accounting isn't as straightforward as you may think.

Housing services include payments for all services, including real-estate agent commissions, home inspection fees, attorney fees, and loan origination fees. What makes GDP's accounting for housing unusual is the attempt to capture the value of services provided by your home rather than its value as an investment.

Here's the short explanation. Your home is a place you can cook dinner and entertain guests. GDP considers your consumption of your home's features and tries to capture their value.

In addition, PCE housing services include the *imputed rental value* of owner-occupied housing. In other words, PCE treats owner-occupied housing as if it were a rental business and the owner rented the home to himself. The idea is that GDP shouldn't care who owns the housing. For the purposes of GDP, a landlord and a homeowner are one and the same. Housing services include the value of rent charged for similar tenant-occupied housing for all owner-occupied homes.

GDP's treatment of housing is unique. For example, the Commerce Department doesn't estimate the value of the services provided by your car and include that value in GDP.

If you'd like to read the long explanation, the Bureau of Economic Analysis (BEA) has written a white paper that makes the whole thing at least a little clearer. You can find this explanation on the BEA website: `www.bea.gov/papers/pdf/RIPfactsheet.pdf`.

Historically, new-home construction leads an economic expansion. As a recession ages, even a small increase in new-home building can help jump-start a slumbering economy. Builders take out construction loans to purchase and improve property, buy the necessary building materials, and hire various contractors. An increase in new-home construction is the start of a virtuous cycle that continues as long as interest rates remain low, unemployment rates continue to fall, and the economy continues to grow.

As interest rates rise (as they typically do during an economic expansion), mortgage rates become less attractive and fewer people want to buy homes. This decrease in the housing demand leads to a slowdown in home construction, which tends to falter in advance of a recession. In fact, the only time since World War II that the economy entered a recession while housing was strong was during 2001, and that recession was brief and mild.

Following the subprime mortgage crisis in 2008, demand for residential housing fell, housing prices fell, and home builders became an endangered species. Although new-home construction tends to recover about the same time as the rest of the economy, the recent recession triggered by the subprime lending crisis shows that every rule has an exception.

Recently, the new-home construction component of GDP has lagged badly (presumably due to a glut of recently built but unsold homes and the large number of foreclosed properties). In 2010, new housing represented only 2.5 percent of GDP, half of its average annual contribution. Had housing contributed its 5 percent average, the 2010 GDP growth rate, compared to 2009, would have soared from a pretty good 2.9 percent to a robust 5.4 percent.

Understanding U.S. housing demand

To fully grasp the impact housing has on the U.S. economy, you need to comprehend some basic information about the housing market and the demand for housing. Currently, the United States is home to about 111 million homes, and each year builders build between 1 and 2 million new homes. About 68 percent of households own their own homes; the rest rent.

Several factors affect the demand for housing:

- **Household formation:** Marriage, divorce, children leaving their parents' home, and single adults leaving shared housing all create new households, which, in turn, increase the demand for housing.
- **Replacement housing:** Houses deteriorate as they age and must occasionally be replaced. Also, people usually have to rebuild homes that are destroyed by fires, floods, hurricanes, tornados, or earthquakes. Sometimes people demolish older homes just to make way for newer, larger, or more modern homes.
- **The economy:** The current economic cycle, the employment situation, and the current level of interest rates all impact the demand for housing. When interest rates and unemployment rates are high, household formation and the demand for housing are muted. After all, people aren't likely to take on new mortgages when they're feeling anxious about their livelihoods. On the other hand, when jobs are plentiful, interest rates are low, and the economy is doing well, the housing sector and all the industries that participate in the multiplier effect perform well.
- **Government policy:** U.S. tax policy encourages homeownership. Any change in the deductibility of mortgage interest would likely reduce residential construction. Government encouragement to make mortgage loans to lower-income families played some role in the recent housing bubble.

Even during the horrible climate for home builders following the subprime mortgage crisis, more than 500,000 new homes were built in both 2009 and 2010. During that time, mortgage rates were very low, but lenders were very selective when offering mortgages to applicants. Only the most qualified buyers were eligible for a loan at any rate.

Studies done by the National Association of Home Builders (NAHB) suggest that the housing malaise from 2009 was the result of a steep decline in demand for new homes, not just overbuilding. This analysis suggests that demand for new housing would exist if only consumers were able to afford new homes. If this analysis is correct, the housing market will recover only when the job market recovers, personal finances improve, and the pent-up demand for housing is unleashed.

Counting One Start at a Time: The New Residential Construction Report

One of the most prominent measures of home-building activity is the Census Bureau's *New Residential Construction report*, more commonly known as the *Housing Starts* or *Building Permits report.* The statistics in this report are useful for investors and business leaders because they're a very good indicator of future economic activity. In fact, the number of authorized building permits is so prescient that the Conference Board includes it in the Leading Economic Index, or LEI (see Chapter 10 for info on the LEI). Table 11-1 provides a brief overview of the New Residential Construction report.

Table 11-1 New Residential Construction Report

Release Schedule	*Agency*	*Web Address*	*Sensitivity*
Monthly: Published schedule, 8:30 a.m. ET	U.S. Census Bureau	`www.census.gov/const/www/newresconstindex.html`	High

The following sections outline the data you can find in this report and explain how you can decipher the data and use it to your advantage in your investments.

Eyeing the data: Where the stats come from

Knowing where the information on the New Residential Construction report comes from can help you better understand what it means. The report considers both single-family homes and multifamily dwellings. It counts each unit in a multifamily dwelling, so for example, when a contractor builds a new 50-unit apartment complex, the report counts it as 50 new residences. The report counts only privately owned residences; however, those residences don't have to be owner occupied. The report counts privately owned rental property, but it doesn't count government housing, dormitories, mobile homes, or nursing facilities.

The New Residential Construction report features five important statistics in its data tables:

- **Table 1 — Building permits:** This statistic shows the number of building permits issued. Most U.S. cities and counties require builders to secure a permit before they can begin any work at a construction site. I discuss building permits more fully in the next section.
- **Table 2 — Construction authorized but not started:** This statistic shows how many projects have been authorized but not yet started. Obtaining a building permit is a bureaucratic chore and entails some cost, so builders don't usually secure a permit and then delay construction. But sometimes factors outside of the builder's control delay the project. Several factors, including bad weather, logistical delays, and labor issues, can cause this statistic to rise. Changing economic or financial conditions can also impact this statistic, so analyze this stat carefully to determine the cause of its rise or fall.
- **Table 3 — Housing starts:** This statistic shows how many projects have actually started. The report counts each new-construction project or each complete rebuild on an existing foundation as a housing start. But it doesn't count room additions or other improvements. I discuss housing starts later in the section "Correlating housing and economic activity."
- **Table 4 — Housing under construction:** This statistic shows the number of projects in process but not yet complete. Building an average home typically takes six months. Growth in this statistic is a sign of either production delays or financial problems.
- **Table 5 — Housing completions:** This stat shows the number of housing units completed and ready for occupancy.

The New Residential Construction report categorizes data into three groups. The largest category is single-family homes. The other two categories are two- to four-unit dwellings and multifamily dwellings with five units or more.

The report also subcategorizes the data into four U.S. regions: Northeast, Midwest, South, and West. Except for Table 2, all the data are shown both seasonally adjusted and annualized and not seasonally adjusted or annualized. Table 2 shows only the nonadjusted and nonannualized data. The published release dates are available on the Census Bureau website at `www.census.gov/const/www/newresconstdates.html`.

Monitoring building permits and other housing stats

The number of authorized building permits, which you find in Table 1 of the New Residential Construction report, is a good indicator of planned home-building activity and future economic activity. Almost every U.S. municipality requires a building permit before lot preparation or construction can begin. Getting a permit costs money and is a bit of a hassle, so builders usually only apply for a permit if they intend to build.

The Census Bureau surveys almost 20,000 builders and municipalities throughout the United States to find the number of authorized permits. Figure 11-1 shows an example of the building permits data in Table 1.

All the data tables in the New Residential Construction report follow the format shown in Figure 11-1 except Table 2 (see the preceding section for details on that table).

The current month's data shown in each table are preliminary and are shown along with results from the previous 12 months. Minor revisions to the data may be made in subsequent reports. The permit data in Table 1 will be revised once, but the other data tables may be revised for up to two months following the preliminary release.

All the tables except Table 2 show the data in two formats. The top section of the table shows seasonally adjusted, annualized data. The lower section of the table shows the raw data that aren't adjusted for seasonality or annualized. (See Chapter 2 for a refresher on annualizing data and adjusting for seasonality.) Each table also shows the percentage difference between the current month and the previous month and the current month and the same month from the previous year.

In Figure 11-1, the preliminary data for February 2011 show an annualized rate of 517,000 permits issued. In other words, based on the 35,900 actual permits issued in February, as shown in the lower section of the table, the Census Bureau statisticians estimate that 517,000 total permits will be issued in 2011.

Consider the number of authorized permits to be a forecast of housing starts. When the number of authorized permits rises, you can expect the economy to rise as well. The converse is equally true. When the number of authorized permits falls, you can expect the economy to slow, too. Keep in mind, though, that these numbers give you little information to help you estimate the timing or the magnitude of the economic growth or contraction.

Table 1. New Privately-Owned Housing Units Authorized in Permit-Issuing Places
[Thousands of units. Detail may not add to total because of rounding]

Period	United States				Northeast		Midwest		South		West	
		In structures with --										
	Total	1 unit	2 to 4 units	5 units or more	Total	1 unit	Total	1 unit	Total	1 unit	Total	1 unit
	Seasonally adjusted annual rate											
2010: February	650	523	20	107	85	68	106	85	311	258	148	112
March	685	542	22	121	68	52	117	90	356	287	144	113
April	610	486	17	107	68	47	114	84	310	258	118	97
May	574	436	18	120	65	48	102	72	294	232	113	84
June	583	421	20	142	85	49	93	74	283	215	122	83
July	559	406	19	134	66	44	94	69	283	209	116	84
August	571	403	18	150	68	42	92	70	279	208	132	83
September	547	402	25	120	75	46	91	70	267	204	114	82
October	552	404	24	124	72	44	108	73	259	202	113	85
November	544	417	20	107	67	50	90	77	264	209	123	81
December	627	442	24	161	117	75	94	66	255	207	161	94
2011: January (r)	563	421	19	123	79	51	92	64	282	216	110	90
February (p)	**517**	**382**	**14**	**121**	**57**	**40**	**87**	**59**	**278**	**206**	**95**	**77**
Average RSE (%)[1]	1	1	8	4	5	4	2	2	1	1	3	2
Percent Change:												
February 2011 from January 2011	***-8.2%***	***-9.3%***	***-26.3%***	***-1.6%***	***-27.8%***	***-21.6%***	***-5.4%***	***-7.8%***	***-1.4%***	***-4.6%***	***-13.6%***	***-14.4%***
90% Confidence Interval[3]	*± 3.3*	*± 1.2*	*± 16.9*	*± 12.1*	*± 8.8*	*± 11.0*	*± 6.1*	*± 7.2*	*± 5.3*	*± 6.2*	*± 2.4*	*± 2.8*
February 2011 from February 2010	***-20.5%***	***-27.0%***	***-30.0%***	***13.1%***	***-32.9%***	***-41.2%***	***-17.9%***	***-30.6%***	***-10.6%***	***-20.2%***	***-35.8%***	***-31.3%***
90% Confidence Interval[3]	*± 3.5*	*± 1.5*	*± 3.1*	*± 11.1*	*± 10.6*	*± 13.3*	*± 5.7*	*± 6.7*	*± 5.3*	*± 6.2*	*± 3.0*	*± 3.4*
	Not seasonally adjusted											
2009:	583.0	441.1	20.7	121.1	68.5	45.8	100.3	74.9	297.4	231.8	116.7	88.7
2010:	598.0	446.6	20.8	130.6	75.5	49.9	100.4	75.2	293.9	230.4	128.3	91.2
RSE (%)	1	1	5	(Z)	3	3	1	1	1	1	2	2
2010: Year to Date[2]	83.5	65.8	2.6	15.2	9.0	6.5	9.8	8.0	44.6	37.1	20.1	14.2
2011: Year to Date[2]	71.9	52.6	2.2	17.1	7.8	5.0	8.7	5.9	41.2	30.8	14.1	10.8
RSE (%)	1	1	8	(Z)	6	5	2	2	1	1	1	2
Year to Date Percent Change[4]	***-13.9%***	***-20.1%***	***-15.4%***	***12.9%***	***-13.1%***	***-23.1%***	***-10.7%***	***-26.4%***	***-7.8%***	***-16.9%***	***-29.6%***	***-23.7%***
90% Confidence Interval[3]	*± 2.1*	*± 1.4*	*± 19.2*	*± 7.4*	*± 10.1*	*± 12.6*	*± 3.3*	*± 4.0*	*± 2.8*	*± 3.2*	*± 1.9*	*± 2.2*
2010: February	44.1	35.0	1.3	7.8	4.8	3.6	5.3	4.6	23.0	19.2	10.9	7.6
March	62.1	49.9	2.2	10.0	5.6	4.2	9.7	7.7	33.6	27.5	13.1	10.4
April	56.3	46.3	1.6	8.5	6.2	4.4	11.0	8.5	28.3	24.0	10.8	9.3
May	51.0	40.1	1.6	9.3	5.9	4.5	9.4	7.2	25.5	20.5	10.2	7.9
June	58.9	43.0	1.9	14.0	9.2	5.0	9.6	7.9	27.4	21.1	12.6	9.0
July	50.4	37.5	1.7	11.2	6.2	4.2	9.1	6.8	24.8	18.7	10.3	7.8
August	53.2	37.2	1.7	14.3	6.3	4.1	9.1	6.8	25.9	18.9	11.9	7.4
September	47.1	34.5	2.1	10.5	7.0	4.3	8.5	6.4	21.7	16.8	9.8	7.0
October	44.0	31.8	1.9	10.4	6.2	3.8	10.0	6.5	19.0	15.1	8.8	6.3
November	39.6	29.4	1.7	8.5	5.3	3.9	7.2	5.7	18.8	14.5	8.3	5.3
December	46.7	30.2	1.9	14.6	8.7	5.4	6.0	3.6	19.5	14.7	12.5	6.5
2011: January (r)	36.0	26.3	1.2	8.5	4.6	2.9	4.4	2.7	19.9	15.1	7.2	5.5
February (p)	**35.9**	**26.3**	**0.9**	**8.7**	**3.3**	**2.1**	**4.4**	**3.2**	**21.3**	**15.7**	**7.0**	**5.3**
Average RSE (%)[1]	1	1	8	4	5	4	2	2	1	1	3	2

(p) Preliminary. (r) Revised. RSE Relative standard error. S Does not meet publication standards because tests for identifiable and stable seasonality do not meet reliability standards.
X Not applicable. Z Relative standard error is less than 0.5 percent.
[1] Average RSE for the latest 6-month period. [2] Reflects revisions not distributed to months.
[3] See the Explanatory Notes in the accompanying text for an explanation of 90% confidence intervals. [4] Computed using unrounded data.

Figure 11-1: New housing units authorized in permit-issuing places.

Correlating housing and economic activity

Although no economic indicator is 100 percent accurate, housing data can give you a somewhat clear picture of the direction the economy is going. Authorized building permits show anticipated building activity, while housing starts show that people are putting real money to work. When the builder clears the lot and starts laying a foundation, either he is under contract with a buyer or he has enough confidence in the economy to commit his own money to build a home in the hopes that a buyer will soon come along.

Figure 11-2 shows the housing starts data series from the late 1950s to the present, with periods of economic recession shown in gray. (Go to `www.census.gov/const/www/newresconstindex.html` to see all the housing starts data in Table 3 of the New Residential Construction report. Note that Table 3 is formatted like the table shown in Figure 11-1.)

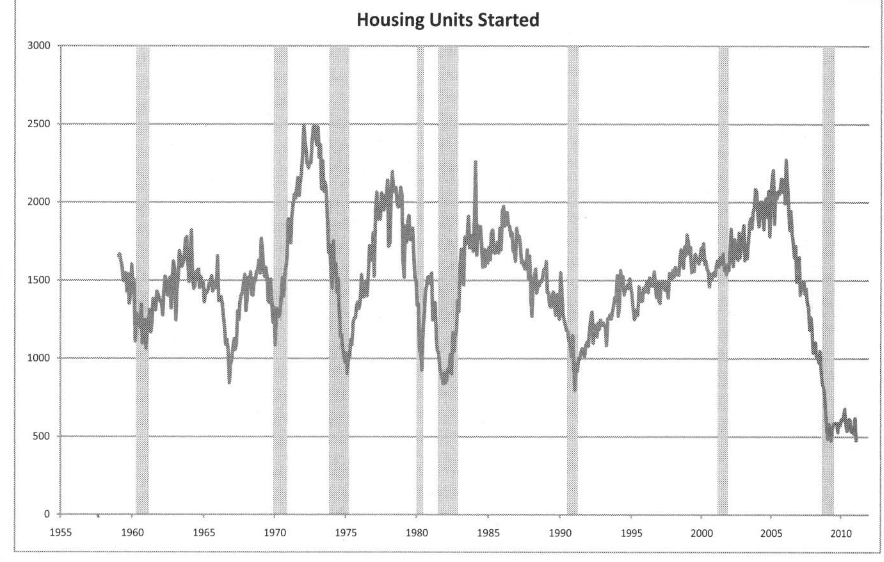

Figure 11-2: The relationship between housing units started and economic recessions.

As you can see in the figure, the housing starts data regularly fall off in advance of economic contractions. However, you can also see that not every fall in housing starts leads to a declared recession (as declared by the National Bureau of Economic Research; see Chapter 7 for details). Timing a recession is difficult when using any economic indicator, but it's especially hard when using housing data. Sometimes housing starts decline years before an economic contraction officially begins.

The housing starts data series in Figure 11-2 shows the characteristic up-and-down jaggedness of erratic, volatile data. The cure is to smooth the data by using a moving average so that you can identify the underlying trend (see Chapter 2 for a refresher on using moving averages). The Census Bureau recommends using a four-month moving average, but given the lag between the turning point in housing starts and an actual recession, the penalty for using a longer moving average is very small and offers the benefit of greater certainty.

From Figure 11-2, you may also notice that the most recent data on housing starts is remarkably low. In fact, the number of housing starts in 2010 is at a 50-year low! By 2011, the economy was performing relatively well (although below average for the early stage of a recovery), and preliminary reports showed GDP growing 2.9 percent in 2010. Yet new housing starts showed very little improvement, and housing contributed only half of its 5 percent long-term average to the 2010 GDP.

You can expect this situation to correct itself, although when it will do so is open to intense debate. Demand for new housing is being tempered by poor job market conditions and the very tight lending standards imposed after the subprime mortgage collapse. These new standards are understandable but very likely overdone. (***Note:*** The recovery may have already occurred by the time you read this book, but at the time of this writing, it hadn't happened yet.)

Remodeling your investment portfolio

Investment markets keep a close watch on authorized building permits and new housing starts. Business managers, especially those in the construction industry and those in the related building-materials and finance industries, also watch the housing data for significant changes that may require adjustments to their business plans. Keep the following bits of information in mind, depending on which type of investments you have.

Building bond interest

Bond investors don't care to see strength in the housing markets. After all, housing growth leads to economic growth, which causes interest rates to rise, and those higher interest rates can fuel inflation. Higher interest rates cause bond prices to deteriorate, and inflation erodes the value of bond interest payments.

Bond investors need to follow housing starts carefully. A single-month rise is no reason to panic, but a persistent trend of improving housing starts is reason enough for bond investors to become vigilant. As the economy comes out of recession, increases in housing starts will likely have little impact on interest rates. But as the recovery gains steam, start shortening the duration of your bond portfolio when you see growth in the housing sector. Likewise, if the trend in housing starts deteriorates, start looking for longer-term bond investments and extending the maturity of your portfolio.

Stocking up on housing

As long as housing starts continue to trend higher, equity investors are a happy bunch. However, as the trend in housing starts declines, investors need to start looking for the exits.

Although a downward trend for housing starts doesn't mean that the economy is going into recession immediately, recession is a likely outcome. Therefore, the first obvious move is to pare back any home-builder stocks in your portfolio, along with companies that supply the building industry. Building-material manufacturers and retailers that service both home builders and remodelers perform better during a downturn than those that service new construction alone. As the housing starts downtrend progresses, an economic contraction becomes likely. Investors need to plan to move away from growth stocks.

Homing in on commodity markets

Investors in commodity markets also need to pay attention to housing trends. Home builders use several tradable commodities to construct single-family houses and multifamily apartments, townhomes, and condos. You can expect decreased demand for lumber, steel, and copper as housing trends decline. Conversely, you can expect demand for these raw materials to increase as the trend in housing starts grows.

Reporting New-Home Sales: The New Residential Sales Report

Some homes are built *on contract,* meaning that a home buyer signed a contract and paid a deposit to the builder to build the home. Others are built on *spec,* or *speculation,* meaning that the builder builds the house before identifying a buyer. For spec homes, the builder must secure construction financing, buy the lot or tract, and then pay for materials, contractors, and direct labor. Not surprisingly, builders are more willing to risk their capital by building spec homes when real estate is doing well.

As long as buyers reward builders by buying their spec homes, all is right in the builders' world. But as soon as the economy starts to drop off, home sales fall and spec builders are left with homes that nobody is willing to buy. As a result, the home builders may have to pay expensive finance charges if their homes remain unsold after they complete them. If things get bad enough and the builder can't pay these expenses, the firm will go out of business.

Getting a handle on the number of spec homes under construction or for sale isn't easy. The Census Bureau's *New Residential Sales report* comes the closest to providing the necessary data. Table 11-2 provides an overview of this report.

Table 11-2 New Residential Sales Report

Release Schedule	*Agency*	*Web Address*	*Sensitivity*
Monthly: Published schedule, 10:00 a.m. ET	U.S. Census Bureau	`www.census.gov/const/www/newressales index.html`	Moderate

Keep reading for more information about this report, including what data you can find in this report, how you can decipher the information, and how you can modify your investments accordingly.

Comparing new starts with new sales: Is it possible?

Correlating the data in the New Housing Starts table (Table 3) of the New Residential Construction report with the data in the New Residential Sales report is next to impossible. After all, the number of new homes started and completed each month is larger, sometimes much larger, than the reported number of new homes sold and for sale.

The reason for this discrepancy is the way the Census Bureau collects and reports the data for the two reports. The housing starts data include all residential construction, while the New Residential Sales report measures only homes that are built *for sale* (meaning only speculatively built homes that the builder offers along with the developed land for sale as a single transaction).

The New Residential Sales report doesn't count all homes that are built under contract. Home buyers and builders can sign a contact at any stage of the home-building project. About 25 percent of new homes are reported sold after construction is complete. Reporting of the remaining transactions is more or less evenly split between those homes under construction and those not yet started. If a home is under contract before construction begins, it probably won't show up in the New Residential Sales report.

Figure 11-3 is an example of Table 1 from the New Residential Sales report. It shows the number of newly constructed homes that sold during the reporting period and the number that remain for sale at the end of that period. The table includes the preliminary estimate for the current month as well as 12 months of historical data. The current month's data are likely to be revised over the course of the next several months. The table also includes the percentage changes from the current month to the previous month and the percentage change from the current month to the same month a year earlier.

Table 1. New Houses Sold and For Sale

[Thousands of houses. Detail may not add to total because of rounding.]

Period	Sold during period[1]					For sale at end of period					Months' Supply[2]	Median sales price ($)	Average sales price ($)
	United States	North-east	Mid-west	South	West	United States	North-east	Mid-west	South	West			
	Seasonally adjusted												
2010: February	347	30	49	180	88	232					8.0		
March	384	33	53	206	92	228					7.1		
April	414	36	56	213	109	216					6.3		
May	282	28	39	152	63	216					9.2		
June	310	34	46	174	56	211					8.2		
July	283	30	43	166	44	210					8.9		
August	274	29	31	149	65	207					9.1		
September	317	35	52	162	68	202					7.6		
October	280	30	40	160	50	200					8.6		
November (r)	286	21	34	164	67	195					8.2		
December (r)	333	21	39	166	107	188					6.8		
2011: January (r)	301	35	40	158	68	186					7.4		
February (p)	**250**	**15**	**29**	**148**	**58**	**186**					**8.9**		
Average RSE (%)[3]	8	25	25	11	15	4					8		
Percent Change:													
February 2011 from January 2011	***-16.9%***	***-57.1%***	***-27.5%***	***-6.3%***	***-14.7%***	***0.0%***					***20.3%***		
90% Confidence Interval[4]	*± 19.1*	*± 32.6*	*± 43.5*	*± 21.3*	*± 48.6*	*± 0.9*					*± 23.0*		
February 2011 from February 2010	***-28.0%***	***-50.0%***	***-40.8%***	***-17.8%***	***-34.1%***	***-19.8%***					***11.3%***		
90% Confidence Interval[4]	*± 14.8*	*± 33.2*	*± 33.4*	*± 19.4*	*± 21.5*	*± 3.8*					*± 22.3*		
	Not seasonally adjusted												
2009:	375	31	54	202	87	232	27	38	118	48	(X)	216,700	270,900
2010: (r)	323	31	45	174	74	188	22	27	98	41	(X)	221,000	272,400
RSE (%)	4	8	14	6	5	3	8	14	6	5	(X)	3	2
2010: Year to Date	50	5	7	25	13	(X)	(X)	(X)	(X)	(X)	(X)	(X)	(X)
2011: Year to Date	40	3	5	22	10	(X)	(X)	(X)	(X)	(X)	(X)	(X)	(X)
RSE (%)	6	20	21	7	7	(X)	(X)	(X)	(X)	(X)	(X)	(X)	(X)
Year to Date Percent Change[5]	***-21.1%***	***-31.1%***	***-33.4%***	***-13.5%***	***-24.9%***	(X)	(X)	(X)	(X)	(X)	(X)	(X)	(X)
90% Confidence Interval[4]	*±9.1*	*±33.0*	*±23.5*	*±14.4*	*±12.0*	(X)	(X)	(X)	(X)	(X)	(X)	(X)	(X)
2010: February	27	2	4	13	7	229	26	36	119	47	8.6	221,900	284,100
March	36	3	5	19	9	227	25	36	118	47	6.3	224,800	262,900
April	41	4	5	21	10	216	24	35	113	45	5.3	208,300	270,500
May	26	3	4	14	6	215	24	34	114	44	8.3	230,500	281,100
June	28	3	4	16	5	213	24	32	111	45	7.5	219,500	256,700
July	26	3	4	16	4	210	24	31	109	46	7.9	212,100	252,100
August	23	3	3	12	6	209	23	31	108	46	8.9	226,600	268,800
September	25	3	4	12	6	204	22	29	109	44	8.2	228,000	270,800
October	23	3	3	13	4	199	22	29	104	44	8.7	204,200	254,400
November (r)	20	2	2	12	4	195	22	28	102	43	9.5	219,600	281,700
December (r)	23	2	3	12	7	188	22	27	98	41	8.3	236,800	290,800
2011: January (r)	21	2	3	11	5	185	21	26	98	40	8.9	234,800	265,300
February (p)	**19**	**1**	**2**	**11**	**5**	**183**	**21**	**25**	**98**	**39**	**9.6**	**202,100**	**246,000**
Average RSE (%)[3]	8	25	25	11	15	4	13	13	5	6	8	5	5

(p) Prelminary. (r) Revised. RSE Relative standard error. (X) Not applicable. (Z) Less than 500 units or less than 0.5 percent.

[1]Seasonally adjusted houses sold are published at annual rates. [2]Ratio of houses for sale to houses sold. [3]Average RSE for the latest 6-month period.
[4]See the Explanatory Notes in the accompanying text for an explanation of 90% confidence intervals. [5] Computed using unrounded data.

Note: The sales price includes the land.

Figure 11-3: New homes sold and for sale.

As you can see in the figure, Table 1 categorizes the data into regional results for the Northeast, Midwest, South, and West and shows both seasonally adjusted and annualized data (in the upper section) and nonadjusted and nonannualized data (in the lower section).

The *For sale at end of period* column shows the number of homes that are either under construction or have been completed and remain unsold. Perhaps the most watched number from this report is the one listed in the *Months Supply* column, which is the inventory-to-sales (I/S) ratio of unsold homes. It shows how many months it would take to clear the unsold homes at the current rate of sales.

Recognizing the connection between new-home sales and the economic cycle

Home buyers with the wherewithal to make a financial commitment during a struggling economy can often find good housing values and low mortgage rates. When enough of these value buyers come forward, their home purchases can push a recession into the early stages of economic growth.

These early-stage home buyers show up in the New Residential Sales statistics as increased houses sold. Of course, not every economic expansion begins with a nudge from the housing sector. You don't have to look past 2009 to find economic growth without the housing sector's participation. Nonetheless, housing jump-starts economic growth often enough that it's worth watching.

Generally speaking, reports of new-home sales pick up before those of existing homes. This has nothing to do with the age or condition of the house being purchased and everything to do with the way the sales data are collected and reported. New-home sales are recorded when the contract is signed and a deposit is accepted. Existing-home sales, which I discuss later in this chapter, are generally reported after the transaction closes.

As the economy grows, housing prices and interest rates climb and eventually make home purchases financially less attractive. As a result, the housing sector slows down, and the economy may follow.

Forecasting investment market reactions

Although investment markets may not react to the New Residential Sales report as emphatically as they do to the New Residential Construction report, this report does have an impact. I explain this impact in the following sections.

Be mindful of the volatility of the New Residential Sales data. This data can be very erratic, and you must smooth out the peaks and valleys in this report with a moving average (see Chapter 2 for more about moving averages). A four- to six-month moving average makes sense for this report.

Bonds

Depending on the state of the business cycle, unexpected strength in the New Residential Sales report may be met with selling in the bond pits. Bond investors prefer placid rather than hot housing markets. Increasing home sales correspond with a growing economy, rising interest rates, and the potential for price inflation. None of these results is good for the bond investor. Bond investors should shorten the duration of their portfolios as home sales grow. Weakness in home-sales data is usually a good time to start lengthening the duration of your bond portfolio.

The current business cycle influences the severity of any bond market reaction. Price inflation isn't a huge risk as the economy emerges from a recession, but it becomes a big concern after the economy has been trending higher. Bond investors need to be especially careful when home sales data show escalating sales prices. It can be a harbinger of inflation.

Stocks

Stock market investors like to see lots of homes being sold. After all, consumers and builders show their optimism and confidence in the future when they make large financial commitments. But because of the volatile nature of this report, stocks rarely show strong reactions to it. Still, stocks of home builders and builder-supply companies, as well as other cyclical company stocks, are likely to do well as long as home sales are growing. Investors are advised to focus on these economically sensitive sectors as home sales increase and move their portfolios to stocks, such as consumer staples, during periods of weakness in the housing market.

Reporting Existing-Home Sales

Although new-home construction gets most of the attention, new-home sales represent fewer than 20 percent of all residential real-estate transactions. The vast majority of sales are for existing homes. However, the economic impact of existing-home transactions is muted, at least compared to the impact of new-home construction. Although people buying an existing home may need to buy some of the same consumer durables and supplies as people moving into a newly constructed home, the sale of an existing home drives very few sales of building materials and has no impact on the local construction market.

Still, a correlation is evident between existing-home sales and GDP (see Chapter 7 for more about GDP). Whether they're buying new or existing homes, new homeowners often need furnishings, window coverings, appliances, and other high-ticket consumer durables for their homes.

Of course, mortgage bankers, transfer agents, title firms, and property insurers all benefit from existing-home transactions in much the same way that they do when new homes are sold. And real-estate agents are very pleased when people buy existing homes because those purchases generate sales commissions. New-construction sales don't always include sales commissions.

In short, a strong market for existing housing helps keep the economy humming along. The National Association of Realtors (NAR) tracks home sales, pending contracts, and home affordability and presents this information in its *Existing-Home Sales report*. Table 11-3 provides an overview of this report.

Table 11-3 Existing-Home Sales Report

Release Schedule	***Agency***	***Web Address***	***Sensitivity***
Monthly: Published schedule, 10:00 a.m. ET	National Association of Realtors	`www.realtor.org/research/research/ehsdata`	Moderate

The Existing-Home Sales report shows preliminary data for the current month and revised figures for the previous 12 months of home sales. The report also includes three years of annual home sales data. Figure 11-4 shows an example of the Existing-Home Sales report. As you can see, the report adjusts the data for seasonality and shows nationwide data alongside regional data for the Northeast, Midwest, South, and West.

Existing Single Family Home Sales

Year		U.S.	Northeast	Midwest	South	West	U.S.	Northeast	Midwest	South	West	Inventory*	Mos. Supply
2008 r		4,350,000	623,000	1,022,000	1,721,000	984,000	*	*	*	*	*	3,110,000	10.0
2009 r		4,566,000	641,000	1,067,000	1,745,000	1,113,000	*	*	*	*	*	2,760,000	8.3
2010 r		4,308,000	604,000	984,000	1,669,000	1,051,000	*	*	*	*	*	3,020,000	9.1
		Seasonally Adjusted Annual Rate					Not Seasonally Adjusted						
2010	Feb	4,370,000	610,000	1,010,000	1,640,000	1,110,000	262,000	39,000	63,000	98,000	62,000	2,960,000	8.1
2010	Mar	4,760,000	660,000	1,120,000	1,810,000	1,170,000	375,000	51,000	91,000	141,000	92,000	3,040,000	7.7
2010	Apr	5,060,000	790,000	1,220,000	1,940,000	1,110,000	459,000	69,000	111,000	173,000	106,000	3,410,000	8.1
2010	May	5,010,000	660,000	1,210,000	1,960,000	1,180,000	462,000	56,000	119,000	176,000	111,000	3,250,000	7.8
2010	Jun	4,580,000	660,000	1,090,000	1,770,000	1,060,000	489,000	73,000	118,000	185,000	113,000	3,310,000	8.7
2010	Jul	3,390,000	470,000	730,000	1,380,000	810,000	338,000	51,000	75,000	134,000	78,000	3,340,000	11.8
2010	Aug	3,720,000	520,000	790,000	1,480,000	930,000	362,000	53,000	76,000	148,000	85,000	3,500,000	11.3
2010	Sept	3,860,000	550,000	850,000	1,520,000	940,000	330,000	47,000	74,000	132,000	77,000	3,340,000	10.4
2010	Oct	3,850,000	550,000	840,000	1,520,000	940,000	316,000	46,000	66,000	126,000	78,000	3,260,000	10.2
2010	Nov	4,080,000	560,000	900,000	1,570,000	1,050,000	317,000	41,000	65,000	124,000	87,000	3,200,000	9.4
2010	Dec	4,580,000	650,000	1,030,000	1,740,000	1,160,000	354,000	46,000	77,000	139,000	92,000	3,020,000	7.9
2011	Jan r	4,700,000	620,000	1,050,000	1,790,000	1,240,000	253,000	32,000	51,000	98,000	72,000	2,920,000	7.5
2011	Feb p	4,250,000	580,000	920,000	1,620,000	1,130,000	254,000	37,000	57,000	97,000	63,000	2,970,000	8.4
vs. last month:		**-9.6%**	**-6.5%**	**-12.4%**	**-9.5%**	**-8.9%**	**0.4%**	**15.6%**	**11.8%**	**-1.0%**	**-12.5%**	**1.7%**	**12.0%**
vs. last year:		**-2.7%**	**-4.9%**	**-8.9%**	**-1.2%**	**1.8%**	**-3.1%**	**-5.1%**	**-9.5%**	**-1.0%**	**1.6%**	**0.3%**	**3.7%**
year-to-date:							**0.507**	**0.069**	**0.108**	**0.195**	**0.135**		

Note: Annual inventory figures are from December of each year

Figure 11-4: Existing-home sales.

Source: National Association of Realtors®. Used with permission.

This report lists the number of homes currently on the market in the *Inventory* column, and it includes an estimation of the number of months required to sell this inventory at the current sales pace (called the *inventory-to-sales,* or *I/S, ratio*) in the *Months Supply* column. The final rows of the figure show the change from the previous month and the previous year. The release schedule for the Existing-Home Sales report is available on the NAR website: `www.realtor.org/press_room/news_release_schedule`. The following sections provide more in-depth information about this report.

Tracking housing prices

The Existing-Home Sales report also tracks average home prices. Although sales of existing homes have little direct impact on the economy, they do have an indirect effect. As home prices rise, homeowners feel wealthier, and they may tap into that increasing value with a home equity loan (which can fuel additional consumer spending). Conversely, falling home prices make it more difficult for homeowners to qualify for home equity loans and can make homeowners think twice before putting their homes on the market. Figure 11-5 shows an example of the Sales Price of Existing Single-Family Homes table.

Sales Price of Existing Single-Family Homes

Year		U.S.	Northeast	Midwest	South	West	U.S.	Northeast	Midwest	South	West
				Median					Average (Mean)		
2008 r		$196,600	$271,500	$150,500	$169,400	$276,100	$241,700	$301,200	$178,100	$212,000	$316,800
2009 r		172,100	243,200	142,900	155,000	215,400	217,000	279,300	168,700	194,700	261,100
2010 r		173,100	243,900	140,800	153,700	220,700	220,600	282,200	170,700	196,500	270,200
				Not Seasonally Adjusted					Not Seasonally Adjusted		
2010	Feb	163,900	261,900	126,700	143,200	206,000	208,200	290,800	153,600	180,900	253,700
2010	Mar	169,500	243,100	134,000	151,000	222,000	214,700	276,800	159,800	191,100	269,000
2010	Apr	172,500	249,100	139,700	152,000	223,400	218,200	283,800	164,300	193,000	270,900
2010	May	174,500	220,800	148,200	156,700	225,400	221,100	267,100	173,100	198,700	276,700
2010	Jun	183,500	252,800	155,600	163,200	226,200	231,200	291,500	184,700	209,600	274,100
2010	Jul	183,000	265,500	150,900	159,600	231,000	233,000	299,300	184,800	206,300	281,400
2010	Aug	178,100	254,600	146,800	157,100	224,200	227,100	290,300	180,500	202,200	273,500
2010	Sept	172,400	239,600	138,800	153,400	223,100	219,100	275,300	169,500	194,200	273,500
2010	Oct	171,500	242,400	138,900	153,100	216,300	219,600	280,600	170,500	196,300	267,700
2010	Nov	170,900	244,600	138,600	150,800	216,900	219,400	284,700	170,700	194,100	267,900
2010	Dec	169,300	234,200	140,100	153,300	209,900	218,600	276,200	173,100	197,600	261,600
2011	Jan r	158,500	236,100	126,400	141,400	196,700	207,000	273,900	159,100	185,200	247,400
2011	Feb p	157,000	230,500	121,700	139,900	196,500	203,700	268,600	154,500	182,300	246,300
	vs. last year:	**-4.2%**	**-12.0%**	**-3.9%**	**-2.3%**	**-4.6%**	**-2.2%**	**-7.6%**	**0.6%**	**0.8%**	**-2.9%**

Source: National Association of Realtors®. Used with permission.

Figure 11-5: Sales prices of existing homes.

The Sales Price of Existing Single-Family Homes table includes preliminary data for the current month and revised figures for the previous 12 months of home prices. The table shows the median and average prices for the United States as well as for four geographic regions — the Northeast, Midwest, South, and West. The table also includes three years of annual home prices, and none of the data is adjusted for seasonality.

Qualifying for a home: The Housing Affordability Index

The National Association of Realtors (NAR) is understandably interested in how much home most buyers can afford. NAR's Housing Affordability Index attempts to show whether a typical family can qualify for a mortgage on an average home. Although the investment community doesn't generally follow the Housing Affordability Index, people in the real-estate and construction industries do pay close attention because most people need a mortgage loan to buy a home. If the average family is financially unable to qualify for a mortgage, realtors and home builders suffer.

NAR defines a *typical family* as one that earns the median family income. A *typical home* is defined based on the national median-priced existing single-family home. Several factors affect affordability, but prevailing home prices and current mortgage rates have the largest impact.

The index itself is reported on a scale in which 100 means that a typical family has just enough income to qualify for a mortgage on an average home. Above 100 means that the family has more than enough money, and less than 100 means that the family is unable to qualify.

Check out the Housing Affordability Index on the NAR website at `www.realtor.org/research/research/housinginx`.

National home sales activity tends to fall off during the fall and winter months and pick up again in the late spring. You can see this general trend in Figure 11-5. This seasonality isn't as strong in the South, but it does exist.

Although home-sale prices aren't adjusted for seasonality, seasonal factors do affect prices. Weather can be a factor of the seasonality of home sales, especially in snowy climates, but school and vacation schedules likely play a bigger role. Most home sales occur during the late spring and summer seasons, which are when average home prices are the highest. (See the later section "Pricing the S&P/Case-Shiller Indices" for more info on U.S. home pricing.)

Understanding how existing-home sales affect investment markets

Given the correlation between housing and the economy and the relative size of the existing-home market compared to the new-construction market, you may expect investors to react more forcefully to the Existing-Home Sales report. Yet although markets do occasionally react to surprising results in the Existing-Home Sales report, investor reactions to the report are otherwise subdued. Generally speaking, the Existing-Home Sales report doesn't have the investment market or economic impact of the New Residential Sales report.

Both stock and bond investors pay closer attention to the Existing-Home Sales report as the economy approaches turning points. Although the report isn't an exceptional forecasting indicator, it's a useful tool to fine-tune and confirm your investment strategies.

Buying bonds as housing falters

The only two times when bond investors care about the Existing-Home Sales report are after the economy starts showing signs of economic contraction (at this point, bond buyers sense an opportunity) and when the economy shows signs of overheating (at this point, bond investors begin to worry).

Bond investors' cause for concern is always the same. They worry about rising interest rates and price inflation. Rising rates depress the price of current bond holdings, and inflation erodes the value of interest payments. Therefore, after a period of economic growth, bond investors grow anxious if housing shows unexpected strength.

The opposite is also true. Bond investors find opportunity when the economy cools and interest rates fall. Although those conditions are harder to spot in the Existing-Home Sales report, any unexpected weakness as the economy contracts may get bond investors' attention.

Bond investors need to treat this report as a second-tier indicator. If you decide to factor it into your longer-term investment planning, use it primarily as a confirming indicator. In other words, use it to confirm your analysis about the current state of the economy, not as a primary decision-making tool.

Stocking up on housing strength

When the economy is coming out of a recession, seeing early strength in the housing sectors isn't unusual. Unfortunately, the Existing-Home Sales report has a built-in lag that trails the data shown in the New Residential Sales report, making it an unsuitable leading indicator.

Stock investors can use the Existing-Home Sales report to anticipate improved profitability in sectors like banking and insurance. Other than that, you should use this report only to confirm your analysis based on other indicators.

Monitoring Pending Home Sales

Unlike new-home sales, which are generally reported when the contract is signed and a deposit is accepted, existing-home sales are reported after the transaction closes. This reporting can occur two or more months after the contract is signed. The difference in the reporting structure means that existing-home sales data tend to lag behind the new-home sales data by two or three months.

To address this issue, the National Association of Realtors (NAR) began reporting figures for existing-home contract signings in 2005 in what it calls the *Pending Home Sales Index.* Using contract signings makes the Pending Home Sales Index more like the New Residential Sales report that I discuss earlier in this chapter. Although this report is still relatively new, its influence is growing.

In fact, the NAR believes that this index is the best predictor for actual home sales activity available. But until investors and economists have a better sense of this indicator's performance, it's unlikely to move markets in any significant way. However, if its predictive capabilities are proved, it will become a more prominent housing indicator. Table 11-4 gives an overview of this index.

Table 11-4 Pending Home Sales Index

Release Schedule	*Agency*	*Web Address*	*Sensitivity*
Monthly: Published schedule, 10:00 a.m. ET	National Association of Realtors	`www.realtor.org/research/research/phsdata`	Low but growing

The Pending Home Sales Index shows existing-home sales in which a contract has been signed but the transaction has not yet closed. The report's main purpose is to provide better insight into future sales of existing homes so as to align existing-home sales data with the data collected for new-home sales. Figure 11-6 shows an example of the Pending Home Sales Index.

In this index, the year 2001 is set to 100 (100 is the baseline; see Chapter 2 for more about baseline indexes). Sales include single-family homes, condos, co-ops, and townhomes. The current month's data are preliminary and may be revised.

As you can see in the figure, the table includes the results from the previous 12 months as well as three annual indexes. It also shows the percentage changes from the previous month and from the previous year and includes regional reports from the Northeast, Midwest, South, and West. The data are presented as both seasonally adjusted annualized rates and not seasonally adjusted rates.

NATIONAL ASSOCIATION OF REALTORS®

Pending Home Sales Index (PHSI)

Year		United States	Northeast	Midwest	South	West	United States	Northeast	Midwest	South	West
2008 r		87.1	74.1	80.8	89.8	99.6	*	*	*	*	*
2009 r		95.0	76.8	88.9	98.5	110.0	*	*	*	*	*
2010 r		89.3	71.2	80.3	97.1	100.7	*	*	*	*	*
		Seasonally Adjusted Annual Rate					Not Seasonally Adjusted				
2010	Jan	90.3	75.8	80.6	98.1	99.6	74.3	52.5	64.1	77.5	96.8
2010	Feb	98.9	80.2	96.5	105.9	105.0	88.3	70.1	94.0	92.2	90.4
2010	Mar	106.2	77.7	100.1	123.1	108.2	119.7	101.4	116.1	136.3	111.8
2010	Apr	111.5	96.9	106.2	125.0	107.2	133.4	124.8	134.4	152.3	109.4
2010	May	78.3	66.3	70.6	82.9	88.6	89.0	87.0	81.2	93.9	91.3
2010	Jun	75.9	57.7	63.1	83.3	91.9	92.7	78.9	79.1	106.1	96.9
2010	Jul	78.4	61.5	66.6	86.2	91.9	85.4	65.5	69.3	99.3	96.2
2010	Aug	82.3	62.8	70.4	90.1	97.8	90.9	66.0	72.3	97.8	119.2
2010	Sept	79.4	58.3	63.7	87.2	100.2	77.1	50.1	62.9	80.5	107.7
2010	Oct	85.5	69.0	78.3	90.7	97.6	84.0	66.6	74.9	85.1	105.3
2010	Nov	94.5	77.3	83.7	95.5	117.8	75.9	51.7	62.7	74.8	110.3
2010	Dec	91.5	75.3	84.1	96.4	104.1	61.1	40.3	52.8	69.6	72.5
2011	Jan p	88.9	73.5	78.0	97.7	98.7	71.0	47.9	60.3	75.5	93.2
	vs. last month:	**-2.8%**	**-2.4%**	**-7.3%**	**1.4%**	**-5.2%**	**16.2%**	**18.9%**	**14.2%**	**8.5%**	**28.6%**
	vs. last year:	**-1.5%**	**-3.0%**	**-3.2%**	**-0.4%**	**-0.9%**	**-4.4%**	**-8.8%**	**-5.9%**	**-2.6%**	**-3.7%**

Figure 11-6: An example of the Pending Home Sales Index.

Source: National Association of Realtors®. Used with permission.

The Pending Home Sales Index has a few limits you need to keep in mind. First of all, most closings happen within one or two months of the contract signing, but they can take longer. Also, not all contracts for existing homes are ultimately closed (this issue affects new-home sales contracts as well). For example, if a home fails inspection, if a buyer is unable to qualify for a mortgage, or if the buyer just gets cold feet, the transaction may not be completed.

Surveying Mortgages

You can find another source of information about home-buying activity in mortgage application data. A home purchase is usually the largest expense people make, and very few home buyers can buy a home outright with cash. Instead, they use a mortgage to borrow the money to buy their home.

Applying for a mortgage requires filling out a remarkable amount of paperwork and sometimes paying a fee just to submit the application. Because only the truly committed home buyer will go through this process, the number of mortgage applications is a very good indicator of home buyers' intentions.

The Mortgage Bankers Association (MBA) tracks mortgage applications for home purchases and refinancing through its *Weekly Applications Survey*. This survey provides the number of applications and the dollar amount of traditional fixed-rate and adjustable-rate loans. Table 11-5 offers more information on this survey.

Table 11-5 Weekly Applications Survey

Releases	*Agency*	*Web Address*	*Sensitivity*
Weekly: Every Wednesday, 7:00 ET	Mortgage Bankers Association	`www.mbaa.org/ResearchandForecasts/ProductsandSurveys/WeeklyApplicationSurvey`	Low

The following sections provide a basis for what data comprises the survey, how you can interpret the information, and how you can use the report in your investing.

Eyeing what data you get at no cost

Although the full Weekly Applications Survey is available only by subscription, the MBA provides the top-line indexes at no charge in a short press release. The indexes in the press release include

- **Market Composite Index:** Measures all mortgage applications, including those for new purchases and refinancing
- **Purchase Index:** Measures mortgage applications for home purchases
- **Refinance Index:** Measures mortgage applications for refinancing existing mortgages

The press release usually shows only the percentage change for each index from the previous week, as well as the percentage change for a four-week moving average from its value the previous week (see Chapter 2 for more information about moving averages). In addition, the press release provides the average rates for 30-year fixed-rate mortgages and 15-year fixed-rate mortgages, as well as the percentage of adjustable-rate mortgages to the total number of applications. Finally, the press release includes a short mortgage-market analysis.

Tracking delinquent mortgages

The flip side of mortgage applications are the homeowners who fall behind on their monthly payments. Just as rising mortgage applications are an indicator of future housing and economic growth, rising mortgage delinquencies are a stark warning that some consumers have taken on financial obligations that they can't satisfy.

Homeowners historically would do whatever was necessary to avoid late mortgage payments and foreclosure. Keeping their home was their highest priority. Pride of ownership coupled with the seemingly old-fashioned requirement for a 20 percent down payment made the home an asset worth keeping. Homeowners had a real financial incentive to keep up with their mortgage payments. But all that changed in the era of subprime lending standards. The housing crisis that began in 2008 was a direct result of too many under-qualified mortgage applicants buying homes that they couldn't afford without the traditional large down payment.

The MBA tracks mortgage delinquencies and foreclosures and publishes the quarterly results in the *National Delinquency Survey.* The complete survey is available for a fee, but you can get the gist of the survey's results by reading the most recent press release, which you find at `www.mbaa.org/ResearchandForecasts/ProductsandSurveys/NationalDelinquencySurvey.htm`. Investors and business leaders use this survey for its insight into the health of mortgage lenders and the mortgage market. The survey also offers a peek at consumers' financial condition and their ability to keep up with their financial obligations.

The survey categorizes mortgage delinquencies and foreclosures according to the type and quality of the loan and geographic location. Mortgages are listed as prime, subprime, or government-guaranteed loans and as either fixed- or adjustable-rate mortgages. Delinquencies are measured by how far the homeowner is behind in payment — over 30 days, over 60 days, or over 90 days.

The National Delinquency Survey also reports foreclosure statistics. Generally, after a homeowner is 90 days delinquent, the mortgage holder can begin foreclosure proceedings but isn't obligated to do so.

Identifying potential market changes

Although mortgage application activity is usually a good indicator of future economic activity, the Weekly Applications Survey rarely has a significant impact on the investment markets. Until recently, neither stock nor bond investors hade given the National Delinquency Survey much attention.

Bonding with the mortgage market

A large, unexpected rise in mortgage applications may spook bond traders who are worried about inflation. From the investment market's perspective, timing of the increase is just as important as the magnitude. Bond investors are more likely to care if the application increase happens after a period of growth rather than as the economy is coming out of a recession.

Until the subprime mortgage debacle, even mortgage-backed bond investors rarely gave the National Delinquency Survey a second look. These bonds were generally considered low-risk investments because people assumed they were backed by the full faith and credit of the U.S. Government (even if that backing was never explicitly made). You can bet bondholders won't make that mistake again. A rise in delinquency rates is likely to drive bond prices lower — especially prices for mortgage-backed bonds — and interest rates higher as investors try to sell these bonds.

Mortgaging stock investments

Except for investors who follow specific banks or mortgage companies, equity investors generally pay little attention to the MBA's mortgage-related reports. Financial stocks can suffer when delinquencies rise, and their profitability generally improves when mortgage applications rise. However, stock market investors have better, timelier indicators for monitoring the health of the housing market and, by inference, the mortgage market, like the New Residential Construction report and Existing-Home Sales report discussed earlier in this chapter.

Pricing the S&P/Case-Shiller Indices

Many indicators track home prices in the United States. For example, the National Association of Realtors tracks the sales prices of existing homes in its Existing-Home Sales report, which I discuss earlier in this chapter. But Standard & Poor's *S&P/Case-Shiller Home Price Indices* receive the most attention in the media and investor circles. Check out Table 11-6 for more information about these indexes.

Table 11-6 S&P/Case-Shiller Home Price Indices

Release Schedule	*Agency*	*Web Address*	*Sensitivity*
Monthly: Last Tuesday, 9:00 a.m. ET	Standard and Poor's (S&P)	`bit.ly/case-shiller-report`	Low

The S&P/Case-Shiller Home Price Indices actually consist of 23 indexes — 20 metro areas throughout the United States and 3 composite indexes.

The goal of these indexes is to track repeat sales of single-family homes in specific regions. S&P uses a matching technique called *sale pair* to match the recent selling price for a home with its first-sale price. The aggregate sale-pair data for each region are then converted into an index.

This process sounds easier than it is. The studies must monitor the condition of the sale-pair homes to make sure that the homes remain in good condition and that any additions or remodeling is factored into the index.

Each month's release provides detailed commentary about the results, graphs showing the indexes over time, and tables showing the index values and the percentage changes from the previous two months and the corresponding month from the previous year.

Another unique feature of these indexes is that *futures and option contracts* (specialized financial derivatives) are traded on the Chicago Mercantile Exchange (CME). The contracts are designed and priced to help large financial institutions manage housing risk. But they're clearly not intended for the novice investor. These derivative contracts are relatively new and are very lightly traded. As they become more widely used, they will make the already useful Case-Shiller indexes even more attractive. See the CME Group website for details at `www.cmegroup.com/trading/real-estate`. (I briefly cover futures contracts in Chapter 15; for more information, check out *Trading Futures For Dummies* by Joe Duarte and *Trading Options For Dummies* by George Fontanills, both published by John Wiley & Sons, Inc.)

Although home prices don't have a direct impact on investment markets, they do have an indirect effect. As home prices rise, fewer people can afford to buy homes. In turn, you see a slowdown in both new- and existing-home sales as well as a corresponding slowdown in the economy. Also, after the subprime mortgage crisis, investors, business leaders and policy analysts are paying close attention to home prices to assess the strength of the current economic expansion.

Part IV

Inflation, Productivity, Interest Rates, and Commodities: Oh My!

"I was so into my charts that one day she came in and told me she was running away with the pool boy. Now there's a trend I didn't see coming."

In this part . . .

This part helps you discover some of the things that can either gum up the economic pipeline or really get the economy moving. First, I explain the very real impact price inflation has on the economy (and everyone in it) and show you how to monitor it. Then I show you how businesses can boost profitability by improving productivity. As it turns out, productivity improvements help the economy, too, so they're definitely worth watching. I finish up by looking at the effects interest rates and commodities have on the economy.

Chapter 12

Determining Inflation's Economic Impact

In This Chapter

- Taking note of the prices consumers pay
- Figuring out how much production materials cost
- Identifying inflation in employee compensation

Inflation has an impact on stock and bond investments, individuals, businesses, and the economy, and it isn't a fun one; at least, not for most people. Simply put, *inflation* is a rise in the general level of prices over time. For most of you, it means that you can't afford to buy as many products and services as you used to. But for people who owe money (through a fixed-rate mortgage or any other large fixed-rate debt), it means that they can pay back the loan with dollars that are worth less than the ones they borrowed. Of course, the person who made the loan isn't happy with this arrangement.

Consider the last time the United States experienced a major inflation problem. The annual inflation rate had grown from less than 2 percent in 1965 to 13.5 percent by 1980. Inflation caused enormous economic damage. For one, the interest rate for a 30-year, conventional mortgage was more than 18 percent by October 1981, and the prime rate exceeded 21 percent in 1982. By 1985, unemployment peaked over 10 percent, which was even worse than what the nation experienced after the 2008 subprime lending crisis. Industries like home building, auto manufacturing, and steel production were badly damaged. The savings and loan industry was all but destroyed. It took the better part of a decade for some industries to recover.

Inflation concerns resurfaced in early 2011. At the time, inflation was growing worldwide, and some wondered whether U.S. monetary policies were at least partly to blame.

This chapter looks at popular indicators for measuring inflation. In addition, it briefly discusses inflation's causes and explains how investors can stay ahead of inflation's impact.

Gauging Inflation from the Consumer's View: The Consumer Price Index

The most well known of all inflation measures is the *Consumer Price Index* (CPI), which measures the average price changes of household goods and services over time.

CPI has a real impact on people's lives. After all, this indicator determines the *cost-of-living adjustment* (COLA) for Social Security, as well as for some alimony payments, child support payments, food stamp programs, pension and collective bargaining agreements, minimum wage laws, and insurance policies with inflation protection. (COLA provides a simple mechanism to ensure that benefit payments keep up with rising prices due to inflation; it's sometimes referred to as a *price escalator.*)

Table 12-1 provides some basic information about the CPI. You can find the CPI publication schedule on the U.S. Bureau of Labor Statistics (BLS) website at www.bls.gov/schedule/news_release/cpi.htm.

Table 12-1 Consumer Price Index

Release Schedule	*Agency*	*Web Address*	*Sensitivity*
Monthly: Published schedule, 8:30 a.m. ET	U.S. Bureau of Labor Statistics	www.bls.gov/cpi/	Very high

The following sections delve deeper into the CPI and explain what it comprises, how you can utilize the information to gauge inflation, what revelations you can find in the index, and how you can use it in your investments.

Eyeing the parts of the CPI

The CPI is actually several related indexes. Here are the most important parts of the CPI:

- **CPI-U:** This index covers about 87 percent of the population, including wage earners, clerical workers, professionals, managerial staff, technical workers, self-employed people, short-term workers, unemployed workers, retirees, and others not in the labor force. It doesn't include people in rural areas, those in the armed forces, or people imprisoned or committed to mental hospitals. The CPI-U is the most widely reported of all the CPI indexes and is the focus of this section.

- **CPI-W:** Although the CPI-W covers only wage earners and clerical workers and represents only 32 percent of the population (it's a subset of CPI-U), it's important because it determines the Social Security COLA escalator, as well as many other price escalator clauses.
- **C-CPI-U:** This is the chained-dollar CPI-U for all urban consumers. (See Chapter 2 for details about chained-dollar indexes.)

Distinguishing between inflation, deflation, and disinflation

Inflation isn't the only "flation" condition that you'll encounter. Here's a brief description of the three currency valuation conditions and what they mean:

- *Inflation* is a rise in the level of prices over time.
- *Disinflation* is a general reduction in the rate of price increases. Prices are still rising during disinflation, but they're doing so at a slower pace.
- *Deflation* is a general decrease in the level of prices over time. Deflation is at least as worrisome as inflation because as prices fall, people tend to horde currency and delay purchases, which can make a weak economy even weaker. (The last bout of general deflation in the U.S. economy occurred during the Great Depression. More recently, the Japanese economy has wrestled with the deflationary problem.)

Inflation used to refer to increases in the money supply. Today, though, some economists use the term *monetary inflation* when referring to the money supply. For clarity, some economists use the term *price inflation* when referring to rising price levels, but *inflation* is generally understood to mean price inflation.

Most economists believe that an imbalance in the money supply causes long-term inflation, especially high rates of long-term inflation trends. In other words, too many dollars are chasing too few goods. If you took economics in school, you may recognize this as the monetarist's definition of inflation. (*Monetarism* is a school of economic thought favored by Milton Friedman, a professor and leader of the influential Chicago school of economics.)

The monetarists stick with their money supply argument even when explaining the causes of modest rates of inflation. In short, if the money supply grows faster than national income, inflation increases.

In contrast, Keynesian theory, a school of economic thought popularized by John Maynard Keynes, argues that money supply growth doesn't directly affect inflation. Instead, an imbalance in the supply and demand for products causes inflation. Money growth is one factor that can help increase the demand for products, but there are many others.

The distinction between these two camps is important because they offer competing solutions to tame high inflation rates (and just about every other economic problem, too). The monetarists' inflation remedy is to tightly control the money supply. Keynesians argue that tax hikes and government spending cuts are the solution. (Although I tend to favor the monetarist argument, it's strictly academic. Policymakers have yet to ask my opinion.)

The CPI includes additional indexes that are based on city size, region, and population. It also provides metro-area indexes for large population centers, like New York City, Los Angeles, and Chicago, as well as selected other metro areas.

The CPI uses a 36-month period from 1982 to 1984 for its reference base, with a reference value of 100. This type of index allows you to easily identify percentage changes from one month to the next or from one year to the next. For example, if CPI grows from 100 in one year to 102 in the next, inflation has grown by 2 percent. Here's another way to look at it: If the CPI index is 221, as it was in February 2011, then inflation has grown by 121 percent since the 1982-to-1984 base reference was established.

Generally, the percentage changes are more important than the absolute value of the CPI itself. Although the various indexes don't move in exactly the same way over the short run, longer-term differences tend to average out. Published data are both seasonally adjusted and unadjusted, but consumers are most interested in the unadjusted data because they provide a better reflection of the prices consumers have to pay. The main use for the adjusted data is in escalation clauses in pension plans, collective bargaining agreements, and Social Security.

Professional economists, including those at the Federal Reserve (the Fed), generally prefer other measures of inflation over the CPI. For example, the Fed favors the GDP price deflator (see Chapter 7) because it covers a broader range of products and services. However, it's published quarterly, so the GDP price deflator isn't the timeliest inflation tool for investors. The personal consumption expenditures (PCE) price index (see Chapter 6) is another favorite of the pros. It also covers a broader range of products and services than the CPI and is published monthly in the Bureau of Economic Analysis's Personal Income and Outlays report.

In a basket: How CPI is measured

CPI is calculated based on the current prices for a basket of frequently purchased household goods and services. The basket includes the following categories:

- **Food and beverages**: Breakfast cereal, milk, coffee, meat, beer, wine, restaurant meals, and snack foods
- **Housing**: Rent, or the equivalent for an owner-occupied house, heating oil, furniture, homeowner's or renter's insurance, and appliances
- **Apparel**: Shirts, sweaters, dresses, jewelry, footwear, and swimsuits
- **Transportation**: New vehicles, airline fares, gasoline, and automobile insurance

- **Healthcare**: Physicians' services, prescription drugs, medical supplies, eye care, eyeglasses, and hospital services
- **Recreation**: Televisions, toys, pets and pet products, sporting goods, and tickets for concerts, movies, and sporting events
- **Education and communication**: College tuition, postage, telephone services, computer hardware, and software
- **Other goods and services**: Personal services, such as haircuts and funeral expenses, personal care products, and some tobacco products

The CPI includes state, local, and federal usage fees, such as water and sewage charges, auto registration, and tolls, as well as sales or excise taxes. But it doesn't include income and Social Security taxes or stock, bond, real estate, or life insurance investments.

You can see the relative weights for the various basket categories in Figure 12-1.

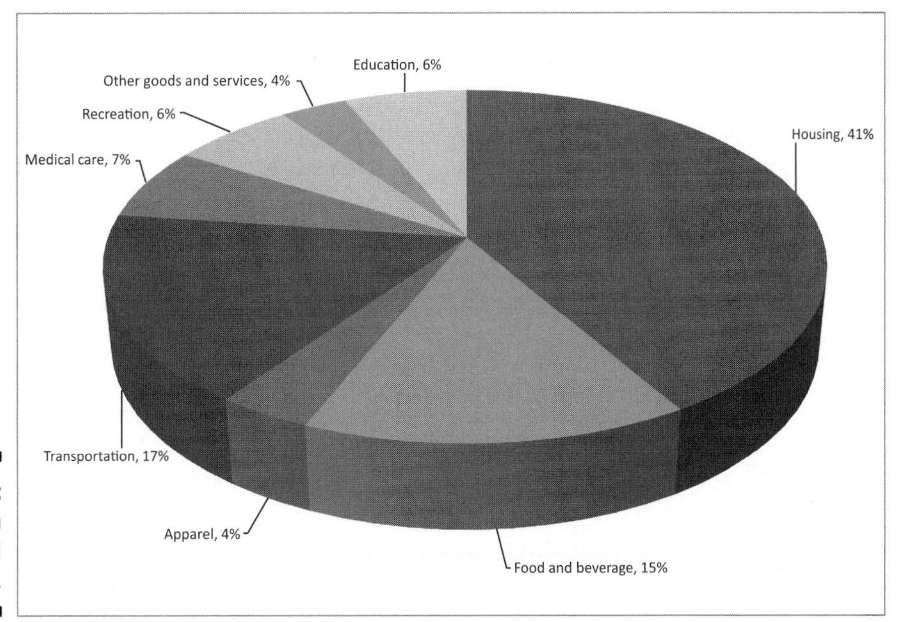

Figure 12-1: Composition of the CPI basket.

Although the CPI basket is based on consumers' purchasing habits, it won't ever precisely match your family's purchases. The basket's purpose is to measure the experience of an average household, not a specific family or individual. If your family, for example, spends a larger percentage of your income on medical expenses than the average family, then your costs are likely to rise faster than average because medical expenses tend to rise more rapidly than other products. On the other hand, if you're very frugal or you live in a temperate climate, your cost to heat your home may be well below average, and your personal CPI may be below average, too.

How the BLS gathers the data

Trained BLS representatives collect the pricing data that make up the CPI basket by surveying approximately 4,000 housing units and 26,000 retail and service vendors. They visit retail stores, like gas stations, department stores, and supermarkets, as well as service companies, like hospitals and hair salons, and use telephone surveys to collect the rest of the pricing data.

The components of the CPI basket are based on the Consumer Expenditure Survey (CES) and are periodically adjusted to reflect current consumption trends. The CES is actually two different large-scale surveys. One of the surveys asks about 7,000 families to provide a summary of their quarterly spending habits over a period of five quarters. The other survey asks about 7,000 families to keep a diary that lists every purchase they make during a two-week period. (Go to `www.bls.gov/cex/` for details on the CES.)

How the BLS interprets sticky data

Sometimes the BLS statisticians and data collectors have to make judgment calls about price changes. The following situations present some challenges to the BLS number crunchers:

- **Changes in packaging:** Manufacturers sometimes change a product's packaging by changing the size, weight, or amount of product in the package. These packaging changes may represent a stealthy price change. If, for example, the packaging for a jar of mayonnaise changed from 32 to 36 ounces but the price remained the same, the BLS would determine that the mayo's price decreased. Conversely, if the price of a box of laundry detergent stayed the same but the amount of product in the package decreased, the BLS would classify it as a price increase.
- **Advancing technology:** Computer and communications industries regularly introduce faster or smaller replacements for existing products. For example, if Apple introduces an update to its iPad product line that makes the iPad faster or gives it additional features but keeps the price constant, should that be considered a price decrease? In general, the BLS says that it is.
- **Product substitutions:** Products in the CPI basket sometimes become obsolete or are replaced by alternative products. The BLS must determine if these substitutions represent a price increase, a decrease, or an entirely new product. For example, consumers may soon have to abandon incandescent bulbs and switch to either compact fluorescent or LED bulbs. The alternative bulbs are much more expensive, but they should also last longer. Is that a price increase or decrease? The BLS makes these kinds of decisions on a case-by-case basis. In the case of light bulbs, the BLS recognizes that the cost per lumen (a measure of light output) is falling; however, it has categorized the compact fluorescent and LED bulbs as new products rather than a general price decrease for lighting.

- **Services:** Collecting pricing data about some services can be very difficult. For example, the CPI considers housing a service. The goal is to measure the costs of home ownership in roughly the same manner as rental housing, so it attempts to remove the investment component of home ownership when reporting CPI. Doing so makes for a very complicated math problem.

Understanding why inflation matters

Mild inflation has been a constant companion of U.S. consumers for decades. High inflation was a serious problem in the late 1970s and early 1980s, and consumers started worrying about increasing prices again in 2011. In small doses, inflation generally has a positive economic effect. The Fed tries to keep annual inflation in the 1 to 2 percent range. The problem occurs when inflation gets far outside of that range, which can mean bad news for consumers.

As the general level of prices increases, the value of the dollar decreases, taking consumers' and businesses' purchasing power with it. Consumers must make do with less. Businesses must pay more for materials and services. Eventually, workers demand more pay to offset their increased costs of living. As corporate profits are squeezed, companies may feel forced to lay off employees.

In situations where inflation gets very high (perhaps when inflation reaches 5 or 6 percent, but certainly when it approaches double digits), consumers may start hoarding nonperishable goods in anticipation of future price increases. These goods can sometimes hold value better than currency. Of course, this action only exacerbates the problem, driving demand for scarce products artificially higher. Consumers also become acclimated to paying off credit with cheaper dollars. As fixed-rate credit becomes scarce, consumers will load up on variable-rate debt in an attempt to stay ahead of inflation.

On the flip side, deflation is at least as damaging as inflation. From the consumers' point of view, seeing the general level of prices fall may seem attractive, but it's ultimately harmful to both consumers and businesses. For one thing, debt becomes more burdensome because the borrower must repay the loan with more valuable dollars. Initially, consumers see some benefit because they can buy more with their money. However, as people ultimately realize that their dollars become worth more as prices fall, they tend to hoard cash. When consumers' purchases slow, businesses' profits suffer. As a result, businesses have a hard time paying their workforces, but employees resist wage decreases, which means that deflation increases labor costs and causes layoffs. As businesses and the economy shed jobs, consumers purchase even fewer products. The deflationary cycle is very difficult to repair.

Seeing the different reactions to inflation and the CPI

Realize that not all industries, products, and services react to inflation the same way. Prices for different products and services may rise at significantly different rates. Figure 12-2 illustrates this fact by showing the CPI percentage changes for several categories of products and services. Specifically, Figure 12-2 shows Table A from the CPI report, which lists the seasonally adjusted percentage changes from the previous month and the unadjusted CPI percentage change from the previous year.

Table A. Percent changes in CPI for All Urban Consumers (CPI-U): U.S. city average

	Seasonally adjusted changes from preceding month							Un-adjusted 12-mos. ended Feb. 2011
	Aug. 2010	Sep. 2010	Oct. 2010	Nov. 2010	Dec. 2010	Jan. 2011	Feb. 2011	
All items	.2	.2	.2	.1	.4	.4	.5	2.1
Food	.1	.3	.1	.2	.1	.5	.6	2.3
Food at home	.0	.4	.1	.2	.2	.7	.8	2.8
Food away from home [1]	.3	.3	.1	.1	.1	.2	.2	1.6
Energy	1.6	1.1	2.5	.1	4.0	2.1	3.4	11.0
Energy commodities	2.6	2.2	4.4	.7	6.4	4.0	4.8	19.3
Gasoline (all types)	2.9	2.2	4.5	.7	6.7	3.5	4.7	19.2
Fuel oil [1]	.9	.8	4.7	4.2	4.9	6.8	5.8	27.1
Energy services	.4	-.4	.0	-.8	.6	-.6	1.1	.2
Electricity	.1	-.1	.2	.6	.3	-.5	.4	2.2
Utility (piped) gas service	1.4	-1.4	-.6	-5.3	1.7	-1.2	3.4	-5.9
All items less food and energy	.1	.0	.0	.1	.1	.2	.2	1.1
Commodities less food and energy commodities	.1	-.2	-.2	.0	-.1	.2	.2	.0
New vehicles	.2	.1	-.1	-.2	-.1	-.1	1.0	.9
Used cars and trucks	.9	-.4	-.6	.1	-.1	-.3	.1	1.9
Apparel	.0	-.5	-.2	.1	.1	1.0	-.9	-.4
Medical care commodities [1]	.2	.3	.1	.2	.1	.5	.7	2.7
Services less energy services	.0	.1	.1	.2	.1	.1	.2	1.5
Shelter	.0	.0	.1	.1	.1	.1	.1	.8
Transportation services	.0	.3	.3	.4	.2	.6	.5	3.5
Medical care services	.2	.7	.2	.2	.3	-.1	.4	3.0

[1] Not seasonally adjusted.

Figure 12-2: Percent changes in CPI for all urban consumers.

Notice how energy price increases overwhelm all other categories in this table, especially the unadjusted percentage changes from the previous year. If you look at the detail lines, you can see that gasoline is 19 percent more expensive than it was a year earlier and fuel oil is more than 27 percent more expensive.

The media commonly report only two of the statistics from Table A:

- **All items:** The first line of the table shows the CPI percentage change for the complete basket of goods.
- **All items less food and energy:** The 12th line of the table shows the core inflation rate, which doesn't count food or energy, the CPI's two most volatile components.

Looking at long-term trends: Core inflation

Most economists, including those at the Federal Reserve (the Fed), are more interested in long-term inflation trends caused by persistent increases in most or all prices rather than temporary price increases in a few products. The same holds true for price decreases. Prices for food and energy products change more rapidly than most other products, which is why economists prefer to focus on inflation without these volatile components. Otherwise, price changes in food and energy might provide a misleading picture of long-term inflation. The BLS calculates *core inflation* by removing the effects of food and energy prices from the CPI.

The price volatility of food and energy is the result of a number of factors. For example, extreme weather conditions can cause some food prices to skyrocket temporarily, and Middle Eastern instability can dramatically increase gasoline and other energy prices.

Yet although these prices tend to rise dramatically without warning, the long-term indexes for food and energy are in line with the average CPI. Even so, this volatility makes it very hard for consumers to budget for food and fuel prices for products that they consume daily. Rising food prices mean that consumers may have to forgo another purchase, and rising energy prices impact everything from gasoline prices to transportation costs for goods throughout the economy.

The Cleveland Federal Reserve Bank takes a different approach to measure core inflation. The Cleveland Fed calculates and publishes the *median CPI,* which it defines as the price change that's right in the middle of a long list of price changes. The Cleveland Fed believes this indicator does a better job of determining the long-term inflation trends compared to the CPI-based core inflation. (Find the median CPI at `clevelandfed.org/research/data/US-Inflation/mcpi.cfm`.)

In the example in Figure 12-2, the annual percentage change in the core rate is almost half of the value of the annual *All items* CPI percentage change. Although the percentage change in food prices is higher than the core inflation rate, the difference is small compared to the energy price spike.

Also notice that not everything in the CPI basket moves in the same direction. Even in the energy sector, prices for natural gas actually fell during the period shown in Figure 12-2.

The CPI's Table A provides a summary of the CPI data. More complete details are available in seven data tables that accompany the CPI report. Figure 12-3 is an excerpt from the first of these data tables, Table 1, which shows the relative importance of each product and service category for the current report, the actual index values, and both the seasonally adjusted and unadjusted monthly percentage changes for each category.

Although food and energy are the CPI's most volatile components, you can see in Figure 12-3 that the medical care categories show the highest growth over time. Look in the column showing the unadjusted index values to see the growth of these indexes relative to the base year 1982 (1982 = 100).

(1982-84=100, unless otherwise noted)

CPI-U	Relative importance, December 2010	Unadjusted indexes		Unadjusted percent change to Feb. 2011 from—		Seasonally adjusted percent change from—		
Expenditure category		Jan. 2011	Feb. 2011	Feb. 2010	Jan. 2011	Nov. to Dec.	Dec. to Jan.	Jan. to Feb.
All items	100.000	220.223	221.309	2.1	0.5	0.4	0.4	0.5
All items (1967=100)	-	659.692	662.943	-	-	-	-	-
Food and beverages	14.792	223.160	224.039	2.2	.4	.1	.5	.5
Food	13.742	222.912	223.799	2.3	.4	.1	.5	.6
Food at home	7.816	220.016	221.241	2.8	.6	.2	.7	.8
Cereals and bakery products	1.090	253.349	254.238	1.1	.4	.4	.8	.0
Meats, poultry, fish, and eggs	1.813	214.344	216.175	6.8	.9	-.3	.9	1.2
Dairy and related products [1]	.839	202.349	203.510	2.4	.6	.4	.1	.6
Fruits and vegetables	1.152	285.619	286.766	4.3	.4	1.8	1.3	2.2
Nonalcoholic beverages and beverage materials	.926	164.019	163.734	.6	-.2	-1.1	1.5	.2
Other food at home	1.996	191.468	193.055	.8	.8	.1	.2	.6
Sugar and sweets [1]	.297	202.648	204.168	1.1	.8	1.3	-.2	.8
Fats and oils	.232	207.813	210.508	4.8	1.3	-.4	2.1	.9
Other foods	1.466	203.610	205.174	.1	.8	-.1	-.1	.5
Other miscellaneous foods [1 2]	.432	120.930	121.438	.2	.4	1.5	-1.2	.4
Food away from home [1]	5.926	228.181	228.606	1.6	.2	.1	.2	.2
Other food away from home [1 2]	.329	160.643	161.836	2.1	.7	.2	.0	.7
Alcoholic beverages	1.051	224.975	225.749	1.5	.3	.0	.2	.2
Housing	41.460	216.739	217.259	.7	.2	.2	.1	.3
Shelter	31.955	249.462	249.886	.8	.2	.1	.1	.1
Rent of primary residence [3]	5.925	251.555	251.829	1.1	.1	.2	.2	.1
Lodging away from home [2]	.776	128.630	131.572	2.0	2.3	1.0	-1.0	.0
Owners' equivalent rent of residences [3 4]	24.905	257.775	258.073	.6	.1	.1	.1	.1
Owners' equivalent rent of primary residence [3 4]	23.310	257.764	258.060	.6	.1	.1	.1	.1
Tenants' and household insurance [1 2]	.349	126.192	126.529	1.7	.3	-1.0	.0	.3
Fuels and utilities	5.096	214.045	215.587	2.3	.7	.8	-.1	1.2
Household energy	4.000	187.704	189.006	1.4	.7	.8	-.2	1.3
Fuel oil and other fuels [1]	.309	314.130	326.919	17.9	4.1	4.1	5.4	4.1
Energy services [3]	3.691	189.088	189.837	.2	.4	.6	-.6	1.1
Water and sewer and trash collection services [2]	1.095	175.754	177.194	5.4	.8	.5	.3	.8
Household furnishings and operations	4.409	124.342	124.576	-1.9	.2	-.1	.1	.1
Household operations [1 2]	.772	151.189	151.358	1.1	.1	.3	.4	.1
Apparel	3.601	116.664	118.369	-.4	1.5	.1	1.0	-.9
Men's and boys' apparel	.882	109.985	110.962	-.3	.9	-.3	1.0	-.9
Women's and girls' apparel	1.520	102.438	105.076	-1.6	2.6	.0	1.5	-1.2
Infants' and toddlers' apparel	.192	110.096	110.101	-3.7	.0	.4	-1.9	-1.6
Footwear	.700	126.286	126.830	-.7	.4	-.1	.8	-.4
Transportation	17.308	200.835	203.037	7.1	1.1	2.0	1.3	1.9
Private transportation	16.082	196.087	198.073	6.9	1.0	2.0	1.3	1.9
New and used motor vehicles [2]	6.333	97.128	97.633	.6	.5	-.1	-.2	.5
New vehicles	3.513	138.925	140.158	.9	.9	-.1	-.1	1.0
Used cars and trucks	2.055	142.555	142.937	1.9	.3	-.1	-.3	.1
Motor fuel	5.079	265.703	271.843	19.4	2.3	6.5	3.9	4.8
Gasoline (all types)	4.865	264.979	270.822	19.2	2.2	6.7	3.5	4.7
Motor vehicle parts and equipment [1]	.408	140.487	140.912	3.9	.3	.3	.9	.3
Motor vehicle maintenance and repair [1]	1.172	250.726	250.851	2.0	.0	.1	.2	.0
Public transportation	1.227	259.634	265.327	9.7	2.2	1.4	1.7	1.9
Medical care	6.627	393.858	397.065	2.9	.8	.2	.1	.4
Medical care commodities [1]	1.633	318.929	321.186	2.7	.7	.1	.5	.7
Medical care services	4.994	417.025	420.567	3.0	.8	.3	-.1	.4
Professional services	2.830	331.921	334.296	2.6	.7	.1	.0	.5
Hospital and related services	1.703	625.817	633.413	5.8	1.2	0.7	-0.1	0.5

See footnotes at end of table.

Figure 12-3: Excerpt from Table 1 of the CPI report.

The February 2011 index for the medical care services component is 420, almost double the index for all items. The February 2011 index for hospital and related services index is 633, and that's almost three times greater than the index for all items. (Although BLS adjusts CPI for quality improvements in products and services, including healthcare, it's unlikely that these adjustments fully account for improvements in healthcare.) You can also see in Figure 12-3 that in the long run, the volatile food and energy indexes are roughly in line with the long-term CPI.

Inflating investment returns

The release of the CPI report can surprise the markets and cause wide price swings in stocks and bonds. Although it's not really a leading indicator (because the CPI reports inflationary pressures that have already occurred, not future inflation), investors and traders still worry about inflation and the CPI's impact on the market and act accordingly.

Identifying bondholders' expectations

Compared to other investors, bondholders have the most at stake when inflation rises. After all, bond investors lend money to borrowers, usually for a fixed rate of return. As inflation grows, lenders suffer when their borrowers pay them back in currency that's worth less over time. Borrowers, on the other hand, see an advantage.

The purchasing power of a bond's future payments erodes as inflation grows. Bond prices fall as investors liquidate long-term bonds and interest rates head higher. Bondholders experience the double whammy of falling prices and the reduced value of future payments.

Although the CPI can affect bond prices, it's not a good predictor of future inflation. For that, bondholders should look to other indicators such as the PCE category of the Personal Income and Outlays report (see Chapter 6) and the Employment Situation report (see Chapter 4). True leading indicators can help foretell the direction of future inflation trends.

Stocking up for inflation

In small doses, inflation may actually help equity investors by supporting rising stock prices. However, during periods of increasing inflation, stock holdings can suffer in several ways. Inflation may cause consumers to forgo some purchases as prices rise and their budgets become strained. This can harm corporate profits and drive equity prices lower. As inflation rises, investors can expect the Fed to raise the federal funds rate (see Chapter 8) to try and slow the economy.

An equity investment's total return, including price appreciation and any dividend payments, must compensate for any loss of purchasing power caused by inflation. As long as inflation remains tame, that compensation is relatively easy. However, stock investments struggle to keep up with higher inflation and generally fail to maintain purchasing power. During the late 1970s and early 1980s, stocks' total inflation-adjusted return was inadequate to maintain purchasing power.

The CPI reports inflation only after it has occurred. It doesn't give investors any advance warning that inflation may become an issue. Stock investors must keep up with leading indicators such as the Manufacturing ISM Report On Business® (*ISM* stands for Institute for Supply Management; see Chapter 10) and the Employment Situation report (see Chapter 4) to adjust their portfolio positions in advance of growing inflation.

Investing in currencies and commodities

Currency investing is tricky in any environment, but it's especially difficult when inflation becomes an issue. When inflation is localized to a single country, cross-currency positions can work as an inflation hedge. For example, if the United States were to experience a bout of inflation without the rest of the world's economies joining in, then currency positions in the Euro or Japanese yen could provide some purchasing-power protection against inflation. Unfortunately for U.S. investors, that hypothetical situation is unlikely. Because the United States imports so much from around the world, prices for many products rise when the U.S. experiences inflation. If the United States is experiencing inflation, expect it to export that problem to the rest of the world.

Meanwhile, commodities in general, and precious metals in particular, can act as an imperfect hedge against rising inflation. In fact, rising commodity prices can serve as an early warning of future inflation. Commodity prices are generally set in very liquid and competitive commodity markets. They react quickly to changes in demand and to underlying price pressure, so rising prices across a wide range of commodities can be an indication of inflation (see Chapter 15 for more about using commodity pricing as an inflation indicator).

Using Manufacturing Costs to Measure Inflation: The Producer Price Index

For a different view of price inflation, you can look at the costs of manufacturing. The BLS *Producer Price Index* (PPI) measures price changes from the seller's perspective. The index tracks the prices of products used by manufacturers and other producers to make consumer products, business consumables, and capital equipment.

Table 12-2 provides a quick overview of this index. (***Note:*** The PPI used to be called the *Wholesale Price Index,* and some people still refer to it by that name.) The PPI release schedule is posted on the BLS website at `www.bls.gov/schedule/news_release/ppi.htm`.

Table 12-2 Producer Price Index

Release Schedule	*Agency*	*Web Address*	*Sensitivity*
Monthly: Published schedule, 8:30 a.m. ET	U.S. Bureau of Labor Statistics	`www.bls.gov/ppi/`	High

The following sections explain how the PPI differs from the CPI, what it measures, and how you can incorporate it into your investment strategy.

Comparing the PPI and CPI

PPI gets a lot of media attention because it's the first inflation measure reported each month and because it sounds like it's cut from the same cloth as the CPI. After all, both the CPI and the PPI measure inflation, and the two reports are released within a day of each other. However, these two indexes have very little in common.

For one thing, the techniques used to collect the PPI data are different from those used to collect the CPI data. For another thing, the PPI measures the prices producers receive, while the CPI measures the costs consumers pay. The PPI doesn't include excise taxes or transportation charges; the CPI does. Also, the PPI includes very few services, but services are a large component of the CPI.

The PPI monthly news release shows more than 200 indexes that are based on price changes for more than 100,000 products. In addition, the BLS creates hundreds of industry indexes and more than 10,000 individual-product and product-group indexes each month. These indexes are available for most U.S. industries in the manufacturing and mining sectors. The BLS also introduces new indexes periodically.

Only a few of the PPI indexes have broad appeal. Investors and business leaders are most interested in the following stage-of-processing indexes:

- **Crude goods index:** This index includes materials that have not been processed, such as natural gas, crude oil, coal, cattle, chickens, hogs, corn, oilseeds, wheat, raw cotton, leaf tobacco, and metal ores.

- **Intermediate goods index:** This index includes products that have been partially processed but are not yet finished goods, such as flour, crude vegetable oils, industrial chemicals, paperboard, milled steel, glass, plastic auto components, and lumber. This category also includes manufacturing supplies such as electric power, natural gas, motor fuels, lubricating grease, shipping enclosures, animal feeds, hand tools, and office supplies.
- **Finished goods index:** This index gets most of the attention. It measures the average price changes for domestically produced and consumed goods and includes both consumer goods and capital equipment used for manufacturing. Examples of finished consumer goods include furniture, processed foods, fresh fruits and vegetables, children's apparel, prescription drugs, cosmetics, gasoline, home heating oil, residential electric power, cars, and household appliances. Capital equipment includes machine tools, farm machinery, heavy trucks, ships, boats, computers, and office furniture.

All producer indexes exclude imported products and most services. However, the BLS has begun incorporating some service sectors into the PPI. Examples include wireless telecommunications, data processing services, stockbrokers, investment bankers, property and casualty insurers, life insurance companies, engineering firms, software companies, and Internet service providers.

Like with the CPI, the BLS publishes a core-inflation PPI that excludes both food and energy prices. (See the sidebar "Looking at long-term trends: Core inflation" for details on core inflation.) The base year for the PPI — where the index value is 100 — is currently 1982. The PPI includes data that are both adjusted and unadjusted for seasonality.

Inflating the price of business supplies

The PPI shows the march of price increases through the chain of production. Crude goods prices typically rise before intermediate goods prices, and intermediate goods prices increase before finished goods prices. However, these increases don't happen instantaneously, so you must take a longer-term view. The year-over-year changes in the PPI show this change well, although you can sometimes see it in quarterly measures, too.

Figure 12-4 shows the summary table (Table A) from the PPI, which shows the finished goods index, the core finished goods index, the intermediate goods index, and the crude goods index.

Table A. Monthly and 12-month percent changes in selected stage-of-processing price indexes, seasonally adjusted

Month	Finished goods					Intermediate goods	Crude goods
	Total	Foods	Energy	Except foods and energy	Change in finished goods from 12 months ago (unadj.)		
2010							
Feb.............	-0.4	-0.5	-2.3	0.0	4.2	0.1	-1.7
Mar.............	0.7	2.5	0.7	0.2	5.9	0.6	-1.0
Apr.............	-0.1	-0.2	-0.2	0.1	5.4	0.8	-1.9
May.............	-0.2	-0.4	-1.0	0.2	5.1	0.2	-3.3
June............	-0.3	-2.4	0.2	0.1	2.7	-0.7	-3.0
July.............	0.1	0.7	-1.0	0.2	4.1	-0.4	1.5
Aug.............	0.6	-0.1	2.5	0.1	3.3	0.6	3.3
Sept............	0.3	0.9	0.0	0.2	3.9	0.4	0.6
Oct[1]............	0.6	0.5	3.0	-0.3	4.3	1.0	4.8
Nov[1]............	0.7	0.8	2.4	0.0	3.5[r]	1.2	1.2
Dec.............	0.9	0.8	2.8	0.2	4.0	0.9	6.5
2011							
Jan.............	-0.8	0.3	1.8	0.5	3.6	1.1	3.3
Feb.............	1.6	3.9	3.3	0.2	5.6	2.0	3.4

1 Some of the figures shown above and elsewhere in this release may differ from those previously reported because data for October 2010 have been revised to reflect the availability of late reports and corrections by respondents.

r Revised

Figure 12-4: Table A of the PPI shows the monthly and annual changes in stage-of-processing indexes.

Table A shows the seasonally adjusted month-to-month changes, as well as the unadjusted annual change from the current month and from the previous 12 months. Notice that the indexes jump around quite a bit from month to month, but the annual changes all march higher.

The PPI report provides a lot more information for each of the index categories in its data tables and even more information on the BLS website (see Table 12-2 for the web address). You can find out how specific industries or specific products affect the PPI by digging into these additional data sources.

Correlating the PPI and economic growth

The relationship between rising producer prices and a growing economy is strong. Price increases that are the result of increased demand rather than supply disruptions are usually a good indicator that the economy is growing. Unfortunately, though, the PPI provides little information to help you forecast the economic future, so it's not a leading indicator. Instead, it's a coincident indicator.

The PPI shows price increases that have already occurred. You'll see some correlation between current crude goods indexes and future intermediate goods indexes, as well as between the current intermediate goods indexes and future finished goods indexes.

However, increases in one production stage or category may not flow to the next stage. Producer prices experience a lot of volatility, and manufacturers can handle short-term increases in manufacturing supplies before they have to increase finished goods prices.

Over periods of six months or less, a rise in the PPI's finished goods index doesn't necessarily mean that consumer prices will increase. The retail environment is very competitive and keeps PPI increases from automatically raising consumer prices. Producers must sometimes absorb cost increases when consumers can simply switch to another product or do without their particular product when prices increase. Similarly, retailers often can't pass along manufacturers' price increases and must absorb some or all of these increases, at least for a period of time.

When people argue that the PPI finished goods index is a good predictor for CPI, they assume that a price change at the producer level will eventually make its way to the CPI. Although the logic makes sense, experience shows that it isn't always true. The simple fact is that month-to-month PPI changes don't predict CPI changes. However, over longer periods, these two indexes do show a stronger correlation.

Showing PPI's investment market impact

As the business cycle matures and product prices start to rise, both stock and bond investors start to worry about inflation. If the economy begins to overheat, investors can expect the Fed to tighten credit to slow growth.

Producing bonds

The bond markets are particularly sensitive to inflation worries, so bond investors often pay very close attention to the PPI reports. Although these indexes aren't leading indicators, they are one of the earliest inflation reports that the government releases. Even though bond investors may give the PPI report more attention than it really deserves, any hint of unexpected inflation will cause bond traders to sell now and ask questions later.

To keep from being caught off guard, savvy bond investors don't depend solely on the PPI inflation gauge. Instead, they keep track of leading indicators like the Employment Situation report (see Chapter 4) and the Manufacturing ISM Report On Business® (see Chapter 10). Doing so helps keep PPI surprises at a minimum. Within the PPI report, the crude goods and intermediate goods indexes offer the earliest inflation warnings, but even they're rarely the first indicator to report worrisome inflation pressures.

Inflating stocks

Like bondholders, stock investors react immediately to any surprises in the PPI report. After all, higher prices mean that consumers can't continue their buying spree. As a result, business profits and then stock prices will fall. Equity investors don't want to be holding inflation-sensitive investments as inflation grows.

If you're a stock investor, you can use the PPI as a coincident indicator to confirm your current economic forecasts. Smart stock buyers also use PPI's industry indexes to identify individual products and industry trends. These indexes can provide insight into the strength of select industries that you can't find easily anywhere else.

The PPI doesn't work well as a forecasting tool. Instead, keep close tabs on the leading indicators, such as the Employment Situation report (see Chapter 4), the Manufacturing ISM Report On Business® (see Chapter 10), and the Personal Income and Outlays report (see Chapter 6), to get early inflation warnings.

Banking on currencies and commodities

Currency trading becomes very complicated as inflationary pressures grow. Although a little inflation is good for the value of the U.S. dollar, higher rates of inflation all but guarantee a response from the Fed. If the Fed's actions slow the economy enough to stop inflation's rise, they'll also dampen enthusiasm for the U.S. dollar.

Meanwhile, the PPI report's crude goods index is a good confirming indicator for commodity traders. Industrial metals, feedlot and grain products, and even precious metals are used as raw materials for manufacturing. Rising prices in these indexes should mirror what's happening in the commodities' futures markets.

Tracking Inflation through Labor Costs: The Employment Cost Index

Another indicator that business leaders, policymakers, and some investors use as an inflation gauge is the *Employment Cost Index* (ECI). This quarterly index is part of the BLS's National Compensation Survey. The ECI shows how total labor costs change over time and tracks changes to the average hourly compensation for U.S. employees.

Although the average hourly earnings statistics from the Employment Situation report (see Chapter 4) are reported monthly rather than quarterly, they measure only the earnings for hourly wage earners. The Employment Situation report doesn't include the earnings for salaried employees or any information about benefit costs for either salaried or hourly employees.

On the other hand, the ECI includes the earnings of most nonfarm employees, including salaried employees, and monitors benefit costs along with direct compensation. The ECI may not be as timely as the Employment Situation report, but it is more thorough.

Table 12-3 gives you a brief overview of this index. The release schedule for the ECI is posted on the BLS website at `www.bls.gov/schedule/news_release/eci.htm`.

Table 12-3 Employment Cost Index

Release Schedule	***Agency***	***Web Address***	***Sensitivity***
Quarterly: Published schedule, 8:30 a.m. ET	U.S. Bureau of Labor Statistics	`www.bls.gov/ncs/ect/`	Moderate

The following sections provide more information about the ECI, including how the BLS monitors labor costs, how labor costs are connected to inflation, and how you can use this report in your investments.

Monitoring and tracking labor costs

Employees are expensive. In fact, total employee costs are usually an employer's largest expense. Because of the nature of the job market, monitoring labor costs is a pretty good way to monitor inflation.

Early in an economic recovery, labor costs usually rise modestly. When business recovers and employers start hiring new staff, labor costs rise but productivity improves, too. As long as productivity grows faster than labor costs, most economists discount the potential for employment costs to drive inflation higher. (See Chapter 13 for the lowdown on measuring productivity.)

However, when employment costs begin to outpace productivity, economists see those rising costs as a symptom that inflationary pressures are growing. Generally, the economy feels inflation's impact only after the business cycle has been in expansion for some time.

Absorbing increases in labor costs is difficult for companies. Some manufacturing companies can move production overseas or retool factories by using new automated processes. But not all companies have these options. For service companies, labor costs are simply part of the business model. When companies pass along labor price increases, inflation tends to rise even higher.

The BLS surveys private employers and state and local governments (but not federal) to collect employment cost data for the ECI. The surveys report information about the actual hourly compensation for hourly employees, the hourly equivalent for salaried employees, as well as benefits such as medical insurance, paid leave, retirement plans, life insurance, performance bonuses, and mandated benefits like Social Security, Medicare, and unemployment insurance. They don't report overtime.

The BLS converts the wage and benefit data into an index that's scaled to the 2005 base year. Data are reported both seasonally adjusted and not adjusted.

Seeing how the Fed uses the ECI

The Fed uses the ECI when making monetary policy decisions (see Chapter 8 for details). The federal government also uses the ECI when making adjustments to government-employee salary schedules.

One reason why the ECI works better in these applications than the Employment Situation report is the way the BLS handles pay-scale differences between industries. For example, if high-wage industries were growing faster than low-wage industries, employee costs would appear to be rising faster than they actually were because of the pay differences. Fortunately, the BLS compensates for these types of industry differences when reporting the ECI, making it a clearer representation of employee costs.

The BLS measures earnings for occupational groups rather than employees in general. The idea is to measure a fixed set of labor, similar to how CPI measures a fixed basket of goods. This allows the BLS to monitor labor migration between high-wage and low-wage industries and even between high-wage and low-wage positions within a single industry. Employees are assigned to these groups based on what they do rather than their job title, education, or training. You can find more about how the data are collected and massaged on the BLS website at `www.bls.gov/opub/hom/pdf/homch8.pdf`.

Although the ECI is highly correlated with the business cycle and the overall economy, it's a lagging indicator. Rising employment costs are almost always visible elsewhere before this indicator is released, which means that you can see signs of increasing labor costs in the Employment Situation report (see Chapter 4) and the Manufacturing ISM Report On Business® (see Chapter 10) before you even get the ECI.

Employing labor costs in investment analysis

Bond markets pay close attention to any inflation gauge, including the ECI, and all investors watch for any inflation surprises that can move the markets. As an inflation gauge, the ECI is useful because employee compensation costs are eventually passed along to consumers.

From an investor's perspective, the ECI is very late to the party. Although bond investors watch the ECI carefully, the reality is that most of the information in this report has already been shown to the market in the Employment Situation report. This report very rarely provides any additional market-moving information.

Chapter 13

Taking a Closer Look at Productivity and Economic Growth

In This Chapter

- Showing productivity improvements
- Compensating workers' productivity
- Determining employees' real cost

Stock and bond markets don't often agree on anything. Economic growth is good for stocks but bad for bonds. Rising unemployment is good for bondholders but ultimately bad for stock investors — and just about everyone else. Productivity, on the other hand, is one thing that both stock investors and bondholders actually do like. Both types of investors love when productivity is growing. What's not to like? Productivity growth is as close to free money as you can get. If you can create more stuff with the same employees, your company becomes more profitable and more competitive without much additional cost.

Even if you must upgrade production equipment, information technology, or your employees' skills to improve productivity, you often come out ahead. As long as the training and equipment upgrades cost less than the value of the productivity improvements, the investment is an easy one to make.

This chapter looks at several economic indicators that track business productivity so that you can see what impact it has on the economy. I focus on employee productivity; that is, business output compared to employee input. After all, employees make up the largest expense for most companies, and anything that can improve employees' productivity is almost always beneficial to the business.

Measuring Productivity and Costs: The Labor Productivity and Costs Report

Today, productivity growth is the most direct path to economic growth and improved living standards in the United States and throughout the world. Measuring U.S. productivity is the responsibility of the Bureau of Labor Statistics (BLS). The bureau reports the utilization and efficiency of workers and the labor costs associated with their productivity.

So what exactly is productivity? *Productivity* measures the quantity of products and services that businesses and their employees produce, per unit of labor used in production. The BLS tallies the total output of U.S. businesses and the total quantity of labor they use and converts the data into a series of indexes called the *Labor Productivity and Costs report.*

The BLS productivity statistics cover most of the U.S. economy. They include workers who produce about 78 percent of the gross domestic product (GDP; see Chapter 7 for details), but they don't include government workers, not-for-profit organizations, or employees of private households. They also don't include any work that you do for yourself, such as making repairs or improvements to your own home.

The BLS gets its data for the Labor Productivity and Costs report from a variety of sources. For example, the Employment Situation report (see Chapter 4) provides the aggregate data for the number of employee hours worked. The GDP report provides the quantity of products and services. Data for employee compensation comes from the National Compensation Survey (see `www.bls.gov/ncs` for details).

The BLS delivers its productivity findings quarterly in the Labor Productivity and Costs report. However, the BLS releases each quarterly report twice. One month after the report's preliminary release, the BLS releases a revision; the data revisions to this report can be quite extensive. Table 13-1 provides an overview of this report.

Table 13-1 Labor Productivity and Costs Report

Release Schedule	*Agency*	*Web Address*	*Sensitivity*
Quarterly: Published Schedule, 8:30 a.m. ET	U.S. Bureau of Labor Statistics	`www.bls.gov/lpc/`	Moderate

The baseline year for the Labor Productivity and Cost indexes is 2005. The 2005 index value is 100 (see Chapter 2 for a refresher on baseline indexes).

The following sections outline what productivity is, how it relates to job growth, and what you need to know about productivity when making your own investments.

Defining productivity

Productivity measures how effectively businesses use labor and capital to generate products and services. The BLS is interested in labor productivity, which it calculates by summing the number of all goods and services produced in the United States and then comparing that total to the number of hours worked to produce those goods and services.

Generally speaking, only two economic inputs are necessary to produce products and services: labor and capital. *Labor* represents the people employed by businesses. *Capital* represents the equipment, technology, and specialized training that businesses buy to help employees produce products and services.

The most important measures of productivity from the Labor Productivity and Costs report are the following three indexes:

- **Output per hour of all persons:** This productivity measure is the essence of labor productivity and is the one most often reported in the news media. Output per hour measures total production — that is, all the goods and services produced by U.S. businesses — divided by the number of employee hours required to produce all those goods and services.
- **Compensation per hour:** Average hourly compensation includes the total compensation for both hourly and salaried staff. (It excludes government workers and not-for-profit employees.) The BLS measures all employee costs, including wages, salaries, benefits, commission payments, bonuses, Social Security payments, and pension contributions.
- **Unit labor costs:** The math is easy: Divide compensation per hour by output per hour of all persons. As productivity increases, unit labor costs decrease. As hourly labor costs rise, so do unit labor costs. If both productivity and labor costs rise equally, unit labor costs remain unchanged.

The Labor Productivity and Costs report presents these indexes as percentage changes from the previous quarter and the previous year, as you can see in Figure 13-1. The figure shows a graphic representation from the March 2011 BLS news release. The bars on the chart represent quarter-by-quarter changes. The superimposed line graph shows changes from the same quarter in the previous year.

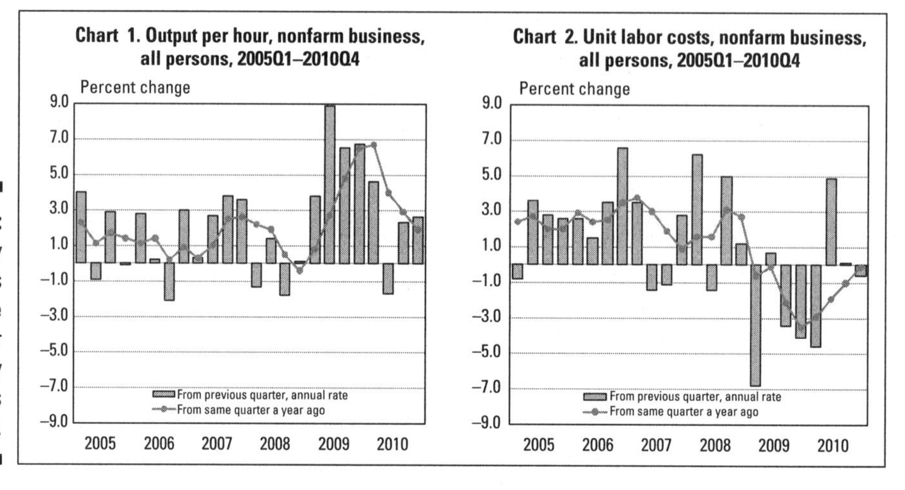

Figure 13-1: Productivity indexes from the Labor Productivity and Costs report.

The Output per hour and Unit labor cost data series are very volatile. Although quarterly percentage changes don't appear to trend, productivity growth does trend over longer periods of time, as I explain in the next section. Figure 13-2 shows the actual data series from the March 2011 Labor Productivity and Costs report; in the report, this data appears in Table 2.

Figure 13-2 shows three years of seasonally adjusted and revised data. You can identify the data revisions; they're shown with a lowercase *r* next to the revised numbers. If you want to see the prior unrevised data, it's available in Table A of the Labor Productivity and Costs report.

The second column of the table shows productivity, which is labeled *Output per hour of all persons*, and the fifth and seventh columns show *Compensation per hour* and *Unit labor costs,* respectively, along with the data used to calculate these statistics. All the columns include both quarter-to-quarter percentage changes and annual percentage changes.

Table 2. Nonfarm business sector: Productivity, hourly compensation, unit labor costs, and prices, seasonally adjusted

Year and quarter	Output per hour of all persons	Output	Hours of all persons	Compen-sation per hour (1)	Real compen-sation per hour (2)	Unit labor costs	Unit nonlabor payments (3)	Implicit price deflator (4)
Percent change from previous quarter at annual rate(5)								
2010 ANNUAL	3.9 r	3.7	-0.2 r	2.4 r	0.7 r	-1.5	4.2	0.8
2010 IV	2.6	4.0 r	1.4 r	2.0 r	-0.6	-0.6	-1.2 r	-0.8 r
III	2.3 r	3.8	1.4	2.5 r	1.0 r	0.1 r	4.3 r	1.9
II	-1.7 r	1.6	3.3 r	3.1 r	3.8 r	4.9	-0.4	2.6
I	4.6 r	5.0	0.4 r	-0.2 r	-1.6 r	-4.6	9.7 r	1.2
2009 ANNUAL	3.7 r	-3.8	-7.2 r	2.0 r	2.4 r	-1.6	4.6	0.8
2009 IV	6.7 r	6.7	0.1 r	2.3 r	-0.5 r	-4.1 r	3.4 r	-1.1
III	6.5 r	1.4	-4.8 r	2.9 r	-0.8 r	-3.4 r	8.1	1.1
II	8.9 r	-0.2	-8.4 r	9.7 r	7.8 r	0.7 r	-2.9	-0.8
I	3.8 r	-6.4	-9.8 r	-3.3 r	-1.2 r	-6.8 r	15.4	1.4
2008 ANNUAL	1.0	-1.1	-2.1	3.3	-0.6 r	2.2	1.2	1.8
2008 IV	0.1 r	-9.5	-9.6 r	1.3 r	11.5 r	1.2	-6.5	-1.9
III	-1.8 r	-6.2	-4.5 r	3.1 r	-3.1 r	5.0	6.1 r	5.4
II	1.4 r	-0.3	-1.7 r	0.0 r	-4.9 r	-1.4	13.5 r	4.2
I	-1.3 r	-2.5	-1.2	4.8 r	0.0	6.2	-7.0	0.8
Percent change from corresponding quarter of previous year								
2010 ANNUAL	3.9 r	3.7	-0.2 r	2.4 r	0.7 r	-1.5	4.2	0.8
2010 IV	1.9 r	3.6 r	1.6 r	1.8 r	0.6 r	-0.1 r	3.0 r	1.2
III	2.9 r	4.3	1.3 r	1.9 r	0.7 r	-1.0 r	4.2 r	1.1
II	4.0 r	3.7	-0.3 r	2.0 r	0.2 r	-1.9	5.1 r	0.9
I	6.7 r	3.2	-3.2 r	3.6 r	1.2 r	-2.9	4.5	0.1
2009 ANNUAL	3.7 r	-3.8	-7.2 r	2.0 r	2.4 r	-1.6	4.6	0.8
2009 IV	6.5 r	0.3	-5.8 r	2.8 r	1.3 r	-3.5	5.8	0.2
III	4.8 r	-3.8	-8.2 r	2.5 r	4.2 r	-2.1 r	3.2	0.0
II	2.7 r	-5.6	-8.1 r	2.6 r	3.6 r	-0.1	2.7	1.0
I	0.8	-5.7	-6.5 r	0.2	0.4 r	-0.6	6.8	2.2
2008 ANNUAL	1.0	-1.1	-2.1	3.3	-0.6 r	2.2	1.2	1.8
2008 IV	-0.4	-4.7	-4.3	2.3	0.7	2.7	1.2	2.1
III	0.5	-1.7	-2.1 r	3.6	-1.6	3.1	1.6	2.5
II	1.9	0.5	-1.3	3.5	-0.8	1.6	1.4	1.5
I	2.2	1.6	-0.6	3.8	-0.4 r	1.6	0.7	1.2
Indexes 2005=100								
2010 ANNUAL	111.5 r	104.0 r	93.2 r	116.4 r	104.2 r	104.4 r	116.6 r	109.2 r
2010 IV	112.2 r	105.3 r	93.8 r	117.4 r	104.4 r	104.6 r	116.9 r	109.5 r
III	111.5 r	104.3	93.5 r	116.8 r	104.6 r	104.7 r	117.3 r	109.7
II	110.9 r	103.3	93.2 r	116.1 r	104.3 r	104.7 r	116.0 r	109.2
I	111.4 r	102.9	92.4 r	115.2 r	103.4 r	103.5 r	116.2 r	108.5
2009 ANNUAL	107.4 r	100.3	93.4 r	113.7 r	103.5 r	105.9 r	111.9 r	108.3
2009 IV	110.1 r	101.7	92.3 r	115.3 r	103.8 r	104.7 r	113.5 r	108.2
III	108.4 r	100.0	92.3 r	114.6 r	103.9 r	105.8 r	112.6 r	108.5
II	106.7 r	99.7	93.5 r	113.8 r	104.1 r	106.7 r	110.4 r	108.2
I	104.4 r	99.7	95.5 r	111.2 r	102.2 r	106.5 r	111.2 r	108.4
2008 ANNUAL	103.6 r	104.2	100.6 r	111.4 r	101.0 r	107.6 r	107.0 r	107.4
2008 IV	103.4 r	101.4	98.0 r	112.1 r	102.5 r	108.4 r	107.3 r	108.0
III	103.4 r	104.0	100.5 r	111.8 r	99.7 r	108.1 r	109.1 r	108.5
II	103.9 r	105.6	101.7 r	110.9 r	100.5 r	106.8 r	107.5 r	107.1
I	103.5 r	105.7	102.1 r	110.9 r	101.8 r	107.2	104.2 r	106.0

See footnotes following Table 6.
r=revised

March 3, 2011
Source: Bureau of Labor Statistics

Figure 13-2: Percentage changes for nonfarm productivity, hourly compensation, and unit labor costs.

Correlating productivity to job growth and costs

Productivity usually gives you a clear picture into how the economy is doing. Although productivity can rise during a recession, as labor usage falls faster than output, it's more common to see the economy rise as productivity grows.

How so? Almost every business process employs some amount of labor. Whether a company makes light bulbs, pencils, or water bottles or provides a service, such as carpentry, computer repair, or advertising, people are a necessary part of the production process. Even fully automated manufacturing processes require people to program and monitor the control systems and maintain the machinery.

Some employee representatives argue that productivity growth leads to lower employment and lower wages. After all, if you can get more production from the same number of people, you may be able to get by with fewer employees. Although that may be the case at individual businesses, causing hardship for individual employees, it doesn't appear to be an issue for the economy as a whole.

In the economy as a whole, the reallocation of labor to more profitable and productive endeavors is good for businesses and, ultimately, for employees. For example, when agricultural workers moved away from the farm in search of more productive employment, living standards improved for everyone. And although productivity increases have outpaced employee compensation over the last decade or two, those productivity improvements have allowed U.S. companies to better compete with low-cost foreign competitors.

In addition to the correlation between economic growth and productivity, a link also exists between productivity and the business cycle. Productivity falls during economic contractions and rises during expansions. In terms of productivity, the typical business cycle looks like this:

- **Slowdown after economic expansion:** Productivity declines along with the economic slowdown. After the economy has been in expansion and nears an economic peak, business begins to slow. Initially, companies are reluctant to lay off staff even in the face of declining sales. Instead, companies may assign existing staff to other projects or offer them advanced training. Total labor hours remain more or less constant, but fewer products and services are produced.
- **Economic recession:** The rate of productivity decline increases. As the economy declines after an economic peak, businesses sometimes have to reduce expenses and may lay off idle workers. The pace of layoffs is almost always slower than the production slowdown.

- **Beginning of economic recovery:** Productivity grows rapidly. When the economy recovers as sales pick up, employers are slow to hire staff until they're confident that the recovery will continue. In the meantime, businesses try to make the best use of existing staff. Using a limited number of employees to grow production makes for robust productivity growth.
- **Economic expansion:** Productivity growth continues, but it does so at a slower rate. Production increases require businesses to hire new staff.

Figure 13-3 shows the long-term growth in productivity and the correlation between productivity growth and the business cycle.

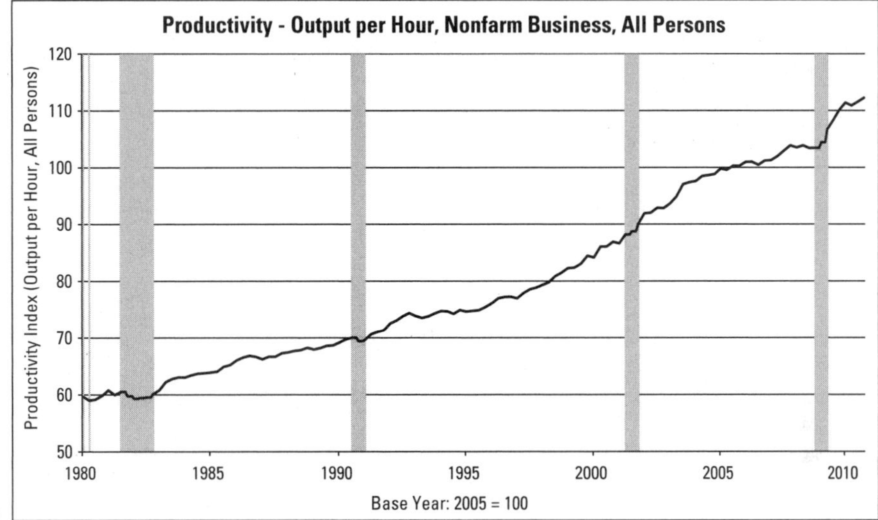

Figure 13-3: Productivity and the business cycle.

Productivity tends to trend higher over time, as you can see in Figure 13-3. However, it almost always falls in advance of recessions, which are shown in gray in the graph. The one exception occurred in 2001 when productivity did not slow. Normally, though, productivity follows the business cycle.

Producing investment returns

Although both stock and bond investors have a vested interest in business productivity, the Productivity and Costs report rarely moves markets. Investors do pay attention to this report, but it's rarely a high priority.

For one thing, investment markets don't react as forcefully to quarterly indicators as they do to more frequently released indicators. Also, most of the report's information has already been reported by the time the report is released. Plus, you can easily estimate productivity growth on your own by looking at the source data. Nonetheless, investors react to productivity data in the following ways.

Loaning money in the face of productivity growth

As long as productivity remains high and growing, bondholders are relatively complacent. After all, the risk of inflation is low when productivity is rising, even if wages are rising.

However, when productivity growth slows, the risk of wage increases triggering a new round of inflation is much higher. Inflation means rising interest rates, falling bond prices, and reduced purchasing power from interest payments.

Bond investors can avoid productivity surprises by keeping up with related data sources, including the Employment Situation report (see Chapter 4), the GDP report (see Chapter 7), various income statistics (see Chapter 6), and industrial production data (see Chapter 8).

Investing in stocks to profit from productivity improvements

Increases in productivity improve business profitability and competitiveness, both of which are good for stock investors. Of course, as productivity wanes, stockholders are likely to suffer, too. The same risks facing bondholders apply to stockholders. If productivity falls while wage and product prices are increasing, the risk for inflation grows.

Stock investors need to follow a similar regimen as bondholders do to avoid productivity surprises. Keeping up with the Employment Situation report (see Chapter 4), various income statistics (see Chapter 6), and industrial production data (see Chapter 8) can help stock investors identify productivity problems before the Labor Productivity and Costs report is released.

Affecting currency markets

Strong productivity growth is usually associated with a stronger dollar. Currency investors are wise to follow the same reports and data as stock and bond investors do to avoid surprises in the Labor Productivity and Costs report.

Watching Employee Compensation Costs: The ECEC Report

Employee compensation (the amount employees are paid) is an integral part of the BLS Labor Productivity and Costs report that I discuss in the preceding section. However, the compensation data in that report are reported as indexes, which may be fine for statisticians but are less useful to investors. Most investors and business managers prefer to see employee compensation costs reported in dollars and cents.

The BLS *Employer Costs for Employee Compensation (ECEC) report* provides the appropriate remedy, albeit a few months after the fact. Unfortunately, data collected for the March ECEC report isn't released until June.

The ECEC report provides total employee compensation costs for private industry as well as for state and local governments. The report's averages don't include compensation costs for the self-employed, farm workers, private household employees, or federal government workers.

The ECEC report measures the average hourly cost for employees' wages, salaries, and benefits, as well as commissions and bonuses. Benefits include health insurance costs, paid leave, vacation pay, retirement plans, Social Security, Medicare, and unemployment insurance.

The report includes national and regional compensation averages along with industry and occupation averages. State and local government data are reported separately from the private industry data, and the two data series are aggregated for the civilian employment category.

The BLS cautions against making compensation-cost comparisons between state and local government occupations and the private sector. (For example, comparing the total state and local government compensation costs average $40.54 per hour with the $29.72 average for civilian workers is misleading.) These two types of employers have different occupational profiles. For example, state and local governments don't employ sales or manufacturing staff. Also, the percentage of professional and administrative support positions in government is much higher than it is in the private sector. These differences generally explain the differences in average compensation costs.

Table 13-2 shows an overview of the ECEC report. The following sections provide more in-depth information about this report, including what it monitors and how you can use it.

Table 13-2 Employer Cost for Employee Compensation Report

Release Schedule	*Agency*	*Web Address*	*Sensitivity*
Quarterly: Published schedule, 10:00 a.m. ET	U.S. Bureau of Labor Statistics	`www.bls.gov/news.release/ecec.htm`	Low

Monitoring labor costs

The ECEC report can provide important information to help you keep track of labor costs in the economy. This information is important because it gives you a quick comparison of how employees are compensated across different occupations.

The ECEC report is based on the National Compensation Survey (see `www.bls.gov/ncs` for details) and covers approximately 63,000 private industry occupations and about 11,500 government occupations. The National Compensation Survey covers more than 12,000 private companies and about 1,800 state and local governments, including public schools and hospitals.

The ECEC report includes average hourly data for all occupations. It converts compensation for salaried employees into an hourly rate based on the approximate number of hours worked. Figure 13-4 shows an example of Table 2 of the ECEC report, which provides aggregate compensation averages for all civilians (private industry plus state and local government employees).

According to Figure 13-4, the average total compensation for all workers in December 2010 was $29.72 per hour based on an average wages and salary amount of $20.71. From this table, you can see how different occupations and industries are compensated and how benefits affect total compensation.

The ECEC report includes 13 other data tables, which slice and dice employee compensation data in ways that are very useful to business managers, especially those in human resources. For example, you can see how compensation differs for union and nonunion employees and for goods-producing companies compared to service companies. You can compare regional compensation differences and the compensations for different-sized companies. Check out the website in Table 13-2 to see these other tables.

Using labor costs to improve investments

Unfortunately, the long lag between the time the ECEC data are collected and the time they're reported dilutes the report's usefulness for investors. If the report were timelier, its data might have better predictive capability for the economy and for inflation.

Investors can and should find timelier data to measure employee costs. The average hourly compensation data from the Employment Situation report may not be as thorough as the data in the ECEC report, but it's reported monthly soon after it's collected (see Chapter 4 for details on this report). The Labor Productivity and Costs report that I discuss earlier in this chapter also provides a timelier look at employee compensation.

Table 2. Employer costs per hour worked for employee compensation and costs as a percent of total compensation: Civilian workers, by occupational and industry group, December 2010

Series	Total compen-sation	Wages and salaries	Benefit costs					
			Total	Paid leave	Supple-mental pay	Insurance	Retire-ment and savings	Legally required benefits
	Cost per hour worked							
Civilian workers[1]	$29.72	$20.71	$9.02	$2.07	$0.69	$2.62	$1.33	$2.30
Occupational group								
Management, professional, and related	49.30	34.50	14.80	3.93	1.13	3.96	2.54	3.23
Management, business, and financial	56.63	39.01	17.62	5.16	2.12	4.01	2.69	3.64
Professional and related	46.56	32.82	13.74	3.48	0.76	3.94	2.49	3.08
Teachers[2]	53.85	38.57	15.28	2.79	0.14	5.29	3.97	3.10
Primary, secondary, and special education school teachers	53.82	38.04	15.78	2.52	0.15	6.00	4.21	2.90
Registered nurses	47.82	33.45	14.37	3.84	1.51	3.66	1.86	3.51
Sales and office	22.27	15.74	6.53	1.45	0.42	2.16	0.75	1.74
Sales and related	20.67	15.50	5.17	1.11	0.45	1.38	0.50	1.72
Office and administrative support	23.22	15.89	7.33	1.65	0.41	2.62	0.90	1.75
Service	16.39	11.65	4.73	0.91	0.29	1.39	0.63	1.51
Natural resources, construction, and maintenance	31.06	21.01	10.05	1.70	0.89	2.77	1.63	3.06
Construction, extraction, farming, fishing, and forestry[3]	31.19	20.87	10.32	1.30	0.96	2.64	1.99	3.43
Installation, maintenance, and repair	30.92	21.16	9.76	2.11	0.81	2.90	1.26	2.69
Production, transportation, and material moving	23.80	15.85	7.95	1.43	0.77	2.59	0.90	2.26
Production	24.41	16.17	8.24	1.58	0.92	2.69	0.80	2.25
Transportation and material moving	23.24	15.56	7.68	1.30	0.64	2.49	0.98	2.26
Industry group								
Education and health services	34.55	24.13	10.42	2.44	0.42	3.37	1.85	2.33
Educational services	42.60	29.52	13.08	2.70	0.15	4.68	3.05	2.50
Elementary and secondary schools	42.49	29.29	13.19	2.29	0.15	5.12	3.26	2.37
Junior colleges, colleges, and universities	45.39	31.43	13.96	3.77	0.14	4.24	3.00	2.81
Health care and social assistance	28.71	20.22	8.49	2.25	0.62	2.43	0.97	2.21
Hospitals	37.22	24.89	12.33	3.26	1.11	3.79	1.55	2.63
	Percent of total compensation							
Civilian workers[1]	100.0	69.7	30.3	7.0	2.3	8.8	4.5	7.8
Occupational group								
Management, professional, and related	100.0	70.0	30.0	8.0	2.3	8.0	5.2	6.6
Management, business, and financial	100.0	68.9	31.1	9.1	3.7	7.1	4.8	6.4
Professional and related	100.0	70.5	29.5	7.5	1.6	8.5	5.3	6.6
Teachers[2]	100.0	71.6	28.4	5.2	0.3	9.8	7.4	5.8
Primary, secondary, and special education school teachers	100.0	70.7	29.3	4.7	0.3	11.1	7.8	5.4
Registered nurses	100.0	70.0	30.0	8.0	3.2	7.6	3.9	7.3
Sales and office	100.0	70.7	29.3	6.5	1.9	9.7	3.4	7.8
Sales and related	100.0	75.0	25.0	5.4	2.2	6.7	2.4	8.3
Office and administrative support	100.0	68.4	31.6	7.1	1.8	11.3	3.9	7.6
Service	100.0	71.1	28.9	5.5	1.8	8.5	3.9	9.2
Natural resources, construction, and maintenance	100.0	67.6	32.4	5.5	2.9	8.9	5.2	9.9
Construction, extraction, farming, fishing, and forestry[3]	100.0	66.9	33.1	4.2	3.1	8.5	6.4	11.0
Installation, maintenance, and repair	100.0	68.4	31.6	6.8	2.6	9.4	4.1	8.7
Production, transportation, and material moving	100.0	66.6	33.4	6.0	3.2	10.9	3.8	9.5
Production	100.0	66.2	33.8	6.5	3.8	11.0	3.3	9.2
Transportation and material moving	100.0	67.0	33.0	5.6	2.7	10.7	4.2	9.7
Industry group								
Education and health services	100.0	69.8	30.2	7.1	1.2	9.8	5.3	6.8
Educational services	100.0	69.3	30.7	6.3	0.3	11.0	7.2	5.9
Elementary and secondary schools	100.0	68.9	31.1	5.4	0.4	12.1	7.7	5.6
Junior colleges, colleges, and universities	100.0	69.2	30.8	8.3	0.3	9.3	6.6	6.2
Health care and social assistance	100.0	70.4	29.6	7.9	2.2	8.5	3.4	7.7
Hospitals	100.0	66.9	33.1	8.7	3.0	10.2	4.2	7.1

[1] Includes workers in the private nonfarm economy excluding households and the public sector excluding the Federal government.
[2] Includes postsecondary teachers; primary, secondary, and special education teachers; and other teachers and instructors.
[3] Farming, fishing, and forestry occupations were combined with construction and extraction occupational group as of December 2006.

Note: The sum of individual items may not equal totals due to rounding.

Figure 13-4: Average hourly compensation of civilians by occupational group.

Calculating What Workers Really Make: The Real Earnings Report

You can find another look at employees' earnings in the BLS *Real Earnings report.* This report is unique because it adjusts its earnings data for inflation. For this reason, the Real Earnings report is of interest to economists and policymakers, as well as business leaders and the employees themselves. But investors pay it no attention, mostly because the Consumer Price Index (CPI), which is much more important to investors, completely overshadows the release of the Real Earnings report.

The Real Earnings report gets its employee compensation data from the Current Employment Statistics survey (see www.bls.gov/ces for more information). This is the same survey used for the Employment Situation report (see Chapter 4). The BLS makes seasonal adjustments before it indexes the data for inflation. It then adjusts month-to-month and year-over-year percentage changes in earnings for inflation, using the CPI (specifically the CPI-U; see Chapter 12 for details.)

The Real Earnings report considers only private sector employee compensation. The report presents data in all nonfarm employees and production and nonsupervisory nonfarm employees, which is a subset of the first category. Table 13-3 gives you a brief overview of the Real Earnings report. You can find the CPI publication schedule on the BLS website at www.bls.gov/schedule/news_release/cpi.htm.

Table 13-3 Real Earnings Report

Release Schedule	*Agency*	*Web Address*	*Sensitivity*
Monthly: Published same day as CPI, 8:30 a.m. ET	U.S. Bureau of Labor Statistics	www.bls.gov/news.release/realer.toc.htm	Low

Chapter 14

Eyeing Business and Municipal Borrowing in the Bond Market

In This Chapter

- Understanding how borrowing works
- Getting the lowdown on interest rates and knowing where to find current rates
- Protecting your bond investments with Treasury Inflation-Protected Securities
- Using the yield curve to gauge the state of the market
- Investing based on bond returns

Businesses borrow money. In fact, they borrow a lot of money. The availability of financial capital impacts businesses' ability to grow, improve productivity, hire workers, and expand their markets.

Loans are available to businesses from a variety of sources. Small businesses are typically dependent on bank loans. Larger companies, on the other hand, can utilize bank loans, but they can also access domestic and global bond markets to raise funds.

Big or small, businesses use long-term loans to finance facilities for manufacturing and offices, purchase machine tools, and outfit offices with furniture and equipment. They use short-term loans to fund operations and help manage cash flows to pay for inventories and receivables.

Of course, businesses aren't the only big borrowers. Local, state, and federal governments also borrow huge quantities of cash. Local governments use the proceeds of borrowing to finance projects like municipal stadiums, libraries, and school buildings. The federal government uses borrowed money to fund interstate highways, corporate bailouts, military equipment, and other projects not covered by current tax revenues, including day-to-day operating expenses.

All this borrowing comes at a price. After all, every loan must be repaid — with interest. Investors and business leaders need to carefully watch current interest rates and how they're changing. The price of business borrowing has a direct effect on stock and bond investments and impacts businesses' ability to grow. This chapter looks at interest rates, how they're set, what types of loans borrowers use, and how the debt markets affect the economy, the business cycle, and the investment markets.

Simplifying the Fixed-Income Market

When investors talk about fixed-income investments, they're talking about bonds and the bond market — the market most people use for debt securities. When big businesses, big banks, and big governments need to borrow big money, they turn to the *fixed-income market.* To understand how business borrowing works, you need to be familiar with bonds and the fixed-income market. This section provides a brief overview.

Bond-market terminology may be a little odd, but the process of borrowing and lending money in the market through bonds is actually quite simple. To borrow money, borrowers issue bonds. In other words, borrowers sell bonds to investors, and investors make loans to borrowers by buying bonds.

Borrowers agree to pay interest on the bonds they issue. Usually, the interest rate and the term of the bond are fixed. For example, a large business may issue a ten-year bond at 4 percent interest. For most bonds, that means the borrower makes two interest payments to the lender each year. At the end of the ten-year term, the bond matures and the bond issuer makes the final interest payment along with the principal repayment.

The process can get a little more complicated than that — with callable bonds, convertible bonds, zero-coupon bonds, and inflation-adjusted bonds — but at the end of the trading day, the basic idea is still that the bond issuer is borrowing money from the bond investor (regardless of which type of bond is being issued).

Other sources of funds are available to borrowers, of course. For instance, businesses and governments can borrow from commercial banks, and commercial banks can borrow from each other and from the Federal Reserve.

Variations on the bond-market concept also exist. Money markets, for example, are a way for large borrowers to get short-term loans. Certificates of deposit are ways for banks to borrow money from local depositors and other investors.

Still, the bond market is the main way that big organizations borrow big money. Not surprisingly, it's a big market. In fact, the market for bonds is at least double the size of the stock market in the United States and throughout the world.

Showing Some Interest in Interest

One important aspect of borrowing includes the interest associated with the lending. With bonds, interest is the investor's compensation for making the loan. Understanding how investors and lenders determine the interest rate is crucial to understanding the bond market's economic impact. The following sections examine how interest rates are set with bonds and what bondholders have to look at when considering investing in bonds.

Grasping how interest rates are set

The market of buyers and sellers determines the interest charged on a bond or any other loan. In other words, supply and demand determine the bond's interest rate. When a bond is first issued, it's generally sold at its *face value* or *par value*, which is usually $1,000 per bond. The *coupon rate* is the bond's initial interest rate. The issuers set the coupon rate so that it's attractive to bond buyers. Although a few exceptions do exist, the coupon rate generally doesn't change throughout the life of the bond. In other words, the interest payment from a 4 percent coupon rate will always pay the same amount. The coupon rate is based on the bond's face value. In this case, the 4 percent coupon rate means 4 percent of the $1,000 face value, or $40 per year (paid in two $20 installments).

Yield is the income return from the bond investment and is usually expressed as an annualized percentage based on the bond's price (but can sometimes be expressed as a percentage of its market value or its face value). As long as the bond sells at par (its par value), the bond's coupon rate is generally equivalent to its yield.

Things get a little tricky when the bond sells for some price other than par. The coupon rate doesn't change, but the yield changes with the bond's price. If interest rates rise, bond prices fall enough so the bond's yield matches current interest rates. In other words, if interest rates rise to 6 percent and you decide to sell your bond that has a 4 percent coupon, the price you receive must be low enough so that the buyer's yield is 6 percent.

The baseline interest rate for all bonds is based on the prevailing rates for U.S. Government debt, which is why loaning money to the U.S. Treasury through bonds is considered a risk-free investment. Loaning money to other borrowers is — by definition — riskier.

Determining risk

Because of the higher risk, non-government-issued bonds pay higher interest rates than the U.S. Treasury. How much higher depends on the amount of risk involved. Ultimately, the bond buyer has to determine if the *risk premium* (the higher interest rate) is sufficient to compensate for the higher risk. The bond buyer considers several factors to determine the risk:

- **Length of the loan:** When everything else is equal, the interest rate for short-term loans is lower than the rate for long-term loans because longer-term loans are riskier. Why? Here I talk mostly about interest risk, not default risk, and, of course, investors demand a bigger return when making riskier loans.
- **Collateral:** Most bonds are backed by the full faith and credit of the issuer. In other words, borrowers don't put up any collateral. In this case, the interest rate is based solely on the borrower's creditworthiness. In case of default, corporate bonds offer the investor some claim on the borrower's assets, but that claim isn't strong enough to allow the investor to recover 100 percent of the principal or interest owed. *Municipal bonds* (those issued by local or state governments) are usually backed by the full taxing authority of the issuing government body.

  In some situations, corporate or government borrowers pledge an asset, or the cash flow from an asset, to secure a loan. In the case of corporate bonds, such a pledge usually results in a modestly lower risk and a lower interest rate on the bond. However, asset-backed municipal bonds may be riskier because they're backed not by the government's taxing authority but by the revenue-generating capability of the asset itself. As a result, asset-backed municipal bonds often pay a higher interest rate than unsecured debt.
- **Creditworthiness:** If you were to take out a personal loan, you'd expect the lender to check your credit history. The same is true in the bond market. Instead of checking a bond issuer's credit score, bond investors look to several rating agencies (Moody's, Standard & Poor's, and Fitch) to determine the risk of default. The rating scales are similar from one agency to the next, but they're not identical. The highest rated AAA (or Aaa) bonds pay the lowest interest rates. Lower-rated bonds pay higher interest rates because they're riskier.

- **Inflation rate**: Interest rates are affected by expectations about inflation over the terms of the loans. Low expected inflation corresponds with low interest rates. High expected inflation means that borrowers must pay higher interest rates to compensate investors for the loss of purchasing power, and possibly also for the risk that inflation will be even higher than expected.
- **Availability of credit:** The overall availability of money to lend in the United States is often the single-largest factor determining interest rates. In other words, borrowers need willing lenders. If money is plentiful because many bond buyers are willing to invest in bonds, then interest rates are low. If the Federal Reserve believes the economy is overheating and drives the federal funds rate higher, money becomes scarce because it becomes more costly for banks and bond buyers to lend. Borrowers must pay higher interest rates to secure a loan (see Chapter 8 for details on the federal funds rate).

Finding Current Interest Rates: The Selected Interest Rates Report

U.S. Treasury securities are actively traded in public markets. You can usually get up-to-the-second rate quotes from your broker. If your broker doesn't offer real-time rate quotes, you can find U.S. Treasury quotes that are 10 to 20 minutes out of date on many investment websites (and you may want to find a different broker).

Real-time quotes for other debt securities are more difficult to find. Unless you're a very active bond trader, keeping track of these rates in real time probably isn't worth the expense or effort. Just ask your broker for the rate quote when you want to buy or sell a specific bond.

If you want to stay abreast of prevailing interest rates, you can get a pretty good estimate of current yields from the Federal Reserve. The Federal Reserve publishes average rates for a wide range of debt securities and various maturities in a report called *Selected Interest Rates* (or more formally, the *H.15 Data Series*). This report is issued weekly and updated daily and is available at no charge from the Federal Reserve's website. Check out Table 14-1 for an overview of the report.

Table 14-1 Selected Interest Rates Report

Release Schedule	*Agency*	*Web Address*	*Sensitivity*
Weekly: Monday, 2:30 p.m. ET	Federal Reserve Board of Governors	`federalreserve.gov/releases/h15/current/`	Low
Daily Update: 2:30 p.m. ET	Federal Reserve Board of Governors	`federalreserve.gov/releases/h15/update/`	Low

The weekly report shows average daily rates for the previous week, average weekly rates for the two previous weeks, and average monthly rates for the previous month. The daily update adds the average daily rates from the previous trading day. Figure 14-1 shows an example of what the report looks like.

The Selected Interest Rates report lists interest rates for the following types of debt securities:

- **Federal funds:** The Federal Open Market Committee (FOMC) sets the target range for the *federal funds rate,* which is the overnight rate for loans between member banks. The supply of money available from member banks determines the daily federal funds rates. In other words, the member banks negotiate the loan rate among themselves for each loan, within the guidelines set by the Federal Reserve. The Selected Interest Rates report shows the effective federal funds rate, which is the weighted average of the daily federal funds rates. (See Chapter 7 for details about the FOMC and the federal funds rate and Chapter 2 for details about weighted averages.)
- **Commercial paper:** Everyone who has a brokerage account is familiar with money market funds. *Commercial paper* is a short-term, unsecured form of money market debt that's issued by large corporations and commercial banks to fund operating expenses, inventories, and receivables. Maturities range from 1 to 270 days but are generally 30 days or less. Typically, this type of loan doesn't pay interest in the traditional sense. Instead, the investor buys the commercial paper at a discount to its face value (also called *par value*). At maturity, the investor receives the paper's face value. The difference between the face value and the discounted purchase price represents the interest on the loan.
- **Certificates of deposit and secondary market certificates:** Your local bank offers *certificates of deposit* (CDs; also called *consumer CDs*) as saving vehicles for depositors. The term of the CD is usually fixed, and investors pay a substantial penalty to withdrawal early. *Secondary market certificates,* sometimes called *negotiable CDs,* are similar in that they have fixed terms and are often offered with fixed interest rates, but they're issued by commercial rather than local banks. Although investors are

restricted from cashing in secondary market CDs before maturity, they can resell them in the open market. Secondary market CDs are issued with maturities as long as five years, however the Selected Interest Rates report lists only those CDs with a maturity of one year or less. Secondary market CDs are also considered money market instruments.

FEDERAL RESERVE statistical release

H.15 (519) SELECTED INTEREST RATES — For use at 2:30 p.m. Eastern Time

Yields in percent per annum — April 18, 2011

Instruments	2011 Apr 11	2011 Apr 12	2011 Apr 13	2011 Apr 14	2011 Apr 15	Week Ending Apr 15	Week Ending Apr 8	2011 Mar
Federal funds (effective)[1 2 3]	0.09	0.08	0.08	0.09	0.12	0.09	0.10	0.14
Commercial Paper[3 4 5 6]								
Nonfinancial								
1-month	0.13	0.17	0.17	0.15	0.19	0.16	0.15	0.17
2-month	0.17	0.13	0.15	0.16	0.16	0.15	0.19	0.21
3-month	0.18	0.22	0.20	0.19	0.20	0.20	0.20	0.23
Financial								
1-month	0.15	0.14	0.14	0.13	0.15	0.14	0.17	0.17
2-month	0.17	0.15	0.17	0.15	0.16	0.16	0.20	0.20
3-month	0.20	0.28	0.23	0.20	0.19	0.22	0.25	0.23
CDs (secondary market)[3 7]								
1-month	0.18	0.17	0.18	0.18	0.17	0.18	0.20	0.23
3-month	0.23	0.22	0.23	0.22	0.23	0.23	0.24	0.28
6-month	0.32	0.31	0.31	0.32	0.30	0.31	0.33	0.37
Eurodollar deposits (London)[3 8]								
1-month	0.24	0.24	0.25	0.25	0.25	0.25	0.29	0.30
3-month	0.42	0.42	0.40	0.40	0.40	0.41	0.42	0.42
6-month	0.56	0.56	0.54	0.54	0.54	0.55	0.53	0.56
Bank prime loan[2 3 9]	3.25	3.25	3.25	3.25	3.25	3.25	3.25	3.25
Discount window primary credit[2 10]	0.75	0.75	0.75	0.75	0.75	0.75	0.75	0.75
U.S. government securities								
Treasury bills (secondary market)[3 4]								
4-week	0.02	0.02	0.03	0.04	0.04	0.03	0.03	0.06
3-month	0.05	0.05	0.06	0.07	0.07	0.06	0.05	0.10
6-month	0.12	0.11	0.11	0.13	0.12	0.12	0.13	0.16
1-year	0.25	0.23	0.22	0.24	0.23	0.23	0.26	0.24
Treasury constant maturities								
Nominal[11]								
1-month	0.02	0.02	0.03	0.04	0.04	0.03	0.03	0.06
3-month	0.05	0.05	0.06	0.07	0.07	0.06	0.05	0.10
6-month	0.12	0.11	0.11	0.13	0.12	0.12	0.13	0.16
1-year	0.26	0.24	0.23	0.25	0.24	0.24	0.27	0.26
2-year	0.85	0.77	0.75	0.77	0.71	0.77	0.82	0.70
3-year	1.35	1.28	1.26	1.27	1.20	1.27	1.32	1.17
5-year	2.31	2.22	2.19	2.23	2.14	2.22	2.28	2.11
7-year	2.98	2.89	2.86	2.88	2.81	2.88	2.95	2.80
10-year	3.59	3.52	3.49	3.51	3.43	3.51	3.54	3.41
20-year	4.42	4.35	4.33	4.32	4.25	4.33	4.35	4.27
30-year	4.64	4.58	4.55	4.53	4.47	4.55	4.57	4.51
Inflation indexed[12]								
5-year	-0.07	-0.10	-0.11	-0.02	-0.09	-0.08	-0.05	-0.09
7-year	0.55	0.52	0.50	0.57	0.50	0.53	0.57	0.54
10-year	0.96	0.90	0.88	0.89	0.82	0.89	0.96	0.96
20-year	1.56	1.50	1.48	1.47	1.40	1.48	1.56	1.58
30-year	1.87	1.81	1.80	1.78	1.71	1.79	1.87	1.89
Inflation-indexed long-term average[13]	1.66	1.59	1.58	1.57	1.49	1.58	1.64	1.65
Interest rate swaps[14]								
1-year	0.44	0.41	0.41	0.41	0.40	0.41	0.44	0.44
2-year	1.00	0.92	0.93	0.91	0.88	0.93	0.98	0.87
3-year	1.59	1.49	1.50	1.46	1.43	1.50	1.56	1.40
4-year	2.09	1.98	1.99	1.94	1.91	1.98	2.05	1.89
5-year	2.52	2.39	2.42	2.36	2.33	2.40	2.47	2.31
7-year	3.14	3.02	3.04	2.98	2.97	3.03	3.08	2.96
10-year	3.69	3.57	3.60	3.54	3.52	3.58	3.61	3.52
30-year	4.42	4.32	4.35	4.31	4.27	4.33	4.33	4.29
Corporate bonds								
Moody's seasoned								
Aaa[15]	5.23	5.19	5.16	5.15	5.08	5.16	5.19	5.13
Baa	6.14	6.10	6.07	6.06	5.99	6.07	6.10	6.03
State & local bonds[16]				5.06		5.06	5.04	4.92
Conventional mortgages[17]				4.91		4.91	4.87	4.84

Figure 14-1: The Federal Reserve's Selected Interest Rates report.

- **Eurodollar deposits (London):** These are dollar-denominated deposits held in London-based banks. Eurodollar deposits often pay higher interest rates than comparable U.S.–based deposits. These loans aren't subject to federal regulations.
- **Bank prime loan:** This is the *prime rate,* which used to be the rate banks charged to their most creditworthy commercial clients. Today banks use the prime rate as a benchmark to set interest rates for their commercial clients. The most creditworthy clients usually pay something less than the prime rate. Commercial clients with less than stellar credit pay more than the prime rate, sometimes a lot more.
- **Discount window primary credit:** The Federal Reserve charges this overnight interest rate when it lends money to member banks. Don't confuse this "discount rate" with the federal funds rate, which is for loans between member banks.
- **U.S. Government securities:** The Selected Interest Rates report lists several types of Treasury debt, including current rates for short-term bills (maturities less than one year), *Treasury constant maturity rates* (which are composite rates based on outstanding bonds across all maturities), and *inflation-indexed* and *inflation-indexed long-term average rates* (which are based on Treasury Inflation-Protected Securities; see the next section for details).
- **Interest rate swaps:** Corporations and commercial banks use these derivative securities to help manage interest rate risk. The Selected Interest Rate report lists only swaps based on the three-month London Interbank Offered Rate (LIBOR) rate. (LIBOR is the rate commercial banks charge each other when lending money in the London wholesale money market. In a sense, it's like the federal funds rate, but it measures the interest rate for transactions outside the control of the Federal Reserve.)
- **Corporate bonds:** The Selected Interest Rate report lists the average yield for bonds rated Aaa and Baa by Moody's Investor Services. Aaa is Moody's highest rating and represents the highest-quality bonds with the lowest level of default risk. The Baa rating represents a medium-grade bond with a higher-risk profile.
- **State and local bonds:** The Selected Interest Rate report lists the average rate for general-obligation bonds issued by state and local municipalities (often called *municipal* or *muni bonds*).
- **Conventional mortgages:** The Federal Home Loan Mortgage Corporation (Freddie Mac) provides data for the average interest rate for fixed-rate first mortgages, and that average rate appears in the Selected Interest Rates report.

Taming the TIPS (Treasury Inflation-Protected Securities) Spread

Treasury Inflation-Protected Securities (TIPS) help shield bond investors from inflation's impact. The value of the principal of these Treasury bonds is raised or lowered based on inflation or deflation as measured by the Consumer Price Index (CPI; see Chapter 12 for details).

Like most bonds, interest on a TIPS bond is paid twice per year at a fixed rate. The actual interest payment is based on the fixed interest rate, but it's applied to the adjusted principal value rather than to the bond's original issue value. (Each payment is calculated by multiplying the adjusted principal by one-half of the interest rate.) At maturity, you receive the greater of the original principal amount or the adjusted principal.

The initial TIPS interest rate is usually lower than the rate for a comparable Treasury bond. A traditional bond is priced to produce a yield to maturity that compensates investors for today's inflation expectations. A TIPS bond is designed to adjust its repayments to compensate for inflation, so its price or yield doesn't include expected inflation.

The difference between the yield of a TIPS bond and a Treasury bond of the same maturity is called the *TIPS spread.* If the TIPS spread widens, the market expects future inflation to be higher than it expected before. If it narrows, the market expects future inflation to be lower than it expected before.

The spread may become very narrow if the market expects little inflation. The yield on the TIPS bond may even rise above the Treasury bond yield if the market expects deflation rather than inflation to prevail in the future.

You can find the current yields for TIPS bonds in the Selected Interest Rates Report referenced in Table 14-1 (under the heading Inflation Indexed). A chart showing the TIPS spread is available on the Federal Reserve Economic Data (FRED) website at `bit.ly/TipsSpread`. Visit the U.S. Treasury Direct website to see how the principal values for specific TIPS bonds are adjusted at `www.treasurydirect.gov/instit/annceresult/tipscpi/tipscpi.htm`.

Following the Treasury Yield Curve

The Treasury offers debt securities in maturities ranging from 3 months to 30 years. Depending on the maturity, Treasury debt goes by different names:

- **Treasury bills**: The maturities for bills range from a few days to 52 weeks. These securities are sold at discount to face value (par value). No interest is paid until the bill reaches maturity.
- **Treasury notes**: The maturities for notes range from one to ten years.
- **Treasury bonds**: The maturities for bonds can be up to 30 years.

The following sections further explain how the interest rates for the various maturities of Treasury securities can tell you a great deal of information about the current economic condition.

Interpreting the yield curve

The yields for various Treasury securities differ as their maturities lengthen. Normally, Treasury bills offer the lowest yield, while 30-year Treasury bonds offer the highest yield.

If you plot the Treasury yields on a graph with the bond's remaining term to maturity along the *x*-axis and its yield along the *y*-axis, you can create a *yield curve.* This yield curve shows the relationship between interest rates and the time to maturity for various U.S. Treasury securities. The shape of the yield curve tells you a great deal about the state of the bond market and the market's inflation concerns. It can even foretell the economy's future. In fact, this is one of the better economic forecasters out there, although its signals are sometimes very early; it may forecast a recession long before one occurs. Investors and business leaders can use the yield curve to improve their economic forecasts. In fact, one measure of the yield curve is included in The Conference Board's Leading Economic Index (LEI; see Chapter 10 for more information).

You can find current Treasury yields on the U.S. Treasury website at `www.treasury.gov/resource-center/data-chart-center/interest-rates/Pages/default.aspx`. You can also find historical yields for Treasury securities at the St. Louis Federal Reserve website: `research.stlouisfed.org/pdl/67`. You can find current charts of the U.S. Treasury Yield Curve many places online. The yield-curve chart on the Bloomberg website is a good example; check out `www.bloomberg.com/markets/rates-bonds/government-bonds/us/`.

Identifying how the curve can look and what the shapes mean

The yield curve takes four easily recognizable shapes. These shapes are useful for visually identifying the condition of the bond market and the economic forecast. The following sections explain what these shapes are and what they mean.

Normal yield curve

When the U.S. Treasury market is operating normally, the interest rate or yield for short-term bills is less than the yield for intermediate-term notes, and the yield for notes is normally less than the yield for long-term bonds. This scenario defines a *normal yield curve,* where the various maturities show a gradual upward slope. Figure 14-2 shows a stylized representation of a normal yield curve. (A real-world yield curve will show some jaggedness rather than a completely smooth curve.)

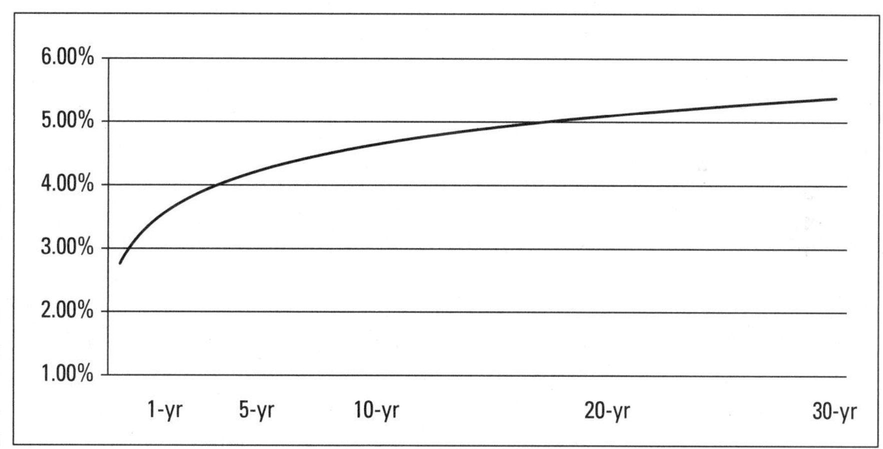

Figure 14-2: Normal yield curve.

A normal yield curve generally occurs during periods of economic expansion. Stock investors should position their portfolios for growth, with an emphasis on cyclical and technology stocks. Bond investors should anticipate that interest rates will eventually rise over time and that future inflation is a possibility. Rising rates mean falling bond prices, so bond portfolios should be weighted toward relatively short-duration maturities.

Steep yield curve

As the economy comes out of recession and begins to grow, bond investors demand a greater premium for longer-dated bonds, which leads to a *steep yield curve.* In other words, investors demand higher rates for bonds with longer maturities than for shorter-maturity bonds. You can see how this curve looks in Figure 14-3.

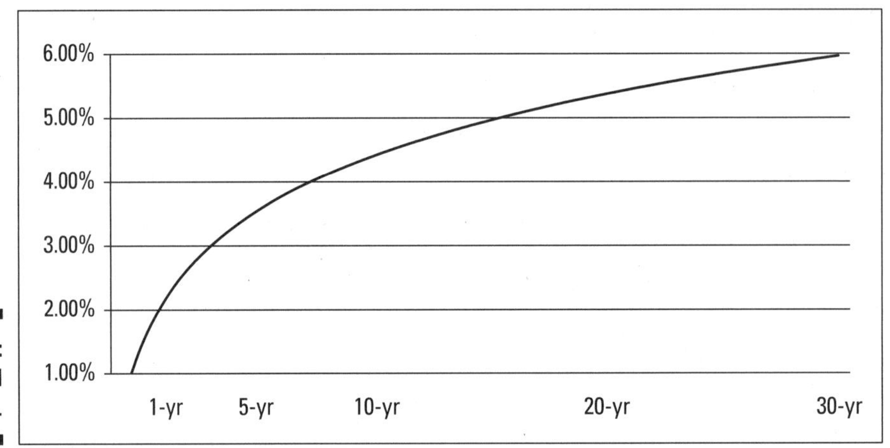

Figure 14-3: Steep yield curve.

It's common to see a steep yield curve at the beginning of an economic expansion. Stock investors should be moving away from consumer staples and into growth stocks of technology companies and manufacturers of durable goods. Bond investors should anticipate rising short-term interest rates. It's also possible that longer-term rates may begin to fall. Although locking in the higher longer-term rates is tempting, remember that these rates are likely to rise as the expansion continues and the risk of inflation grows.

Flat yield curve

When the Federal Reserve wants to slow the economy, one of its few available tools is to raise the federal funds rate (see Chapter 8 for details). If it does so, the rates for short-term debt securities are likely to rise faster than the rates for intermediate- and long-term securities. Why? According to standard theory, longer rates are averages of current and expected future short rates. Sometimes all these rates are bunched very close together, causing a *flat yield curve.* In the example shown in Figure 14-4, the curve is flat, but in a real-world yield curve, a few bumps may show up in the middle of the graph.

When you see the yield curve flatten, start planning for an eventual turn in the economy. Occasionally, a flat yield curve can turn into an inverted yield curve (see the next section).

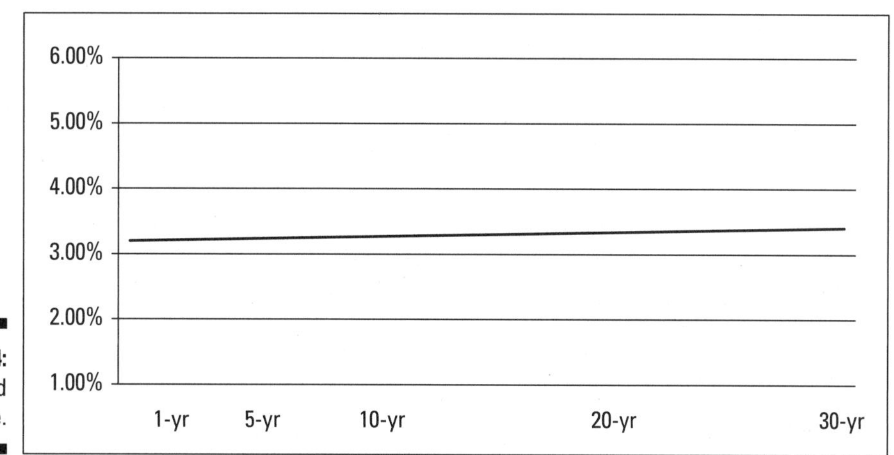

Figure 14-4: Flat yield curve.

Inverted yield curve

In this rare scenario, short-term yields are actually higher than long-term yields, causing the curve to become an *inverted yield curve*. You can see an example in Figure 14-5.

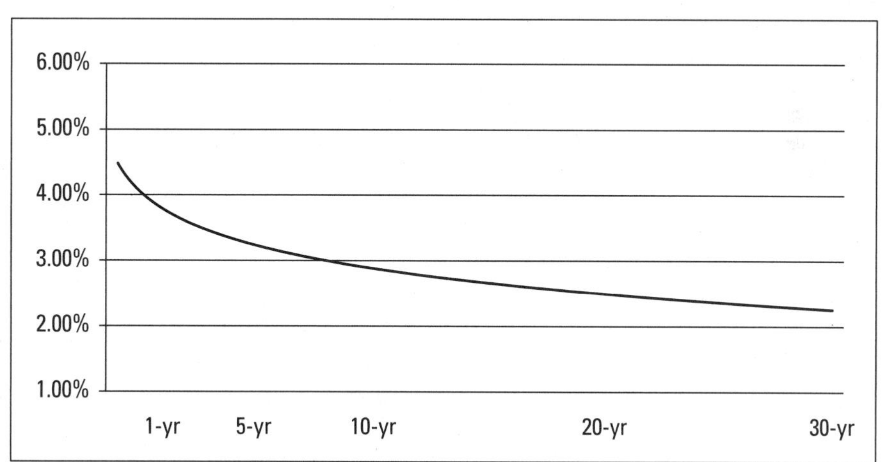

Figure 14-5: Inverted yield curve.

What investor in his right mind would ever accept lower rates for riskier long-maturity bonds? Usually a smart one. As the Federal Reserve raises short-term rates, the economy is likely to slow, and the risk of future inflation falls. Bond investors respond by bidding up the prices for long-term bonds, which lowers their yield. This situation isn't common, but when it does happen, it's usually a good time to lock in those long-term yields. In the past, whenever this situation has occurred, an economic slowdown or recession has always followed. On average, you can expect the slowdown to come within 6 to 12 months, but it may take more or less time.

Seeing the Bond Market's Impact on the Rest of the Market

The bond market has a dramatic impact on businesses' ability to improve productivity and grow. Investors feel its effects in the stock markets, in the currency markets, and throughout the economy, which I discuss in the following sections.

Yielding interesting returns

The bond market is keenly aware of the current interest rate climate. Prices of bonds rise or fall based on expectations for the economic future. In fact, the bond market is a very efficient signaling mechanism. Watch the yield curve for clues about the economic future.

Inflation directly affects current interest rates. Rising inflation raises interest rates because it diminishes the purchasing power of a bond's interest and principal payments, making them less valuable. Bond prices fall as inflation rates rise. Longer-maturity bonds suffer the most from inflation's impact. For any fixed inflation rate, the longer an investor has to hold a bond to recover the principal payment, the less valuable that payment becomes.

On the other side of the transaction, bond issuers must offer higher interest rates to compensate for higher inflation rates. Rising interest rates reduce businesses' profitability and competitiveness, harm the job market, and make improving businesses' productivity more expensive.

Investing in yield

In today's momentum-driven investment markets, stock investors need to pay closer attention to the bond market and its yield curve. At the very least, you can use them to see the warning signs that an economic turn is ahead. Stock investors can use the shape of the yield curve to help forecast recessions. The yield curve may not tell you whether the turn is going to happen during the next quarter or the next year, but you can be confident that the economic change is coming.

If the first decade of the new century has taught investors anything, it's that equities are a risky place to invest. You better know how your stocks' potential returns compare to the relatively placid world of bond investing. If the total returns on your stock investments aren't substantially higher than what you can get in the bond market, you should consider bond investments instead.

Not too long ago, investors did make a connection between the bond market and the stock market. In fact, investors used to compare expected stock returns to current bond yield. If the cash flows from an equity investment couldn't outperform a fixed-income investment, the investor had no reason to take an extra risk in the stock market. Fortunately, people like Warren Buffet remind today's investors that this kind of investing hasn't gone out of style. Buffet's Berkshire Hathaway remains an investment powerhouse by following cash flow investing principles.

Forecasting the currency's value

The yield curve can also help you forecast the U.S. dollar's value. Overseas currency traders react to changes in the debt market the same way that domestic bond investors do. If they see a flat or inverted yield curve, they know that the economy is going to slow at some point. As a result, the U.S. dollar becomes much less attractive because interest rates will fall along with overseas demand for U.S. dollars. On the other hand, when the yield curve is relatively steep, overseas investors usually take the opportunity to take a position in the U.S. currency because it's likely to strengthen along with the U.S. economy.

Chapter 15

Harvesting Commodity Data

In This Chapter

- Taking a closer look at commodities and their relationship with the economy
- Gathering data about economically sensitive commodities
- Distinguishing between spot and futures prices and knowing where to find them
- Indexing commodities for fun and profit

At one time, commodities and the U.S. economy were synonymous. The country's fertile farmlands and abundant natural resources gave rise to mighty industries that powered the U.S. economy.

During the Gilded Age (the late 19th century), the United States grew by producing natural and agricultural commodities and turning them into useful products. Sawmills turned timber into lumber that Northeastern shipyards used to build fishing fleets and trading ships. Iron mills sprouted around the Great Lakes and used Appalachia coal to forge iron from Midwestern ore. Oil came from Pennsylvania, copper from Michigan, and silver from Nevada. The South produced cotton, tobacco, indigo, and rice.

Although the service sector has eclipsed U.S. manufacturing over the past century, commodities are still an integral part of the U.S. economy. Corn, wheat, aluminum, steel, copper, nickel, oil, lead, zinc, tin, crude oil, sugar, oats, rice, hogs, beef, cotton — they're all part of the U.S. economic landscape.

Commodity pricing is very sensitive to changes in the economy. Prices rise during expansions and fall during recessions. In short, commodity price trends are very good economic indicators. This chapter explores the link between commodities and interest rates, stock prices, the business cycle, and the economy.

Understanding Commodities: Focusing on Supply and Demand

Using commodity prices as an indicator of economic health isn't a new concept. In fact, commodity prices were likely the original economic indicator, in use long before Columbus set sail from Spain.

Traditionally, *commodities* are products from agriculture or mining — things like lumber, iron ore, cotton, and rice. Today's definition is a bit more expansive and includes manufactured or processed products, like chemicals and gasoline, that are all but identical from one manufacturer to another.

A direct correlation exists between a nation's economy and the prices of its commodities. When economic activity is strong, demand for commodities is also strong, and strong demand usually results in higher prices. Likewise, when the economy slows, so does the demand (and, therefore, the price) for commodities.

Despite the fact that service industries account for the largest part of today's U.S. economy, the correlation between economic growth and commodity prices remains strong. Consider the following major service companies and their use of commodity products to see why:

- **Pulte Homes:** Home builders use steel and cement for the home's foundation, lumber for framing, and copper in electrical wiring, plumbing, and roofing.
- **American Airlines:** Airliners require fuel, and the planes themselves contain rubber for the tires, glass for the windows, textiles for the seating, and metal for the framing and fuselage.
- **Starbucks:** Coffee shops use coffee and sugar for brewed beverages, dairy for lattes, and wheat for pastries.

Commodity products can get to market several different ways, which means that you can monitor their prices several ways. The next sections examine the three most common ways to purchase and sell commodity products: cash markets, forward contracts, and futures markets.

Paying cash upfront: Cash markets

One way that people buy and sell commodities is through *cash market,* or *spot market,* transactions. Buyers and sellers complete these cash transactions at the current market price, sometimes called the *spot price.* The seller expects payment upon delivery, thus, completing the transaction. (Spot prices are published and available for many commodities. I discuss data sources for these spot prices in the later section "Pricing Commodities.")

For example, when you go to the farmers' market to buy a few ears of corn, you deal directly with the farmer, paying him as soon as you receive the corn. That situation describes a cash transaction. The farmer posts his price next to a stack of corn. You decide how much corn you want, maybe you haggle a little, and then you both agree on a price. The deal is done. You take delivery of the corn right there on the spot. Even if your friendly farmer uses the latest technology and can accept debit card payments by using a smartphone, it's still a cash transaction.

The same cash transaction takes place when the farmer sells his product directly to a large company. The two parties agree on a price and arrange the delivery and payment, and the deal is done.

Specifying the purchase terms before you buy: Forward contracts

Forward contracts are common in the world of commodities. The buyer and seller negotiate the terms of these agreements. There are no standard forward contracts, although effective forward contracts specify the product to be delivered, the quantity, the price and delivery terms, and the penalties for failure to deliver. Normally, the buyer makes the payment at the time of delivery, but forward contracts don't have to be structured this way. Many of these contracts are private, so prices are rarely posted.

To get a better idea of what a forward contract is, say that you own a small organic bakery that sells artisan breads. You support your local farmer and buy his organically grown wheat because he practices sustainable agricultural methods. Now say that you run out of flour. You go to your local organic farmer to buy some more, but he's out, too. He sold it all. Though he has already planted the next crop, he won't harvest it for several months.

Obviously, you need another source for organically grown wheat right now, but you also want to make sure that this situation doesn't happen again. So you offer to buy enough of the farmer's current crop (the one that hasn't been harvested yet) to hold you over until the next harvest.

The farmer likes this idea because it's good for both you and his farm. You get a steady supply of organic wheat for your bakery, and the farmer gets to lock in a buyer for part of his harvest. You agree on a price and the payment and delivery terms, and the deal is done.

You may have a problem if the harvest isn't large enough to satisfy your contract, but as long as the contract details how the two of you will handle missed deliveries or payments, it's a good forward contract.

This example is for two small businesses, but forward contracts also take place between large commodity producers and large manufacturers.

Bidding for a price: Futures markets

The main difference between forward contracts and futures contracts is standardization; in other words, futures markets provide a standardized way for commodity buyers and sellers to transact business. In *futures markets,* standardized contracts specify the product details, quantity, quality, delivery date, and delivery location, and these contracts are traded on a futures exchange.

Commodity pricing in the futures market is similar to pricing in the stock and bond markets. They're all double-auction markets: Buyers bid for a product (by posting a *bid price*), and sellers offer their product for sale (by posting an *offer* or *ask price*). The difference between the highest bid and the lowest offer price is called the *spread.*

Transactions occur at either the bid price or the ask price or sometimes in between the two. When a transaction occurs, that transaction becomes the current *market price.* The market price is transitory, meaning that it can change when the next transaction occurs.

Farmers and commercial bakers enter into futures contracts for the same reason the organic baker executed a forward contract with the local farmer in the earlier section "Specifying the purchase terms before you buy: Forward contracts." Commercial bakers need a steady supply of wheat throughout the year, and farmers like to have at least some of their crop under contract before harvest.

Plus, futures contracts can help manage price risk. Prices for wheat are extremely volatile throughout the year. As long as farmers have a good harvest, prices at harvest are often the lowest of the year, which is great for the baker but not for the farmer.

The only time prices are high at harvest is when farmers experience widespread crop failure, which can be the result of natural disasters like tornadoes or floods, drought, disease, or pests. In the case of widespread crop failure, the commercial baker is at a disadvantage because he must pay higher prices for the now-scarce commodity.

If the farmer waits until harvest to sell his wheat, he may get the lowest prices available for his efforts. On the other hand, if the baker waits until harvest to purchase the farmer's wheat, he's at the whim of the market.

Futures contracts can help mitigate these price risks, at least to some degree, by allowing the farmer and baker to hedge against wide price swings. When hedging, the farmer sells enough wheat futures contracts to cover some or all of his crop when prices are high enough to grow the wheat profitably. Rather than deliver his wheat to satisfy the contract, he can buy back an equal amount of futures contracts to effectively close his position. The same hedging strategy applies to the baker but in reverse.

Delving into Commodities Reports

To make use of commodity pricing as an economic indicator, investors and business leaders must understand how and where commodities are used. A vast amount of information is available about the supply and demand for commodities. Some of this info is freely available from U.S. Government agencies. Private sources fill in the details not provided by the government.

Pricing for individual commodity products can be extremely volatile; this volatility sometimes makes identifying economy-wide price trends difficult. One way to overcome this problem is to aggregate commodity products into a single price index (I discuss such indexes in the later section "Tracking Commodity Indexes"). Nonetheless, it's also useful to understand how supply and demand changes affect pricing for individual commodities. The production reports I describe in the following sections give you the data you need to identify supply disruptions or isolated changes in demand.

Digging for gold and other precious metals

Gold is the hot commodity, at least recently. Inflation fears and other economic concerns pushed gold prices over $1,500 per ounce for the first time in 2011. However, gold isn't an income-producing investment. It doesn't offer a yield of any sort. Also, its price is sensitive to both deflation and inflation. If investors fear deflation, the price of gold is likely to fall.

So why is gold such a popular commodity? The biggest reason is that its value doesn't correlate with the stock or bond markets. (In other words, gold's price is independent of stock and bond prices.) Thus, people use gold to do two things:

- **Some investors use gold as a hedge against inflation.** When investors fear the risk of inflation is growing, some think that gold holds its value better than other assets. (Others argue the point, but for our purposes, knowing that many view gold as an inflation hedge is enough.)
- **Some investors use gold as a safe haven against economic calamity.** Historically, gold has held its value during periods of war, famine, and political unrest. It has held its value even when the currency is completely debased.

Unfortunately, gold's use as a safe haven makes it less than perfect as an economic indicator. Segregating investors who use gold as an inflation hedge from those who use it as a safe haven (of course, they're sometimes one and the same) is difficult. As a result, knowing how much of gold's price increase is directly attributable to inflation isn't easy. Still, gold is a good way to measure investors' fears, which is why tracking price trends for this precious metal is important.

The U.S. Geological Survey (USGS) provides information about U.S. and worldwide gold mine production, as well as gold reserves held in countries around the world, in its monthly *USGS Gold Report.* This report also includes details on U.S. refining, imports and exports, and U.S. Treasury inventories. Table 15-1 provides an overview of the USGS Gold Report.

Table 15-1 USGS Gold Report

Release Schedule	*Agency*	*Web Address*	*Sensitivity*
Monthly	U.S. Geological Survey	`minerals.usgs.gov/minerals/pubs/commodity/gold`	Moderate

The United States is a net exporter of gold. In fact, the United States is the fourth-largest gold producer after Australia, South Africa, and China. The USGS estimates that almost 70 percent of the gold used in the United States is used for jewelry and the arts. Less than 10 percent is used in electronics manufacturing. Other uses include dentistry, decoration (gold leaf), medicine, and medals.

The market for gold is very liquid. In addition to investing directly in the metal itself, you can invest in gold-related mutual funds and exchange-traded funds (ETFs). Most mutual funds invest in the stocks of gold mining companies. Some ETFs use the same approach. Others invest in the precious metal itself. (If you need a refresher on mutual fund or ETF investing, check out the latest edition of *Mutual Funds For Dummies* written by Eric Tyson and published by John Wiley & Sons, Inc.)

Investors use other precious metals, like silver, platinum, and palladium, as a hedge against inflation in the same way they use gold, so price trends in these metals can serve as economic indicators, too. (However, be aware that silver prices tend to be volatile and have occasionally been subject to illegal price manipulation, which diminishes its usefulness as an economic indicator.) Like gold, these metals have both industrial and jewelry uses. The USGS offers production reports for these metals, as well, although the reports for platinum and palladium are combined. You can find the reports at the following websites:

- **Silver**: `minerals.usgs.gov/minerals/pubs/commodity/silver/`
- **Platinum and palladium**: `minerals.usgs.gov/minerals/pubs/commodity/platinum/`

Drilling into the energy markets

Energy prices generally rise during periods of economic expansion and fall during recessions, and they're certainly subject to inflationary pressures. In addition, rising energy prices can impact pricing for products and services across the economic spectrum, including heavy industry, transportation, and even retail. However, energy prices are also highly subject to supply disruptions caused by hurricanes, floods, and geopolitical tensions. For this reason, investors need to be aware of any supply constraints that may account for changes in energy pricing.

The U.S. Department of Energy (DOE) makes keeping track of the energy markets easy to do. The DOE follows production, current supplies, and current utilization for all energy products, including coal, electricity, nuclear power, geothermal energy, hydropower, natural gas, crude oil (also called *petroleum*), and renewable sources like bioenergy, solar power, and wind. Crude oil and natural gas are the most interesting to investors, so I focus on them in the following sections.

Refining crude oil

Crude oil isn't the only energy product investors need to watch, but it may be the most economically sensitive commodity of all. Because the United States is dependent on crude oil for transportation, its price directly affects consumer prices for a number of products. To underscore the extent of crude oil's economic sensitivity, consider this: Spikes in the price of crude oil have coincided with almost every economic recession since the OPEC-fueled gas shortage in 1973 (*OPEC* stands for *Organization of the Petroleum Exporting Countries*).

When crude oil is refined, it yields a number of other commodity products (sometimes called *petroleum products*), including gasoline, diesel fuel, and jet fuel, as well as plastics, resins, and petroleum jelly. One standard 42-gallon barrel of oil can create about 44 gallons of petroleum products (see Figure 15-1 for a visual representation of what you get from one gallon of oil).

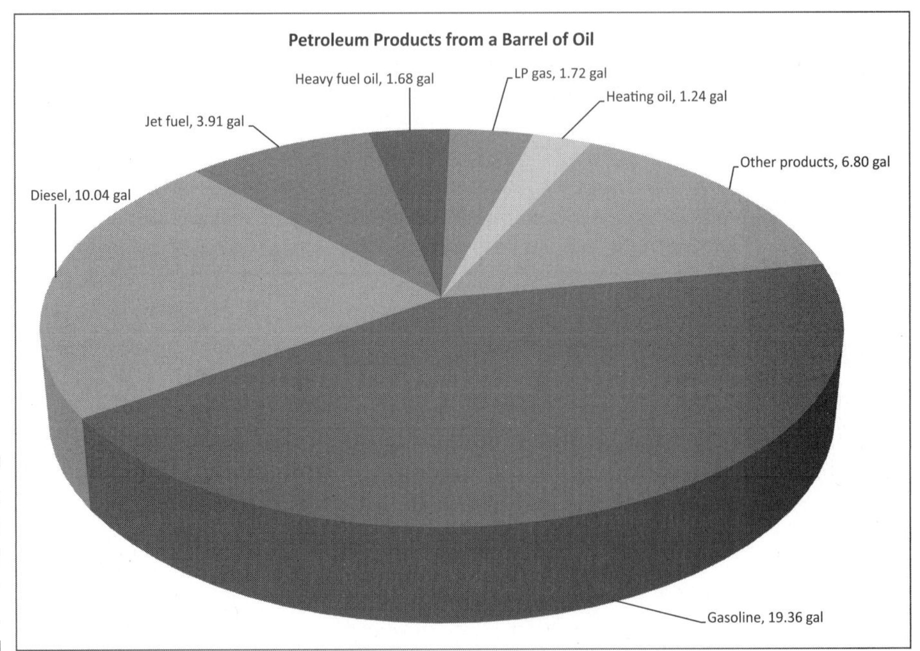

Figure 15-1: Petroleum products from a barrel of oil.

The *Other products* category in Figure 15-1 includes products like ink, dishwashing liquids, ammonia, tires, plastics, and crayons. To explain the increase in volume (from 42 to 44 gallons), the DOE says that refining oil is like making popcorn. It gets bigger when it's refined. (More precise explanations of the phenomenon are certainly available, but the popcorn analogy is good enough for most investors.)

Table 15-2 tells you what you need to know to follow the DOE's weekly petroleum report, called *This Week in Petroleum*.

Table 15-2 This Week in Petroleum

Release Schedule	*Agency*	*Web Address*	*Sensitivity*
Weekly: Every Wednesday, after 1:00 p.m. ET	U.S. Energy Information Administration, Department of Energy	`eia.doe.gov/oog/info/twip/twip.asp`	Moderate

This Week in Petroleum shows domestic and worldwide oil production, crude oil inventories, drilling rig counts, retail and futures prices for petroleum products, and refinery output. Additional reports are available on this site for heating oil, propane, diesel (or distillate), and gasoline.

In addition to the info you get from the U.S. DOE's report, you can find a lot more details about the energy markets from other sources. Here are just a few examples:

- **American Petroleum Institute:** Much of the detailed data are available only by subscription, but many summary reports are available at no charge (`www.api.org`).
- **Oil & Gas Journal:** This trade publication reports on the worldwide oil industry (`www.ogj.com`).
- **Organization of the Petroleum Exporting Countries (OPEC):** The OPEC's monthly *Oil Market Report* provides worldwide supply and demand statistics, product markets, refinery operations, market price analysis, futures analysis, as well as analysis of other futures markets (`www.opec.org`).
- **Chemical Week:** This publication offers news reports covering the chemical industry (`www.chemweek.com`).
- **Plastics News:** This trade publication reports on the plastics industry (`www.plasticsnews.com`).
- **International Energy Agency (IEA):** Many of this organization's reports are available only by subscription, but some statistics are available at no charge (`www.iea.org`). A two-week-old version of the IEA *Oil Market Report* is available at this link: `omrpublic.iea.org`.

Tapping natural gas

Natural gas is another widely used and economically sensitive energy commodity. Half of the homes in the United States use it for heat, although if you look at just the Midwest, more than 80 percent of homes use natural gas for heat. Some homes also use it for cooking.

In addition, natural gas generates about 22 percent of the electricity used in the United States, is a component in fertilizer, and is used in some commercial transportation applications, like city buses and other fleet vehicles. It can also be used to produce hydrogen.

Investors need to keep an eye on supply and demand for natural gas. Industrial and residential prices rise and fall with demand. Prices have a clear seasonality, but they're also affected by economic conditions. Because natural gas is a very clean-burning hydrocarbon, demand is expected to outpace other types of hydrocarbon-based fuel in the coming decades. You can use the DOE's *Natural Gas Storage Report* to stay informed about natural gas markets (see Table 15-3).

Table 15-3 Natural Gas Storage Report

Release Schedule	*Agency*	*Web Address*	*Sensitivity*
Weekly: Every Thursday, 10:30 a.m. ET	U.S. Energy Information Administration, Department of Energy	`www.eia.doe.gov/naturalgas/`	Moderate

The Natural Gas Storage Report provides current inventory levels as well as historical usage patterns. The companion report, *Natural Gas Weekly Update,* provides a summary of the previous week's daily spot and futures prices and is available on the same site (see the later section "Pricing Commodities" for details on spot and futures prices).

Monthly production reports, analysis of the number of natural gas rigs in operation, and natural gas spot prices and residential prices are also available on the DOE's natural gas website, which I list in Table 15-3. You can see the seasonal and economic effects on natural gas demand and pricing in Figure 15-2, which shows commercial and residential gas prices from 1985 through April 2011.

The cyclicality of residential prices caused by seasonal demand is obvious, but this seasonal cyclicality also affects commercial prices. Although the effects of the business cycle on natural gas pricing aren't as obvious, you can see that they play a role, especially from the late 1990s through 2011.

Figure 15-2 also shows how supply and demand constraints can overwhelm seasonal and economic factors. The price spike in 2005 corresponds to supply disruptions that occurred when Hurricane Katrina destroyed some natural gas infrastructure. The price spike in 2008 is probably the result of rising crude oil prices.

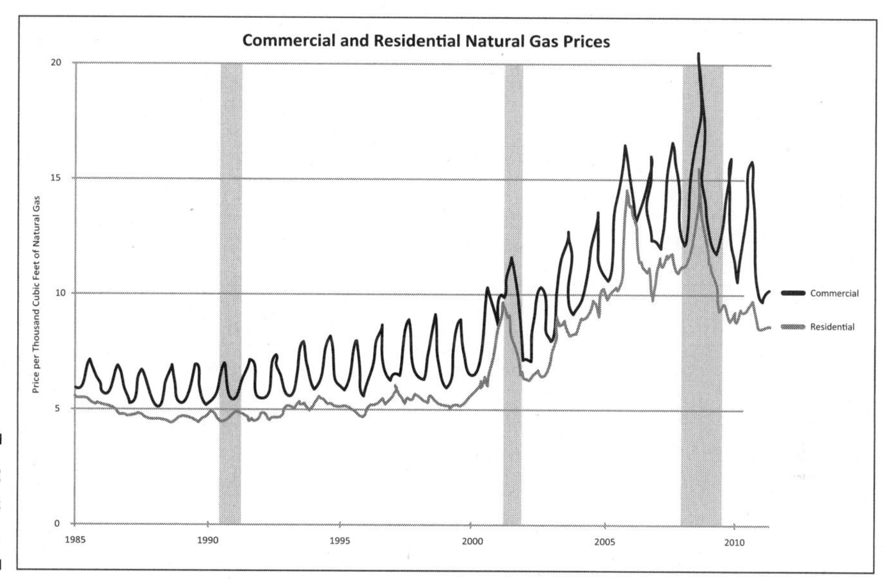

Figure 15-2: Natural gas prices.

Growing the agricultural markets

Though agricultural products are very sensitive to the current state of the economy, food prices are also at the whim of the weather. That's why keeping track of agricultural markets and disruptions in food prices makes sense for investors.

Agricultural products are inputs for a wide range of consumer and business industries. Grains and meats end up in human food and livestock feed. Cotton and wool are primarily used for textiles. Leather can be used in furnishings, fashion accessories, and footwear. Lumber is often the single-largest commodity used in home construction; it's used for framing, flooring, and cabinetry.

The commodities markets categorize agricultural products into three broad groups:

- **Grains:** Wheat, corn, soy (soybeans, soybean meal, soybean oil), oats, rough rice (rice that still has the husk intact), red wheat, spring wheat, and canola
- **Meats and dairy:** Livestock, including live cattle and feeder cattle, hogs, pork bellies (bacon), milk, dry whey, nonfat dry milk, and butter
- **Softs:** Coffee, sugar, cocoa, frozen concentrated orange juice, cotton, wool, lumber, and container board

The good news is that the U.S. Department of Agriculture (USDA) provides an enormous amount of information about agricultural products in its *outlook reports.* Table 15-4 gives an overview of this collection of reports.

Table 15-4 Outlook Reports

Release Schedule	***Agency***	***Web Address***	***Sensitivity***
Monthly	Economic Research Service, U.S. Department of Agriculture	`www.ers.usda.gov/publications/outlook/`	Moderate

The USDA publishes one report for each of the agricultural commodities it follows. Separate reports are available for bioenergy; cotton and wool; feed grains; livestock, dairy, and poultry; oil crops; U.S. agricultural trade; rice; sugar and sweeteners; and wheat.

Each outlook report covers worldwide consumption, domestic and international production, current and projected inventories, as well as data tables specific to each commodity. The *U.S. Agricultural Trade report* provides a summary of all the outlook reports. You can find it at the link listed in Table 15-4.

The following USDA agencies provide even more specialized information that investors can use to track supply and demand for agricultural products and to help determine the cause of price-trend changes:

- **Economic Research Service (ERS)**: The ERS is the USDA's economic research service. The reports that interest investors the most provide research on animal products, biotechnology, the farm economy, the food sector, and trade. The ERS has an extensive collection of databases about feed grains, food prices, wheat data, and meat prices. It also provides research on global food markets, trade agreements, and agricultural exports. Find all this research at `ers.usda.gov`.
- **National Agricultural Statistics Service:** This agency provides acreage reports, agricultural prices, grain stocks, cattle reports, crop production reports, and crop progress and condition reports for each state. Go to `www.nass.usda.gov` for details.
- **Agricultural Research Service (ARS):** The ARS provides educational and tutorial products, daily news, and the monthly *Agricultural Research* magazine. Find all this info at `ars.usda.gov`.
- **Office of the Chief Economist:** The Chief Economist publishes commodity forecasts, daily weather highlights, the *Weekly Weather and Crop Bulletin*, a drought monitor, crop calendars, and the *Global Crop Production Review*. Check out `www.usda.gov/oce` for details.

Mining industrial metals

Industrial metals are another important commodity for investors to follow. Although investors rarely use these metals to hedge against inflation risk (except occasionally copper), prices for these products are very sensitive to the business cycle. The USGS provides statistical briefs on almost 100 different nonfuel minerals. Some of the most economically sensitive ones include

- **Aluminum:** The United States is a net importer of aluminum. It's used in beer and soda cans, automobiles, airliners, building construction, electrical equipment, machinery, and consumer durable products.
- **Copper:** Copper, which is sometimes called *red gold,* is very sensitive to economic trends. It's used in home construction for electrical wiring, plumbing, and HVAC (heating and cooling) systems, electronics manufacturing, automobiles, and industrial applications.
- **Nickel:** The most common use for nickel is in stainless and alloy steel. That steel is then used in the transportation, chemical, and electrical equipment industries, as well as in construction and household appliances.
- **Gypsum:** A typical new home contains more than 7 tons of gypsum. It's used for walls and ceilings and as a component in concrete. It's also useful as a soil conditioner.
- **Titanium:** Approximately 95 percent of all titanium is used in the form of *titanium dioxide,* a white pigment in paints, paper, and plastics. When used in its metal form, titanium is resistant to corrosion and exhibits a high strength-to-weight ratio.
- **Zinc:** Most zinc is used to galvanize metal, protect iron and steel from corrosion, and make bronze and brass. It's also used to make rubber, some chemicals, paint, and agricultural products.

The USGS provides industry indicators for each of these commodities in its *Commodity Statistics and Information reports.* These reports provide worldwide supply and demand information, U.S. and worldwide production statistics, inventory levels, utilization statistics, and a brief analysis of industry trends for each commodity. You can find links to these reports on the USGS website (see Table 15-5 for an overview of these reports).

Table 15-5 USGS Commodity Statistics and Information Reports

Release Schedule	*Agency*	*Web Address*	*Sensitivity*
Monthly	U.S. Geological Survey	`minerals.usgs.gov/minerals/pubs/commodity/`	Moderate

The USGS produces other publications that you may find useful in your investing. They include the following:

- **Metal Industry Indicators:** This monthly newsletter analyzes the economic health of the metal industries. It includes leading indexes developed in conjunction with Columbia University. Find this newsletter at `minerals.usgs.gov/minerals/pubs/mii/`.
- **Minerals Yearbook:** This annual publication provides statistical data and industry analysis and includes details about domestic industries, government programs, tariffs, imports and exports, and inventories for more than 90 individual minerals and materials. Although it's published annually, it may not be released until as many as 15 months after the end of the publication year. Go to `minerals.usgs.gov/minerals/pubs/commodity/myb/` for more info on this annual publication.
- **Mineral Commodity Summaries:** This annual report provides summaries from the Minerals Yearbook. Find out more at `minerals.usgs.gov/minerals/pubs/mcs/`.

Pricing Commodities

When researching commodity prices, investors need to be aware of the difference between spot and futures prices. *Spot prices* are priced for current delivery of a product. *Futures prices* are contract prices for future delivery. Futures prices are often higher than the spot prices, although they may occasionally be lower. The following sections help you tell the difference between the two prices and explain how to find them.

Pricing for individual commodity products may not show a dramatic correlation with the economy or the business cycle. However, some commodities do show a direct correlation with the predominant industries where they're used. Lumber and gypsum, for example, are strongly correlated with the housing industry, and aluminum is closely related to consumer product packaging and transportation.

Finding spot prices

One thing you'll notice when you start looking for spot prices is how many more commodities trade in spot markets than in futures markets. Commodities like burlap, eggs, lard, palm oil, mustard seed, potato, cardamom, jute, and coal trade in spot markets but not in futures markets. (Refer to the section "Paying cash upfront: Cash markets" for more on spot markets.)

One of the best places to stay up-to-date with spot prices is the *Wall Street Journal* online. You can find a link to their spot listings at `online.wsj.com/mdc/public/page/mdc_commodities.html`. Scroll down to the Complete Commodities and Futures Data box and click on one of the links listed under Spot Prices. Notice that this resource offers a long list of commodity prices but no charts. The prices represent actual sales prices for physical commodities. Historical data is available but only one day at a time.

Finding futures prices

Several places list commodity futures pricing and trend charts. Although real-time pricing would cost you, you can find delayed quotes and end-of-day prices at no charge on a number of websites:

- **CRB Trader:** Provides price quotes (including intraday delayed price quotes), charts, and contract specifications (including trading symbols, trading units, trading months, trading hours, contract limits, and contract expiration); `www.crbtrader.com/data.asp`
- **Bloomberg:** Provides a price summary for the most actively traded commodities but doesn't include charts, intraday pricing, or contract details; `www.bloomberg.com/markets/commodities/futures/`
- **Wall Street Journal:** Provides price quotes, intraday delayed prices, charts, and option chains; `online.wsj.com/mdc/public/page/mdc_commodities.html`

Depending on the website, delayed prices may be 10 to 20 minutes old. If you're a commodities trader, those delays are probably too long for you to trade effectively, so you likely need to pay for a real-time data service. However, if you're just trying to stay abreast of commodity price trends, delayed prices work just fine. In fact, end-of-day prices are usually all you need.

Of course, commodity futures exchanges also offer delayed pricing, usually at no charge. The primary U.S. exchanges are

- **CME Group:** Includes the Chicago Mercantile Exchange (CME), the Chicago Board of Trade (CBOT), the New York Mercantile Exchange (NYMEX), and the Commodity Exchange (COMEX); `www.cmegroup.com/`
- **Kansas City Board of Trade:** Provides pricing for listed grains only; `www.kcbt.com`
- **Minneapolis Grain Exchange:** Provides pricing for listed grains only; `www.mgex.com`

Tracking Commodity Indexes

Some experts feel that the real money involved in commodity trading makes commodity pricing a better economic indicator than those indicators based on surveys or other techniques. Commodity prices, interest rates, and inflation tend to move together. In addition, commodity prices, especially as represented by composite commodity indexes, correlate very well with the equity markets and the business cycle. In other words, composite commodity indexes offer investors an excellent tool to monitor the business cycle and the current economic condition. In fact, aggregate commodity indexes often correlate better with the overall economy than prices for individual commodities.

Even though making investment decisions based solely on pricing indicators from the commodities markets may not be wise, these tools are valuable for the investor and business manager to monitor. This section looks at several commodity indexes and shows how they perform as economic forecasters.

Following Standard & Poor's GSCI

Standard & Poor's (S&P) purchased the Goldman Sachs Commodities Index (GSCI) from Goldman Sachs in 2007 and renamed it the *Standard & Poor's GSCI,* although most people still refer to it simply as the *GSCI.* Information about the index is available in Table 15-6.

Table 15-6 Standard & Poor's GSCI

Release Schedule	*Agency*	*Web Address*	*Sensitivity*
Daily: 4:15 p.m. CT	Standard & Poor's	`http://bit.ly/SandP-GSCI`	Moderate

Goldman Sachs began publishing the original GSCI in 1991 as a broad aggregate of many commodities. The makeup of the index has changed over the years. Figure 15-3 shows the various commodity components in the S&P GSCI as of December 2010.

Currently, the S&P GSCI is a *production weighted index,* which means that the commodity's average quantity of worldwide production over the past five years determines the weighting. The idea is to have the index represent the relative significance of the commodities in the world economy. Today's S&P GSCI is heavily weighted in energy products, as you can see in Figure 15-3.

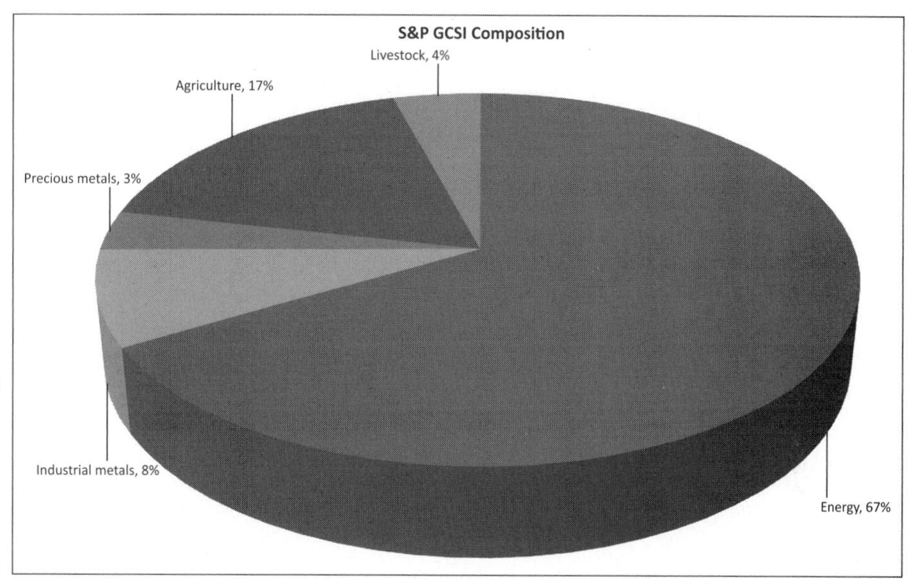

Figure 15-3: Composition of Standard & Poor's GSCI.

Source: Standard & Poor's Financial Services, LLC

The S&P GSCI is really a family of indexes that measures a variety of commodities and commodity groups. The S&P GSCI series includes a variety of subindexes, including commodity sectors like agriculture, metals, as well as single component indexes. However, most investors still favor the aggregate S&P GSCI.

One unique feature of this index series is the availability of indexes in currencies other than the U.S. dollar, including the Euro, Australian dollar, Japanese yen, Swiss franc, and pound sterling.

Several exchange-traded products use the S&P GSCI or one of its subindexes as a benchmark. Exchange-traded funds (ETFs), exchange-traded trusts (ETTs), and exchange-traded notes (ETNs) trade either on the major stock exchanges or on the commodities exchanges. Here are several of the existing funds that use the GSCI as a benchmark:

- **iShares S&P GSCI Commodity-Indexed Trust**: `us.ishares.com/product_info/fund/overview/GSG.htm`
- **iPath S&P GSCI Total Return Index ETN**: `www.ipathetn.com/GSP-overview.jsp?investorType=pro`
- **iPath S&P GSCI Crude Oil Total Return Index ETN**: `www.ipathetn.com/OIL-overview.jsp`

Other GSCI tracking funds, notes, and trusts also trade on various world exchanges.

Commodity-indexed funds differ from traditional mutual funds and ETNs. These funds may be lightly traded and extremely volatile. ETNs have different risks than ETFs. For example, the ETNs sponsored by iPath are a debt obligation of the issuer (Barclays Bank, PLC), so the issuer, not the fund, holds the actual assets.

Digging into the Thomson Reuters/Jefferies CRB Index

The *Thomson Reuters/Jefferies CRB Index* is the oldest of the publicly available commodity price indexes. (In case you're wondering, *CRB* stands for *Commodity Research Bureau.*) This index has been published in one form or another since 1958. It has undergone several revisions and changes in ownership, and is now owned by Thomson Reuters, LLC, and Jefferies Financial Products, LLC. Check out Table 15-7 for some general information about this index.

Table 15-7 Thomson Reuters/Jefferies CRB Index

Release Schedule	*Agency*	*Web Address*	*Sensitivity*
Daily: 4:15 p.m. CT	Thomson Reuters/Jefferies	`www.jefferies.com/cositemgr.pl/html/ProductsServices/SalesTrading/Commodities/ReutersJefferiesCRB/index.shtml`	Moderate

After you navigate to the website listed in Table 15-7, click on the Index Data link to view a chart for the CRB Index data. Then choose what chart you want to view from the drop-down menus and click the See Chart button. You can also download historical data by clicking on the Download to spreadsheet link underneath the chart.

In its current iteration, the CRB Index includes 19 commodities that represent all sectors traded on futures exchanges. The index is rebalanced monthly to keep it from being overweight in commodities whose prices have trended higher. The target balance of commodities is shown in Figure 15-4.

Compared to the S&P GSCI, the CRB Index is weighted less heavily in energy and includes a heavier weighting in agricultural products. Like the S&P GSCI, several funds use the CRB Index or related indexes as a benchmark.

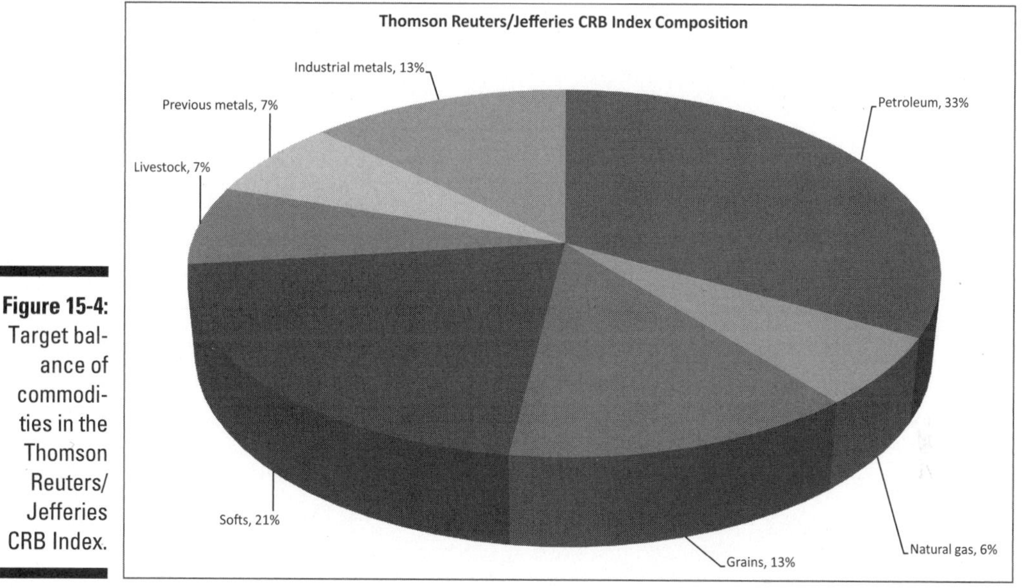

Figure 15-4: Target balance of commodities in the Thomson Reuters/Jefferies CRB Index.

Reading *The Economist*'s commodity index

Subscribers to *The Economist* can keep up with their own version of the *Commodity-Price Index* in print and on the web. Table 15-8 offers an overview of this index.

Table 15-8 *The Economist* Commodity-Price Index

Release Schedule	*Agency*	*Web Address*	*Sensitivity*
Weekly: Each Tuesday (with publication of the print magazine)	*The Economist*	`www.economist.com/markets-data`	Moderate

To find the commodity index values, go to the site listed in Table 15-8 and click on *The Economist* commodity-price index link in the right-hand column under Indicators.

Surveying the Dow Jones-UBS Commodity Indexes

The *Dow Jones-UBS Commodity Indexes* track traded futures contracts. Though a few of the contracts are listed on the London Metals Exchange, most are listed on U.S. commodities exchanges. Table 15-9 shows you where to find information about the Dow Jones-UBS Commodity Indexes.

Table 15-9 The Dow-Jones-UBS Commodity Indexes

Release Schedule	*Agency*	*Web Address*	*Sensitivity*
Daily: 4:15 p.m. CT	Dow Jones USB	`www.djindexes.com/commodity/`	Moderate

Dow Jones-UBS also provides subindexes and single commodity indexes. Examples of the aggregate subindexes include agriculture and livestock, industrial metals, precious metals, softs, grains, and petroleum.

iPath also offers ETNs that track the Dow Jones-UBS Commodity Indexes. Like other ETNs, they represent a debt obligation of iPath's sponsor, Barclays Bank, PLC, and not an equity position in a fund.

Part V

International Intrigue: Indicators beyond the United States

The 5th Wave By Rich Tennant

"As an emerging-market investment I like the land of Oz, and Middle Earth, but I'd stay away from Never Never Land."

In this part . . .

In this part, I focus on international trade, explaining how it both helps and hurts the U.S. economy and showing you how to monitor the economies of the United States' international trading partners. I highlight the many opportunities that exist for both businesses and investors to profit from overseas trading, and I show you how to evaluate the trading environment to protect your assets from fluctuating currency prices.

Chapter 16

Trading with the United States

In This Chapter

- Understanding why foreign trade is important
- Surveying the U.S. trade deficit
- Tracking how much the United States owes foreign countries

With all the hand-wringing people do about the trade deficit every time foreign trade statistics are released, you probably won't be surprised to discover that the United States is the world's largest importer. In fact, the United States imports almost as many goods and services as the entire European Union combined. U.S. imports account for a bit more than 15 percent of all imports worldwide.

However, you may be surprised to find out that the United States is still one of the world's largest exporters. China recently took the top spot away from Germany, but the United States is number three in total exports.

Imports and exports are important components in the U.S. economy. Exports add to the value of the gross domestic product (GDP). Although consumers are generally attracted to low-price (or high-quality) imports, imported products are a real cost to the economy. In fact, every dollar's worth of imported products or services is subtracted from the total GDP. Investors and business leaders must pay close attention to the economic indicators that track this large portion of the U.S. economy.

This chapter discusses foreign trade from the U.S. perspective. It examines U.S. imports and exports, the trade deficit, and the impact foreign trade has on the U.S. economy.

Tracking Trade: U.S. International Trade in Goods and Services Report

Trade is a crucial part of the U.S. economy. The value that exports add to the economy is probably obvious. Large U.S. manufacturing and service companies depend on foreign markets for a significant percentage of their revenue, profit, and growth. Even smaller firms regularly profit from opportunities in foreign trade.

On the other side of the ledger, U.S. consumers and businesses spend more than 16 percent of GDP on imported goods and services. The benefit of imports to consumers is difficult to deny. Many U.S. shoppers choose attractively priced foreign goods, like food, clothing, and footwear, over more expensive domestically produced products. For some product categories, like computer laptops and popular cellphones, only imported products are available.

The U.S. Bureau of Economic Analysis (BEA) tracks the value of all imports and exports in its *U.S. International Trade in Goods and Services report* (or *U.S. International Trade report,* for short). Table 16-1 tells you what you need to know to stay up-to-date with this foreign trade report.

Table 16-1 U.S. International Trade in Goods and Services Report

Release Schedule	*Agency*	*Web Address*	*Sensitivity*
Monthly: Published schedule, 8:30 a.m. ET	U.S. Bureau of Economic Analysis, Department of Commerce	`www.bea.gov/newsreleases/international/trade/tradnewsrelease.htm`	Usually low, sometimes moderate

This extensive report, which I give an overview of in the following sections, is issued about six weeks after the end of the reporting month. For example, the November 2010 report was issued in the middle of January 2011. You can find the release schedule on the BEA website: `www.bea.gov/newsreleases/news_release_sort_international.htm`.

Reporting U.S. exports and imports

The U.S. International Trade report starts with a brief analysis of the value of imports and exports for all goods and services. It describes changes from the previous month and identifies the product or service categories that caused the changes. The data are volatile and exhibit seasonality, so the BEA offers analysis by using three-month moving averages alongside the raw data.

Small data revisions are common, but large revisions are occasionally required. Benchmark revisions are usually published in June and can cover several of the previous years. (See Chapter 2 for a refresher on moving averages and benchmark revisions.)

At first glance, this report may seem a bit overwhelming. It's typically about 50 pages long and includes 18 primary data tables (which are called *exhibits* in this report) and 6 supplementary data tables. After you get past the sheer bulk of the report and begin to see how the U.S. International Trade report is organized, it becomes much more manageable.

The rest of this section guides you through the detailed data tables.

Tracking monthly and annual trade

A few of the report's exhibits, including Exhibit 1, provide a summary of the monthly and annual foreign trade data for the previous two to three years. Figure 16-1 shows an example of Exhibit 1.

Exhibits 1, 2, and 12 show variations of the same information:

- **Exhibit 1 — U.S. International Trade in Goods and Services:** This exhibit provides a summary overview of monthly exports, imports, and the balance of trade data, as well as two years worth of annual data. *Balance of trade* is the difference between the monetary value of all exports minus the monetary value of all imports. The seasonally adjusted value of goods and services are provided for each data category. (I discuss balance of trade more thoroughly later in this chapter. See Chapter 2 for more about adjusting for seasonality.)
- **Exhibit 2 — U.S. International Trade Three-Month Moving Averages:** This exhibit provides three-month moving averages for the data in Exhibit 1. Foreign trade data tend to bounce around a lot. Instead of focusing on small one- or two-month changes, which are rarely meaningful, look for developing trends. In other words, focus more attention on Exhibit 2 than 1. (I don't include an example of Exhibit 2 here because the format is almost identical to that shown in Figure 16-1. See Chapter 2 for more information about calculating and using moving averages.)

- **Exhibit 12 — U.S. Trade in Goods:** The BEA provides the same summary data you see in Exhibit 1, without seasonal adjustments, in Exhibit 12; the format of Exhibit 12 is almost identical to that of Exhibit 1.

Part A: Seasonally Adjusted

Exhibit 1. U.S. International Trade in Goods and Services

In millions of dollars. Details may not equal totals due to seasonal adjustment and rounding. (R) - Revised.

Period	Balance			Exports			Imports		
	Total	Goods (1)	Services	Total	Goods (1)	Services	Total	Goods (1)	Services
2009									
Jan. - Dec.	-374,908	-506,944	132,036	1,570,797	1,068,499	502,298	1,945,705	1,575,443	370,262
Jan. - Feb.	-62,429	-82,596	20,167	252,385	170,210	82,175	314,814	252,806	62,008
January	-36,067	-45,912	9,845	125,461	84,285	41,176	161,528	130,197	31,331
February	-26,362	-36,684	10,322	126,923	85,925	40,998	153,286	122,610	30,676
March	-28,009	-38,601	10,592	125,994	84,834	41,160	154,002	123,435	30,568
April	-28,445	-39,366	10,920	124,119	82,685	41,435	152,565	122,050	30,514
May	-24,855	-35,900	11,044	125,841	84,757	41,084	150,696	120,656	30,040
June	-27,139	-38,241	11,102	127,869	86,580	41,290	155,009	124,821	30,188
July	-33,086	-43,746	10,660	129,616	88,233	41,384	162,702	131,979	30,724
August	-31,072	-42,105	11,033	130,350	88,611	41,739	161,421	130,716	30,705
September	-35,164	-46,268	11,104	134,180	92,014	42,165	169,343	138,282	31,061
October	-32,302	-43,976	11,674	138,094	95,217	42,877	170,396	139,193	31,203
November	-35,273	-47,063	11,790	138,997	95,729	43,268	174,270	142,792	31,478
December	-37,132	-49,082	11,950	143,353	99,631	43,723	180,485	148,713	31,772
2010									
Jan. - Dec.	-495,728	-647,077	-151,349	1,834,166	1,288,663	545,502	2,329,894	1,935,740	394,153
Jan. - Feb.	-74,365	-98,634	24,269	289,351	200,883	88,467	363,715	299,517	64,198
January	-34,647	-47,109	12,463	144,747	100,555	44,192	179,394	147,664	31,730
February	-39,718	-51,525	11,806	144,603	100,328	44,275	184,321	151,853	32,469
March	-39,506	-52,259	12,753	150,270	105,275	44,995	189,776	157,534	32,242
April	-40,571	-52,598	12,027	148,011	104,298	43,713	188,582	156,896	31,686
May	-41,996	-54,480	12,484	152,252	107,294	44,958	194,248	161,774	32,474
June	-49,941	-62,065	12,124	150,302	105,089	45,212	200,242	167,154	33,088
July	-42,226	-54,875	12,648	153,788	107,895	45,893	196,014	162,770	33,244
August	-46,316	-58,933	12,617	153,624	107,745	45,879	199,939	166,677	33,262
September	-44,079	-57,033	12,955	154,350	107,893	46,456	198,428	164,927	33,502
October	-38,227	-51,134	12,907	158,681	112,183	46,498	196,908	163,317	33,591
November	-38,239	-51,438	13,199	160,239	113,593	46,645	198,478	165,032	33,446
December	-40,264	-53,629	13,365	163,297	116,514	46,783	203,561	170,143	33,418
2011									
Jan. - Feb.	-92,727	-119,640	26,912	332,663	238,377	94,286	425,390	358,016	67,374
January (R)	-46,969	-60,298	13,329	167,542	120,417	47,125	214,511	180,715	33,795
February	-45,758	-59,341	13,583	165,121	117,960	47,161	210,880	177,301	33,578
March									
April									
May									
June									
July									
August									
September									
October									
November									
December									
January data as published last month:	-46,341	-59,754	13,414	167,744	120,500	47,244	214,084	180,254	33,830

(1) Data are presented on a Balance of Payments (BOP) basis.

NOTE: For information on data sources and methodology, see the information section on page A-1 of this release, or at www.census.gov/ft900 or www.bea.gov/newsreleases/international/trade/tradnewsrelease.htm.

Figure 16-1: Exhibit 1 of the U.S. International Trade in Goods and Services report.

The columns showing the total values of exports and imports provide the most significant data in these three exhibits. Export growth often coincides with an economy coming out of recession. Import growth usually accompanies an expanding U.S. economy.

Trading services

Exported services (services provided by U.S. companies to non-U.S. residents, companies, or governments) and imported services (services provided by non-U.S. companies to U.S. residents, companies, or governments) are reported in Exhibits 3 and 4, respectively. Significant changes in the growth rate for foreign trade services are rare. Services are often provided under long-term contracts, which help keep the aggregate growth rate for foreign trade services relatively stable. Here's what you need to know about the exhibits that deal with foreign trade services:

- **Exhibit 3 — U.S. Services by Major Category: Exports:** Service categories in this exhibit include travel and transportation, passenger fares (fares paid by foreign nationals to U.S. carriers), royalties and licensing fees, and U.S. Government services, including military contract sales. The category *Other Private Services* is a catch-all category that includes education, financial services, insurance, telecommunications, data processing, advertising, professional fees, and a long list of other specialized services.
- **Exhibit 4 — U.S. Services by Major Category: Imports:** This exhibit reports on the same categories as Exhibit 3, but it focuses on imports rather than exports. Rather than military sales, this exhibit reports defense purchases from overseas and services purchased by the U.S. Government from non-U.S. vendors.

Service exports generally exceed service imports and represent a net gain for the U.S. GDP. (Notice that intellectual property exports, which are shown under the category *Royalties and License Fees,* represent one of the largest areas where exports exceed imports.) Investors and business leaders can use these exhibits as one additional tool to determine the health of the U.S. economy. Growth of service exports is more beneficial to the economy when compared to growth of service imports.

Trading products

Manufactured products, commodities, and agricultural products account for the majority of foreign trade. Exhibits 5 through 8 provide increasing levels of detail about these exported and imported products. Exhibits 10 and 13 show variations on this same data. All exhibits in this list, except for 13, are adjusted for seasonality.

- **Exhibit 5 — U.S. Trade in Goods:** This exhibit reports the values of products that make up U.S. foreign trade, listed by month and year.
- **Exhibit 6 — Exports and Imports of Goods by End-Use Category:** This exhibit expands on Exhibit 5; it categorizes imports and exports as food and beverage, industrial supplies, capital goods, automotive vehicles, and consumer goods. The exhibit includes monthly and annual aggregate values for exports and imports in each category.

  Exhibit 7 — Exports of Goods by End-Use Category and Commodity: This exhibit provides additional detail about exports for each category from Exhibit 6. Figure 16-2 shows an excerpt from Exhibit 7. (Check out the nearby sidebar "Measuring foreign trade products" for the lowdown on what some of the terms in this table mean.)

  As you can see in Figure 16-2, under the *Foods, feeds, and beverages* category, Exhibit 7 details specific types of products, including food oils, animal feed, fish and shellfish, nuts, rice, dairy products, wine and beer, fruits, vegetables, and meat and poultry.
- **Exhibit 8 — Imports of Goods by End-Use Category and Commodity:** This exhibit lists the same categories as Exhibit 7 (refer to Figure 16-2), but it reports imports rather than exports.
- **Exhibit 10 — Real Exports and Imports of Goods by Principal End-Use Category, 2005 Chain-Weighted Dollars:** This exhibit adjusts the data for inflation, which is helpful for tracking the volume of foreign trade products. The effects of inflation can inflate the value of foreign trade products but not the volume.
- **Exhibit 13 — Exports and Imports of Goods by Principal End-Use Category:** This exhibit provides the same information and layout as Exhibit 6, but the data aren't seasonally adjusted.

Investors can find Exhibit 10 to be particularly useful. It's the only one of these product exhibits that's adjusted for inflation. That adjustment makes it the best way to monitor the actual volume of export and import goods. That's not to say that investors and business leaders should ignore the other exhibits. The detail in these exhibits highlights industries that are performing well overseas and where foreign corporations are making advances into U.S. markets.

Part A: Seasonally Adjusted

Exhibit 7. Exports of Goods by End-Use Category and Commodity

In millions of dollars. Details may not equal totals due to seasonal adjustment and rounding. The commodities in this exhibit are ranked on the monthly change within each major commodity grouping. (-) Represents zero or less than one half of measurement shown. (R) - Revised.

Item (1)	February 2011	January 2011 (R)	Monthly Change	Year-to-Date 2011	Year-to-Date 2010	Year-to-Date Change
Total, Balance of Payments Basis	**117,960**	**120,417**	**-2,457**	**238,377**	**200,883**	**37,493**
Net Adjustments	**1,413**	**1,162**	**251**	**2,576**	**1,858**	**717**
Total, Census Basis	**116,547**	**119,255**	**-2,708**	**235,801**	**199,025**	**36,776**
Foods, feeds, and beverages	**10,548**	**10,708**	**-160**	**21,256**	**17,765**	**3,491**
Oilseeds, food oils	335	466	-131	801	657	144
Animal feeds, n.e.c.	593	685	-92	1,278	1,366	-88
Soybeans	1,753	1,838	-84	3,591	3,397	194
Fish and shellfish	384	438	-55	822	664	159
Other foods	801	844	-43	1,645	1,507	138
Nuts	420	451	-31	872	833	38
Rice	197	228	-31	426	455	-30
Sorghum, barley, oats	50	74	-24	124	154	-31
Nonagricultural foods, etc.	112	114	-2	226	205	21
Dairy products and eggs	286	280	6	566	351	215
Alcoholic beverages, excluding wine	149	142	6	291	211	79
Wheat	1,190	1,181	9	2,370	1,059	1,311
Wine, beer, and related products	148	138	10	286	225	61
Bakery products	444	421	23	865	754	112
Vegetables	516	492	24	1,008	915	92
Fruits, frozen juices	756	722	33	1,478	1,264	214
Meat, poultry, etc.	1,323	1,254	69	2,578	2,104	474
Corn	1,091	938	153	2,029	1,643	386
Industrial supplies and materials	**39,200**	**39,769**	**-570**	**78,969**	**58,753**	**20,216**
Chemicals-organic	2,949	3,307	-357	6,256	5,222	1,035
Petroleum products, other	4,020	4,269	-249	8,288	4,666	3,622
Gas-natural	493	680	-187	1,173	794	379
Chemicals-fertilizers	665	832	-167	1,498	1,235	263
Crude oil	75	197	-122	272	197	74
Nuclear fuel materials	151	264	-113	415	364	51
Cotton, raw	1,368	1,470	-102	2,838	938	1,900
Chemicals-other	2,270	2,340	-70	4,610	3,963	647
Pulpwood and woodpulp	845	892	-47	1,737	1,331	407
Finished metal shapes	1,382	1,427	-45	2,808	2,404	404
Natural gas liquids	255	299	-44	554	722	-168
Agric. industry-unmanufactured	384	424	-40	808	630	179
Fuel oil	3,490	3,520	-30	7,010	3,859	3,151
Mineral supplies-manufactured	456	472	-16	928	813	115
Logs and lumber	452	467	-15	919	720	198
Plastic materials	2,973	2,987	-14	5,960	5,419	541
Iron and steel products, other	548	559	-11	1,107	941	166
Finished textile supplies	219	230	-10	449	411	38
Leather and furs	82	90	-8	173	148	25
Agriculture-manufactured, other	203	211	-8	414	367	47
Iron and steel mill products	1,002	1,010	-8	2,012	1,552	461
Agric. farming-unmanufactured	248	254	-6	501	443	58
Chemicals-inorganic	650	656	-5	1,306	1,095	211
Tobacco, unmanufactured	70	75	-5	146	205	-59
Tapes, audio and visual	41	45	-4	86	86	0
Industrial rubber products	325	329	-4	654	565	89
Newsprint	1,121	1,124	-3	2,246	2,008	237
Hair, waste materials	56	58	-2	114	93	20
Glass-plate, sheet, etc.	127	126	1	253	265	-12
Hides and skins	205	203	2	408	280	128
Cotton fiber cloth	273	267	6	541	372	169
Wood supplies, manufactured	108	102	7	210	192	19
Nontextile floor tiles	51	42	9	93	84	9
Shingles, molding, wallboard	389	380	9	769	648	122
Nonmetallic minerals	70	59	10	129	99	30
Electric energy	53	41	13	94	112	-18
Synthetic rubber-primary	377	358	19	735	569	166
Manmade cloth	562	538	24	1,100	919	181
Other industrial supplies	1,915	1,887	28	3,802	3,428	373
Aluminum and alumina	745	715	30	1,460	1,137	323
Precious metals, other	1,207	1,161	46	2,367	1,744	623
Coal and fuels, other	397	338	59	735	287	449
Nonferrous metals, other	774	695	79	1,468	1,099	369
Metallurgical grade coal	938	847	91	1,785	1,053	732
Copper	709	608	100	1,317	932	385
Steelmaking materials	1,213	1,029	184	2,242	1,530	712
Nonmonetary gold	2,293	1,887	406	4,180	2,814	1,366

Figure 16-2: Exhibit 7 shows the exports of goods by end-use category and commodity.

Measuring foreign trade products

Foreign trade products can be measured on either a *census basis* or a *balance of payments basis.* (You see these terms in Exhibit 7 in Figure 16-2.) Here's a quick explanation of these two terms:

- **Balance of payments basis (BOP)**: This measurement technique makes adjustments to eliminate duplicate transaction data. The goal in using this technique is to provide a more accurate accounting of U.S. trade.
- **Census basis**: This measurement technique provides the difference between total U.S. exports based on free alongside ship export values and U.S. general imports based on customs values.

The *free alongside ship export (FAS) value* is the total transaction price for the merchandise, including inland freight, insurance, and any other fee charged to get the product to the export port and to prepare it to be loaded onto the ship. The FAS value doesn't include actual loading fees or any fees attributable to the transaction after the product is loaded onto the ship (or airplane).

Also called *customs import value,* the *customs value* is the value of the merchandise sold for export to the United States; it doesn't include transportation costs, insurance, delivery, or import duties.

Accounting for crude oil

The U.S. imports a lot of crude oil, and its value has a significant impact on the total foreign trade value. Segregating petroleum products from the rest of the trade statistics is helpful because the price of these products is so volatile. Ideally, the inflation-adjusted exhibits would negate the effect of this volatility, but unfortunately they don't completely compensate for it. The following exhibits deal specifically with crude oil:

- **Exhibit 9 — Exports, Imports, and Balance of Goods, Petroleum and Non-Petroleum End-Use Category Totals:** This exhibit shows the value of imports, exports, and balance of trade for petroleum products compared to non-petroleum products. Petroleum products include crude oil, petroleum preparations, liquefied propane, as well as products like ethane, butane, benzene, and toluene.
- **Exhibit 11 — Real Exports, Imports, and Balance of Goods, Petroleum and Non-Petroleum End-Use Commodity Category Totals, 2005 Chain-Weighted Dollars:** This exhibit indexes the data from Exhibit 9 for inflation. The format of the two exhibits is almost identical.

Exhibits 9 and 11 show the significant impact petroleum imports have on the balance of trade and on GDP (recall that imports are subtracted from GDP). Depending on the price of oil, the impact can range from 35 percent to 65 percent of the total trade deficit (which I discuss later in this chapter).

Examining foreign trade by country

Exhibits 14 and 14a show trade information categorized by country and geographic region. The data in these exhibits aren't adjusted for seasonality. Figure 16-3 shows an excerpt from Exhibit 14.

- **Exhibit 14 — Exports, Imports, and Balance of Goods by Selected Countries and Areas:** This exhibit shows exports, imports, and balance of trade statistics for the largest U.S. trading partners. The table segregates the data by geographic region and then by individual country.
- **Exhibit 14a — Exports, Imports, and Balance of Goods by Selected Countries and Areas:** This exhibit is the same as Exhibit 14, except that it shows geographic and country data for the previous year.

Although the United States imports more products than it exports to most countries, that isn't true for all countries. Australia, Hong Kong, the Netherlands, and several South American countries all import more U.S. products than the U.S. imports from them. Investors can use these exhibits to see how trade with other countries is affecting the U.S. GDP.

Tracking foreign trade by product category

Exhibits 15 through 18 provide foreign trade data for specific products and product categories:

- **Exhibit 15 — Exports and Imports of Goods by Principal SITC Commodities:** *SITC* stands for *Standard International Trade Classification.* This two-page list shows monthly and year-to-date exports and imports of manufactured, agricultural, and commodity products.
- **Exhibit 16 — Exports, Imports, and Balance of Advanced Technology Products:** This exhibit lists export, import, and trade balance data for advanced materials, aerospace products, biotechnology products, electronics, and other advanced technology products.
- **Exhibit 17 — Imports of Energy-Related Petroleum Products, Including Crude Oil:** This exhibit shows the quantity of energy-related products, reported in barrels of oil or their equivalent, alongside the dollar value of these petroleum products.
- **Exhibit 18 — Exports and Imports of Motor Vehicles and Parts by Selected Countries:** This exhibit reports the exports and imports of automotive products, listed by country.

Part B: NOT Seasonally Adjusted

Exhibit 14. Exports, Imports, and Balance of Goods By Selected Countries and Areas--2011

In millions of dollars. Details may not equal totals due to rounding. (-) Represents zero or less than one half of measurement shown.
(R) - Revised. (X) - Not applicable.

Item (1)	Balance			Exports			Imports		
	February 2011	January 2011	Year-to-Date 2011	February 2011	January 2011	Year-to-Date 2011	February 2011	January 2011	Year-to-Date 2011
Total Balance of Payments Basis	**-47,844 (R)**	**-57,649**	**-105,493**	**111,210 (R)**	**111,317**	**222,527**	**159,055 (R)**	**168,965**	**328,020**
Net Adjustments	-828 (R)	-1,058	-1,886	1,413 (R)	1,162	2,576	2,241 (R)	2,220	4,461
Total Census Basis	**-47,016 (R)**	**-56,591**	**-103,607**	**109,797 (R)**	**110,155**	**219,952**	**156,813 (R)**	**166,745**	**323,559**
North America	-8,153 (R)	-8,687	-16,840	34,431 (R)	35,407	69,838	42,584	44,094	86,678
Canada	-2,890 (R)	-3,792	-6,682	20,586 (R)	20,567	41,153	23,476	24,359	47,835
Mexico	-5,263	-4,895	-10,158	13,845	14,840	28,684	19,108	19,735	38,843
Europe	-6,803	-7,236	-14,039	24,489	24,520	49,010	31,293	31,756	63,049
European Union	-6,946	-5,614	-12,560	19,997	20,253	40,250	26,943	25,867	52,810
Austria	-509	-410	-919	184	176	360	693	586	1,279
Belgium	786	865	1,651	2,346	2,102	4,449	1,560	1,237	2,797
Czech Republic	-100	-115	-214	114	116	230	213	231	444
Finland	-182	-166	-348	157	197	354	340	362	702
France	-482	-557	-1,039	2,331	2,242	4,572	2,813	2,798	5,611
Germany	-3,322	-3,120	-6,442	3,860	3,648	7,508	7,182	6,768	13,950
Hungary	-83	-162	-245	118	100	218	201	262	463
Ireland	-2,569	-1,917	-4,486	771	710	1,481	3,340	2,627	5,967
Italy	-1,007	-1,271	-2,278	1,245	1,189	2,434	2,253	2,460	4,712
Netherlands	974	1,654	2,628	2,924	3,164	6,088	1,950	1,510	3,460
Poland	-63	-95	-158	221	236	457	284	332	615
Spain	141	235	376	822	1,005	1,827	680	770	1,451
Sweden	-360	-634	-995	425	371	795	785	1,005	1,790
United Kingdom	164	538	703	3,698	4,136	7,835	3,534	3,598	7,132
Other EU	-334	-460	-794	781	860	1,641	1,115	1,320	2,435
Norway	-112	-349	-461	300	248	547	411	597	1,009
Russia	-974	-2,126	-3,100	581	451	1,032	1,554	2,577	4,131
Switzerland	-227	73	-153	1,527	1,665	3,193	1,754	1,592	3,346
Other Europe	1,454	781	2,235	2,084	1,904	3,988	630	1,123	1,753
Euro Area	-6,229	-4,868	-11,097	15,060	14,841	29,900	21,289	19,709	40,998
Pacific Rim Countries	-22,477	-27,995	-50,472	28,738	27,866	56,604	51,215	55,861	107,076
Australia	1,372	1,174	2,546	1,953	1,859	3,812	581	686	1,266
China	-18,842	-23,271	-42,113	8,437	8,078	16,515	27,279	31,350	58,628
Indonesia	-864	-1,037	-1,902	591	509	1,100	1,455	1,547	3,001
Japan	-5,240	-4,981	-10,220	5,292	4,993	10,286	10,532	9,974	20,506
Malaysia	-723	-826	-1,549	1,152	1,258	2,410	1,875	2,083	3,958
Philippines	23	-78	-55	650	606	1,256	627	684	1,311
Newly Industrialized Countries (NICS)	1,535	1,001	2,536	10,156	10,311	20,467	8,621	9,310	17,931
Hong Kong	2,481	2,174	4,655	2,763	2,524	5,287	282	350	633
Korea	-811	-1,003	-1,814	3,082	3,197	6,279	3,893	4,200	8,093
Singapore	778	773	1,551	2,284	2,308	4,592	1,506	1,535	3,041
Taiwan	-913	-942	-1,855	2,026	2,283	4,309	2,939	3,225	6,164
Other Pacific Rim	261	24	285	507	251	758	246	227	473
South/Central America	126	-405	-279	11,835	12,629	24,464	11,709	13,034	24,743
Argentina	369	201	570	635	653	1,288	267	452	718
Brazil	948	988	1,936	2,909	3,212	6,121	1,961	2,224	4,184
Chile	199	192	391	945	1,059	2,004	745	867	1,612
Colombia	-66	-551	-618	1,121	1,082	2,202	1,187	1,633	2,820
Other S/C A	-1,324	-1,235	-2,559	6,225	6,624	12,849	7,549	7,859	15,408
OPEC	-9,384	-9,945	-19,329	4,208	4,286	8,494	13,592	14,231	27,824
Nigeria	-2,528	-2,876	-5,404	331	269	600	2,859	3,145	6,004
Saudi Arabia	-2,573	-1,594	-4,167	811	932	1,744	3,384	2,526	5,910
Venezuela	-2,073	-2,817	-4,890	780	830	1,611	2,854	3,648	6,501
Other OPEC	-2,211	-2,658	-4,868	2,285	2,255	4,540	4,496	4,913	9,409
Timing Adjustments	(X)	-452	-452	(X)	20	20	(X)	472	472

Figure 16-3: Exhibit 14 shows exports, imports, and balance of goods by selected countries and geographic regions.

A few product categories account for the majority of trade between the U.S. and its major trading partners. Investors and business leaders can use Exhibits 15 through 17 to monitor changes in net exports and imports. This information can help identify areas of economic strength and also potential threats to U.S. businesses.

Finding more trade data in the supplemental tables and online

Additional exhibits in supplemental data tables reslice the trade data in a variety of interesting ways. For example, you can find out how each of the U.S. states benefits from foreign trade, which countries provide the most petroleum to the United States, and what the balance of trade is between the United States and specific trading partners. (I go into more detail about the balance of trade later in this chapter.)

Even more information is available on the U.S. Census Bureau website. If you want to know, for example, what products and services the United States and China trade, the Census Bureau has the tools to help you find out. Just go to `censtats.census.gov/naic3_6/naics3_6.shtml` and click on China from the second drop-down menu.

Correlating trade and economic growth

Foreign trade is strongly correlated with economic growth, but it isn't a leading indicator. At best, it's a concurrent indicator, although some consider it to lag behind the economy.

The state of the U.S. economy and the state of the economies of its trading partners affect foreign trade. Specifically, the following economic factors can impact the volume and value of foreign trade:

- **Currency exchange rate:** The value of the U.S. dollar can have a significant effect on foreign trade. A strong U.S. dollar makes imports less expensive for U.S. consumers. It also makes U.S. exports more expensive for foreign buyers. A weak dollar makes products manufactured in the United States less expensive to the foreign buyer and, thus, more attractive to U.S. trading partners. In a similar manner, a weak dollar makes imported products more expensive for U.S. consumers.
- **Growth rate:** Strong economic growth in the United States generally translates into more product imports. Consumers have more to spend when the economy is growing, and the dollar tends to be strong. However, the price of U.S. goods is usually less attractive to foreign buyers when the U.S. economic growth rate is high.
- **Inflation:** Inflation directly affects product prices and the value of the local currency. When the U.S. suffers periods of inflation, the value of the dollar falls and product prices climb. It's a double-whammy. U.S.

exports are less attractive, and imports are more expensive. Why are imports more expensive? The dollar price of an item is higher. Foreign goods are priced in foreign currency. If the exchange rate remains fixed in the face of U.S. inflation, the relative price should fall. The reverse is true when U.S. trading partners experience inflation. The value of the dollar may appreciate against the foreign currency and make imports more attractive.

- **Tariffs:** *Tariffs,* or taxes, on imported products make them more expensive for domestic consumers. Tariffs on exported products make them more expensive for U.S. trading partners.
- **Other barriers:** Regulatory hurdles also affect the volume and value of trade. These hurdles may include environmental considerations, health considerations, or safety standards.

Trading information for investment returns

For stock investors and bondholders, trade reports aren't easy to analyze. Your first thought may be that strong exports and weak imports would be good for bondholders. After all, a strong dollar often corresponds with high interest rates, which bondholders generally prefer. But then you remember that GDP grows when exports grow *and* when imports fall. Strong GDP growth is rarely good for bonds. If you're confused, you're not alone. The markets don't react consistently to trade reports.

For several reasons, trade indicators don't lead the economy, which means that they're coincident indicators at best, and occasionally exhibit characteristics of lagging indicators. Those reasons include the following:

- **Foreign trade happens on a slow pace.** A long lag exists between the time when foreign-trade orders are placed and the time when the products are delivered. After all, transporting products across national borders takes time, and sometimes unexpected delays occur when getting products to market.
- **The value of trade reports decreases somewhat because they're released so long after the data are collected.** Of course, the markets don't generally like surprises, so unexpected trade results can have an outsized impact on the markets. Unfortunately, predicting market reaction to trade data is difficult at best. Few analysts can reliably anticipate market reaction to surprises in the foreign trade reports.

The only reliable generalization you can make is that demand for U.S. dollars grows as U.S. exports grow and, as a result, the value of the dollar increases. Conversely, the demand for U.S. dollars falls, along with their value, as U.S. imports grow. Currency traders can profit from either scenario.

Figuring Out the Balance of Trade

When people talk about the *trade deficit,* what they're really talking about is the *balance of trade*. Segments of the balance of trade appear in almost every exhibit in the U.S. International Trade in Goods and Services report (see Figures 16-1, 16-2, and 16-3). Calculating the balance of trade is easy; it's the difference between the total value of U.S. exports and imports. When the value of exports exceeds the value of imports, the balance of trade is a positive number and represents a *trade surplus.* When the value of imports exceeds the value of exports, the balance of trade is a negative number and represents a trade deficit. Some people refer to the trade deficit as the *trade gap.*

The U.S. runs large deficits with many countries, including China and Japan, members of the Organization of the Petroleum Exporting Countries (OPEC), like Saudi Arabia and Venezuela, and India and Thailand. However, not every foreign trading partner is a net exporter to the United States. The United States runs a trade surplus with countries like Australia, Singapore, the Netherlands, Belgium, and Brazil (refer to Figure 16-3).

Following the TIC (Treasury International Capital) System

If you want to know how much money the United States owes to foreign countries, you may want to check out the *Treasury International Capital (TIC) System report.* It's available from the U.S. Treasury at no charge. This extensive series of reports tracks foreign investments in U.S. Treasury securities, common stocks, commodities, currencies, and derivatives.

Of course, capital flows both into and out of the United States. The TIC System report also reports on U.S. investments made overseas. Table 16-2 provides what you need to know to keep track of the TIC System report.

Table 16-2 Treasury International Capital System Report

Release Schedule	*Agency*	*Web Address*	*Sensitivity*
Monthly: Published schedule, 9:00 a.m. ET	U.S. Treasury	`www.treasury.gov/resource-center/data-chart-center/tic/Pages/index.aspx`	Low

The TIC System report actually consists of a number of reports. You can find release dates for all the TIC reports, charts, and data on the Treasury website at www.treasury.gov/resource-center/data-chart-center/tic/Pages/release-dates.aspx.

The U.S. Treasury publishes a press release about 45 days after the reporting month. It provides a general summary of all these reports, including, for example, details about the cross-border financial transactions made by domestic and foreign governments, central banks, investors, and corporations. The summary includes the net value of long-term and short-term securities transactions (including U.S. Treasury securities), as well as monthly net flows into and out of the U.S.

This report is rarely useful for investors, but it's crucial for economists and analysts trying to understand the financial condition of the United States. If you want to understand the true impact of the trade deficit and its relationship to the U.S. budget deficit, the TIC is an invaluable resource.

Making sense of the trade deficit

Every month, the news reports the value of the trade deficit. From the way it's presented, concluding that the deficit is a significant problem that the United States must solve is easy, or is it? Nobel-prize-winning economist Milton Friedman took the view that trade deficits aren't important in and of themselves. After all, foreign exporters have to do something with the dollars that consumers used to buy the imports. If the trading partner doesn't use the dollars to buy U.S. exports, then the dollars must ultimately return to the United States in the form of equity or debt investments. The United States gets the imported products and incremental investment, too. (He also made the point that concern about deficits is often an attempt to push economic policies that favor exporters.)

Well-known businessman Warren Buffet is clearly in the opposing camp and believes deficits are a serious problem. His position is that other countries effectively own trillions of dollars' worth of the United States, quite a bit more than the United States owns of them. He views this debt and the associated interest payments as an expensive drain on U.S. resources and the economy as a whole.

Although this is a terrible oversimplification, both the experts are right. A trade deficit means that the U.S. is purchasing more goods, by value, than it's producing. Though that isn't sustainable over the long term, the trade deficit isn't a problem in and of itself. The problem is how much money the United States owes to foreign countries.

Chapter 17

Following Economies Worldwide

In This Chapter

- Evaluating overseas investment opportunities
- Finding reliable international indicators in English
- Keeping track of the economies in Germany, Japan, and China

Few U.S. investors look beyond the border when investing. Although overseas investing may lack safety measures that U.S. investors rely on, the profit opportunities can be significant enough to compensate for the extra risk. Of course, investing all your assets overseas isn't prudent, but ignoring the diversification offered by overseas investing is equally imprudent.

Big companies act where most individual investors are too timid to tread. For example, 75 percent of Coca Cola's operating income comes from overseas operations, and Yum Brands (KFC, Pizza Hut, and Taco Bell) has a large presence in China. In fact, most of the S&P 500 companies derive a significant percentage of their revenues and profits outside the United States. Even small companies can find opportunities to operate successfully in this international environment.

Fortunately, a wealth of information exists to help you evaluate the risks and opportunities involved in investing outside the United States. For some countries, the thoroughness of their economic indicators rivals those of the United States.

This chapter helps you find economic indicators for the largest foreign economies — in English. I discuss economic indicators for the smaller emerging markets in Chapter 18.

Investing in Overseas Markets

You may be surprised to discover that some overseas investment returns can dwarf those found in the United States. If you focus strictly on the United States, you may miss out on some profitable investments overseas.

For example, recently, the economic growth rate in the United States has been less than half of the average worldwide growth, and growth rates for individual countries can be significantly above average. In 2009, China's growth rate was 9.1 percent, and in 2010, it was 10.3 percent. India's 2009 growth rate was also 9.1 percent, and its 2010 growth rate was 8.3 percent. Compare those rates to the U.S. rates of –2.9 percent in 2009 (yes, the U.S. GDP growth was negative in 2009!) and 2.7 percent in 2010.

When you're thinking about investing in overseas markets, take the time to compare the results for global stock markets. One source for this data is the World Bank website: `http://data.worldbank.org/indicator/CM.MKT.INDX.ZG`. Because overseas markets are volatile, you need to look for both recent and long-running economic strengths. Focus on long periods of growth rather than a single jump in growth. Figures 17-1 and 17-2 show the best- and worst-performing stock markets in 2010.

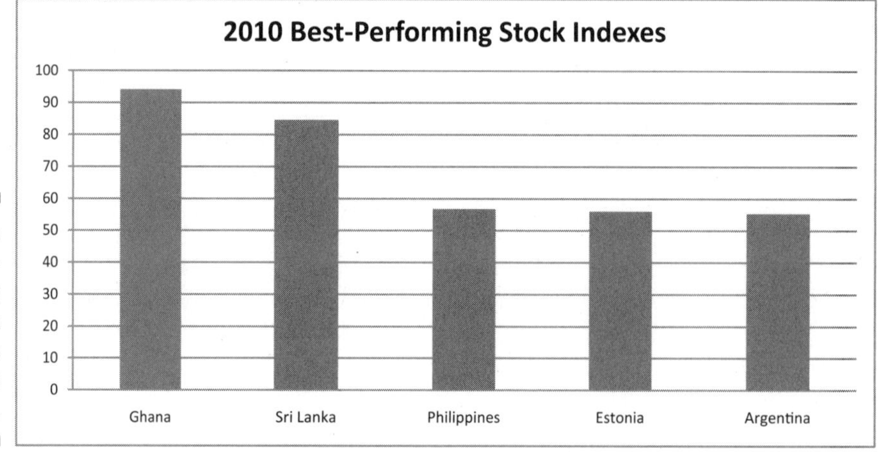

Figure 17-1: Best-performing stock markets worldwide in 2010.

Notice that the United States isn't in either figure. The U.S. stock market is rarely the worst- or best-performing stock market in the world. In 2010, the U.S. market was in the middle of the pack; as measured by the S&P 500, the U.S. stock market grew 12.8 percent for 2010.

My point here isn't that you should invest your assets in any random country. Rather, my point is that you need to carefully investigate where the best returns are before you make any overseas investments. You also need to make sure that you diversify your investments; otherwise, you magnify your risk because overseas markets are often more volatile than U.S. markets and you have the added risk of potentially adverse changes in the rate for currency exchange.

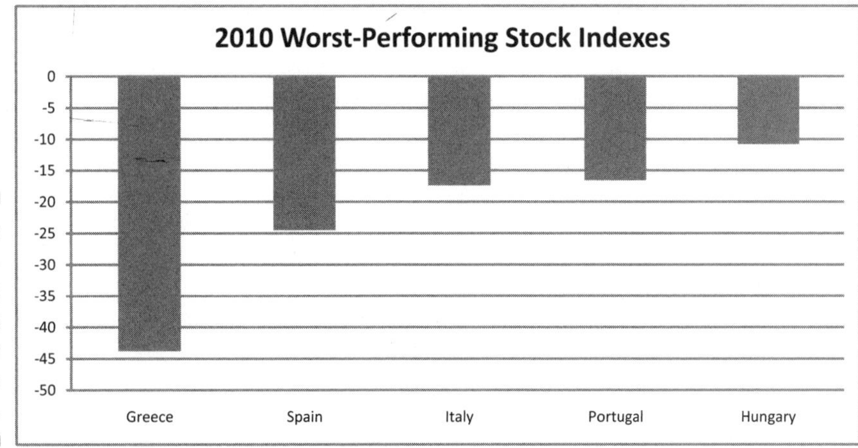

Figure 17-2: Worst-performing stock markets worldwide in 2010.

If you invest in bonds, you can find attractive opportunities overseas. In fact, overseas bond prices are often lower with higher yields than comparable U.S. Government and corporate bonds. So don't be afraid to look overseas for higher-paying bonds; just be careful about the risks, including the potential for an adverse change in currency exchange rates.

Taking a closer look at the risks involved in overseas investing

From the perspective of a U.S. investor, two things have to happen for an overseas investment (either equity or debt) to work out well:

- **The investment must provide a positive return in the local currency.** Although an appreciating foreign currency can partially compensate for a losing investment and, on rare occasions, may make it profitable, that's a poor substitute for investing in an appreciating asset.
- **The relationship between the U.S. dollar and the foreign currency must move in the investor's favor.** If the foreign currency appreciates against the dollar, the U.S. investor is happy, at least about that part of the investment. After all, appreciation of the foreign currency can actually improve the profitability of the foreign investment. However, if the dollar appreciates against the foreign currency, the value of any asset held in that currency will decrease.

Currency risk isn't the only risk overseas investors face. U.S. investors need to be especially aware of the local laws, rules, and regulations wherever they invest. U.S. markets are relatively stable in part because regulatory agencies monitor them closely. Overseas investment markets don't always offer the same stability and regulatory oversight that domestic markets do. Further, laws of foreign countries don't always work in favor of U.S. investors.

Using Reliable Sources to Find Info on International Indicators

The trick to finding success in overseas investments is finding sources of information that you can trust. Researching an investment idea only to find that the indicators mean something different overseas than they do in your home country doesn't do you much good.

Good economic indicators conform to international conventions. Fortunately, the indicators in many countries do so. Large European countries all follow similar accounting practices. Even smaller *Eurozone countries* (European Union members that have adopted the Euro currency) are being forced to adopt these generally accepted reporting conventions.

You have to be especially careful when dealing with reports from some (mostly non-European) countries. China is probably the most obvious example. Even the Chinese government recognized that it needed to clean up its economic reporting, and it claims that it has done so. Unfortunately, verifying that the current Chinese economic reports are more reliable is difficult for outsiders to do.

So how do you know which economic reports are reliable? The following sources have a good track record for providing summary reports about international indicators:

- **The CIA World Factbook:** Yes, *that* CIA. The Central Intelligence Agency publishes an overview of most countries in the world; that overview includes a brief economic report. Although the details in this overview aren't enough for you to make an informed investment decision, they can help you validate information you've collected elsewhere. (Go to `https://www.cia.gov/library/publications/the-world-factbook/index.html` to check out the CIA overview. Just click on the region or continent you want to investigate on the map and then click on the country's name. You can then click on any of the topic areas, such as Economy, that you're interested in.)
- **The World Bank:** The World Bank offers economic analysis and data for most countries in the world. (Go to `data.worldbank.org` and click the By Country link to find a list of country reports. Click on the Indicators link to see the long list of indicators available from the World Bank. Another World Bank site, `econ.worldbank.org`, provides links to analysis, research books, and other tools that can help you stay current with international indicators.)

- **The International Monetary Fund (IMF):** The IMF offers analysis as well as country statistics. (Go to `www.imf.org` and click on the Country Info tab for country-level economic indicators. The Research tab provides access to valuable economic analysis.)

The following sections point out a couple of indexes that can help you find trustworthy data overseas.

Surveying purchasing managers globally

Purchasing managers (you know, the people who purchase almost everything a company needs, from office supplies to manufacturing materials) are an exceptionally good resource for economic information. (Refer to Chapter 10 for more information.) The *JPMorgan Global Manufacturing Purchasing Managers Index* (PMI) takes this concept to a global level. It offers an excellent source of aggregated data for economies across the globe. Table 17-1 gives an overview of what you need to know about this report.

Table 17-1 JPMorgan Global Manufacturing PMI

Release Schedule	*Agency*	*Web Address*
Monthly: First business day of the month, 11:00 a.m. ET	JPMorgan, Markit Economics, Institute for Supply Management (ISM), and International Federation of Purchasing and Supply Management (IFPSM)	`bit.ly/jpmorgan-global-pmi`

The JPMorgan Global Manufacturing PMI is compiled from purchasing manager surveys in 26 countries. It provides an early indication of manufacturing conditions and global production levels. The report presents the data as a series of *diffusion indexes,* which show how much and in what direction survey results have changed from the previous survey (see Chapter 2 for details on diffusion indexes). In this report, index readings above 50 indicate an increase, and readings below 50 represent a decrease. A brief analysis, as well as a companion report covering global service companies, accompanies the index readings.

Surveying purchasing managers in Europe

Another widely followed purchasing manager report is the *Markit Eurozone Composite PMI.* It follows a format similar to that of the JPMorgan Global Manufacturing PMI and offers an excellent source of aggregated data for the European economies. Table 17-2 provides the need-to-know info about this report.

Table 17-2 Markit Eurozone Composite PMI

Release Schedule	*Agency*	*Web Address*
Monthly: First business day of the month, 11:00 a.m. ET	Markit Economics	`bit.ly/markit-eurozone-pmi`

To find this particular PMI, go to the website listed in Table 17-2 and click on the Eurozone: Markit Eurozone Composite PMI link. (Unfortunately, the list isn't well organized. The easiest way to find it is to use your browser's search function; that's Ctrl + F5 for most browsers.)

The Markit Eurozone Composite PMI surveys about 4,500 firms in Germany, France, Italy, Spain, the Netherlands, Austria, the Republic of Ireland, and Greece. Both manufacturing and service firms are surveyed. The information provided by this report is very similar to that provided by the JPMorgan Global Manufacturing PMI; it provides comparisons between the member countries as well as an analysis.

While you're searching for this report, you'll encounter a long list of country-specific PMI reports. These PMI reports follow a similar format. They're an excellent resource for investigating the results from specific countries.

Tracking the German Economy

Germany is Europe's largest economy, the fourth-largest single-country economy in the world, and the world's second-largest exporter, behind China. The country is also one of the United States' largest trading partners. As a result, if you're considering investing overseas, you need to get a good handle on the German economy.

Germany's economic reporting follows a model similar to that of the U.S. Bureau of Economic Analysis, which uses National Income and Product Accounts (NIPA) to track gross domestic product, or GDP (see Chapter 7 for details about GDP). Many of Germany's economic reports are published in English and are often as thorough and useful as those published in the United States.

The following sections explain where to go to find German economic statistics that you can use to keep track of the country's economic well-being.

Measuring German productivity

The Federal Statistics Office (FSO, or, in German, *Statistisches Bundesamt Deutschland*) produces a number of indicators to evaluate Germany's economic condition. These reports are similar to the reports issued in the United States by agencies like the Bureau of Labor Statistics, the Census Bureau, and the Federal Reserve and are all available in English. Table 17-3 explains more about the German FSO reports.

Table 17-3 German Federal Statistics Office Economic Indicators

Release Schedule	*Agency*	*Web Address*
Monthly and some quarterly	German Federal Statistics Office	`bit.ly/german-statistics`

The following list is a sample of the reports you can find on the FSO website:

- **Building permits:** Measures the number of permits issued for building construction, the construction work completed, the volume of unfinished building projects at the end of the year, and the retirement of structures. This report is roughly analogous to the U.S. Census's Bureau New Residential Construction report (see Chapter 11), but the German version covers both residential and commercial projects.
- **Consumer price index (CPI):** Shows the average change in price for goods and services purchased for household consumption. This index is similar to the U.S. CPI produced by the Bureau of Labor Statistics (see Chapter 12).
- **Employment:** Measures the number of people employed in gainful activity (wage earners, salaried employees, public officials, marginal part-time workers, and soldiers), self-employed people, and unpaid family workers. It also reports the seasonally adjusted unemployment rates. This report is analogous to the U.S. Employment Situation report (see Chapter 4).
- **Foreign trade balance:** Measures cross-border trading of goods between the Federal Republic of Germany and other countries. This report is similar to the U.S. Bureau of Economic Analysis's U.S. International Trade in Goods and Services report (see Chapter 16).

- **Gross domestic product (GDP):** Measures the value of the goods and services produced in Germany. GDP is calculated at current prices and then adjusted for inflation. The rate of change of the price-adjusted GDP serves as a measure of economic growth in a national economy. The German GDP report is similar to the one produced by the U.S. Bureau of Economic Analysis (see Chapter 7).
- **Labor costs:** Measures labor costs per hour worked. Costs are subdivided into wages and salaries as well as nonwage costs. This quarterly report is similar to the U.S. Bureau of Labor Statistics Employment Cost Index (see Chapter 12).
- **Orders received in manufacturing:** Measures the total value of orders received by manufacturing companies that have 50 or more employees. This report is similar to the U.S. Census Bureau's Full Report on Manufacturers' Shipments, Inventories, and Orders (see Chapter 9).
- **Private consumption:** Measures the value of goods and services purchased by individuals. The concept is similar to the U.S. Bureau of Economic Analysis's personal consumption expenditures (PCE) found in the Personal Income and Outlays report (see Chapter 6).
- **Producer prices:** Measures the average price for raw materials and industrial products produced in Germany and sold within the country. It's analogous to the U.S. Bureau of Labor Statistics' Producer Price Index (see Chapter 12).

One prominent report from the FSO website is the Production Index. Like the United States, Germany reports its GDP quarterly. Investors wanting a more timely measure of German productivity can find it in the FSO's *Production Index.* The Production Index is similar to the U.S. Federal Reserve's Industrial Production and Capacity Utilization report (see Chapter 8). Table 17-4 shows you where to find the German Production Index in English.

Table 17-4 German Production Index

Release Schedule	*Agency*	*Web Address*
Monthly; 11:00 a.m. CET (Central European Time; 5:00 a.m. ET)	German Federal Statistics Office	`bit.ly/german-production-index`

The Production Index measures the monthly performance of German industry. It reports index values along with percentage changes from the previous month and the previous year. The index's base year is 2005.

The link in Table 17-4 takes you to the overview page for the Production Index. You can access data tables for the Production Index by clicking the tabs across the top of the web page.

Although Germany's service sector is larger than its manufacturing sectors, this report correlates well with Germany's quarterly GDP report. The Production Index provides results for specific economic sectors and is released within several weeks after the data are collected. Figure 17-3 shows a sample from the German Production Index.

Production index in production industries
original value
current month, preliminary
% changes on the previous year

Year, month		Production industries	Production industries (excluding building services)	Mining and quarring	Manufacturing	Energy supply	Construction industry
2011	Feb	16.4	14.9	-3.9	16.8	-2.7	58.3
	Jan	16.1	14.8	-1.9	17.3	-4.6	57.7
2010	Dec	13.7	15.6	-12.9	17.6	-0.6	-21.4
	Nov	12.2	12.7	-4.5	13.7	3.2	6.5
	Oct	8.6	9.0	-5.2	9.9	0.7	2.6
	Sep	8.1	8.4	5.2	9.3	-4.0	3.5
	Aug	14.9	15.6	7.4	17.1	-1.2	6.7
	Jul	7.6	8.2	3.2	8.8	0.0	0.3
	Jun	14.2	14.8	-4.2	16.1	1.1	7.7
	May	12.6	13.2	-9.9	13.3	16.3	4.3
	Apr	13.6	14.3	-5.3	14.8	13.0	4.7
	Mar	13.0	13.6	-21.7	14.5	9.8	4.0
	Feb	6.0	7.2	-25.3	7.5	9.4	-17.9
	Jan	0.4	1.0	-20.9	0.9	4.9	-18.7
2009	Dec	-2.3	-2.5	-13.7	-3.2	6.2	1.9
	Nov	-4.4	-5.2	-12.0	-5.5	1.0	6.8
	Oct	-11.6	-12.4	-16.9	-13.0	-3.2	2.7
	Sep	-12.2	-13.1	-24.9	-13.5	-4.8	3.2
	Aug	-15.5	-16.9	-27.4	-17.9	0.0	4.7
	Jul	-16.5	-17.7	-24.4	-18.6	-2.6	2.9
	Jun	-18.9	-20.0	-16.8	-21.1	-4.8	-0.3
	May	-18.1	-19.3	-17.8	-19.6	-13.9	1.5
	Apr	-27.0	-28.4	-24.9	-29.1	-20.4	-2.4
	Mar	-11.3	-12.6	0.9	-13.0	-9.8	13.8
	Feb	-23.6	-23.7	-2.1	-25.2	-6.7	-23.0
	Jan	-22.0	-21.7	-8.5	-23.8	1.2	-27.9
2008	Dec	-7.3	-7.8	-19.3	-7.4	-8.9	2.1
	Nov	-11.0	-11.4	-21.7	-11.3	-11.4	-4.8
	Oct	-3.7	-3.8	-15.7	-3.4	-4.9	-2.3
	Sep	5.4	5.3	-14.5	6.0	-0.3	7.5
	Aug	-5.1	-4.9	-14.4	-4.5	-7.6	-7.7
	Jul	3.4	3.4	-10.7	4.0	-0.6	1.4
	Jun	4.4	4.5	-14.4	5.3	-2.5	2.8
	May	-1.0	-0.8	-10.3	-0.7	-0.3	-3.8
	Apr	16.2	16.5	-0.7	17.2	11.1	11.7

Source: Federal Statistical Office of Germany, Wiesbaden, Germany

Figure 17-3: German Production Index.

The sample in Figure 17-3 shows the month-to-month changes for the overall Production Index as well as for the mining, manufacturing, energy, and construction sectors.

Surveying German businesses

Another report you may find useful if you're considering German investments is the *IFO Business Climate Survey.* The IFO, which stands for Information and Forschung (meaning "research" in German), is part of the CESifo group, which is the Center for Economic Studies and the ifo Institute for Economic Research.

The Business Climate Survey is an excellent leading indicator. It has been shown to correlate with Germany's GDP as well as with the economies of other major European countries. Results are released during the same month the survey is taken, which makes the IFO a timely report of current business conditions and future expectations. Table 17-5 briefly overviews the Business Climate Survey.

Table 17-5 German IFO Business Climate Survey

Release Schedule	*Agency*	*Web Address*
Monthly: 10:30 a.m. CET (Central European Time; 4:30 a.m. ET)	CESifo Group	`bit.ly/german-business-survey`

The Business Climate Survey is based on surveys of companies in the manufacturing, construction, wholesale, and retail sectors. The survey asks about the current business situation and respondents' expectations for the next six months. The current situation is either good, satisfactory, or poor. Future expectations are either favorable, unchanged, or unfavorable.

Figure 17-4 shows a sample of the data table from the Business Climate Survey.

Germany (Index, 2000 = 100, seasonally adjusted)

Month/year	04/10	05/10	06/10	07/10	08/10	09/10	10/10	11/10	12/10	01/11	02/11	03/11	04/11
Climate	101.8	101.6	101.9	106.3	106.8	106.9	107.7	109.3	109.9	110.3	111.3	111.1	110.4
Situation	99.5	99.7	101.3	106.9	108.3	109.8	110.2	112.2	112.9	112.9	114.8	115.8	116.3
Expectations	104.2	103.6	102.5	105.6	105.2	104.0	105.2	106.4	106.8	107.8	107.8	106.5	104.7

Source: Ifo Business Survey.

Source: CESifo GmbH (Munich Society for the Promotion of Economic Research)

Figure 17-4: Sample of the German Business Climate Survey.

The survey's results are presented as three indexes: the *Business Climate Index* (labeled *Climate* in Figure 17-4), the *Present Situation Index* (labeled *Situation*), and the *Expectations Index* (labeled *Expectations*). The values for each of the indexes are calculated by subtracting the number of poor/unfavorable responses from the number of good/favorable responses.

The report shows 13 months of the survey results. The Expectations Index looks forward, and most economists consider it an excellent leading indicator. Figure 17-5 shows a summary of the survey results for the four business sectors — manufacturing, construction, wholesale, and retail.

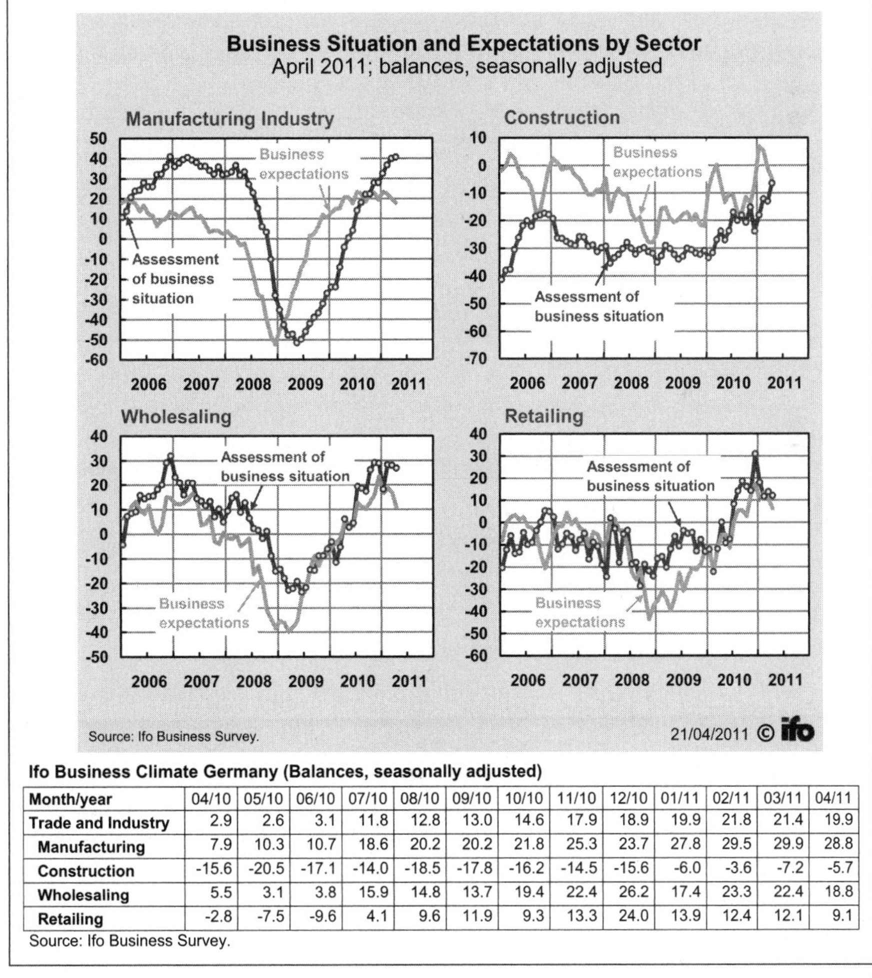

Ifo Business Climate Germany (Balances, seasonally adjusted)

Month/year	04/10	05/10	06/10	07/10	08/10	09/10	10/10	11/10	12/10	01/11	02/11	03/11	04/11
Trade and Industry	2.9	2.6	3.1	11.8	12.8	13.0	14.6	17.9	18.9	19.9	21.8	21.4	19.9
Manufacturing	7.9	10.3	10.7	18.6	20.2	20.2	21.8	25.3	23.7	27.8	29.5	29.9	28.8
Construction	-15.6	-20.5	-17.1	-14.0	-18.5	-17.8	-16.2	-14.5	-15.6	-6.0	-3.6	-7.2	-5.7
Wholesaling	5.5	3.1	3.8	15.9	14.8	13.7	19.4	22.4	26.2	17.4	23.3	22.4	18.8
Retailing	-2.8	-7.5	-9.6	4.1	9.6	11.9	9.3	13.3	24.0	13.9	12.4	12.1	9.1

Source: Ifo Business Survey.

Figure 17-5: A summary of the Business Climate Survey results for the four main business sectors.

Source: CESifo GmbH (Munich Society for the Promotion of Economic Research)

The lines labeled *Assessment of Business Situation* in the graphs in Figure 17-5 correspond to the Present Situation Index for each of the sectors. The lines labeled *Business Expectations* represent the Expectations Index.

You may recognize a similarity between the IFO Business Climate Survey and the U.S. Manufacturing ISM Report On Business® from the Institute for Supply Management (ISM). The survey technique is similar, as is the reporting. (See Chapter 10 for details.)

Tracking the Japanese Economy

Japan is the third-largest single-country economy (behind the United States and China), the world's fourth-largest exporter, and one of the United States' most significant trading partners. No wonder you need to be aware of the Japanese economy if you're considering overseas investing.

You don't have to look hard to find reliable Japanese economic statistics in English. In fact, the country provides several reports that are more than thorough and, thus, make for excellent economic resources for investors and business leaders. The Japanese indicators are well documented, using everyday language. You don't need a degree in economics or statistics to understand these reports.

Check out the following sections for details on how to find out more about the Japanese economy.

Surveying Japanese businesses

Japan produces one of the most unique business surveys on the planet. Its name, *Tankan,* roughly translates as the *Short-Term Economic Survey of Enterprises in Japan.* Although the Tankan is basically just a nationwide business confidence survey, it contains much more detail than any other country's business survey.

The Bank of Japan (BOJ), Japan's central bank, conducts the Tankan survey. The BOJ then uses the results to help implement and fine-tune its monetary policy. Each quarter, the BOJ surveys more than 11,000 representative companies about a wide range of corporate activities. The BOJ conducts the surveys in March, June, September, and December and releases the results in April, July, October, and mid-December.

The return rate for these surveys is remarkable. Typically, fewer than 2 percent of surveyed companies fail to respond. Table 17-6 shows you where to go to find the latest Tankan survey results in English. You can find the publication schedule for the Tankan survey at `bit.ly/tankan-release-schedule`.

Table 17-6 Bank of Japan Tankan Survey

Release Schedule	*Agency*	*Web Address*
Quarterly: Published schedule; 8:50 Japan Standard Time (7:50 p.m. ET the previous day)	Bank of Japan	`bit.ly/japan-tankan-survey`

The Tankan survey consists of two parts: a quantitative survey based on actual and forecast quarterly data and a judgment survey asking for projected results. The judgment survey is the more interesting of the two parts of the survey because its responses look forward and represent the economy's future. Table 17-7 shows you some of the topics that the judgment survey asks about.

Table 17-7 Tankan Judgment Survey Topics

Topic	*What It Asks Participants about Their Company*	*Responses*
Business conditions	To judge their company's general business conditions	Favorable, not so favorable, or unfavorable
Domestic supply and demand conditions for your industry (including overseas conditions if they can't easily be extracted)	To evaluate demand levels from domestic customers relative to the industry's ability to supply product	Excess demand, almost balanced, or excess supply
Overseas supply and demand conditions for your industry	To evaluate demand levels from overseas customers relative to the industry's ability to supply product	Excess demand, almost balanced, or excess supply
Inventory level of finished goods	To evaluate the current finished goods inventories at the time of the survey	Excessive, adequate, or insufficient
Wholesalers' inventory levels	To evaluate the finished goods inventories for the company's wholesalers, including overseas wholesalers	Excessive, adequate, or insufficient

(continued)

Table 17-7 *(continued)*

Topic	*What It Asks Participants about Their Company*	*Responses*
Production capacity (not including down-time for repairs)	To determine whether their company has sufficient business equipment to meet customer demand at the time of the survey	Excessive, adequate, or insufficient
Employment conditions	To evaluate the number of employees needed to meet customers' product requirements	Excessive, adequate, or insufficient
Financial position	To measure the cash position of their company	Easy, not tight, or tight
Lending attitude of financial institutions	To evaluate their company's lenders	Accommodative, not severe, or severe
Change in interest rate on loans	To evaluate the interest rate changes on outstanding loans	Rise, unchanged, or fall
Conditions for commercial paper (CP) issuance	To judge whether the market is receptive to new commercial paper issued by their company	Easy, not severe, or severe
Change in input prices	To evaluate raw material pricing trends	Rise, unchanged, or fall

For each topic listed in Table 17-7, the survey asks respondents to provide actual results for the previous quarter and forecast results for the next quarter. In addition, the survey asks respondents to provide actual annual and forecast results for total sales, sales for export, exchange rate, material costs, personnel costs, depreciation, operating profits, income, expenses, current profit, and net income.

The survey also requests quarterly information about total liabilities, loans from institutions, commercial paper outstanding, corporate bonds, total assets, cash and deposits, securities listed as assets, the number of full- and part-time employees, and new hires of recent college graduates.

Unfortunately, the Bank of Japan has not authorized me to include excerpts of the Tankan in this book. However, you can download an archived copy of the December 2010 Tankan Survey by going to `http://bit.ly/japan-tankan-dec-2010`. I refer to this release throughout the rest of this section.

The results you see on the first page of the Tankan survey are categorized by the size of the business (large, medium, or small), by the type of business (manufacturing or nonmanufacturing), and then by the specific business sector. The numbers you see are a result of a diffusion calculation (see Chapter 2 for details on diffusion indexes). In the case of the business conditions diffusion index, when the value is above zero, business conditions are improving. When the value is below zero, business conditions are deteriorating.

For example, the actual result for large manufacturing enterprises fell three points from September to December 2010 , from 8 to 5, which represents a decline in business conditions. The forecast value fell from 5 to –2, a decline of seven points and a sign of further deterioration. Results for medium-sized and small businesses were even worse.

You find the aggregate business condition judgment for all industries at the bottom of page 1. In the December 2010 Tankan report, that aggregate judgment was –11 (minus 11), a decline of one point from the previous report.

Notice the number of surveys returned (look at the table in the upper-left-hand corner of page 1 of the report). The response rate for all enterprises was 98.9 percent. Another forward-looking statistic in this report is the predicted exchange rates, which you can find in the table in the upper-right-hand corner. In the December 2010 Tankan, the value of the yen is predicted to continue depreciating compared to the U.S. dollar.

On page 8 of the December 2010 Tankan report, the chart in the upper-left-hand corner shows a long-term look at the business conditions diffusion index for manufacturing businesses. Notice how the business conditions forecasts correspond to economic recessions, which are indicated by the shaded areas.

Keep in mind that the report on business conditions is only one part of the Tankan survey. Each of the judgment survey topics listed in Table 17-7 receives similar treatment in the quarterly Tankan report.

Following the Tohoku-Pacific Ocean Earthquake that occurred on Mach 11, 2011, responses to the Tankan survey understandably fell by several points. The BOJ took the extraordinary step of splitting the survey into two parts for that reporting period. The BOJ segregated the results received before the earthquake from those received after the earthquake. In addition, the BOJ warned that the data have validity issues due to the major disruptions caused by the disaster.

Measuring Japan's productivity

Since the Tohoku-Pacific Ocean Earthquake, the international investment community has become concerned about the recovery of the Japanese business sectors. Exports account for a significant percentage of Japan's manufacturing capacity, and Japan's exporters have an outsized influence on the economy as a whole.

One way to track the recovery in Japan is with the Japanese Industrial Production report, which is produced by the Ministry of Economy, Trade, and Industry (METI). Table 17-8 briefly outlines this report. You can find the release schedule for the Japanese Industrial Production Report at `http://bit.ly/japan-meti-schedule`.

Table 17-8 Japanese Industrial Production Report

Release Schedule	*Agency*	*Web Address*
Monthly: Published schedule, 8:50 Japan Standard Time (7:50 p.m. ET the previous day)	Japanese Ministry of Economy, Trade, and Industry	`bit.ly/japan-meti-statistics`

The Industrial Production report is extensive, regularly running more than 70 pages. The METI first issues the report with preliminary data and then revises the initial report one month later. Revisions can be extensive. The index's base year is 2005.

Note: The website listed in Table 17-8 is translated into English. However, unlike the Tankan survey, the Industrial Production report doesn't include a separate English version of the data tables. Instead, the same report includes both Japanese and English descriptions.

The METI hasn't authorized me to include excerpts of the Industrial Production report; however, you can download an archived copy of the March 2011 report at `http://bit.ly/japan-ind-production-march-2011`; it's long, so give it a few moments to download. I refer to that report throughout the rest of this section.

The Industrial Production report covers industries such as mining and manufacturing, general machinery, information and communication equipment, transportation equipment, chemicals, petroleum products, pharmaceutical drugs, and plastic products. In addition, it categorizes products as capital goods, durable consumer goods, and nondurable consumer goods.

On page 6 of the report, you find an example of one industry's summary profile. (Note that the page is labeled 6 but the PDF file counts it as page number 8.)

The summary page, shown on page 6, covers all mining and manufacturing industries. It shows changes from the previous month, the previous quarter, and the previous calendar and fiscal years. The English-language legend is on the right-hand side of the page. (The black upward-facing triangle isn't intuitive; it represents a decline.) The summary page includes an overview of the following data:

- **Industrial production:** This part of the report represents actual reported production. From calendar year 2009 to 2010, production rose from 81.1 to 94.4, an increase of 13.4 points.
- **Shipments:** The report shows sales as shipments. Shipments rose from 82.1 in 2009 to 95.8 in 2010 (an increase of 16.7 percent). Growing sales typically mean inventory reductions and future production gains, which are generally a sign that the economy is growing.
- **Inventory:** Growing inventory represents declining sales. Inventories rose from 93.1 in 2009 to 96.6 in 2010 (an increase of 3.8 percent). Normally, when shipments improve, inventories shrink, but that didn't happen in this case. This discrepancy is an indication that sales may not be as robust as mining and manufacturing managers had anticipated; it may be one of the first signs that the economy is starting to slow.
- **Inventory ratio:** Unlike the inventory/sales ratio used in the United States, the Industrial Production report represents the inventory ratio as an index. It doesn't represent the number of months of supplies at the current shipment rate. The index fell from 131.6 in 2009 to 108.1 in 2010 (a decrease of 17.9 percent). This is another sign that shipments and sales are not keeping up with the growth of inventories.

Tracking China's Economy

In 2010, China became the world's largest exporter. This huge economy is expanding at an extraordinary rate. Unfortunately, finding reliable economic information about China is difficult. The problem isn't that the country doesn't produce the data. It does. In fact, the National Bureau of Statistics of China generates reams of economic data and translates much of it for English speakers.

The problem is the quality of the data. The Chinese government itself has recognized that its reports may have been less informative over the years than they could have been. To help improve the quality of the data, China assigned both collection and dissemination responsibilities to the National Bureau of

Statistics in 2005. As a result, you need to be a bit skeptical of the data. China offers businesses and investors the potential for significant growth. However, until the economic community becomes more comfortable with Chinese economic reports, make sure that any investments you make in China are well diversified and that they represent only a small percentage of your entire business or investment portfolio.

Table 17-9 shows you where to find English translations for the main Chinese economic statistics.

Table 17-9 Chinese National Bureau of Statistics Indicators

Release Schedule	*Agency*	*Web Address*
Monthly, some quarterly, and some annual	National Bureau of Statistics of China	`stats.gov.cn/english/`

Links on the left-hand side of the webpage listed in Table 17-9 take you to monthly, quarterly, and annual reports. These reports include

- **Growth Rate of Value-Added by Industry, Region, and Sector:** Rather than an index, this monthly report shows an estimate of the value added during production processes.
- **Investment in Fixed Assets by Industry and Region:** This monthly report shows investment amounts in yuan.
- **Consumer Price Index:** This monthly index shows the percentage change in consumer prices across a variety of products, using the previous year as the base index value.
- **Consumer Confidence Index:** This monthly index shows the values for consumer expectations, consumer satisfaction, and aggregate consumer confidence.
- **Gross Domestic Product (GDP):** This very brief quarterly report shows the aggregate growth rate.
- **Producer Price Index:** This quarterly index provides the price index for major agricultural products.

Figure 17-6 shows an example of the quarterly GDP report.

Gross Domestic Product (GDP) (First Quarter, 2011)

National Bureau of Statistics of China

	Absolute Value (100 million yuan)	Growth Rate over the Same Period Last Year (%)
Gross Domestic Products	**96311**	**9.7**
Primary Industry	5980	3.5
Secondary Industry	46788	11.1
Tertiary Industry	43543	9.1

Notes:
1. Absolute value is computed at current price, growth rate is computed at constant price.
2. Statistical data in this table are preliminary verification results.

Gross Domestic Product Growth Rate on Quarterly Bases

Gross Domestic Product	Pd. Ago(%)
2011 Q1	2.1
2011 Q2	
2011 Q3	
2011 Q4	

Note: Data in this table are seasonally adjusted.

Figure 17-6: Example of the China GDP report.

Source: Quoted from the website of the National Bureau of Statistics of the People's Republic of China

As you can see, the GDP report is extremely brief. The three categories included in this report are

- **Primary industry:** GDP based on mining, agriculture, and fishing
- **Secondary industry:** GDP based on the manufacturing sector
- **Tertiary industry:** GDP based on the service sector

If you want more data than what you see in the monthly or quarterly reports, you can download an annual rollup of the National Accounts data in Excel format. From the link listed in Table 17-9, click on the Yearly link under Statistical Data in the left-hand column. Then select a year from the drop-down menu next to the National Accounts entry in the table and click Search. In the left-hand column, click on the little book icon next to the part of the report you want to read. Then click on the specific section you want to read. (Unfortunately, this link doesn't work in all browsers. For example, I can access the data by using Internet Explorer but not with Firefox.)

Chapter 18

Monitoring Emerging Economies

In This Chapter

- Keeping an eye on emerging markets
- Evaluating India's economy
- Tracking Brazil's economic progress

Emerging markets are those countries that are experiencing phenomenal rates of growth. As an investor, you definitely want to be aware of this growth. Fortunately, you can use economic indicators to find potential business and investment opportunities in these high-growth environments.

This chapter introduces you to several tools you can use to find economic data that'll help you identify and investigate the fastest high-growth economies in the world. Specifically, it takes a look at the emerging economies in India and Brazil, two high-profile, high-growth success stories.

Following Emerging Markets

Finding reliable economic data about emerging markets can be challenging. Too few countries publish economic data in English. Even fewer provide the explanations you need to understand how the data was collected or what the results mean. Fortunately, a few sources do provide reliable English reports to help you get started.

Chapter 17 suggests three research resources for international economic data: the CIA World Factbook, the World Bank, and the International Monetary Fund (IMF). These sources offer viable research data for emerging economies, but you may want a little more info before you make the jump into emerging markets. This section introduces you to a couple of other sources of economic information that are especially useful for evaluating emerging markets.

Seeing the world through Google's Public Data Explorer

One resource you can use to gauge emerging economies is Google's *IMF Public Data Explorer* (*IMF* stands for *International Monetary Fund*). It offers a convenient way to compare a variety of economic indicators from multiple countries. This experimental yet helpful extension of Google's public data search feature is part of Google Labs. Though it may never become part of Google's formal product offering, as long as it's available, it offers an excellent resource for researching emerging economies. I provide a quick glance at this resource in Table 18-1.

Table 18-1 Google's IMF Public Data Explorer

Release Schedule	*Agency*	*Web Address*
Periodically	International Monetary Fund; Google Labs	`bit.ly/google-dataset-imf`

The Public Data Explorer provides data from the IMF that include economic indicators from most countries throughout the world. For example, the IMF dataset includes

- **National accounts:** Gross domestic product (GDP) data in several variations, including indexed for inflation and *purchasing power parity* (PPP), a method used to standardize economic statistics based on consumers' purchasing power rather than the currency exchange rate
- **Demographic data:** Population and unemployment rate data
- **Trade:** Export and import data
- **Monetary:** Inflation rates
- **Government finance:** Government debt, revenue, and expenditures as a percentage of GDP

Google's Public Data Explorer allows you to examine economic statistics from individual countries, as well as compare economic results from one country to another or to a number of other countries.

The IMF's dataset is only one of many in Google's Public Data Explorer. You can find a complete list of Google's public datasets at `www.google.com/publicdata/directory`.

Using other sources to track emerging markets

Other sources of useful economic data that you can use to follow emerging markets include white papers and economic studies published by universities, think tanks, and even management consulting firms. For example, the management consulting firm McKinsey & Company offers a useful source of economic insight for many countries across the globe. You can access the data in two ways:

- **By regional groupings**: `csi.mckinsey.com/en/Knowledge_by_region.aspx`
- **By topical groupings:** `csi.mckinsey.com/Knowledge_by_topic.aspx`

Monitoring India's Economy

India considers itself the world's fourth-largest economy, based on the GDP you get when you use purchasing power parity, or PPP. (PPP is based on consumers' purchasing power rather than the currency exchange rate.) Although PPP is a valid statistical approach, I generally prefer the more traditional currency-based GDP calculation. India's traditional GDP ranking is the 10th- or 11th-largest economy in the world, depending on who's doing the ranking.

Regardless of which GDP measure you use, however, India is big and growing fast. Using 2010 estimates, the population exceeds 1.2 billion people, which is second in size only to China's 1.3-billion population. But India doesn't adhere to China's one-child policy, and its population is growing faster than China's. India is likely to overtake China's population size within a decade or two.

Although India's economy isn't as large as China's, it does have several advantages that help it compete effectively in the worldwide economy:

- **Use of the English language:** About 10 percent of India's population speaks fluent English. Others speak English as a second language but not fluently. According to the CIA World Factbook, India uses English for national, political, and commercial communications.

  India's English proficiency helps in two areas. First, English is widely accepted as the basis for international business communications, even in countries where English isn't the primary language (like many countries in the European Union, for example). Second, India's English-speaking population allows the country to host a number of service industries that depend on English-language proficiency. (China lags behind India in both areas.)

- **Well-established democratic institutions:** Although there are obvious exceptions (like China), democratic countries generally outperform the economies of countries operating under autocratic rules.
- **Transparent legal system:** India's legal system is relatively transparent, especially when compared to other emerging economies or even when compared to China. Strong and stable legal traditions are crucial for attracting foreign investment, especially for emerging markets.

About 30 percent of India's population currently lives in its urban centers. Like most developing countries, the population is shifting from rural areas to cities because that's where the work is.

With India's huge population, visualizing the scale of this migration may be difficult. One striking metaphor comes from the McKinsey Global Institute. To accommodate the people migrating into cities, McKinsey estimates that India needs to build commercial and residential space equivalent to one Chicago every year between now and 2030. (You can find this report online at `www.mckinsey.com/mgi/publications/india_urbanization/index.asp`.)

That kind of growth and migration puts a huge strain on the country's infrastructure. But it also provides an important economic opportunity. For example, construction equipment and building material companies already participate in India's booming growth, and, not surprisingly, they expect substantial future revenue and profit growth. The following sections take a closer look at India's economic progress and future growth.

Following India's economic progress

English speakers can keep up with India's economic data relatively easily thanks to the India Central Statistics Office (CSO) website. The CSO website offers a long menu of economic statistics, ranging from energy use to demographic data to business sector reports. It includes monthly reports, like the Consumer Price Index (CPI) and the Production Index, as well as the quarterly GDP report. Table 18-2 gives a brief overview of this site.

Table 18-2 India Central Statistics Office Website

Release Schedule	*Agency*	*Web Address*
Monthly, quarterly	India Central Statistics Office	`bit.ly/india-stats`

India's GDP is one of the most widely used reports on the CSO website. It doesn't provide the depth of data offered by the U.S. GDP report (see Chapter 7), but it does provide a good overview of the current state of the economy and its potential for continued growth. You can see the overview of India's GDP report by following the link listed in Table 18-2.

Included in the GDP report are the following pieces of info:

- **GDP at current prices:** This section of the report provides a good summary of the total economic production and shows the aggregate GDP, not adjusted for inflation. It profiles three broad segments of the economy: agriculture, industry, and services.
- **GDP at constant 2005 prices:** This part of the report shows the aggregate GDP, indexed for inflation. The indexed data show the same economic segments as the current price data: agriculture, industry and services. (All inflation adjustments for India data are based on 2005 dollars, although this is likely to change during the next baseline adjustment. See Chapter 2 for the lowdown on baseline adjustments.)
- **Implicit Price Index:** This part shows another inflation-adjusted GDP index — the Implicit Price Index — which is similar to the U.S. implicit price deflator (see Chapter 7). This index is released quarterly, which makes it less timely than either the Consumer Price Index or the Wholesale Price Index.
- **Production Index:** The Index of Industrial Production (IIP) measures the percentage growth of manufacturing.
- **Consumer Price Index (CPI):** India's CPI is too narrowly focused to accurately gauge inflation for the whole economy. The Wholesale Price Index is the better tool. (See Chapter 12 for details on the U.S. CPI.)
- **Wholesale Price Index (WPI):** This inflation indicator is equivalent to the U.S. Producer Price Index, or PPI (see Chapter 12). It measures the average price level of wholesale products.

Anticipating India's future growth

India presents itself as an investor-friendly environment with good future growth opportunities. For investors and business managers looking for a long planning horizon, India may be a good opportunity.

You may be familiar with one part of India's service sector — the high-tech call centers. Although many U.S. companies employ this service, it represents only a small part of India's service economy. India businesses provide support services for many industries throughout the world, including banking and medical diagnostics. The country also has highly skilled electrical engineering and software development firms.

These services represent a significant competitive strength for India. After all, it's hard to imagine a country like China, or any country without a large English-speaking population, trying to provide services at this level of quality.

The service sector may be the most visible of India's growth industries, but investors and business leaders can't overlook India's manufacturing capabilities. India's skilled workforce is developing and managing many types of manufacturing facilities.

Even so, manufacturing in India isn't without challenges. Infrastructure development is progressing, but housing, hospitality (hotels and restaurants), and transportation are still insufficient to meet today's requirements. This smart, industrious country is addressing these issues to further the country's growth. Development of India's manufacturing base and infrastructure are areas that you should monitor carefully.

Following Brazil's Economic Future

Brazil is another one of the world's growth stories. Its GDP is ranked number eight in the world. Although its current economic growth rate doesn't compare to that of India or China, the country is growing in spite of persistent inflation.

Brazil is a country rich in natural resources. For example, it recently declared its independence from imported oil, partly through extensive exploration and partly by adopting sugarcane ethanol for its transportation needs and for export. In fact, Brazil is the world's largest ethanol exporter, and it mandates the use of E25, a mixture of 75 percent gasoline and 25 percent ethanol throughout the country.

Brazil also builds airplanes, automobiles, and consumer goods. And it's the leading processor of steel, iron, and cement in South America. In addition to ethanol, the country exports orange juice, aircraft, textiles, and soybeans.

In the following sections, I explain a little more about the Brazilian economy, including the investment opportunities it offers and some warning signs to watch out for.

Summarizing Brazil's economy

Banco Central do Brasil (BCB), the Brazilian Central Bank, provides an extensive collection of economic data in English. The data include economic indicators such as the Consumer Price Index, the Wholesale Price Index, construction sector costs, and capacity-utilization reports. Table 18-3 provides what you need to know to follow the BCB indicators.

Table 18-3 Banco Central do Brasil Economic Indicators

Release Schedule	*Agency*	*Web Address*
Monthly, quarterly	Banco Central do Brasil	`www.bcb.gov.br/?indicators`

Other BCB reports provide stats on capital goods production, oil and ethanol production, automotive imports and production, unemployment rates, the GDP, and a whole lot more. One particularly important indicator on the BCB website is the Industrial Production report.

This Industrial Production report provides the collected data and seasonal adjustments for capital goods production, consumer durables and consumables, as well as intermediate goods used as input for further production. The report publishes the data as an index, using the base year 1992 (see Chapter 2 for more about baseline indexes). It also provides month-to-month and year-over-year percentage changes.

Although the available data from BCB is extensive, it does have two main drawbacks you need to consider:

- **The economic data is published without analysis.** If you want a discussion of the data, you have to visit another source for Brazilian economic data. The Brazilian Institute of Geography and Statistics (IBGE) provides some of the same data as the BCB, along with some analysis. Unfortunately, though, only portions of the IBGE website are translated from Portuguese into English. (You can find the IBGE website at this address: `ibge.gov.br/english/`.)
- **You need a spreadsheet program like Microsoft Excel to read the data.** The BCB doesn't publish its data in a format that you can display in a web browser or print easily without a spreadsheet program. After the data is in your spreadsheet program, however, you can do anything you'd like with it. If you're familiar with Excel, this approach makes analyzing the information easier.

  Many of the BCB spreadsheets use acronyms and abbreviations alongside the data. Fortunately, a glossary of terms and a description of the conventions used in the spreadsheets are also available on the BCB website.

Understanding Brazil's inflation issue

Investing in a developing economy like Brazil does have some issues — inflation being the main one — you need to be aware of before you start dropping money.

To understand the inflation issue, consider this: Inflation throughout the 1980s and the early 1990s was horrible, peaking at over 200 percent for a time. Austerity measures implemented during 1994 eventually brought inflation rates back to single digits. At the time of this writing, the official inflation target is 4.5 percent; however, Brazilian inflation rates exceeding 6 percent have been reported in 2011.

Brazil's economic growth makes it an attractive investment candidate for U.S. investors. However, you must keep a careful watch on inflation because it could overwhelm the economic growth. After all, rising inflation makes currency valuations unfavorable for foreign investors, and if it grows too high, equity and debt investments have trouble outperforming the high rates of inflation.

If Brazil is able to keep its inflation problem from getting out of control, it's a country worthy of consideration for future investments and business ventures. At the time of this writing, Brazil's central bank was raising interest rates to try and keep inflation within the target rates. Investors can monitor the success of these efforts by using Banco Central do Brasil's CPI reports, which can be found on the website listed in Table 18-3.

Part VI
The Part of Tens

In this part . . .

Here you find a hallmark of the *For Dummies* series — the Part of Tens. In this part, you discover how to create your own ten-step checklist for monitoring the U.S. economy and how to make your knowledge of economic indicators pay.

Chapter 19

Ten Ways to Track the U.S. Economy

In This Chapter

- Reviewing ten top indicators
- Picking ten that are right for you

Way too much information — indicators and other details — about the economy is available for any one human to absorb it all. If you try to make sense of everything, nothing will make sense.

Even full-time economists don't keep track of *everything*. You have to prioritize and find a way to pare down the huge quantity of economic information into useful, digestible chunks. Otherwise, you'll never have time to invest, manage your business, or even play outside in the sun.

This chapter identifies my personal top ten indicators and my reasons for selecting them. For tips on how to keep up with your top ten economic indicators, go to Chapter 1.

Note: Your investment style may be very different from mine. If it is, you may want a different set of indicators in your top ten list. You may not even need ten. For example, if you're primarily a bond investor, your focus is likely on interest rates and inflation. If you're a home builder, your focus is on interest rates, housing starts, and employment. You get the idea. You need to tailor your short list of indicators to your personal needs. Feel free to use my list if it suits your needs. Or use it as a guide to create your own. Just be sure to select the indicators that will help you meet your goals.

Monitoring Jobs and Employment Data

Changes in employment statistics are often the first omens of an economic problem. They're not much help for identifying when the economy is coming out of recession, but they're usually the first signs that an economic expansion may be coming to an end.

Although employment is almost always late to the party when an economy recovers, rising employment is part of a growing economy. As long as employment statistics continue to rise, the economy is likely to grow.

When monitoring employment, I focus on these two reports:

- **Unemployment Insurance Weekly Claims Report:** This report usually offers the very first sign that unemployment rates are rising. Rising unemployment often leads to a slowing economy. ***Note:*** Seasonal factors affect these statistics, which can make them quite volatile, so you shouldn't depend on the Weekly Claims Report alone. Still, it serves as a timely warning that you need to pay close attention to other signs of economic changes.
- **Employment Situation report:** The Bureau of Labor Statistics (BLS) Employment Situation report is the perfect companion to the Weekly Claims Report. It provides information about the job market, employee compensation, and unemployment. It shows how many people are working full or part time, how many are looking for work, and how many have given up on ever finding a job. This report is an excellent tool for keeping track of U.S. employment.

Rising unemployment goes hand in hand with a recession. High unemployment rates coincide with lower consumer spending. Lower consumer spending leads to production slowdowns, which lead to more layoffs.

Stock investors, business managers, and bondholders differ in their specific reactions to employment statistics, but all three should keep a close eye on employment.

I discuss both the Weekly Claims Report and the Employment Situation report in Chapter 4.

Accounting for Consumer Spending

If you want to know what really makes the economy hum, look no further than consumer spending. As consumer spending grows, so grows the economy. Conversely, when consumers pull back on spending, the economy usually heads for a slump.

The best tool for tracking consumer spending is the Personal Income and Outlays report from the Bureau of Economic Analysis (BEA). Specifically, you want to monitor personal consumption expenditures (PCE) from this report. It's the third indicator on my top ten list. (See Chapter 6 for details about the Personal Income and Outlays report, including PCE.)

PCE reports spending for durable goods, nondurable goods, and consumer services. Of these, spending on durable goods is the most economically sensitive. After all, *durable goods* are big-ticket purchases that consumers can postpone or completely forgo until they're feeling confident about the economy. Any increase or decrease in spending on durable goods often precedes a change in the economy, so it's a good barometer all by itself.

From the economy's point of view, spending (which you track with PCE) is more important than personal income because consumers can unwisely spend more than they make. Consumers can use credit cards, personal loans, and home equity loans to buy durable goods when their income doesn't quite cover the monthly bills. However, if personal consumption gets too far ahead of personal income for too long, there will be bills to pay, and those bills alone can lead to an economic slowdown.

Strong spending almost always coincides with economic growth, while slow spending almost always signifies that the economy is about to lag behind.

Checking Up on Businesses

To check the health of U.S. manufacturers, I turn to the Manufacturing ISM Report On Business®. This report provides an excellent overview of the manufacturing sectors and includes the PMI (formerly known as the Purchasing Managers Index), which summarizes the whole Report On Business® in a numeric single index.

Though the U.S. economy is now mostly service based, the PMI offers excellent correlation with the U.S. gross domestic product (GDP). In fact, it's usually very good at identifying turning points in the business cycle before they actually show up in GDP.

The reason I include the Manufacturing ISM Report On Business® on my top ten indicators list is that stock and bond markets are very sensitive to changes in the PMI. I definitely don't want to miss what this indicator has to say! (See Chapter 10 for details on the ISM, the Report On Business®, and the PMI.)

Showing an Interest in Interest Rates

Interest rates affect the business cycle, and the business cycle affects interest rates. Because interest rates are so closely related to the economy, I include two interest rate indicators on my top ten list:

- **Federal Open Market Committee (FOMC) report:** The FOMC sets the federal funds rate targets and reports them in its FOMC press release. The FOMC meets eight times each year and issues this press release at the end of each meeting. The federal funds rate is one of the few tools the Federal Reserve (the Fed) has to help manage monetary policy — that is, to either stimulate or cool the economy. When the Fed wants to cool the economy, it starts to raise the federal funds rate. That action alone is often enough to eventually slow the economy. Check out Chapter 8 for more on the federal funds rate.
- **The yield curve:** This indicator shows interest rates for the various maturities of Treasury securities. Its shape tells you about the bond market's inflation concerns. You can find the yield-curve chart on the Bloomberg website at `www.bloomberg.com/markets/rates-bonds/government-bonds/us/`.

  The federal funds rate and the yield curve are inextricably intertwined. As long as the Fed is trying to stimulate the economy, the federal funds rate remains low and the yield curve is normal.

  Sometimes, when the Fed is raising rates, the interest rate picture gets out of whack. Short-term rates approach and sometimes exceed rates for longer-term debt. As a result, the yield curve either flattens or inverts, and you can be all but certain that an economic contraction will follow. Chapter 14 includes information on the yield curve.

Building on Housing and Construction

Housing is one of the single-largest components in the U.S. economy. In fact, housing is a leading economic indicator. New-home construction regularly slows before the economy peaks, and it's often one of the first sectors to lead the economy out of recession. When new-home construction slows, start looking for other signs that the economy is weakening.

The New Residential Construction report from the U.S. Census Bureau is the housing indicator on my top ten list. The report measures the following two areas. (Refer to Chapter 11 for more on this report.)

- **New building permits:** They're a good indication that home builders are planning future economic activity. After all, when construction on a new home actually starts, you know that a home builder or home buyer is spending real money and making a very large financial commitment to complete the home. When many people make this commitment (by getting new building permits), the whole economy benefits.
- **New-home construction:** This drives the purchase of building products like lumber, flooring, roofing, and air-conditioning systems. The purchase of new homes also leads consumers to purchase other big-ticket consumer durable goods, like kitchen appliances and household furniture.

Seeing how the business cycle affects housing is fairly easy. High interest rates and falling employment numbers slow new-home construction. When people feel anxious about their income, they're not likely to build or buy new homes. Without consumer demand, home builders and building products companies suffer. Sales of consumer durables are also likely to fall.

Following Inflation

High inflation rates are very harmful to the economy. When prices rise because of monetary inflation, the dollar's purchasing power falls. As a result, bonds become less attractive, and bondholders drive interest rates higher to compensate. Stocks often suffer during periods of inflation, too.

Although professional economists follow other inflation indicators, the Consumer Price Index (CPI) is the most widely followed inflation indicator and is one of my top ten indicators. (Chapter 12 delves into the CPI.)

Though I may backup the CPI with the PCE (see Chapter 6), the Cleveland Fed's Median CPI, or the GDP price deflator (see Chapter 7), the CPI still gets most of my attention.

Surveying Consumers

The University of Michigan's Surveys of Consumers report may be the most popular economic forecasting tool available. One of the components in the report — the Expectations Index — does an especially great job of forecasting economic recovery, so, of course, it's one of my top ten indicators. When the economy has been in recession, start looking for the Expectations Index to begin turning higher. It's usually a sign that the recession is nearing an end.

See Chapter 5 for details about the University of Michigan's Surveys of Consumers report and the Expectations Index.

Following the GDP

The last of my top indicators is the Gross Domestic Product (GDP) report. This mammoth quarterly report tells you everything you need to know about the condition of the economy. Sure, you can find several timelier reports, but this all-encompassing report is too thorough to ignore. I discuss the GDP report in Chapter 7.

Chapter 20

Ten (Or So) Money-Making Tips You Can Use with Economic Indicators

In This Chapter

- Being on the right side of the market
- Following investor trends while sticking to your own strategy
- Investing overseas and achieving balance in your portfolio
- Deciding to act without making big investment mistakes

Economic indicators give you an advantage as both an investor and a business manager. After all, they can help you identify opportunities and turning points in the economy.

When you integrate your newfound knowledge of economic indicators into a complete investment strategy, you can improve your investment results. But, first, you need to figure out how to identify and manage risk and plan for market volatility. This chapter is here to help you do just that. It describes the tools and techniques you need to make the best investment decisions when using economic indicators. You can also check out the latest editions of *Trading For Dummies,* which I coauthored with Lita Epstein, and *Investing For Dummies* by Eric Tyson (John Wiley & Sons, Inc.) for more in-depth information.

Finding the Big Picture: Distinguishing between Bull and Bear Markets

As an investor, your first goal is to identify the current market conditions. Then you have to decide what you're going to do about them. The economic indicators I discuss throughout this book show where the economy and business cycle are heading. Now you just need to integrate information from the investment markets into your plans and figure out which type of market you're dealing with.

- *Bull markets* generally start before the economy shows signs of recovery.
- *Bear markets* begin before the economy is clearly in recession.

You can identify bull and bear markets in many different ways. For example, the media generally use a simple measure that says it's a bear market when the Dow Jones Industrial Average falls by some fixed measure, usually 10 percent or so. However, this definition isn't very helpful, because it doesn't give you any way to identify the risk of a bear market in advance.

My preferred approach is very simple. It's called the *Bullish Percent Index,* and it's created by plotting the percentage of stocks currently on a buy signal. Buy and sell signals are determined based on a very old charting technique called *Point and Figure charting.* Based on this technique, the stock market will always be in one of these six states:

- **Bull alert:** The number of stocks on a buy signal is increasing, and a bull market may be forming. Plan accordingly and make only small investments that will work well if a bull market occurs.
- **Bull confirmed:** The number of stocks on a buy signal has passed the threshold that generates a buy signal on the Bullish Percent Index. You're in a bull market. Your investment strategy should favor equities and growth. If you use investment leverage, now is the time to use it.
- **Bull correction:** A pullback is in progress. Bull corrections can either reverse to the bull confirmed condition or deteriorate to the bear alert condition. Remove all leverage and begin making plans for a bear market if the market deteriorates farther.
- **Bear alert:** The number of stocks on a sell signal is increasing, and a bear market may be forming. Plan accordingly. Don't hold any investment that violates your predetermined selling thresholds.
- **Bear confirmed:** The number of stocks on a sell signal has passed the sell-signal threshold on the Bullish Percent Index. You're in a bear market. Your investment strategy should favor debt vehicles, income stocks, and short-side investments if they're part of your plan.
- **Bear correction:** A pullback is in progress. A bear correction can revert to a bear confirmed or transition to a bull alert. Remove all leverage and plan accordingly.

To see a Bullish Percent Index chart for yourself, head to `www.StockCharts.com` and search for *NYSE Bullish Percent Index.* Make sure to select P&F Chart (Point and Figure chart) from the drop-down menu before pressing Go. Fortunately, this site labels the Bullish Percent Index with one of the six conditions I describe in the preceding list.

Tracking Sector Rotation

Years ago, Sam Stovall, Standard and Poor's chief investment strategist, found that investment market cycles tend to lead business cycles. His *Sector Rotation Model* shows how the stock market bottoms out before the economy is fully in a recession and how it begins its recovery before the economy

This model can help you fine-tune your analysis of the current market environment and identify the stocks in the strongest sectors. Table 20-1 shows the four market categories identified in this model.

Table 20-1 Four Market Categories in the Sector Rotation Model

Market Category	***Effects on***			
	Consumers	***Industrial Production***	***Interest Rates***	***Stocks***
Early recovery	Consumer expectations begin to rise (see Chapter 5).	Industrial production begins to rise (see Chapter 8).	Interest rates bottom out (see Chapters 8 and 14).	Energy sectors, basic materials sectors, and industrial sector stocks rise.
Full recovery	Consumer confidence levels may show consumer expectations beginning to fall.	Industrial production stats flatten out.	Interest rates rise.	Consumer staples and service sector stocks perform best.
Early recession	Consumer confidence falls more sharply. Job losses accelerate.	Industrial production drops.	Interest rates begin to fall.	Dividend-paying utilities and finance stocks are usually safe havens.
Full recession	Consumer confidence may begin to show signs of improving.	Industrial production remains flat to falling.	Interest rates continue to fall.	Cyclical and technology stocks usually lead the way out of a recession.

Following the Herd

Buying low and selling high is good advice, but doing so is harder than it sounds. Too many people think you have to buy at the lowest price and sell at the highest price, but the truth is you're not going to do that very often, if ever. In fact, if you try to time the exact bottoms and tops, you'll likely find yourself with a lot of losing trades.

Although following other investors makes absolutely no sense at times, sometimes following the trend is a very profitable strategy. The philosophy of successful trend followers is that it's okay to buy a little late and sell a little early. After all, you need someone to sell your investments to, and finding that someone is much easier to do when the market's full of eager buyers than when many people are scrambling to sell their investments at the same time.

Some trend followers base decisions on market action alone. I prefer to consider economic indicators as well. If you use the indicator knowledge I provide in this book along with tools like the Bullish Percent Index, the Sector Rotation Model, and trend following, you can be a successful investor.

Taking Three Steps, Then a Stumble

The Federal Open Market Committee (FOMC) is responsible for setting the *federal funds rate* (a very short-term interest rate that the Federal Reserve uses to manage the pace of economic growth; see Chapter 8 for more info). Keep an eye on this rate. When you see the FOMC raising rates after the recovery is well underway, start making plans to adjust your portfolio as the economy starts to slow.

The FOMC very rarely raises rates right before the economy puts on the brakes. Investors know this. So after the first federal funds rate hike, wily investors start making plans for an economic slowdown but usually wait for the FOMC to raise rates a few more times before reacting. The rule of thumb is that the FOMC will rise rates three times (three steps) before the market stumbles; in other words, expect the market to react after the third federal rate hike, probably not before.

Balancing Your Portfolio

Even the Easter Bunny shouldn't put all his eggs in one basket. Although you probably wouldn't even think about putting all your investment assets into a single stock, too many investors do put all their assets into a single type of investment, and too often, they experience bad results.

Investors have a remarkable menu of investments to choose from: growth stocks, value stocks, domestic stocks, foreign stocks, long- and short-term bonds, contracts on futures and options, precious metals, mutual funds, and exchange-traded funds. Getting the mix right is tough but important.

The key is to devise a portfolio strategy that's generally profitable under a variety of volatility and risk scenarios. You need a mix of assets so that some will perform well regardless of the current economic situation. Then you need to regularly adjust the balance of your portfolio to keep the percentage allocation of each asset class in line with your overall plan. For example, when your long-term bonds outperform your equity investments, realize some of the profits and reallocate the assets to match your original plan.

Investing Strategically

Pick the style of investor you want to be and stick with it. If you're going to follow the very successful cash flow models of Ben Graham and his student Warren Buffet, then you can't let the day-to-day meanderings of the market sway you.

Conversely, if you plan to profit from the market's short- or intermediate-term movements, then stick with that plan. Don't try doing both. No matter what, make sure that you have a strategy when investing.

Taking Your Investments Abroad

Today, investing outside of your home country is easy. You just have to remember one important point: Investing abroad entails currency risks and specific country risks that you don't experience if you invest only at home. But those different risk profiles can work to your advantage. For example, when the U.S. dollar is strong, it pays to buy foreign equities and debt. You get more for your money and the potential for additional profit if the dollar ever weakens.

However, U.S. investors need to be aware of the currency risk. As the value of the dollar rises against other currencies, overseas investments suffer. Even if you pick solid investments, your total return could decline because of exchange rates.

Mutual funds and exchange-traded funds (ETFs) can ease the difficulty of foreign investing, but they can't shelter you from currency risk. (*ETFs* are investment funds, that are bought and sold on the stock exchanges.)

Avoiding Big Investment Mistakes

When investing, make sure that you avoid potentially costly mistakes. These mistakes range from the following:

- **Losing your portfolio:** The one huge investment mistake you can make is losing a large portion of your portfolio. Don't do that. Instead, make sure that you know the conditions that will cause you to sell *before* you invest. If an investment meets its price objective, sell at least part of it and lock in some of the profits. If any investment turns into a loser, make sure that you have a plan for how to get out.
- **Getting emotionally attached to your investments:** Don't marry your investments. After spending so much time researching your investments, it's easy to become attached to them. But if you do so, you may have a hard time selling an underperforming investment. Instead, treat every sell decision with the same clear-eyed detachment you had when you were researching the investment in the first place.
- **Thinking you're error proof:** Don't be afraid to admit that you may have made a mistake. It's okay to sell a losing stock. That way, you can keep your assets to invest or trade another day. And whatever you do, don't try to prove that you're smarter than Mr. Market. It doesn't matter if your analysis is 100 percent perfect; if the market disagrees, you're going to lose money.

Avoiding Analysis Paralysis

The simple truth is that you have access to too much information. You can't possibly know everything, so you're going to have to make decisions based on incomplete knowledge. If you try to keep up with every bit of economic news, you'll never be able to make an investment decision.

Don't overwhelm yourself. Figure out a small set of economic indicators to watch and then diligently track them. Find a few investment tools that meet your needs and master them inside and out. Try to stay abreast of the news without getting sidetracked by listening to too many advisors. Everyone has an opinion, and few opinions agree. When everyone starts to agree, it's time for you to start looking for an alternative approach.

Glossary

adjusting for inflation: The process of indexing or otherwise changing a data series or an economic indicator to remove the effects of inflation.

annualize: To mathematically transform data so that you can compare economic indicators that are published at different frequencies, such as a monthly indicator and a quarterly indicator. Annualizing data turns each value into an estimate of the annual growth rate.

balance of payments: A record of a country's exports and imports, including goods, services, and financial transactions.

balance of trade: The difference between the value of imports and exports.

bear alert: An indication that a bear market may be forming.

bear confirmed: An indication that stocks are in a bear market.

bear correction: During a bear market, a bear correction indicates that a pull-back is occurring. Corrections can revert to a bear confirmed or transition to a bull alert condition.

bear market: The stock market condition characterized by generally falling stock prices.

Beige Book: A report that includes anecdotal descriptions of business conditions compiled by the Federal Reserve's regional banks from interviews with local business leaders. The full name is the *Summary of Commentary on Current Economic Conditions by Federal Reserve District.*

benchmark: The reference value used for comparing economic conditions.

benchmark index: A numerical scale that uses a benchmark as a reference value to measure economic conditions.

bond: A type of fixed-income investment that's essentially a loan from the bond buyer to the bond issuer. Bonds generally pay interest two times per year until the bond reaches its contracted term, at which time the principal is repaid along with the final interest payment.

building permit: A legal authorization to construct a residence or commercial building on a specific piece of property. Building permits can be issued to a construction company or an individual and are required for single-family homes and commercial structures in most U.S. localities.

bull alert: An indication that a bull market may be forming.

bull confirmed: An indication that stocks are in a bull market.

bull correction: During a bull market, a bull correction indicates that a pullback is occurring. Corrections can revert to a bull confirmed or transition to a bear alert condition.

bull market: The stock market condition characterized by generally rising stock prices.

Bullish Percent Index: A measurement that shows the percentage of stocks on a buy signal.

Business Climate Survey: A leading German economic indicator that's prepared by the *Institute for Economic Research.* The survey's results are presented in a monthly report that features three indexes: Business Climate, Present Situation, and Expectations. The monthly report is known to be successful in forecasting turning points in economic growth.

business cycle: A series of economic expansions and contractions. One cycle includes one period of expansion, a peak, one period of contraction, and a trough. Sometimes the expansion phase is broken into the recovery phase (where the economy reaches its previous peak) and the expansion phase (where the economy rises above its previous peak).

capacity utilization: Percent of the nation's manufacturing capacity currently in productive use. Capacity-utilization reports are useful in indicating economic slowdowns.

central bank: The financial institution responsible for managing a nation's money supply and providing regulatory oversight for the commercial banking system. The Federal Reserve System is the U.S. central bank.

chaining dollars: A technique that removes the effects of inflation from a series of prices or economic indicators.

civilian workforce: All the people working or available to work in a nation, excluding military and some other institutional employees but including nonmilitary government employees. It also excludes discouraged workers.

coincident indicator: An economic indicator that changes at the same time the economy changes. You use it to confirm economic forecasts made by leading indicators.

commodities: Agricultural products, industrial and precious metals, energy products, and other products that are used as raw materials or as inputs to manufacturing processes.

confidence level: The probability that the reported value from a survey lies within a range around the true population value. Used in the construction of surveys to determine the number of participants required so that results are within the desired range of population values with the specified levels of confidence. Generally specified as 90 percent, 95 percent, or 99 percent.

consensus estimate: An aggregate estimate (of any economic indicator) based on the average of many forecasts produced by independent forecasters. A consensus estimate (also called a consensus opinion) is generally more accurate than any single forecaster.

constant dollars: A measurement of prices or economic indicators that isn't adjusted for inflation. Nominal values, on the other hand, are adjusted for the effects of inflation.

Consumer Price Index (CPI): A measure of the price level based on the prices for a standardized basket of goods and services.

Consumer Sentiment Index: A measure of consumers' economic confidence.

contraction: See ***economic contraction***.

core inflation: A measure of inflation based on a version of the Consumer Price Index that excludes food and energy prices. Core inflation is generally considered to be more representative of inflation's actual economic impact because food and energy prices are extremely volatile and are often subject to price pressures other than inflation. For example, food prices vary based on extreme weather conditions. Energy prices are subject to change due to political instability in energy-producing parts of the world.

correlation: A statistical concept that shows how much one indicator is related to another. Numerically, the statistical scale ranges from zero to one, where zero shows no correlation and one shows perfect correlation.

currency exchange: The process of buying or selling one currency, using another currency. The global currency market is called the ForEx, short for Foreign Exchange Market.

current-dollar value: The value of an economic data series or an economic indicator that hasn't been adjusted for inflation.

custom import value: The price paid for merchandise intended for export to the United States. It doesn't include costs for shipment, delivery, or import duties.

deflation: A general decrease in the level of prices over time. Deflation increases the real value of money, allowing a consumer to buy more goods with the same amount of money over time.

diffusion index: An indicator that shows how much and in which direction the answers to a survey differ from the response that conditions are unchanged.

discouraged worker: An unemployed worker who has stopped looking for a job, usually because jobs are scarce.

disinflation: A general reduction in the rate of price increases. Prices are still rising during disinflation, but at a slower pace.

disposable personal income: The amount of money people have available to spend on goods and services after taxes have been deducted.

durable goods: Products that are generally intended to last three years or longer. Durable goods are the most economically sensitive of all consumer spending categories.

economic contraction: A period of economic decline.

economic expansion: A period of economic growth. Some consider economic expansion and economic recovery to be equivalent. Others consider the period of economic expansion to occur after the economic recovery has reached the peak of the previous expansion.

economic sectors: Broad categories of businesses based on the type of business.

FAS: Abbreviation for free alongside ship. This export value is the total transaction price for the merchandise, including inland freight, insurance, and any other fee charged to get the product to the export port and prepared for loading; it doesn't include loading fees.

federal funds rate: The interest rate banks charge for overnight interbank loans. The Federal Reserves' Federal Open Market Committee sets the target rate, and the Fed conducts monetary policy to try to hit this target . It's also called the fed funds rate.

Federal Open Market Committee (FOMC): The Federal Reserve committee responsible for conducting monetary policy and setting the federal funds rate.

Federal Reserve: The central banking system of the United States. Duties include conducting the monetary policy, regulating banking institutions, and maintaining the stability of the financial systems of the United States. It's also called the Fed.

Federal Reserve banks: Regional branches of the Federal Reserve that provide banking services for member banks and to the federal government.

fixed-income investment: Generally a debt security characterized by fixed-interest payments over a fixed term to maturity; also known as a bond.

fixed-income market: Another term for bond market.

foreclosure: A legal process of taking possession of a mortgaged property in the event of default on the mortgage.

forward contract: A nonstandardized agreement between two parties to purchase a product, usually a commodity product, for delivery in the future. The contract specifies the product to be delivered, the quantity, the price, the delivery terms, and the penalties for failure to deliver. Normally, payment is made at delivery.

full employment: A theoretical condition where everyone who is able and willing to work is able to do so.

futures contract: A standardized type of forward contract traded on one of the futures exchanges.

GDP: Gross domestic product; the total estimated value of all goods and services produced in a country.

GNP: Gross national product; the total value of all goods and services produced by all people of a country, regardless of whether they're in the country or not.

growth rate: A measure of the percentage change of an economic indicator from one period to the next. Generally, the growth rate is annualized to make comparing one growth rate to another easier.

hedge: An investment position designed to offset the risk from another investment position.

household formation: New households created by marriage, divorce, children leaving their parents' home, or single adults leaving shared housing. All new households create demand for housing.

housing completions: Housing units completed and ready for occupancy.

housing starts: Housing construction that has actually been started (or excavated). A start is counted for each new housing construction project or for a complete rebuild on an existing foundation.

index: A ratio that measures the extent of change and is used in data comparisons.

inflation: A rise in the level of prices over time.

inflation-indexed bonds: A type of fixed-income investment in which the principal and interest are indexed to reduce the impact of inflation on the investment's interest payments. See also ***Treasury Inflation-Protected Securities (TIPS)***.

International Monetary Fund (IMF): The intergovernmental organization of 187 countries tasked with fostering global monetary cooperation and financial stability around the world.

international trade: Trade with foreign nations; a key component of the U.S. economy.

lagging indicator: An economic indicator that changes after the economy has changed. You use it to confirm that a recession or expansion has begun.

leading indicator: An economic indicator that changes before the economy has changed. You use it to forecast that an expansion or recession is coming.

London Interbank Offered Rate (LIBOR): The interbank overnight loan rate commercial banks charge each other when loaning money in the London wholesale money market. It's like the federal funds rate, but it measures the interest rate for transactions outside the control of the Federal Reserve.

monetary policy: The responsibility of a nation's central bank to balance the often-conflicting goals of minimizing the damaging effects of currency inflation and encouraging full employment. In the United States, the Federal Reserve has three financial tools to implement monetary policy: open-market operations, federal funds rate targets, and reserve requirements for member banks.

money supply: The total amount of money available at a given time in the economy. It generally includes all currency in circulation, plus checking account deposits, savings accounts, money market accounts, and certificates of deposit.

moving average: A statistics tool used to create a series of mathematical averages to help smooth volatile data sets and to make it easier to visualize data trends that may not be obvious otherwise.

nondurable goods: Products that generally aren't intended to last more than a year or two. They're also called consumer staples or consumables and include food, beverages, pharmaceuticals, and household goods. The purchase of nondurable goods generally isn't very sensitive to the state of the economy.

open-market operations: The Fed's buying and selling of U.S. Treasury securities and other federal agency securities in the open market to influence bond prices and interest rates.

peak: The highest point in one business cycle or one economic cycle.

personal consumption expenditures (PCE): Sum of the value of durable goods, nondurable goods, and services purchased by consumers. This value is part of the GDP report and the Personal Income and Outlays report.

price deflator: An index used to convert current-dollar values into approximate real-dollar (inflation-adjusted) values. The implicit price deflator is the ratio of the current-dollar value of a series, such as GDP, to its corresponding chained-dollar value, multiplied by 100.

price index: Constructing a weighted average of pricing for a specified collection of goods within a specific region and for a specific time period.

private investment: An investment made in an industry by nonpublic sector companies.

productivity: A measure of business efficiency.

real-dollar value: An estimate of an economic data series or economic indicator that has been adjusted for inflation.

recession: A business cycle contraction or general slowdown in economic activity.

reserve requirements: Member banks in the U.S. Federal Reserve System are required to hold in reserve an amount equal to a minimum fraction of customer deposits. These reserves can be in the bank's cash vault or held on deposit at the Federal Reserve. The reserve requirement is set by the Federal Reserve Board of Governors within limits specified by Congress.

seasonal fluctuations: Variations in sales or demand that reoccur based on the time of year or season.

Sector Rotation Model: An investment model that shows how the stock market in general and stocks in specific sectors tend to move in advance of the economy or business cycle.

smoothing: A mathematical technique used to adjust an economic indicator to reveal trends that may not be obvious in the unsmoothed data. See also ***moving average***.

spot price: The current prevailing price at which cash transactions are completed immediately, as contrasted to transactions that occur in the futures markets.

subprime mortgage crisis: Financial crisis propagated by a rise in foreclosures and delinquencies resulting from poorly qualified mortgage applicants.

supply and demand: General economic theory for determining prices of standardized commodity prices in a competitive market. In general, the price of an item rises as the demand for the item increases or as its supply decreases.

survey: A technique used to gather information from consumers or businesses. Surveys are usually implemented by asking questions to randomly selected participants.

sustainable maximum output: A theoretical measure of industrial production capacity, assuming all manufacturing facilities are operating at their theoretical maximum capacity. It's adjusted for downtime and labor constraints.

trade deficit: When the value of imports exceeds the value of exports.

trade surplus: When the value of exports exceeds the value of imports.

Treasury Inflation-Protected Securities (TIPS): U.S. Treasury bonds whose principal and interest payments adjust for inflation.

Treasury International Capital System (TIC): The system that measures cash flows into and out of the United States for investments (including investments in U.S. Treasury securities), common stocks, commodities, currencies, and derivatives.

trough: the lowest point in one business cycle or one economic cycle.

Unemployment Insurance Weekly Claims Report: This indicator provides the number of claims filed by unemployed individuals for unemployment insurance assistance.

unemployment rate: The percentage of the total workforce that is unemployed and currently looking for work.

yield curve: A graph that displays the levels of short-term and long-term interest rates. In the United States, Treasury securities are most often used to measure the interest rates for short-maturity and long-maturity bonds.

Index

• A •

• B •

• D •

• E •

• H •

• I •

• J •

• K •

• L •

• M •

• N •

• P •

• Q •

• R •

• S •

• T •

• U •

• W •

• Y •

• Z •